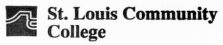

BONES OF THE MAYA

EDITED BY
STEPHEN L. WHITTINGTON AND
DAVID M. REED

BONES OF THE
MAYA

STUDIES OF ANCIENT
SKELETONS

SMITHSONIAN INSTITUTION PRESS
Washington   London

Copyright © 1997 by the Smithsonian Institution.
All rights reserved.

Copy Editor: Nancy P. Dutro
Designer: Janice Wheeler

Library of Congress Cataloging-in-Publication Data

Bones of the Maya : studies of ancient skeletons /
    edited by Stephen L. Whittington and David M.
    Reed.
        p.   cm.
    Includes bibliographical references and
index.
    ISBN 1-56098-684-0 (alk. paper)
    1. Mayas—Anthropometry.   2. Human
remains (Archaeology)—Mexico.   3. Human
remains (Archaeology)—Central America.
4. Mayas—Antiquities.   5. Mexico—Antiquities.   6. Central America—Antiquities.
I. Whittington. Stephen L.   II. Reed, David M.
F1435.3.A56B66   1997
972.81′016—dc21   96-50150
                                        CIP

British Library Cataloguing-in-Publication Data
is available.
Manufactured in the United States of America.
01 00 99 98 97 5 4 3 2 1

♾ The paper used in this publication meets the
minimum requirements of the American National
Standard for Performance of Paper for Printed
Library Materials Z39.48–1984.

For permission to reproduce illustrations appearing in this book, please correspond directly with
the authors, or the owners of the works as listed
in the individual captions. The Smithsonian Institution Press does not retain reproduction rights
for these illustrations individually or maintain a
file of addresses for photo sources.

Cover and title page: original drawing of Tikal
Altar 5 by Linda Schele.

Contents

Contributors

Carl Armstrong, Department of Anthropology, State University of New York, Plattsburgh

Jane E. Buikstra, Department of Anthropology, The University of New Mexico

Diane Z. Chase, Department of Sociology and Anthropology, University of Central Florida

Mark N. Cohen, Department of Anthropology, State University of New York, Plattsburgh

Della Collins Cook, Department of Anthropology, Indiana University

Marie Elaine Danforth, Department of Sociology and Anthropology, University of Southern Mississippi

Andrés del Ángel, Instituto de Investigaciones Antropológicas, Universidad Nacional Autónoma de México

Robert E. Ferrell, Department of Human Genetics, University of Pittsburgh

John P. Gerry, Mesoamerican Laboratory, Department of Anthropology, Harvard University

Karen D. Gettelman, Department of Anthropology, Indiana University

Lorena M. Havill, Department of Anthropology, Indiana University

Keith P. Jacobi, Alabama Museum of Natural History, The University of Alabama

Harold W. Krueger, Geochron Laboratories Division, Krueger Enterprises, Inc., Cambridge, MA

Nora M. López Olivares, Proyecto Atlas Arqueológico de Guatemala, Instituto de Antropología e Historia de Guatemala

Lourdes Márquez, Esquela Nacional de Antropología e Historia, México

Virginia K. Massey, Department of Anthropology, Texas A&M University

D. Andrew Merriwether, Department of Anthropology, University of Michigan

Kathleen O'Connor, Population Research Institute and Department of Anthropology, The Pennsylvania State University

K. Anne Pyburn, Department of Anthropology, Indiana University Purdue University

David M. Reed, Department of Anthropology, The Pennsylvania State University

Frank P. Saul, Biomedical Anthropology Associates, Toledo, OH

Julie Mather Saul, Biomedical Anthropology Associates, Toledo, OH

D. Gentry Steele, Department of Anthropology, Texas A&M University

Rebecca Storey, Department of Anthropology, University of Houston

Diane M. Warren, Department of Anthropology, Indiana University

David Webster, Department of Anthropology, The Pennsylvania State University

Christine D. White, Department of Anthropology, University of Western Ontario

Stephen L. Whittington, Hudson Museum, University of Maine

Lori E. Wright, Department of Anthropology, Texas A&M University

Near the end of *Breaking the Maya Code*, Michael Coe (1992) describes a Dumbarton Oaks conference held in Washington D.C. during the fall of 1989. The conference dealt with the Classic Maya collapse and some of the more highly respected archaeologists working in the Maya area presented papers. The audience was full of other specialists, as well as what might be termed Maya "groupies," all present to hear the most recent pronouncements on the causes of the collapse of Maya civilization through much of the southern lowlands, beginning in the 9th century.

Coe describes his disgust with the conference because a whole class of Maya experts was excluded from the program: epigraphers. He complains that one renowned scholar concerned with interpreting Maya art who was in the audience was treated with disrespect because she was not a "dirt archaeologist."

Coe's dissatisfaction with the conference should strike a chord with researchers working on human skeletons from Maya sites. Through-out the two days of the conference, not a single presenter mentioned evidence relating to the collapse that could be found on human bones, despite almost two decades having passed since the publication of Frank Saul's (1972a) ground-breaking study of the skeletons of Altar de Sacrificios and the subsequent publication of many other papers, site report appendices, and book chapters. One presenter reportedly did plan to discuss demographic and pathological data pertaining to the collapse found in skeletons from Copán, but his presentation ran long and he skipped that part of his paper. Thus, when osteological data were not ignored by the participants, they were treated like site-report appendices, which is where much of the information about Maya skeletons from decades past is to be found.

Frustration with the silence on the rich data set already in existence led one of us (Whittington) to phone Frank Saul soon after the conference and suggest that it was time to organize a conference on Maya osteology. While Frank supported the idea in principle, other concerns quickly forced the abandonment of the notion indefinitely.

A number of papers on Maya osteology were presented at the Society for American Archaeology 1993 annual meeting in St. Louis, but they were spread throughout all the days of the meeting and occurred in many different symposia, general sessions, and poster sessions. It was necessary to read the program and abstracts carefully in order to discover where and when there would be presentations on the subject. During the course of the meeting, the two of us (Whittington and Reed) ran into each other and began to discuss the idea of getting as many of the osteologists producing data today as possible together into a single symposium, something that had never been done before. It seemed clear after the St. Louis meeting that there were enough specialists studying diverse topics, from paleonutrition to mitochondrial DNA to artificial cranial deformation, to put together an exciting session at the next SAA meeting.

The next meeting was held in April 1994 at the Disneyland Hotel in Anaheim, California. Partly because of the venue and partly to convey the excitement of answering significant questions about Maya civilization, the proposed name for the symposium was "Maya Bones!" The meeting organizers rejected that name and the title of the symposium became the lyrical "Recent Studies of Ancient Maya Skeletons." A sizable audience, especially given the early Sunday hour and unfortunate technical difficulties, came to hear 11 presentations by scholars and a discussion by Jane Buikstra.

Those symposium papers form the core of this book. Since the meeting, and after presenting the book concept to the Smithsonian Institution Press, we decided to invite scholars from México and Guatemala to submit papers, to add an introduction by David Webster putting

Maya osteology into the wider context of Maya archaeology, to ask Mark Cohen to synthesize the osteological data from the important Tipu project, to invite Virginia Massey and Gentry Steele to discuss the interesting skull pit at Colha, and to include an indexed bibliography of the first 150 years of Maya osteology. Owing to time restrictions of the original symposium and length restrictions of this book the work of many researchers, past and present, does not appear here, and for this we apologize. However, the indexed bibliography does list the publications, through the end of 1994, of those working in Maya osteology.

We hope that archaeologists who read this book will be made more aware of the potential human skeletons have to help answer important research questions and will begin to give more concern to using excavation techniques which permit recovery of human skeletal remains in better condition and increasing numbers. It is clear from the papers in this book that much more useful information can be extracted from carefully excavated and properly documented skeletons than from carelessly curated bones. Our recent work with the extremely well-preserved but woefully badly documented and stored remains from the Late Postclassic Kaqchikel capital of Iximché have made us very aware of this point.

Little growth can occur within a field as long as its specialists are working in isolation, publishing individual articles in journals, or writing seldom-seen and hard-to-find site-report appendices. A field is maturing when scholars with similar interests get together to talk, begin to collaborate on multidisciplinary projects drawing upon various specialties, such as DNA analysis, stable isotope analysis, and paleopathology, and present their results in concentrated doses to an interested public. With the publication of this book we believe it can be said that Maya osteology is coming of age.

We thank the participants in the symposium and those whom we later invited to submit papers, Peter Cannell of the Smithsonian Institution Press, and William T. Sanders and David Webster for their support through the years. We also thank Christine, Dan, and Joe Whittington, Sissel Schroeder, and our parents, Charles and Alice Whittington and Jesse and Elizabeth Reed, for their patience and for making it all possible. Finally, we dedicate this book to the Maya, living and dead, without whom the world would be a poorer place.

PART 1

Introduction

David Webster

Studying Maya Burials

When I was first a graduate student in the mid-1960s, there were very few specialized studies of Maya burials or osteological remains. Some impressive tombs, such as those discovered at Tikal and Kaminaljuyú, were described in much detail. Skeletal remains from particularly famous tombs, such as that of Pacal at Palenque, were sometimes examined by physical anthropologists. One occasionally ran across an analysis of larger samples, such as E. A. Hooton's (1940) study of bones dredged from the Well of Sacrifice at Chichén Itzá, but these usually emphasized only one or two characteristics such as sex, stature, or dental alteration, and the wider implications were seldom explored except in highly speculative ways. Systematic informtion on the osteometrics, paleodemography, and paleopathology of substantial samples did not exist.

For almost a century Mayanists had recovered large, and sometimes well-controlled, burial samples. An example is the large series from the Carnegie Institution's Group A-V excavations at Uaxactún in the 1930s. Such collec-

tions, however, were generally treated as marginal data sets, serendipitously unearthed for the most part, to be briefly summarized within the context of featured presentations of architecture, stratigraphy, artifacts, art, and inscriptions. Results were seldom compared among sites or regions. No sophisticated biochemical methods applicable to bone were available. Issues of general concern to archaeologists attempting to reconstruct ancient Maya society were only superficially addressed using information from burials.

As the papers in this volume indicate, much has changed very rapidly. Within the professional lifetimes of such pioneers as Frank Saul (still contributing; see Saul and Saul this volume), archaeologists have begun systematically to recover large burial populations and to analyze both their cultural and biological dimensions using increasingly standardized methods that facilitate comparison. Most conspicuously, sophisticated biochemical methods have proliferated, usually borrowed from colleagues in the biological and physical sciences, and more are on the horizon. Enterprising archaeologists combine field experience and laboratory expertise to learn surprising and useful new things about the ancient Maya, many of which pertain to issues of fundamental importance that Mayanists have argued about for generations. While not yet mature, Maya burial and skeletal research has certainly become dynamic and innovative in the last three decades.

Many readers of this volume may be methodologically informed about burial and skeletal analysis, but not know much about the ancient Maya. My contribution in part serves to place the specific studies that follow in the larger context of Maya archaeology. I also consider some important research issues, most notably sampling and contextualization, that affect our ability to analyze skeletal materials and interpret the resulting data, and summarize what seem to me to be some of the more interesting implications and opportunities inherent in the research presented. My personal qualifications are general archaeological ones, not those of a specialist in skeletal analysis, so I am unequipped to evaluate critically the specific procedures and methods fundamental to many of the papers, a task undertaken by Professor Buikstra at the end of the volume. I have, however, participated in many projects that have produced skeletal samples, particularly at Copán, a Maya polity in western Honduras that is archaeologically well known, and where both editors of this volume have also worked. Copán's burial sample is one of the largest available for the Maya region, and results of Copán research figure prominently in several of the following chapters. I draw on my Copán experience to point up some major issues central to burial and skeleton analysis.

Archaeological Background

Although Mayanists have not traditionally been in the forefront of innovation in skeletal studies, Maya archaeology in fact offers a particularly fertile field for recovery of mortuary remains and development and testing of methods for their analysis. Most importantly, there were a lot of ancient Maya. Particularly in Classic times (A.D. 300–900), Maya population densities were extremely high, according to some authorities (Culbert and Rice 1990) among the highest for any preindustrial, agrarian cultures. These populations were spread over an enormous area, about 250,000 km^2 in the Maya lowlands proper, and a much larger area if we include the Maya highlands (Fig. 1.1). Moreover, there was considerable biological and cultural continuity in the populations of this vast region from at least the time of the earliest known agricultural settlements (at about 1200 B.C.) through the Spanish conquests of the 16th century. All this means that unusually large numbers of dead people were disposed of and are out there for archaeologists to find, and that local burial populations are the product of a widely shared and deeply rooted cultural tradition.

Two shared mortuary practices are of particular significance to archaeologists. First, unlike some other Mesoamerican peoples such as the Aztecs, who cremated most of their dead, the ancient Maya preferred inhumation. Second, though they occasionally used what appear to be detached cemetery zones, as at Jaina, or natural repositories, such as caves, and also placed illustrious dead in special burial contexts, such as great tombs beneath specially prepared mortuary buildings as at Palenque (Ruz 1973), most people were buried in and around residential groups. Such groups vary from the tiny clusters of domiciles, kitchens, and storehouses of low-ranked Maya farmers (Fig. 1.2) to the sprawling, multiplaza, palatial establishments of Maya lords and kings (Fig. 1.3). The former were occupied by social groups of nuclear or extended family scale, while the latter sometimes housed hundreds of people (Webster 1989a). Most constructions outside the regal-ritual cores of large Maya centers are in fact parts of residential groups.

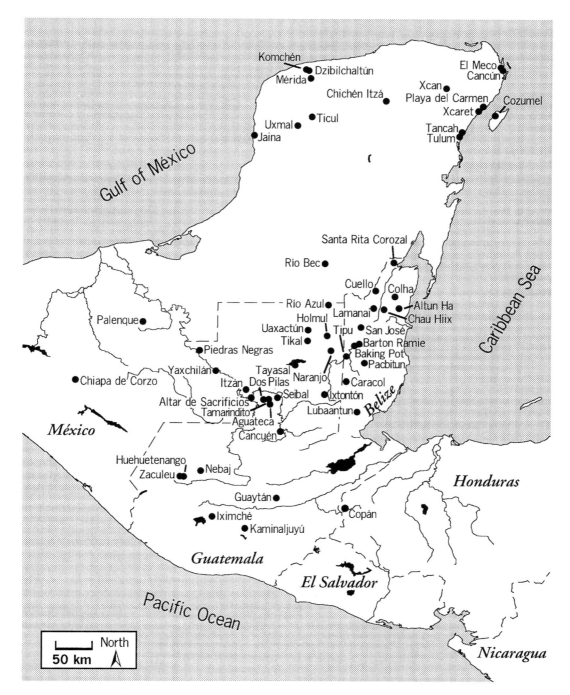

Figure 1.1. Map of the Maya highlands and lowlands showing sites mentioned in this volume.

Within such groups, burials of prominent individuals were often placed in ritually and symbolically special places. Other dead were disposed of under the floors of houses, beneath the adjoining plaza surfaces, in the fill of new construction, or simply in domestic middens. Presumably this pattern partly reflects the veneration of dead ancestors that survives in some

Figure 1.2. Remains of basal platforms of two small Maya residential structures at Group 99B-19-1, a small rural farmstead in the Copán Valley, Honduras. Eight burials were recovered while trenching along south wall of Structure 1 (bottom).

Maya communities today. Patricia McAnany (1995) argues that such veneration had many important functions in Maya society from the earliest times, and demonstrates the transformations of domestic burial places into communal ritual facilities.

One consequence of this domestic burial propensity is that archaeologists encounter burials virtually wherever they investigate architecture. Because the Maya built environment is unusually conspicuous and well preserved, and has long served to structure archaeological research (Webster 1994a), burials are frequent byproducts of excavation, no matter what the specific research issues might be. Also, the burials typi-

cally recovered from remains of ancient households include people of all ages and sexes. A reasonable working assumption is that these individuals share a high degree of social and genetic relatedness, particularly when, as is often the case, burials are collected from small, highly discrete, dispersed residential groups. Architectural stratigraphy often helps sort out relative chronological relationships among burial contexts. Finally, variations in general architectural associations and mortuary treatment provide insights into ranking of burial populations or individuals within them.

The ancient Maya also manipulated skeletal parts to an unusual degree, as several of the following chapters make clear. Bones were fashioned into artifacts of various kinds. Skulls and teeth of the living were remodeled for cosmetic or status purposes (Havill et al. this volume). Bones of the dead were routinely used as ritual implements or trophies. Remains of sacrificed people were deposited in special ritual deposits (Massey and Steele this volume). Even the inhumations of revered ancestors were subject to such manipulation. Tombs were reopened and bones were retrieved, used in ceremonies, and then redeposited, some in different places. Bones of the ancestors seem to have been brought by settlers to newly established households, thus preserving social identity and connections as residences proliferated or moved. Documentation of all this activity provides rich insights into Maya status variation and cultural practices in general, including esoteric dimensions of mortuary behavior and ideology.

Other advantages derive from our extremely rich understanding of ancient Maya culture and society. Archaeologists in some other regions of the world often recover abundant and rich burial data, but know comparatively little about the larger cultural background to which they relate. A good example is the ʿUbaid culture of early Mesopotamia (Hole 1989). Several large ʿUbaidian cemeteries have been excavated, yielding thousands of burials, but very little is

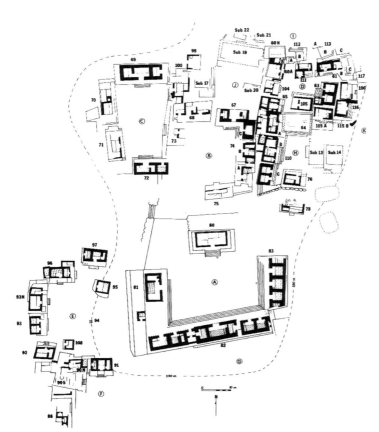

Figure 1.3. Elite Group 9N-8 at Copán, Honduras. This multiplaza complex was the establishment of a major Maya subroyal lord in the late 8th century. Hundreds of burials have been recovered from it.

known about related patterns of settlement, demography, subsistence, diet, economics, ritual, and social and political organization. Mayanists, by comparison, have unusually detailed information about all these things for several reasons. Important insights derive from ethnographic studies of existing, indigenous Maya communities and populations that retain many basic continuities with the past. We also have Spanish ethnohistoric accounts of the 16th century Maya at or shortly after European contact, most notably that of Landa (Tozzer 1941), as well as some native documents written after the Conquest.

The Precolumbian lowland Maya were literate, and have left us reasonably abundant texts that are particularly informative about the Late Classic period (A.D. 600–900) when lowland Maya civilization matured and popula-

tion sizes and densities peaked. These texts contain a wealth of information about chronology, dynasties, political history, and ritual (Culbert 1991; Stuart 1993), and are especially useful in association with the rich tradition of Maya art, often highly representational, that accompanies them. On the elite and especially royal levels, it is sometimes possible to identify the skeletal remains of individuals whose names, titles, offices, life spans, and absolute dates are known.

The long history of Maya archaeology itself, combined with the comparative abundance, accessibility, and good preservation of Maya sites, has produced a huge accumulation of data from which details of social, economic, political, demographic, and ritual behavior may be reconstructed. Finally, on a practical level, objections by modern descendants of the ancient Maya to archaeological excavation of burials have to this point been absent or muted, unlike the situation in the United States.

The downside of all these attractions of the Maya burial record, of course, is preservation. Hot and at least intermittently humid tropical conditions can rapidly degrade bone, and it was not uncommon in the past for Maya archaeologists, discouraged by the condition of the skeletal remains they recovered, simply to discard them. Fortunately, preservation is not uniformly bad. In any large burial population some skeletons are extremely well preserved, especially those from well-built, protected burial contexts (producing in some collections a high-status bias). Others are mush, some detectable only as stains in the earth. Most burials fall between; though they are fragmentary and missing some components, most skeletal parts can be retrieved. Mayanists have become increasingly aware that large amounts of information can be obtained from even fragmentary bone by proper analysis in the field and laboratory. Very small fragments suffice for stable isotope or DNA research, although here the state of chemical degradation may be more of a concern than size or completeness of the bone sample itself.

Contextualization

Our mature understanding of ancient Maya civilization facilitates contextualization of skeletal studies in two main ways. First, archaeologists can knowledgeably integrate recovery and analysis of burial samples into their research designs. Second, they can interpret analytical results within the context of sophisticated understanding of ancient Maya culture, and the archaeology of specific sites or regions. Adequate contextualization is necessary if research is to be appropriately designed, and interpretation of results informed and intelligible. An example from Copán serves as a handy illustration.

Excavations at the multiplaza elite residential Group 9N-8 (shown in Fig. 1.3) turned up burials in all plazas. Rebecca Storey (pers. comm. 1990) identified a surprisingly large ratio (15:2) of adult female to male burials in Plaza E. One plausible explanation for this disparity is polygyny. Prominent Maya men in Classic times almost certainly had senior wives of noble rank, as well as lesser consorts. Plaza E is immediately adjacent to Plaza A, which we believe was the residential courtyard of the lord of the whole compound, and so is a logical place to find such consorts housed, and ultimately buried.

Let us consider how polygyny might introduce noise into attempts to determine whether Copán elites had better diets than commoners, as indicated by isotopic analysis of diet. Suppose we divided our skeletal sample spatially, on the assumption that people buried in large impressive groups were of generally higher rank than those buried in small, rural places. Suppose further that the isotopic signatures indicate general similarity in diet between the two spatially segregated populations. One interpretation is that there was no effective difference between elite and commoner diets. Another interpretation, however, is that the sample populations are inappropriately segregated. If the lord of 9N-8 recruited mature women from rural farming households as subsidiary wives or consorts, their bone chemistry would presumably reflect the diets of their original, more modest social circumstances. Remains of such women in elite residential contexts would thus blur dietary distinctions between elites and commoners. Fortunately, maize consumption is so high across all social groups at Copán that no confusion results from such noise (Reed 1994), but the pattern might be different elsewhere. Awareness of potential problems of this sort could prompt more sophisticated statistical manipulation of observed data, but presupposes informed researchers.

One danger of the increasing specialization of skeletal research is that laboratory analyses may not involve those familiar with the original excavations, or even knowledgeable about Maya culture and archaeology. When excavators and analysts are not the same individuals, extremely close collaboration is therefore necessary if contextualization is properly to inform analytical design and interpretation.

The Maya burial record will provide many unique opportunities if such collaboration is developed and maintained. Consider its potential for DNA analyses of genetic affinity using ancient bone samples, a method now being perfected and applied (Merriwether et al. this volume). To develop and test the utility of this method it will be necessary to apply it to bone from individuals who either demonstrably share, or are highly likely to share, such affinities. Individuals recovered from royal tombs at particular centers can often be linked to textually documented dynastic sequences, and their precise relationships thus known (see, for example, the many dynastic lists provided by Sharer 1994 for centers such as Tikal, Copán, Palenque, Yaxchilán, and Piedras Negras). Such individuals should have extremely close genetic affinities. On a much more mundane level, so should many of the individuals buried around the dispersed houses of rural Maya farmers. Both kinds of contexts provide ideal samples for testing DNA methods, which in turn will greatly refine our archaeological understanding, but only if laboratory and field researchers work very closely.

Sampling

By far the most intractable problem in Maya burial research is that of sampling. Two pioneer studies by William Haviland (1967) and William Rathje (1970), both of which combined cultural and biological dimensions of Maya burials, illustrate sampling limitations. Haviland's attempts to detect stature differences in individuals of different ranks at Tikal, and to track these differences through time, were severely hampered by his tiny sample size (n = 55). Rathje's sample was larger (n = 110), though still arguably insufficient for his research purpose: documenting sociopolitical changes in Classic Maya society over several hundred years. The real problem was the character of this sample. In order to amass a sizable number of reasonably well-documented burials from varied settlement contexts, Rathje was forced to utilize burials from two different Maya centers, when sound research design required they all be from the same one. None of Rathje's burials was collected with his specific research questions in mind, and the sample was produced by different projects at different times by archaeologists using varying procedures of recovery, analysis, and curation.

For the most part Maya archaeologists today, like Haviland and Rathje, must content themselves with availability samples. Projects designed to investigate specific burial populations and related research issues are beginning to appear, as at Tipu (Jacobi this volume, Cohen et al. this volume), but these are still exceptions. More characteristically, burials are opportunistically encountered, and originally recorded and removed by archaeologists who have only a general familiarity with skeletal analysis. Some skeletal material remains unanalyzed long after the original projects that produced it have been completed, many in the absence of intimate understanding of the original contexts or conditions of recovery (Whittington and Reed 1993). Detection, recording, and recovery of burials has been a major focus of some recent projects, notably those at Caracol (Chase 1994, this volume) and Río Azul (Adams and Robichaux 1992). Even in these cases, however, the principal concern was with specific kinds of elaborate tombs that could be detected by surface inspection or that had already been found by looters.

It will probably always be the case that archaeologists will have to content themselves with small samples of certain kinds of Maya burial populations. In the nature of things we will never have remains of many demonstrably royal individuals from any center. We will always encounter the occasional idiosyncratic but extremely revealing ritual deposit, such as the fascinating skull burials described by Massey and Steele (this volume). There are ways, however, to ensure that the more representative run of burials is reliably sampled.

One solution is to design projects *specifically* to recover adequate samples. Here though, the Maya preference for architectural (and particularly residential) burial contexts creates a real problem. Burial concentrations are not high, as they are in formal cemeteries, nor are individual burial locations precisely predictable. Large, representative samples can only be systematically recovered by extensive architectural excavations, which are time-consuming and expensive, and often require costly restoration. Acquisition of burial samples by itself seldom justifies such efforts.

A more workable solution is to devise large projects with many research questions in mind, and to integrate burial recovery and studies into the research design. Sometimes this works quite well. For example, our Penn State University 1980–1984 excavations in the Copán urban core were designed to expose very large portions of several impressive compounds thought to be elite residences. Our basic objectives were to document the domestic and other functions of these compounds, discern patterns of social and political structure, and get some idea of the culture history of occupation.

Many lines of data were appropriate to these objectives, including those derived from burials. We specifically probed likely burial contexts, but our very extensive architectural exposures also turned up burials in unexpected places, as did later restoration work. Burials, as anticipated, were numerous, and they engaged increasing amounts of our time and energy. In 1983 Professor James Hatch of The Pennsylvania State University organized a field school at Copán specifically to streamline burial recovery. He and his specially trained students recorded and removed approximately 150 burials in six weeks, and our total sample from urban core groups is now approximately 500 individuals. These burials, as well as others from outlying sites and other Copán projects, are being studied by a small group of scholars, including Rebecca Storey, Stephen Whittington, and David Reed (all contributors to this volume). Such cooperation helps to standardize observations, facilitates the exchange of information, and also benefits from the different skills, approaches, and interests of multiple researchers. Fortunately, because of the proliferation of large, long-term field projects, large burial samples numbering hundreds of individuals are now common.

Another solution to the problems of burial sampling is to devise projects that are comparatively inexpensive and small in scale, but that yield collections of burials appropriate to certain restricted research issues. Between 1985 and 1986 we explored seven rural residential groups at Copán (Webster and Gonlin 1988). Because these groups were so small, it cost very little to carry out extensive excavations. We anticipated that burials would be recovered at each group, providing useful insights into composition of commoner household populations and burial practices. This was a good idea in the abstract, but the Maya fooled us. Although we tested all the appropriate contexts, burials were recovered only from two of the smallest sites. For unknown reasons, the inhabitants of the other sites disposed of their dead well away from the places they lived. In this case conception and execution of research design were good, but an adequate burial sample still failed to materialize. Exactly the same approach might have produced good samples elsewhere in the Maya lowlands.

A problem of particular intransigence is assembling skeletal samples useful for detecting patterns of temporal change. Although many Maya centers were occupied continuously for centuries, particular projects generally produce sizable burial samples from fairly narrow time ranges. Especially difficult is adequately sampling Early Classic or Preclassic skeletal remains at sites with large Late Classic architectural overburdens. Attempts to detect chronological patterning thus often depend upon lumping burial assemblages of different ages from many sites into the same sample (e.g., Márquez and Ángel this volume), an obviously problematical strategy given the regional variation in all things Maya that is becoming increasingly evident.

Also frustrating is our inability to control chronological relationships adequately within particular ceramic phases. As an example, most burials recovered at Copán date to the period from A.D. 600 to 1000 and are associated with ceramics of the Coner phase, which began around A.D. 600–650. Except where stratigraphic or architectural associations are particularly clear, it is often difficult to place individual burials accurately within this four-century interval, during which many extremely important social, political, and demographic changes occurred that influenced health, nutrition, diet, and life span. I regard acquisition of osteological samples suitable for detailed longitudinal studies at particular centers as one of the greatest challenges of Maya research.

Issues

Cultural and biological information from burials can provide information on many basic issues of concern to Maya archaeologists. Of these issues, most of which are addressed in the following papers, I think the following are most important:

1. The nature of status differentiation in Maya populations
2. The kinds of nutritional states and disease loads characteristic of specific Maya populations

3. The demographic structure of regional Maya populations or segments of them (e.g., household populations)
4. The nature of ancient Maya diets
5. The implications of skeletal trauma for cultural behaviors such as warfare
6. Patterns of regional and chronological variation in all of the above

Data relating to these issues are not only interesting in themselves, but have broader implications. Dietary reconstruction provides a useful example.

Mayanists have long debated the composition of ancient Maya diets. Ethnographic studies indicate that traditional Maya obtain very high proportions of their daily caloric intake from maize, and ethnohistoric accounts suggest the same pattern. If this assumption holds for Preconquest times, and particularly for the Classic period, it would greatly facilitate reconstruction of subsistence practices, population size and density, and help us understand such processes as the collapse of Classic Maya political systems.

Unfortunately there has been considerable debate concerning ancient Maya diets for 25 years, primarily stimulated by the discovery that population densities were far higher than originally thought. Alternative subsistence models emphasize root crops, ramon (*Brosimum alicastrum*), or generalized arboriculture (Harrison and Turner 1978). Macrofossil evidence from many sites reveals the considerable range of plant foods available to the Maya, but cannot directly show dietary contributions. Uncertainty about what staples the Maya depended on have either discouraged the construction of general models of Maya subsistence and its demographic implications, or caused debate over those that were proposed.

Wiseman (1983) long ago suggested that isotopic data could be used to analyze patterns of paleonutrition. Several isotopic studies have now been completed and are resolving the diet issue. As several of the papers in this volume indicate (Wright; White; Gerry and Krueger; Whittington and Reed), high maize signatures are showing up in several well-analyzed samples. There is expected regional and temporal variation, but maize appears to be everywhere an important or dominant dietary staple. Even the variation is falling into comprehensible patterns: less dependence on maize in Belize, where ecosystems are complex and marine resources are immediately available, and high dependence at land-locked sites such as Copán.

These findings are extremely useful. They confirm assumptions made by archaeologists attempting to model ancient Maya subsistence systems. For example, the assumed maize consumption estimate (60%) used by John Wingard (1992) in his simulation of Copán's agricultural and population history turns out to be almost exactly that empirically derived by Gerry and Krueger from burials (this volume). Reed's work (1994) independently confirms very high maize intake at Copán (probably greater than 60%) for a larger, more varied burial sample. Correlation of several major lines of evidence concerning Copán's demographic, agricultural, and political history (Webster 1994b) is much more plausible in light of such dietary reconstructions. The lesson is that even quite basic results of innovative skeletal research can have many general and far-reaching implications for resolving fundamental research issues.

Summary and Conclusions

Maya burial studies have come a long way very quickly. They are revealing many useful things to us, and greatly enhancing our reconstructions of what the ancient Maya were like and how they changed. Accelerating innovations in methods and techniques promise even more exciting insights in the near future. Our rich understanding of Maya society and culture in general enables us to evaluate all this new information effectively.

There are, however, distinct growing pains. Give someone a hammer, and they will find something to pound (Moore and Keene 1983). This "Law of the Hammer" is beginning to apply to Maya burial studies. The power and sophistication of our implements (our statistical and laboratory methods) are outpacing the capacity of archaeologists in the field to produce burial samples to which these methods may be effectively and appropriately applied. Application of such methods to inappropriate samples not only frustrates our attempts to understand what the ancient Maya were like, but can also unnecessarily impede the evaluation and refinement of the methods themselves, because it may be unclear whether ambiguous results reflect problems with the procedures or with the samples.

To avoid these problems field and laboratory researchers must work together not only in the phases of analysis, but also in research design. When, inevitably, availability samples are used, researchers must understand the nature and contexts of the samples, adjust their analytical approaches accordingly, and describe their methods and samples very clearly in their publications. If we do all these things conscientiously, the bones of the ancestors will have much more to tell, and will speak clearly to us.

PART 2

Osteological Studies

2

Southern Lowland Maya Archaeology and Human Skeletal Remains: Interpretations from Caracol (Belize), Santa Rita Corozal (Belize), and Tayasal (Guatemala)

Diane Z. Chase

One class of data that is crucial to archaeological interpretations of prehistoric populations, their health, status, and demographic patterns, is that derived from human burials. These are recovered in what, at first glance, appear to be sizeable quantities in most excavations at most Maya sites (Chase 1994; Saul and Saul 1991; Tourtellot 1990a; Welsh 1988). Yet, how much do we know about the actual remains of the ancient Maya and how can excavated samples be used to define ancient populations?

The sites of Caracol, Santa Rita Corozal, and Tayasal are all Maya sites in the southern lowlands. Each of these sites, however, is located within a distinctive geographic area and maintains a different history of human occupation. Investigations at each site have added important information to our views of the ancient Maya and, when taken together, provide greater insight into both a broader interpretation of the nature of ancient Maya populations and the methodological and theoretical difficulties involved in making intersite comparisons.[1]

Caracol, Santa Rita Corozal, and Tayasal: Temporal and Skeletal Samples

Caracol, the largest of the three sites, is located in the Vaca Plateau of Belize in the foothills of the Maya Mountains at an elevation of over 500 m. Long-term large-scale excavation was started at Caracol in 1985 and has taken place every year since then (Chase and Chase 1987; D. Chase and A. Chase 1994). The earliest

[1] The author acknowledges the problems in comparing health among archaeological populations as identified by Wood et al. (1992). This discussion, however, will place greater emphasis on an equally important phenomenon: determination of sampling problems through correlation of osteological remains with other archaeological information.

settlement at the site epicenter dates to approximately 300 B.C. and occupation continued until about A.D. 1100. However, the primary occupation of Caracol was during the Classic period, or from A.D. 250 to 900, with a population peak occurring at approximately 650. Population estimates based on housemound counts indicate that minimally 115,000, and more probably almost 150,000, people lived at the site in 650 (A. Chase and D. Chase 1994a). The total burial sample recovered thus far at Caracol consists of 183 recorded interments (171 with data retrieved by means of excavation) representing more than 300 individuals.[2] More than 80 of Caracol's investigated interments are located in formally constructed tombs.

Half a country away to the north in Belize is Santa Rita Corozal. Encompassed by, and largely buried under, modern Corozal Town and its suburbs, this site is located directly on Chetumal Bay between the New River and the Río Hondo. Santa Rita has a very long and continuous history of occupation beginning at about 1200 B.C. Its peak settlement, however, dates to the Late Postclassic period (A.D. 1200–1530) when population is estimated to have reached between approximately 7000 and 11,000 people (D. Chase 1990). The Corozal Postclassic Project (Chase 1982; Chase and Chase 1988) excavated 134 interments, including two formal tombs, at Santa Rita Corozal from 1980 through 1985. Some 164 individuals are represented in these burials. At the turn of the present century, Thomas Gann (1900, 1911, 1914, 1918) recovered an additional 26 burials representing 28 individuals at Santa Rita Corozal (Chase 1982).

Tayasal is located in the heart of the Maya lowlands on the tip of a peninsula that juts into Lake Petén Itzá in the northern part of modern-day Guatemala. Tayasal and its surrounding region were occupied continuously from the Middle Preclassic through the Classic and Postclassic periods. Excavation and reconnaissance were undertaken by the University of Pennsylvania in 1971 and 1979 (A. Chase 1983, 1985, 1990). This work recovered 51 burials representing 56 individuals. This total also includes two tombs. Eight additional burials representing eight individuals were excavated at the site early in this century by Carl Guthe (1921, 1922).

Population History: Settlement and Burial Samples

It is common for reconstructions of prehistoric population to be based on excavation data, exclusive of skeletal or burial remains (cf. Ashmore 1981; Culbert and Rice 1990). Generally speaking, population estimates in the Maya area are based on counts of numbers of structures at any one site, with consideration being given to the possibility that not all structures are visible based upon surface remains and to the likelihood that early occupation has not been adequately sampled at multiphase sites. The structure counts, usually derived from reconnaissance and survey, are further modified to account for nonresidential buildings and for limited use-spans for individual constructions. Excavation data are then utilized to estimate the total number of structures in use at any given time. The resultant figures are then multiplied by a standard number of individuals believed to have lived in any single Maya house-

---

[2] The burial totals reflected in this paper and in Table 2.3 are current through the 1994 season at Caracol, Belize. Additional data gathered as a result of the 1995 and 1996 field seasons do not change the conclusions presented here or significantly alter any percentages relative to Caracol burial practices. As of the end of the 1996 field season some 213 formal interments, representing almost 400 individuals, are known from the site; 31 of these interments were disturbed by looters; 7 empty tombs, presumably once used for burial, are not included in this burial total. Additionally, a burial dating to approximately 600 B.C. is now known from the outlying Caracol core settlement.

Table 2.1 Santa Rita Corozal: Relative Population Based on Burials and Settlement (Approximately 5 km²)

Time Period	Percent Based on Structures	Percent Based on Burials	Total Population Based on Structures	n[a]	Percent of Population Seen in Burials
Early Preclassic 1200–900 B.C.	2.19	4.82	150	4	.0044
Middle Preclassic 900–300 B.C.	2.19	3.02	150	5	.0028
Late Preclassic 300 B.C.–A.D. 200	15.77	24.44	1079	34	.0032
Protoclassic A.D. 200–300	26.28	14.38	1798	4	.0011
Early Classic A.D. 300–550	21.02	20.13	1438	14	.0019
Late Classic A.D. 550–900	35.65	29.76	2438	29	.0017
Terminal Classic/Early Postclassic A.D. 900–1200	30.66	7.19	2097	6	.0005
Early Facet Late Postclassic A.D. 1200–1300	26.28	17.97	1798	5	.0014
Late Facet Late Postclassic A.D. 1300–1530	100.00	100.00	6840	64	.0020

[a]n = number of skeletal individuals.

hold (usually 5 or 5.6 people) to arrive at the total projected population for various time periods and an overall population trajectory. While there are problems with this method of population reconstruction, its general use and application in the Maya area provide a relatively standard method for comparing excavated sites.

Although not typically employed, a comparison of relative population derived from skeletal individuals, as opposed to structural dating, may be instructive in identifying places where skeletal sampling is inadequate or where problems exist in population estimates that have been made using nonskeletal data. Burial samples recovered from the sites of Caracol, Santa Rita Corozal, and Tayasal compare favorably in size with those collected at other lowland Maya sites (see Welsh 1988). Any consideration of the total length of time that given

sites were occupied, however, reveals the fact that only an extremely small percentage of the total population alive at any one time is represented in a given skeletal population. Numbers of interments recovered archaeologically, though, may correlate proportionately with relative numbers of excavated structures per time period. Alternatively, they may not, thus indicating a greater possibility of sampling error.

At Santa Rita Corozal (Table 2.1) when the burials per time period are adjusted to indicate maximum individual lifespans (likely overestimated at 50 years), the representative population, as recovered in skeletal remains, is extremely small. For late facet Late Postclassic Santa Rita, the time period for which we have the largest skeletal sample as well as ethnohistoric information that can be correlated with this estimated population peak, only .002% of

Table 2.2 Tayasal-Paxcamán Zone: Relative Population Based on Burials and Settlement (Approximately 90 km^2)

Time Period	Percent Based on Structures	Percent Based on Burials	Total Population Based on Structures	n[a]	Percent of Population Seen in Burials
Middle Preclassic 750–250 B.C.	4	.00	878	0	.000000
Late Preclassic 250 B.C.–A.D. 250	56	2.50	12,293	1	.000008
Early Early Classic A.D. 250–400	71	41.67	15,585	5	.000032
Late Early Classic A.D. 400–550	85	83.33	18,658	10	.000179
Early Late Classic A.D. 550–700	95	50.00	20,853	6	.000096
Late Late Classic A.D. 700–950	100	100.00	21,951	20	.000182
Early Postclassic A.D. 950–1200	37	45.00	8122	9	.000222
Middle Postclassic A.D. 1200–1450	76	35.00	16,683	7	.000084
Late Postclassic A.D. 1450–1700	16	5.00	3512	1	.000057

[a]n = number of skeletal individuals.

any contemporaneous population was recovered archaeologically. For Classic period Tayasal (Table 2.2) the figures are even more dismal, with only .000182% of the coeval population that existed at that area's population peak being recovered. For Caracol (Table 2.3) even though the burial sample of individuals dated to the Late Classic is over ten times that of the Tayasal region (275 vs. 26), only .000591% of the estimated population has been recovered relative to the site's population peak. Thus, our skeletal samples are extremely small, in spite of all the excavation that has been undertaken. The major implication of these figures is that interpretations made from such archaeological samples with regard to health, age of death, and population characterization may suffer from significant sampling errors even if the percentages of relative population derived from both structural counts and skeletal individuals is equivalent.

A second problem in characterizing skeletal populations derived archaeologically becomes evident when one looks at population trajectories over time. Comparisons between population numbers derived from settlement research and numbers of recovered individuals for specific temporal periods reveal severe points of disjunction at some sites. In particular, differences tend to be magnified with regard to the Protoclassic (A.D. 100–300) and Terminal Classic (A.D. 800–1000) periods at many sites (cf. Culbert and Rice 1990). Estimated populations based on settlement, as opposed to numbers of recovered burials, hint at differential burial practices that standard archaeological sampling is not finding. This gulf between the estimated population based on settlement research and the number of burials that may be correlated with this settlement is particularly strong for the Terminal Classic era at both Santa Rita

Table 2.3 Caracol: Relative Population Based on Burials and Settlement (Approximately 177 km^2)

Time Period	Percent Based on Structures	Percent Based on Burials	Total Population Based on Structures	n[a]	Percent of Population Seen in Burials
Late Preclassic 300 B.C.–A.D. 250	1.49	1.47	1714	3	.000583
Early Early Classic A.D. 250–400	8.27	2.94	9513	5	.000210
Late Early Classic A.D. 400–530	17.50	14.71	20,131	27	.000497
Early Late Classic A.D. 530–650	100.00	100.00	115,032	162	.000591
Late Late Classic A.D. 650–780	87.51	63.24	100,665	113	.000427
Terminal Classic[b] A.D. 780–1080	9.64	1.47	11,089	7	.000090

[a] n = number of skeletal individuals.

[b] Low frequency may partially reflect an inability to separate Late and Terminal Classic material in the core of Caracol.

Corozal and Caracol. Assuming that the settlement data are being correctly interpreted, it can be suggested that burial patterning at these two sites for this time period differed substantially from previous Classic period patterns. This would suggest skewing not only of our burial populations but also of our understanding of the changes and processes that occurred during this crucial time of transition.

Caracol

Investigations at Caracol have focused on the Classic period (A.D. 250–1080). Ten seasons of excavation have led to the recovery of a relatively large osteological collection. However, because of the substantial population that inhabited the site, there is still a question of the representative nature of the skeletal sample (Table 2.3). The relative populations at Caracol derived from structures and burials indicate closest correspondence during the late Early Classic (A.D. 400–530) and the subsequent early Late Classic period (A.D. 530–650), even though the largest skeletal samples derive from

the early Late Classic and the late Late Classic periods. While the number of individuals identified in burials during both phases of the Late Classic (162 and 113) may seem large compared with the number of individuals identified for any phase at Santa Rita Corozal or Tayasal, they are extremely small relative to the larger projected population for Caracol. In addition, it would appear that there is underrepresentation of osteological remains for the majority of phases at Caracol. The percentage of estimated population seen in burials varies from a low of .00009% in the Terminal Classic (A.D. 780–1080) to a high of nearly .0006% during the Late Preclassic (300 B.C.–A.D. 250) and early Late Classic periods (A.D. 530–650).

Santa Rita Corozal

Investigations at Santa Rita Corozal were conducted with the intent of producing information on the Maya Postclassic period (Chase and Chase 1988). The site was selected for excavation because of its known Postclassic occupation, but earlier remains were excavated when encountered. Identification of Santa Rita Co- rozal population history has been undertaken based both on structural and burial informa- tion (Table 2.1). Methodologies for these analyses are provided in D. Chase (1990). Even though only securely dated burials and occupa- tion were utilized in these analyses, the two databases provide nearly equivalent informa- tion for only two periods of occupation at the site: the Early Classic period (A.D. 300–550) and the late facet of the Late Postclassic (A.D. 1300– 1530). Burial populations were found to ex- ceed percentages of structurally projected pop- ulations during the Early Preclassic (1200– 900 B.C.), Middle Preclassic (900–300 B.C.), and Late Preclassic periods (300 B.C.–A.D. 200), but structure-based population percentages exceeded those in the burial sample during the Protoclassic (A.D. 200–300), Late Classic (A.D. 550–900), Terminal Classic/Early Post- classic (A.D. 900–1200), and early facet Late Postclassic (A.D. 1200–1300) periods. Thus, one can question the reliability of the exca- vated skeletal sample in comparison to the evi- dence for occupation of structures during at least four time periods totaling 900 years. Sim- ilarly, one can question the structural sample in contrast to the osteological sample during three time periods totaling 1400 years. How- ever, as indicated above, even in those horizons where the relative proportion of osteological samples exceeds or correlates with other ar- chaeological information, the total number of individuals identified represents such a small portion of the total population (from less than .0005% of the Terminal Classic/Early Post- classic estimated population to between .001 and .005% of all other estimated popula- tions) that it is unclear how representative these samples really are relative to the population at large.

Tayasal-Paxcamán

Excavations in the Tayasal-Paxcamán Zone were undertaken in an effort to identify Late Postclassic occupation in the area. However, investigations produced evidence for settlement predominantly on earlier horizons. The basic methodology for undertaking an analysis of population in the Tayasal area is explained by A. Chase (1990). His comparison of relative populations based on burials and settlement has been amplified in Table 2.2. These calcula- tions indicate nearly equivalent structure- and burial-based populations during three periods in Tayasal's history: the late Early Classic (A.D. 400–550), the late Late Classic (A.D. 700– 950), and the Early Postclassic (A.D. 950–1200) periods. During all other periods of occupation (totaling 1800 years) the percentage of relative population derived from structure counts was found to exceed the percentage of relative popu- lation based on skeletal information substan- tially. The estimated population of the approxi- mately 90 km^2 area of the Tayasal-Paxcamán Zone was approximately 22,000 in the late Late Classic period (A.D. 700–950). The rela- tive percentage of coeval population seen in the skeletal sample ranges from 0 to approximately .0002%. The smaller percentage of population seen in burials at Tayasal as opposed to Santa Rita Corozal or Caracol may be related to the number of seasons of work (only one excava- tion season at Tayasal compared with four at Santa Rita Corozal and more than ten at Cara- col) as well as to an excavation strategy that fo- cused both on areal clearing of latest structures and "vacant terrain" tests. Thus, in compari- son to the other two sites, it is even more un- clear how representative the Tayasal sample is relative to the population at large.

Location and Typology of Interments

The location of interments at any Maya site is related both to ancient cultural practices and to contemporary archaeological excavation strat- egies. At Caracol, the majority of interments have been encountered in residential architec- tural compounds or "*plazuela* groups." While interments are present in varying contexts within these groups, the prominent burial location in a Caracol *plazuela* group is in relation to the eastern building. Approximately 65% of Caracol's residential groups are easily recognizable as having an eastern focus (where the eastern building is the focal point in a given group). Even when not recognizably focal, the eastern building was still often used as a shrine or mausoleum at Caracol (A. Chase and D. Chase 1994b). Such eastern constructions generally contain burials in one or more tombs along with subsequently placed interments in crypts, cists, or simple fill. The pattern of eastern interment is fairly clear-cut archaeologically. Most Caracol tombs have entryways permitting multiple use of the same chamber and most of these tombs contain the remains of more than one person. In contrast to other sites practicing sequential multiple-individual interments in tombs (where all bodies remain in the chamber) such as at Guaytán (Smith and Kidder 1943) and at Lubaantun (Hammond et al. 1975), Caracol provides a different and diverse interment picture with regard to its tombs. Some interments were primary with individuals buried immediately in tombs. Other individuals were clearly secondary burials within tombs. Still other individuals were removed from tombs after a period of time and interred elsewhere (D. Chase and A. Chase 1996). Eventually, however, the tomb was given its final use and formally sealed. This final use often consisted of the interment of a primary individual accompanied by other bundled secondary remains. Following tomb closure, crypt or cist interments were then placed tangentally to the lower eastern building step and subsequent burials were then intruded into the stairway itself. While tombs and burials have been noted in other (noneastern) locations (including the north and south buildings in Caracol's residential groups), they do not occur in the same frequency as in an eastern construction. Given the large population projected for Caracol and the archaeologically known residential burial patterns, it

can also be posited that the Classic inhabitants maintained other burial areas that have not yet been located.

The location of more than 120 tombs is known for Caracol, and archaeological information has been recorded for more than 90 of these. All date to the Classic period (and most to the Late Classic period). More collapsed tombs are located whenever settlement pattern research is carried out at the site. In fact, based on the data from tombs, and particularly in their distribution at Caracol, any social dichotomy seen in Maya burial practices in the central lowlands becomes diminished by the Late Classic period, when not only did a greater percentage of the population have final resting places inside tombs, but there was also more distributional equivalency in burial goods and patterns as compared to earlier times (Chase 1992).

Many interments at Caracol, whether in tombs or simple burials, contained the remains of more than one individual. As mentioned previously, not all interments were primary. Archaeological evidence exists for secondary burials of single individuals in tombs and in simple graves as well as evidence of multiple primary interments combined with secondary interments in similarly varied circumstances. The interment of multiple individuals (some of whom may be partially or wholly articulated) is not unknown in the Maya world, but the quantity of multiple-individual burials that have been recovered at Caracol (ca. 39% of the total Late Classic sample; Chase 1994) is striking in comparison to the paucity of these kinds of interments at other lowland sites. For instance, at Tikal only 1.4% of the Late Classic burial sample contains multiple bodies. The prevalence of multiple-individual interments at Caracol is part of a complex of features that can be suggested as correlating with the creation of a strong cultural identity at Caracol during the Late Classic period following a period of successful wars against Tikal and Naranjo (A. Chase and D. Chase 1996). The emphasis on this practice at the site may also conceivably correlate with the need to inter an ever-increasing Late Classic population within a limited space.

At Santa Rita Corozal, interments are encountered in both residential and nonresidential structural locations. Perhaps because of its greater time depth, temporal variation in burial patterns is more evident at Santa Rita Corozal than it is at Caracol. During the Preclassic period, most of the skeletal population was buried in simple primary context in extended or flexed position below houses or house platforms. Most burial offerings included a single ceramic vessel, although some included shell or other artifacts. By the Early Classic period, a dichotomy in burial practices is noticeable at Santa Rita Corozal. Two tombs were found in nonresidential architecture in Structure 7. These are elaborate interments of single individuals (one male and one female) containing a variety of exotic ceramic, jadeite, lithic, and shell artifacts. Elsewhere at Santa Rita Corozal during the Early Classic period, interments were located below houses and consisted primarily of flexed individuals in cists or simple burials that were generally accompanied by no more than a single ceramic vessel that had been "killed" and placed over the head. Similar to Caracol, however, by the Late Classic period any dichotomy in burial practices lessened. During the Postclassic period, while there was variation in burial practices, tombs were no longer used. Elaborate interments during this later time were marked by stone altars and were located in association with multiple-room residential structures and smaller shrines. Individuals in these interments included both males and females, but were usually buried in an upright flexed position. These presumed high-status burials were accompanied by pottery or by jewelry made of shell, jadeite, or metal. Other Postclassic interments consisted of simple graves cut into or behind existing buildings. Multiple interments, both primary and secondary, are much more common in the Postclassic

at Santa Rita Corozal (42 burials with 69 individuals) than during the earlier Classic period (41 burials with 42 individuals). There is no evidence at Santa Rita Corozal for the eastern burial focus found at Caracol.

At Tayasal, the burial sequence starts with a single elaborate Late Preclassic burial that was found in vacant terrain excavations. It was accompanied by eccentric obsidians and a jadeite and shell mosaic ornament. The Tayasal burials datable to the Early Classic exhibit the same dichotomy noticed at Caracol and Santa Rita Corozal. The single tomb noted for this period contained 14 vessels and a host of smaller items, whereas most other coeval burials had only one or two vessels. The Late Classic interments at Tayasal are almost formulaic: an extended supine body accompanied by one to four vessels, one of which is often "killed" and inverted beneath the head of the individual as if to serve as a pillow. The single Late Classic tomb, dating to the beginning of the period, is a slight elaboration on this general theme with seven ceramic vessels and five jadeite beads. No multiple burials are known from Late Classic Tayasal (n = 26); however, two multiple burials, each containing two individuals, are known from both the Early Classic (n = 13) and the Postclassic (n = 12) periods.

Relative Aging, Sexing, and Health Status of Skeletal Populations

The skeletal samples from each of these sites are somewhat fragmentary. Even *in situ* preservation of remains was generally poor. Thus, in-field identification of age and sex often has taken precedence over post-field analyses. Nevertheless, there have been rare cases when post-field assessments have altered in-field interpretations. The author viewed all of the available skeletal material from each of these sites, but not always with the same intensity. The author was not present for the 1971 Tayasal excavations and thus could only review the stored skeletal remains in Guatemala in conjunction with other post-field analyses undertaken during the summer of 1977. A large number of the Santa Rita Corozal burials were excavated by the author and all were viewed in-field and briefly in the Corozal laboratory, but many have not been fully reviewed post-field. A similar situation exists for Caracol. Analysis of the Santa Rita Corozal and Caracol materials is still ongoing and, in fact, the Caracol sample is being increased on a yearly basis. Thus, certain of the following comments may be modified in the future.

In all cases, as many factors as possible were included in the analysis. Age-at-death in each sample population is most accurate for sub-adults in which dental eruption patterns could almost always be used in conjunction with other less reliable factors (such as long-bone length). Age-at-death of adults has generally been based on less reliable, degenerative changes, especially wear in teeth. However, a complete internal scaling of wear following Miles (1963) has yet to be completed. Age-at-death for adults was likely underestimated, rather than overestimated. Some individuals in each of the sample populations are particularly difficult to analyze because of substantial antemortem tooth loss that interfered with assessment of dental wear.

Sexing of skeletal remains also has been undertaken using as many means as possible, but has been hampered by preservation. Sex assessments were made only on adults and only when there was reasonably good evidence, preferably from analysis of features on the pelvis and skull. Other identifications (individual stature, pathological lesions, etc.) were dependent upon preservation and thus were made on an individual case-by-case basis as samples would allow.

The age-at-death of individuals in the skeletal population at Caracol ranges from infants less than one year of age to adults approximately 50 years of age or older. The majority of adults in this skeletal sample, however, likely lived to somewhere between 25 and 35 years of age. This skeletal information compares with historic information from Caracol hieroglyphic texts that record the death of one of Caracol's known rulers, Kan II, at the age of 71 in A.D. 680. Potential problems and discrepancies for other Maya sites (specifically Palenque) have been previously noted between skeletal age and hieroglyphically recorded age (Marcus 1992; Ruz 1977). As Kan II's burial has not been found, we cannot assess the validity of the site's textual statements vis-a-vis skeletal analysis. However, few, if any, individuals at Caracol can be assigned an age of "71." It must be cautioned again, though, that the extant analysis has avoided any over-aging of osteological remains at Caracol.

Even though the samples are extremely small relative to the once extant total populations, the percentages of archaeologically recovered burials at various ages of death may be instructive in viewing the populations of these sites. For instance, in comparing the two inland sites of Caracol (cf. Chase 1994) and Tayasal (cf. Chase 1983) for individuals identified as to age-of-death, 14.79% of the sample at Caracol was composed of infant skeletons, while only 5.36% of the sample at Tayasal was composed of infants. At Tayasal, 23.21% of the sample was composed of skeletons of individuals over 35 years of age, while at Caracol only 11.24% of the sample was composed of such individuals. It is tempting to ascribe such demographic differences to variations in population density and urban environment (cf. Storey 1992b for Teotihuacán). Alternatively, these differences may simply relate to differential sampling at the two sites.

The actual cause of death is rarely evident in the skeletal remains from Caracol. Health problems evident in the skeletal remains rather indicate that a given individual survived a particular health problem. Identifiable health problems include dental problems such as enamel hypoplasia, calculus, caries, tooth loss, and alveolar resorption, as well as other less common maladies such as fused vertebrae, porotic hyperostosis, and arthritis. The most common affliction is enamel hypoplasia, existing in approximately 16% of the burial sample. Moderate to severe calculus is thus far noted in only seven individuals, or 2.1% of the Caracol sample. Porotic hyperostosis, found to be present in relatively high proportions in some Maya populations (cf. Saul 1972a for Altar de Sacrificios), has been identified in only seven individuals at Caracol, equally distributed among adults and subadults. Interestingly, however, the identified cases of porotic hyperostosis cluster within specific household groups. The known cases come from only three locations at the site.

The Santa Rita Corozal individuals show less evidence of ailments than those from either Caracol or Tayasal. Porotic hyperostosis occurs in only three cases and there is only a single recorded case of dental calculus. In comparison, the Tayasal population exhibits no porotic hyperostosis and only a single case of noticeable hypoplasia. Some 13.56% of the adult burials at Tayasal had no caries or calculus in the teeth (n = 8). However, two cases of possible rickets are recorded for Tayasal and 18.64% of the population (n = 11) shows mild to severe calculus build-up, indicative of other potential dietary problems. Evans (1973), in his study of calculus and caries in the Tayasal sample, suggested the presence of a dietary imbalance (specifically a high-carbohydrate, low-protein diet) throughout much of the site's history. How much of a potential role the environment played in the health picture cannot be determined at this time. From this rather limited sample, it is unclear whether the seaside Santa Rita population was healthier than either the lakeside Tayasal or the upland Caracol populations.

Dental Modification (Filing and Inlays)

Dental modification is extremely variable across the three sites. No cases of either inlays or filing have been noted for Santa Rita Corozal. At Tayasal inlays occur in three Late Classic buri-

als while filing occurs in four burials (one Preclassic, two Late Classic, one Early Postclassic). One Postclassic burial additionally exhibits a single supernumerary tooth. Caracol is seemingly anomalous for most Classic era lowland sites in that 34.34% of the burial sample exhibits filing or inlays of jadeite, hematite, and shell, making dental modification relatively common in the skeletal sample of the site. Of the Caracol interments, 11.66% have inlays only, 14.11% have filed teeth only, and 8.57% include teeth that exhibit both inlays and filing. Fully 20% of the excavated interments at Caracol (33 burials in 26 groups) contain individuals with inlaid teeth. This may be compared with 2.6% of the total interments from Tikal (n = 6). The interments that have individuals with inlaid teeth include those located in tombs in the epicenter that presumably represent royalty, as well as many individuals buried in simple graves in the farming areas of Caracol. Thus, the simple presence of filing or inlays has no direct correlation with status (a similar situation is also true for Copán; Whittington 1989). However, the Caracol data also indicate that certain inlay and filing patterns (such as mandibular inlays of jadeite in the incisors and canines bounded by hematite-inlaid premolars) may be indicative of a particular status.

Population History: Further Problems in Intrasite and Intersite Comparison

The osteological sample at each of the three sites or zones considered here was generated using roughly comparable methodologies. Areal clearing, axial trenching, and test excavations were undertaken at each site. In all three sites interments have been encountered in a variety of locations, including placement in residential and nonresidential constructions, as well as in plazas. Individuals have also been placed in a diverse range of interment conditions, from inclusion in trash dumps to formal placement in elaborately constructed tombs. However, the intensity of investigation has varied at each site. Caracol has been the locus of ten years of research, but had a larger overall population. Santa Rita Corozal was a smaller site with four seasons of excavation. Maximal Tayasal populations were larger than Santa Rita Corozal but smaller than Caracol, but digging took place during only a single season. As noted, the temporal foci of investigation also varied among the sites as did the frequencies of differing excavation types and the emphasis on structural as opposed to nonstructural investigations. All of these things have a bearing on the osteological sample that is generated and should be considered in any attempt at making absolute correlations of skeletal remains among these sites.

Analysis of Smaller Household Compounds

Granted that synthetic interpretations relating to skeletal populations at most Maya sites are problematic because of scale, the legitimate question can be raised as to whether sampling problems can be better controlled in smaller, more intensively excavated contexts. A brief answer to this obviously complex question is "yes and no."

Perhaps the best known skeletal samples that have been used to characterize a large population are those derived from the Tlajinga 33 apartment complex at Teotihuacán (Storey 1985, 1992b). Storey (1992b:50,70) notes that this "compound is but one of 2000" and that it was occupied for "a period of 450–500 years." Millon (1976) estimated that each Teotihuacán compound housed populations of up to 100 people. Thus, over the span of its history Tlajinga 33 presumably housed some 900 people. Storey (1992b:130) notes that "the Tlajinga 33 compound residents recovered from skeletal remains numbered 206." Of this number, there were 42 primary burial contexts with 49 individuals, 16 secondary interments with 19 individuals, and 22 "refuse interments" representing 42 individuals. The remainder of the sample derived from secondary fill (and midden) contexts. This combined sample appears to present a representative cross-section of a prehistoric population (Storey 1992b). Thus, Storey sees her skeletal sample as adequately reflecting age and sex distributions. It would also apparently represent some 22.89% of the compound residents, an extremely high total for most Mesoamerican contexts. However, disagreement exists over how representative even this skeletal sample is. While Storey (1992b:70) argues that the Tlajinga 33 sample "will reflect demographic characteristics of the majority of the inhabitants of the city," Sempowski (1992:30) explicitly disagrees, noting that "most burial data from Teotihuacán relate to persons of intermediate status, whose remains were interred in their house and happen to have been well preserved."

Samples from most lowland Maya house compounds or plaza groups are not as representative as those from Tlajinga 33. This is particularly evident in the published data from Tikal. Haviland has presented data from a series of housemound excavations at Tikal, from which the representativeness of a given house compound's skeletal population can be extrapolated. For Group 2G-1 (Haviland 1988), it can be estimated that some 106 people occupied it over its history. Twelve burials of adult males are known from this group. Thus, although 11.32% of the presumed burial population from Group 2G-1 was recovered, the sample is nevertheless skewed, including only males that are all associated with a single building in the group. For Group 7F-1 (Haviland 1981), it can be estimated that some 245 people occupied this compound over its history. Fifteen burials were recovered from excavations in the structures and associated plaza of this group. Thus, some 6% of the total population is represented in this burial sample. For Groups 4F-1 and 4F-2

(Haviland et al. 1985), it can be estimated that some 910 people occupied these locales over a long occupation history. Even though 31 burials (spanning all segments of a potential population) were recovered, this sample represents only 3.41% of the overall population that once lived here. Similar low figures, hovering around 10% of a total group's population, can be obtained from calculations based on the more intensively excavated groups at Caracol. In summary, then, the representativeness of the skeletal samples from even the most detailed excavations in Maya *plazuela* groups of the south-central lowlands must be questioned from an analytic standpoint in regard to both the residential group and the population at large.

Discussion

Comparisons of the skeletal populations from Caracol, Santa Rita Corozal, and Tayasal suggest very different population histories but reveal some interesting similarities. Epicentral Caracol was occupied relatively late (ca. 300 B.C.) compared to both Tayasal (600 B.C.) and Santa Rita (1200 B.C.). However, Caracol reached a much larger peak population during the Late Classic period than either of the other two sites. Santa Rita Corozal is the only site of the three to have its primary population peak occur in the Late Postclassic period. The skeletal populations at all three sites suffered similar health problems. However, the sampled osteological remains of the people from Caracol show more evidence of maladies, a higher percentage of infant skeletons, and a lower percentage of skeletons of individuals older than 35. Differences seen among these populations may be related to a variety of factors such as environment (lacustrine and coastal as opposed to inland), the more urban nature of the densely populated Caracol, or to sampling. Some answers may possibly be garnered from future re-

search, such as the dietary analyses being conducted on the Santa Rita and Caracol samples by Henry Schwarcz and Christine White.

Viewing skeletal and burial information among sites can be misleading if the proper controls of context and scale are not maintained. For example, a comparison of Early Classic interments at Santa Rita Corozal and Caracol might tend to overemphasize the significance of Santa Rita Corozal based on the wealth of exotic items found in that site's tombs (cf. Chase 1992), items of far more beauty and rarity than are presently known from Caracol's many chambers. Santa Rita Corozal was clearly a less important site politically than Caracol during this time. The prominence of its burials likely reflects Santa Rita's closer proximity to trade routes and increased efforts of peripheral rulers to emphasize their status in death.

Coeval differences in cultural practices relating to interments among the sites are also worthy of attention. Early Classic interments at each of the three sites exhibit bimodal distributions. All three sites have elaborate Early Classic tombs sharing broadly similar artifacts. However, a basic similarity in the pattern of placing single ceramic vessels near the heads of individuals in Early Classic and Late Classic primary interments at both Tayasal and Santa Rita Corozal is not reflected in the burials of Caracol. The greater frequency of tombs and inlaid teeth in the Late Classic period at Caracol, as opposed to either Santa Rita Corozal or Tayasal, may reflect the site's prosperity at this time, but also may be indicative of other internal cultural factors (such as the intentional establishment of a distinctive Caracol identity).

Burials have been used to assist in making status distinctions at each site. However, this is never a simple matter. At Caracol, there does seem to be one key factor in status assessments: the amount of tomb volume per individual. The greater tomb volumes (ca. 7 m^3 of space per individual) appear to correlate with other factors, such as painted hieroglyphic texts, that suggest royal status. At Santa Rita Corozal and Tayasal other factors, such as the architecture and artifact contents of the surrounding building, when combined with interment type and contents, have helped to yield better status assessments. Comparative study of interments can also be used to assess relationships among sites within a region. The distributional study of tomb volume in the wider area surrounding Caracol reinforces the existence of a hierarchy of sites subordinate to Caracol (Chase 1992).

When viewing the occupation history of these three sites, it is useful to compare population reconstructions gained from settlement data with the actual skeletal population recovered. Discrepancies between population percentages, as expressed in settlement and skeletal samples, may be suggestive of sampling problems in the recovery of the skeletal population. Such comparisons may also help to demonstrate the severity of cultural changes associated with specific transitions that are evident in the archaeological record.

In summary, not only does contextual analysis of skeletal remains from the lowland Maya sites of Caracol, Santa Rita Corozal, and Tayasal add significantly to the interpretations at each site, but the combined comparisons suggest more about the variability in ancient Maya populations than each of these analyses would indicate in isolation. However, discussion and comparison of skeletal materials within and between sites is not without its difficulties. A number of authors have questioned the overall comparability of data from divergent reports, the ability to view health among different archaeological populations, and whether paleo-epidemiology can be attempted using archaeological data (Ortner and Aufderheide 1991; Wood et al. 1992). There are not only differences in methodology and reporting with regard to skeletal analysis, but there are also problems in the basic sampling of skeletal remains. Differing archaeological research strategies may yield distinctive or skewed skeletal samples, as may past cultural practices. Furthermore, comparison of population percentages based on dated structural occupation as opposed to dated osteological materials reveals even greater potential sampling problems whether one is viewing residential groups, sites, or wider regions. Comparisons within and between sites can only be expected to be meaningful if the parameters involved in defining any set of archaeological data have been carefully explored in an attempt to determine the reliability and comparability of individual sample populations.

Acknowledgments

The investigations reported on above have been funded by a wide variety of institutions. The work in the Tayasal-Paxcamán Zone of Guatemala was supported by The University Museum and the Anthropology Department of the University of Pennsylvania. Investigations at Santa Rita Corozal were funded by the National Science Foundation (Grants BNS-8318531 and BNS-8509304) as well as by the Explorers' Club, Sigma Xi, various agencies at the University of Pennsylvania, and private donations. Investigations at Caracol have been funded by the Dart Foundation, the Government of Belize, the Harry Frank Guggenheim Foundation, the National Science Foundation (Grants BNS-8619996 and SBR-9311773), the United States Agency for International Development, the University of Central Florida, the Institute of Maya Studies, and private donations. The author would also like to thank Arlen F. Chase for his help and input into this paper.

3

The Preclassic Skeletons from Cuello

Julie Mather Saul and Frank P. Saul

Located in northern Belize between the Río Hondo and New River, the Preclassic Maya site of Cuello has been extensively excavated since 1975 (Hammond 1991). Excavations were concentrated on Platform 34, a raised area of about 80 × 70 m upon which sits what is now known to be a small Late Formative pyramid. When test excavations in 1975 revealed continuous occupation from about 1200 B.C. onward, large-scale excavations were undertaken in order to understand the antecedents of Classic Maya civilization better through an increased understanding of the Preclassic Maya.

Platform 34, dating to the Late Formative period, was constructed over an earlier Middle Formative (Swasey, Bladen, Mamom phases, 1200–400 B.C.) patio group. Initial occupation, consisting of low platforms built on the old ground surface, developed into a household patio group of residential platforms around a patio.

Most Swasey and Bladen graves (1200–650 B.C.) were cut into house platforms during house construction, use, and abandonment. Some few others were placed outside the house platforms themselves, but still seemingly within a "domestic" context.

During the Mamom period (650–400 B.C.), while the patio floor apparently shifted from a primarily domestic to a more ceremonial function, most burials continued to be located in or under houses or ancillary structures.

The largest number of burials come from the Chicanel phase (400 B.C.–A.D. 250). The Mamom patio group was covered by a limestone rubble fill more than 1 m in depth during construction of Platform 34 at about 400 B.C. A depression of about 4 × 5 m in the top center of the rubble contained Mass Burial I (approximately 32 individuals), sealed by the plaster surface of Platform 34. Over time, successive plaza floors were laid as Platform 34 was remodeled, and in about A.D. 100 a plain stela was erected in the center of the plaza in front of the pyramid. At about this time Mass Burial II (approximately 12 individuals) was introduced into the plaza floor directly above Mass Burial I and east of the stela. Seven other burials also appear to be "sacrificial events" in honor of the construction of Platform 34.

A succession of what were probably ceremonial structures were constructed on the western side of the plaza, culminating in the Late Preclassic pyramid (Structure 350) and its Early Classic successor, Structure 35. Here, only one burial was found, an adolescent axially placed (east-west) within one of the earlier buildings. Such placement was usually reserved for both prestige and sacrificial burials during later Maya times. The skull of a child was deposited in a bowl as a dedicatory offering for Structure 35.

The remainder of the known Chicanel burials were interred in residential platforms to the north of the plaza (those on the south having been almost entirely removed by erosion). As during Swasey, Bladen, and Mamom times, grave placement indicates continued use of structures after burial of the dead.

We have previously published information on 122 Preclassic burials, excavated from 1975 to 1980, in the site report (Saul and Saul 1991). Further excavations in 1987, 1990, 1992, and 1993 have increased the Middle Formative population by raising the number of Swasey individuals from 1 to 6, Bladen from 11 to 19, and Mamom from 8 to 30, making this possibly the largest skeletal sample from the Middle Formative period. The total number of Preclassic (Middle and Late Formative) individuals is now 166, although 180 burial sites have been discovered at Cuello. Some of the 14 "extra" burials were part of a settlement survey and, as none are definitely Preclassic, will not be discussed here. In at least one case, two burials were "collapsed" into one: the extra pair of tibiae found with Bladen Burial 7 (and given the burial number 8) were found to have been part of Swasey Burial 171 (excavated several years later), whose legs were displaced by the much later cut for Burial 7 and reinterred with Burial 7.

Many burials at Cuello were disturbed during subsequent demolition and construction events, as well as cut through by later burials, with skeletal material usually "disappearing" into fill, or added to the burial whose cut displaced it. In one instance, the grave cut for Mamom Burial 161 disturbed four earlier burials (three Mamom, one Bladen), and Burial 161 was placed into the cut with the shaft of his left tibia resting against the truncated end of the humerus of Bladen Burial 169. In this case, a fragment of ulna found in the fill of the intruding burial (161) was later reunited with a portion of ulna from disturbed Burial 160.

An exception to the seeming rule of "careless" treatment of displaced skeletal material was found in the careful rearrangement of Mamom Burial 162. This female (excavated in 1992) had evidently been disturbed when skeletal by a later, but unused, grave cut. The pelvis and lower extremities were still articulated, and the skull and clavicles in proper position, but only the right arm was present (although fragments of both hands and wrists were found by the pelvis). A few ribs were stacked on the right humerus, with the first two cervical vertebrae carefully placed within the curve of the ribs, odontoid process pointing upward. The missing scapulas, ribs, vertebrae, and left arm were found at a lower level next season, in a jumble in the fill near her left shoulder.

Although in-the-ground preservation in the Maya lowlands is poor owing to root damage and other factors, this unusually large Middle and Late Formative skeletal collection has outstanding stratigraphic documentation, and intensive reconstruction and analysis have produced useful information on population composition, health status, and cultural modifications during this important and still relatively unknown period.

This report will focus primarily on the now larger Middle Formative Swasey, Bladen, and Mamom populations, without ignoring the

Chicanel, or Late Formative, individuals. The reader is referred to the Cuello volume for more detailed information on individual burials excavated before 1987 (Saul and Saul 1991).

Population Composition: Sex and Age

Methods

Initial determinations of sex and age were made independently by both authors and then reconciled if necessary, a rare occurrence (Table 3.1). Standard evaluation techniques were used (i.e., Krogman and İşcan 1986), and integrated with knowledge derived from our previous studies of large numbers of Maya skeletons (Altar de Sacrificios, Seibal, Lubaantun, Tancah, Río Azul, Cozumel, and others), familiarity with other ancient skeletal remains, and experience with modern skeletons from forensic cases.

Owing to the highly fragmentary, eroded, and incomplete condition of these remains, some age or sex determinations either could not be made, or could not be made with any precise certainty. Many of the more reliable indicators no longer existed or were so fragmentary and degraded as to be useless (i.e., pelvises, epiphyseal ends of long bones, rib ends, medial clavicles).

Most individuals, therefore, are of necessity assigned to very general age categories. To state more specific estimates would imply greater accuracy than is possible, given the indicators available. In deference to the condition of these remains, we have used the following categories: Subadult (immature; dental development and skeletal changes as available may provide information leading to more specific age ranges), Young Adult (20 to 34 years), Middle Adult (35 to 54 years), and Old Adult (55+ years). In order to accommodate those individuals whose age estimates appear to fall "between" these ranges, we have added: Young/Middle Adult

(30 to 40 years) and Middle/Old Adult (45 to 55 years).

Teeth were the primary source of information in determining the age of subadults, as even with careful excavation small fragments of only a handful of epiphyseal surfaces could be examined. Although four children under four years were recovered from the earliest Swasey and Bladen levels, it is quite possible that the more fragile bones of young children may not have survived, leading to an underrepresentation of subadults.

In no instances were pubic symphyses or auricular areas present, and very few rib ends could be examined. Therefore, adult ages were assessed through examination of observable cranial suture closure, tooth wear, and arthritic lipping of those rare surviving articular surfaces.

We were also forced to rely on less exact sex indicators such as size and robusticity of longbone shafts, mandible shape, orbital rims, supramastoid crests, and mastoid processes (keeping in mind the effects of tumpline use and head burden-carrying on muscle attachments among Maya females), occasional sciatic notch fragments, tooth size, etc., and in one case, even context. Because of these constraints, sex determinations are, with few exceptions, "probable."

Our presence in the field on those occasions when we were available to do our own excavation impressed upon us the importance of "reading" and measuring such remains in the ground. Much information is lost and can never be recovered upon removal when cancellous bone has become inextricably merged with the soil and cortical bone is riddled with roots and crushed by overburden.

Sample

The total of 166 Preclassic burials (130 adults, 36 subadults) can be divided into six groups (Table 3.2).

The ratio of adults to subadults at Cuello during the Swasey phase is a surprising 2:4.

Table 3.1 Population Composition by Sex and Age in Years

Phase	Subadults				YA 20–34			Y/MA 30–40			MA 35–54			M/OA 45–55			OA 55+			A 20+			All
	0–4	5–9	10–14	15–19	M	F	?	M	F	?	M	F	?	M	F	?	M	F	?	M	F	?	
Swasey	1	1	2		1	1																	6
Bladen	3	1	1		2	4		2			3			1							2		19
Mamom[a]	2	3	3	2	7		1	1	2	1	1	1								2	1	2	30
Chicanel[b]	6	7	2	1	12	2	3	5	7	1	6	5	1							3		3	64
MB I					6		1	5		1	3						1			11	1	3	32
MB II					8			3		1	2		1										15
Totals	12	12	8	3	36	7	5	16	9	4	15	6	2	1	0	0	1	0	0	16	4	8	166

NOTE: M = male; F = female; ? = unknown sex; YA = young adults; Y/MA = young to middle-aged adults; MA = middle-aged adults; M/OA = middle-aged to old adults; OA = old adults; A = adults of unknown age; MB = mass burial.

[a] One Mamom subadult was so fragmentary that age could not be determined, but was probably under 10 years old.

[b] No mass burials.

Table 3.2 Cuello Individuals by Phase

Phase	SA	A	n
Swasey (1200–900 B.C.)	4	2	6
Bladen (900–650 B.C.)	5	14	19
Mamom (650–400 B.C.)	11	19	30
Chicanel (400 B.C.–A.D. 250)[a]	16	48	64
Early Chicanel Mass Burial (ca. 400 B.C.)		32	32
Late Chicanel Mass Burial (ca. A.D. 100)		15	15

NOTE: SA = subadults; A = adults; n = number of individuals.

[a] No mass burials.

Subadults consist of two adolescents in their early to mid teens and two children under 7 years, including one 14- to 18-month-old infant. Both of the adults are Young Adults, one male and one female. One of the teenagers (Burial 179, 12 to 15 years, ca. 1200 B.C.) is also thought to be female, although primarily by context, as the "feminine" shape of her mandible could be due to immaturity rather than sex, and no useful pelvic remains survived. "She" was buried lying on her back with her knees drawn up to her chest and her head turned to her left. Her arms were bent, with her right arm embracing the 14- to 18-month-old child, whose face lay on her cheek (also facing left), its extended body lying on its left side beneath her right arm, legs stretched down between the teenager's knees. This careful and intimate arrangement strongly suggests a mother-child relationship.

The Bladen adult to subadult ratio is 14:5. Subadults consist of three children under 4 years, one 9.5- to 14-year-old and one 6- to 10-year-old. Adults include six Young Adults (two male, four female), two Young/Middle Adults (both male), three Middle Adults (all male), one Middle/Old Adult male and two "Adult" females. The male to female to unknown ratio for Bladen adults is 8:6:0.

The Mamom adult to subadult ratio is 19:11. Subadults consisted of four teenagers, one pre-teen, three children between 5 and 9 years, two infants (6 to 12 months and 6 to 9 months) and one "immature" individual (consisting of a few small long-bone fragments). Eight Young Adults (seven male, one unknown), four Young/Middle Adults (one male, two female, one unknown), two Middle Adults, and five "Adults" make up the adult population. The sex of four adults could not be determined, probable males numbered 11, and probable females numbered four. Two of the teenagers also are quite likely to be males, based on mandible shape, and size and robusticity of long bones. Counting these two as probable males yields a male to female to unknown ratio of 13:4:4 (not including the nine unsexable subadults).

The Chicanel burials, not including two mass burials that may or may not contain Cuello people, yield an adult to subadult ratio of 48:16, and a male to female to unknown sex ratio of 26:14:8. Both mass burials were exclusively adult and virtually exclusively male (one may contain a small female or abnormally small male), which, combined with location and arrangement, leads us to suspect that these were probably ceremonial events, possibly involving individuals who were not part of the immediate Cuello population.

Mass Burial I (Early Chicanel, ca. 400 B.C.) contains the complete or partial skeletons of approximately 32 individuals with an adult to subadult ratio of 32:0, and a male to female to unknown ratio of 26:1:5. The single female (who could be an abnormally small male) is an adult of unspecified age, as are 11 of the males and three of those of unknown sex. The sex of one Young Adult and one Young/Middle Adult could not be determined. Probable males are made up of six Young Adults, five Young/

Middle Adults, three Middle Adults, and one Old Adult. The "centerpiece" of Mass Burial I was an arrangement of two primary males (one Young Adult, one Young/Middle Adult). Into their laps and at their feet were placed "body bundles": the disarticulated, tightly packed (therefore probably excarnate) parts of a minimum of nine Young/Middle Adult males. Around this central core the remains of 21 individuals were interred, mainly as single or double burials, as well as two more body bundles (one a minimum number of three individuals, the other a minimum of four).

Mass Burial II (Late Chicanel, ca. A.D. 100) consisted of approximately 15 adults, with a male to female to unknown ratio of 13:0:2. Eight of the males were Young Adults, three were Young/Middle Adults, and two were Middle Adults; the two individuals of unspecified sex were Young/Middle and Middle Adults. As in Mass Burial I, two primary males (both Young Adults) were accompanied by "body bundles," in this case two bundles containing the disarticulated parts of at least eight individuals. Above this unit was placed a double secondary burial, one individual partly disarticulated, the other both disarticulated and incomplete. Remnants of at least two more individuals were found in the fill.

The construction of Platform 34 appears to have inspired the ritual interment of at least seven other individuals: a double burial of one male and one possible female, both with their skulls and mandibles standing upright some distance from their normal location, with a tooth burial (one individual) accompanying the male; the double burial of two children, ages .5 to 1.5 years and 1.5 to 2.5 years (one with a pot replacing the head); a Young/Middle Adult male found partly disarticulated in fill; and a Young Adult male at the base of a wall. (See Saul and Saul 1991 for comments on "decapitations.")

A pit, partially excavated in 1980 and at that time thought to contain the fragmentary remains of one male, was found on further excavation in 1990 actually to contain the fragmentary, mostly cranial, remains of at least three adult individuals (at least two males), plus the dental remains of at least three adults (Young Adult, Young/Middle Adult, Adult), and one tooth of a 1- to 2-year-old child. Cut marks were found on parietal fragments, and tiny cross-cuts on the deltoid tuberosity of a right humerus and a distal left ulna fragment, all unhealed. The presence of cut marks, as well as the inclusion of multiple fragmentary individuals suggests a ceremonial (possible sacrificial) event.

Chicanel burials (excluding both mass burials) have an adult to subadult ratio of 48:16 and a male to female to unknown ratio of 26:14:8. This suggests a "selection" of males for ceremonial burial (perhaps even ceremonial death) in the "public" area, while in the residential area the population continued their customary burial of family members under and near houses. Certainly the predominance of mass-burial males points to selection.

For the entire Preclassic period the adult to subadult ratio at Cuello is 130:36, and the male to female to unknown ratio is 85:26:19. The population was predominantly Middle Adult (35 to 54) or younger (with only one Middle/Old Adult and one Old Adult) and male (although the 28 "Adults" could have included older individuals and the unsexable individuals could have included females). This apparent shift to adult males appears during the Mamom period, when the function of the "patio" area of Cuello was shifting from domestic to ceremonial use, and shifts farther in this direction during the Chicanel.

Health Status

Most diseases do not leave recognizable markers on bone, and at Cuello post-burial erosion

Table 3.3 Linear Enamel Hypoplasia (Assessable Permanent Dentition)

Phase	Absent				Present				
	M	F	?	Phase %	M	F	?	Phase %	n
Swasey/Bladen	4	2	3	53	3	3	2	47	17
Mamom	4	0	2	35	5	2	4	65	17
Chicanel[a]	12	4	4	48	11	5	6	52	42
Mass Burial I	3	0	1	36	6	0	1	64	11
Mass Burial II	0	0	0	0	7	0	2	100	9
Totals	23	6	10	41	32	10	15	59	96

NOTE: M = males; F = females; ? = unknown sex; n = number of individuals.

[a] No mass burials.

of bones and teeth has made detection of such markers especially difficult. However, some information on potentially significant (and also less significant) lesions and conditions has been obtained. Several less significant, but nonetheless interesting, lesions present in single or small numbers of individuals and described in detail in the Cuello report will not be further discussed here; they include spondylolisthesis, neurofibroma, osteoid osteomas, and sinusitis (Saul and Saul 1991).

In the discussion that follows, individuals are considered to be "evaluable" for a certain trait or lesion if the necessary skeletal element(s) or teeth are sufficiently preserved to permit inspection for the specific trait or lesion in question.

Linear Enamel Hypoplasia

Although occurring in the teeth, linear enamel hypoplasia represents a systemic developmental arrest during the process of tooth crown formation, rather than dental disease in the usual sense. This nonspecific marker, whether caused by malnutrition, infectious disease, or a combination of the two, is common at Cuello, and in the Maya area in general (Table 3.3). The location of the arrest line or groove serves as a clue to the timing of the disturbance. At

Cuello, as at various other Maya sites, groove location tends to indicate systemic problems at around 3 to 4 years of age (Saul 1972a; Saul and Saul 1991). This is about the age of weaning among the Maya as recorded by Bishop Landa at the time of European contact (Tozzer 1941). Always a critical time, the rigors of weaning may have been heightened by malnutrition and infectious disease.

The permanent tooth crowns of both mature and immature individuals have been examined and recorded, as they are a permanent record of nonspecific "stress" during the period of enamel formation of the individual, early childhood. "Presence" of linear enamel hypoplasia requires only one tooth bearing the lesion, whereas "absence" can be determined only if at least one each of the following teeth are present: central incisor, canine, premolar, first molar, and second molar. Percentages here, as throughout this paper, refer to percent of "evaluable individuals" for the particular trait being studied.

Linear enamel hypoplasia is present in 57 (59%) of the 96 evaluable Cuello Preclassic dentitions. It increases from 47% in the combined Swasey and Bladen phases to 65% in the Mamom phase and then decreases to 52% during Chicanel (excluding the two mass burials).

The Early Chicanel mass burial shows a 64% presence, but this increases to 100% in the Late Chicanel mass burial. The magnitude of this last figure further suggests that the backgrounds of the occupants of at least the second mass burial may have been different from that of the rest of the Cuello population.

Females consistently show a higher frequency than males during the Swasey/Bladen (60% female vs. 43% male) and Mamom phases (100% female vs. 56% male), and in the nonmass burial Chicanel population (56% female vs. 48% male). However, frequency of linear enamel hypoplasia in both Chicanel mass burials of males is higher than that of Cuello's Chicanel females, as well as nonmass burial Chicanel males. The Mamom "peak" is much more strongly evident among females, and during the entire Formative period at Cuello (not counting the two mass burials) the occurrence of linear enamel hypoplasia was higher in females (63%) than in males (49%). The change in male to female to unknown ratio during the Mamom phase to 11:4:4 (more "male" than during Swasey and Bladen times) combined with the female peak in hypoplastic lesions may relate to the Mamom change in function from primarily domestic to more ceremonial use.

Although linear enamel hypoplasia formed at about 3 to 4 years of age is common at Cuello, severe, nonlinear hypoplasia on the permanent teeth of one Chicanel child of 5 to 7 years of age indicates problems at 9 to 18 months. In addition, "pinpoint" pits are present midway down the distal surface of the maxillary third molar crowns of a Swasey Young Adult male, and the location of linear defects on the teeth of a Bladen female suggest systemic problems at about 5 to 6 years of age.

In comparison, hypoplasia figures for Preclassic Altar are eight present, two absent, and three unevaluable. Hypoplasia figures for Preclassic Seibal are five present and one unevaluable. These numbers are small but suggest one

or more nutritional, ecological, or cultural differences resulting in comparatively greater frequencies than in the Cuello population.

Spongy or Porotic Hyperostosis

Spongy or porotic hyperostosis is characterized by expansion of the diploë (and reorientation of its trabeculae) between the inner and outer tables of the skull, followed by erosion of the outer table in a sievelike pattern. This lesion is possibly associated with several varieties of anemia, especially iron deficiency anemia, perhaps in conjunction with the anemia of protein deficiency. Iron deficiency anemia can be quite variable in its skeletal manifestations as well as in its potential origins (nutrition, parasites, ceremonial bloodletting, etc.; Saul 1972a; Saul and Saul 1989). Although spongy or porotic hyperostosis seems to be quite common elsewhere in the Maya area, it is virtually absent at Preclassic Cuello (Saul and Saul 1991). Only 2 of the 49 individuals whose cranial remains could be evaluated show outer table porosity and diploic thickening. Both are from Chicanel, one a young adult male ("healed" lesion status) and the other the nonsexable teenager ("active" lesion status) who was apparently sacrificed and found in the first western ceremonial structure.

For comparison, at Preclassic Altar porotic hyperostosis was present in five and absent in two individuals. At Preclassic Seibal it was present in two and unevaluable in four. Again these numbers are small but suggest that one or more nutritional, ecological, or cultural differences may have favored the Cuello population, resulting in Cuello's extremely low frequency of this disorder.

Ossified Subperiosteal Hemorrhages and Periodontoclasia

Ossified subperiosteal hemorrhages are "bleeds" within the fibrous membrane surrounding the bone in life, that have become calcified or later ossified, and are therefore preserved after death. The initial impetus for such a flow would be a blow or some other sort of trauma, and the possibility of hemorrhage is enhanced by previous soft-tissue (especially capillary wall) weakness, such as that resulting from inadequate vitamin C in the diet.

Periodontoclasia is a common form of alveolar soft-tissue inflammation resulting in degeneration of tooth sockets with consequent tooth loss. It may be produced by a variety of interacting factors, such as mechanical irritation, infection and tissue breakdown due to vitamin C deficiency. When the two conditions occur together, vitamin C deficiency can be suspected (Saul 1972a; Saul and Saul 1991).

Although only 27 Cuello individuals were complete enough to be declared to be free of ossified subperiosteal hemorrhages, seven examples of such hemorrhages were found. Both subperiosteal hemorrhages and periodontoclasia were present in two Bladen females, one Chicanel female, and one Mamom male. One Chicanel male and one male in Mass Burial I, although showing ossified subperiosteal hemorrhages, could not be inspected for periodontoclasia, as was the case in an unsexable Chicanel adolescent.

It should be noted that the subperiosteal hemorrhages that we identified in the Cuello remains were somewhat fragmentary and eroded by root action (as was the norm for skeletal remains at Cuello). Our prior experience with the Altar de Sacrificios skeletons (Saul 1972a, Figs. 33–39) where the hemorrhages were varied in form and extent (and undamaged) provided the basis for recognizing similar (although damaged) smooth and dense ossified elevations of the periostium at Cuello. In contrast to the inflammatory cortical response described in our section on possible treponemal infection, these lesions did not involve the underlying cortex, and were generally confined to a small area of the bone involved.

Periodontoclasia was much more evident and very common at Cuello. All eight evaluable individuals from the Swasey and Bladen phases combined showed signs of periodontoclasia. Only 2 Young Adult males of the 13 evaluable Mamom individuals were free of periodontoclasia. Periodontoclasia was present in 22 out of 24 Chicanel individuals, with only 2 Young Adult males lacking this lesion. All four evaluable individuals in Mass Burial I and all five in Mass Burial II showed periodontoclasia.

For comparative purposes, at Preclassic Altar hemorrhages were present in three, absent in three, and unevaluable in seven individuals. Periodontoclasia was present in eight, absent in one, and unevaluable in four. Both conditions were present in three. For Preclassic Seibal, hemorrhages were present in one and unevaluable in five. Periodontoclasia was present in five and unevaluable in one. Both were present in one individual.

Saber-Shin Tibiae and Treponemal Infection?

Inasmuch as syphilis (both venereal and endemic) and yaws and other infections such as pinta are caused by the same organism (*Treponema pallidum*), and because organisms may evolve over time, we believe that it is appropriate to reference our ancient specimens to the general category, "treponema," rather than to a specific modern clinical entity (Table 3.4).

Owing to the fragmentary and incomplete condition of the Cuello remains, we have focused on tibiae, since tibial shafts were available for many individuals when other bones were not, and were frequently abnormal in configuration. We did, however, find potentially related abnormalities of the fibula in eight individuals with tibial abnormalities, including three with additional forearm involvement, and one (Burial 83; see Fig. 3.1) with most of the skeleton, incuding the skull, involved. This last individual was so severely affected that histologic studies were done, eliminating Paget's

Table 3.4 Tibial Abnormalities (Assessable Adults Only)

Phase	Normal				Anterior-Posterior Bowing				Cortical Expansion				Anterior-Posterior Bowing and Cortical Expansion				
	M	F	?	Phase %	M	F	?	Phase %	M	F	?	Phase %	M	F	?	Phase %	n
Swasey													1	1		100	2
Bladen	1	2		30		1		10	2			20	2	2		40	10
Mamom	1	1	1	25	2	1	1	33	2			17	1	2		25	12
Chicanel[a]	8	1		35	2			8					9	6		58	26
MB I	3			38	1			13					4			50	8
MB II													1			100	1
Totals	13	4	1	31	5	2	1	14	4	0	0	7	18	11	0	49	59

NOTE: M = male; F = female; ? = unknown sex; n = number of individuals; MB = mass burial.

[a] No mass burials.

disease as a possible cause (Della Collins Cook, pers. comm. 1988).

Tibial abnormalities included anterior-posterior bowing, cortical expansion, and periosteal reaction striations (Saul and Saul 1991). The combination of these abnormalities, together with medullary canal narrowing and maintainance of a straight and vertical interosseous crest (due to the manner in which remodeling proceeds) results in a tibia shaped like a cavalry saber, or "saber-shin tibia" of the sort that has been associated with congenital and endemic syphilis as well as yaws (Ortner and Putschar 1985).

Using the above criteria, a very significant portion of the entire Preclassic Cuello population (49% or 29 of the 59 evaluable adults) have "saber-shin tibiae" (Figs. 3.1–3.4). Of these, 18 (62%) are males and 11 (38%) are females. An additional eight (14%) show anterior-posterior bowing with no cortical expansion and four (7%) show cortical expansion with no anterior-posterior bowing. The remaining 18 (31%) are apparently normal. Additional information on distribution of tibial abnormalities by culture period and sex will be found in Table 3.4.

Those tibiae that show only anterior-posterior bowing or only an inflammatory cortical response may represent differing degrees or stages of bone reaction to a treponemal infection, or nutritional or usage stresses, or some entirely different infection or inflammatory response that is unrelated to treponemal disease.

The Precolumbian origin of syphilis remains controversial after centuries of discussion (Baker and Armelagos 1988; Ortner and Putschar 1985) and perhaps undeterminable given the concerns we expressed earlier in this section, but we believe that it is reasonable to state that a treponema-like disease, producing tibial abnormalities ("saber-shin") resembling those of modern day syphilis or yaws was present at Cuello as early as 1200–900 B.C. For comparison, saber-shin tibia was present in 1 and unevalu-

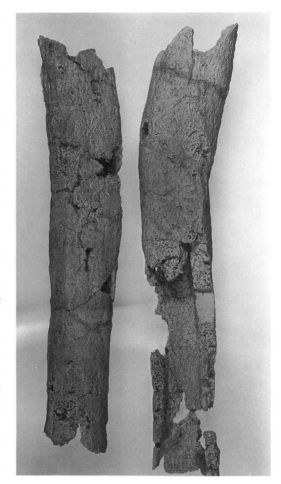

Figure 3.1. Burial 83, Adult Chicanel male. Medial views of left (on left) and right tibiae showing "saber-shin tibia" abnormality. Anterior-posterior bowing is pronounced (+++) in both (although slightly less marked in the left tibia) and cortical expansion extremely pronounced (+++++). Treponemal disease seems to be the most likely diagnosis as radiographic and histologic studies have ruled out Paget's disease.

able in 11 Preclassic Altar individuals and was unevaluable in 6 Preclassic Seibal individuals.

Osteoarthritis

Osteoarthritis or degenerative joint disease is an important indicator of individual and populational activity and stress patterns. Unfortu-

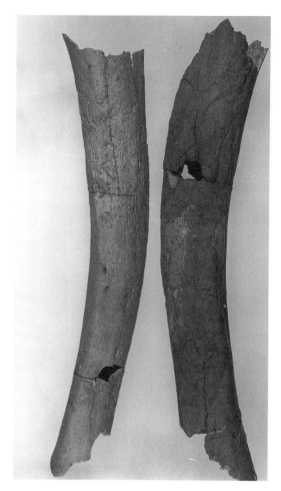

Figure 3.2. Burial 81, Young/Middle Adult Chicanel female. Medial views of left (on left) and right tibiae, showing "saber-shin tibia" abnormality. Anterior-posterior bowing is pronounced (+++) in both and cortical expansion is very pronounced (++++) in both (although the right tibia is more expanded).

nately, surviving articular surfaces were rare at Cuello. As only a few articular surfaces could be examined for signs of arthritis, we can draw no real conclusions about the absence, presence, or location of arthritis on a populational level. Arthritic lipping of the vertebral column was found in at least four males and one female. Several males had lipping of the foot phalanges, while two females and a male showed

lipping of hand phalanges. Most of these changes are probably age and activity related, with the male left distal thumb joint (right not affected) probably related to a more specific (but unknown) left-handed activity, perhaps pressure-flaking of chert or obsidian. A more detailed discussion of osteoarthritis at Cuello will be found in Saul and Saul (1991). In comparison, for Preclassic Altar, 13 individuals were unevaluable, and for Preclassic Seibal 1 individual had cervical osteoarthritis, and 5 were unevaluable.

Dental Health and Abnormalities

The various categories of dental disease must be considered to be interrelated to a great degree. Caries can lead to antemortem tooth loss and abscesses, calculus deposits lead to gum inflammation and thus to periodontoclasia and antemortem tooth loss, abscesses lead to tooth loss, and so forth. Dental disease is common in the Maya area, and Cuello is no exception (Saul and Saul 1991).

Unfortunately, only 7 individuals in all of Cuello had complete dentitions (32 teeth), with 47 individuals represented by fewer than 20 teeth. For this reason, we present data on caries and antemortem tooth loss in table form (Tables 3.5 and 3.6), without attempting to draw possibly misleading conclusions by comparing individuals. The people of Cuello certainly suffered from caries, with caries having destroyed at least 25% of the tooth crown in at least 13 individuals (including 4 Young Adults). Some teeth had been reduced to roots bearing "wear polish," testifying to retention followed by continued use for chewing.

Counting total teeth found during each phase as a "population," the Swasey/Bladen phase (304 teeth) had an 8% caries rate (24 carious teeth), the Mamom phase (313 teeth) a 14% caries rate (44 carious teeth), and the Chicanel phase (616 teeth without the mass burials) a 12% caries rate (74 carious teeth), for a total Cuello (1233 teeth) caries rate of 12% (142

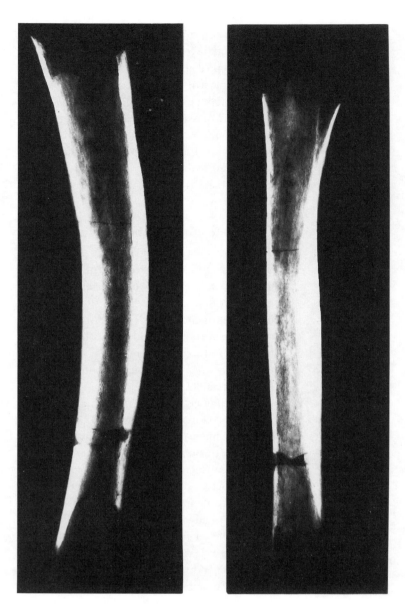

Figure 3.3. Burial 81, lateral (on left) and anterior-posterior radiographs of left tibia showing "sabering" and also medullary stenosis or internal narrowing due to cortical expansion often associated with treponemal infection. Radiographs courtesy of R. E. Miller.

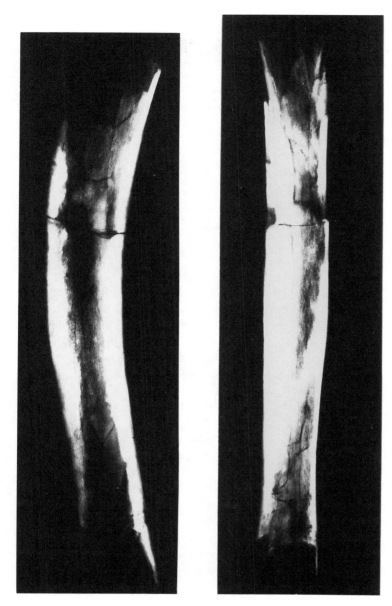

Figure 3.4. Burial 81, lateral (on left) and anterior-posterior radiographs of right tibia showing "sabering" and medullary stenosis. Radiographs courtesy of R. E. Miller.

Table 3.5 Ratio of Number of Carious Teeth to Number of Teeth Present (Adults Only)

		Teeth Present:	1–19				20–31				32	
Phase	Sex	Carious Teeth:	0	1–5	6–15	16+	0	1–5	6–15	16+	0	1–5
Swasey/Bladen	Male			1			2	2	1		1	1
	Female		1	1			2				1	
	Unknown											
	Total		1	2	0	0	4	2	1	0	2	1
Mamom	Male			1	1		2	3	2			
	Female			1				1			1	
	Unknown		2	1								
	Total		2	3	1	0	2	4	2	0	1	0
Chicanel[a]	Male			7			2	5	2	1	3	
	Female		4	4				3				
	Unknown		4	1								
	Total		8	12	0	0	2	8	2	1	3	0
Mass Burial I	Male		5	5	1		2	1				
	Female											
	Unknown		1									
	Total		6	5	1	0	2	1	0	0	0	0
Mass Burial II	Male		1	4			2					
	Female											
	Unknown		1				1					
	Total		2	4	0	0	1	2	0	0	0	0
Total Cuello[a]			11	17	1	0	8	14	5	1	6	1
Total Cuello[b]			19	26	2	0	11	17	5	1	6	1

[a] No mass burials.

[b] Including mass burials.

Table 3.6 Antemortem Tooth Loss

	Absent	Present
Swasey/Bladen phase	4	2
Mamom phase	1	2
Chicanel phase[a]	6	11
Mass Burial I	0	1
Mass Burial II	1	0
Males	9	10
Females	3	6
Totals	12	16

[a] No mass burials.

carious teeth). Mass Burial I had 21 carious teeth out of a total of 149 (14%), and Mass Burial II had 9 carious teeth out of 104 (9%).

Caries in females rose from 3% during the Swasey/Bladen phase to 15% during the Mamom, and then fell to 7% in the Chicanel. Caries in males rose from 10% in the Swasey/Bladen phase to 15% in the Mamom, and stayed virtually the same in the Chicanel (14%).

Subadults had few carious lesions in deciduous and permanent teeth. Seven Swasey/Bladen subadults ranging in age from 14 to 18 months to 11 to 14.5 years (a total of 134 teeth) had only two carious teeth (1.5%). Six Mamom subadults from 3.5 to 5.5 years to teenagers (82 teeth) also had only two carious teeth (2.4%). The caries rate rose in the Chicanel phase, where 120 teeth from seven subadults (the youngest aged 5 to 7 years, the oldest 15 to 19 years) had a caries rate of 5.8% (seven carious teeth).

Dental calculus was present on the dentitions

of virtually all individuals, including some in their teens. "Severe" calculus deposits were found in two Swasey/Bladen males (Middle Adult and Young/Middle Adult), one Young Adult Mamom female, and two Young Adult Chicanel males. All those who could be evaluated for both periodontoclasia and calculus possessed both, with one exception: a Chicanel Young Adult male with severe calculus deposits.

Abscesses were found only in seven males. Mandibular abscesses were present in a Mamom Young Adult and a Chicanel Young Adult. Maxillary abscesses were present in one Bladen Middle Adult, and in a Chicanel Young Adult, Middle Adult, and Adult. The maxillary abscess in the Old Adult in Mass Burial I communicated with an inflammation of the maxillary sinus.

ENAMELOMAS. Since our last publication on this population, one more enameloma has been found in a Mamom male, joining one Bladen female and two Chicanel males. These "pearls" of dental enamel are typically located on the roots of molars. This essentially normal variation is thought to be more prevalent in Asiatics and Northern Europeans. (See also Saul and Saul 1991). Preclassic Altar and Seibal individuals had none.

CONGENITALLY MISSING MANDIBULAR INCISOR. The left central mandibular incisor of an unsexable Mamom teenager (12 to 16 years old) is congenitally absent. While congenitally missing teeth do occur (most commonly third molars), it is extremely rare to find a mandibular incisor missing (Robert A. Burns, pers. comm. 1991). Dental radiographs show no signs of the missing tooth "submerged" in the mandible, nor are there any mandibular third molars forming. No maxilla is present.

RETENTION OF DECIDUOUS TEETH AND IMPACTED THIRD MOLARS. The deciduous left mandibular second molar of the Swasey teenager buried embracing a 14- to 18-month-old child has been retained and is impacting the unerupted permanent second premolar beneath it in the jaw. Its "mate" on the left was shed in more timely fashion, allowing the permanent premolar to erupt completely. The right mandibular third molar of a Young Adult Bladen male is firmly impacted against the root of the second molar, while the left third molar is fully erupted.

Postcranial Trauma

As no new examples of postcranial trauma were found, we will present only a brief summary of healed fractures which are presented in greater detail in our Cuello report (Saul and Saul 1991). Seven postcranial fractures are present, all in Chicanel males. Five healed fractures in at least three males were found in Mass Burial I: a foot phalanx fracture, malaligned "parry" fractures of left radius and ulna, "Colles" fracture (distal left radius), and fractured left capitate and lunate. In the "general" Chicanel population were found a fracture of the distal tibia and a malaligned femoral midshaft fracture with "exuberant" fracture callus. The presence of fractures only in males, combined with the high incidence of healed fractures in the mass burial population (five fractures in at least three individuals) suggests that males, and in particular those within the mass burials, were in some way more "exposed" to such trauma, perhaps through combat or "sports." For comparison, in Preclassic Altar individuals there was one midclavicular fracture. In Preclassic Seibal indiviudals no postcranial trauma was found.

Cranial Trauma

Cranial trauma was also found only in males and is described in the 1991 report. Above the right orbit of one Bladen male are a 15-mm "cut" and a circular perforation (6 mm) of the outer table, both healed. Lesions in two adult Chicanel males affect only the outer table, with a ring of osseous condensaton surrounding a shallow "dent." Campillo (1977) describes such lesions, found predominantly in males and located in vulnerable areas of the skull. A practicing neurosurgeon, he feels these "cranial erosions" represent healed osseous reactions secondary to traumatic injuries to the periosteum, and relates them to clinical cases. (See Saul and Saul 1991 for more detailed information on Cuello cranial trauma and for comments on "decapitations.") In Preclassic Altar individuals there was one left lambdoid "dent." For Preclassic Seibal, no cranial trauma was found.

Cultural Modifications

Intentional modifications of both head shape and teeth were common in the Maya area. We choose to refer to these modifications as "shaping" and "decoration," instead of the more commonly used, but pejorative, terms "deformation" and "mutilation." The Maya themselves, at time of contact, told the Spaniards that customs such as head shaping were "given to our ancestors by the gods, gives us a noble air, and our heads are thus better adapted to carry loads." They said that some body alterations were for the "sake of elegance" and "beauty" while others made them look "ferocious and fierce," thus frightening their enemies (Tozzer 1941:88, 217).

Cranial Shaping

Although other shaping classifications have been proposed, Imbelloni and Dembo's system (Comas 1960) is most frequently used in Latin America. Their basic categories involve "Tabular" shaping produced by fronto-occipital compression, and "Orbicular" or "Annular" shaping using bands that compress the head circumferentially. These categories are further subdivided into the "Erect" variety (the direction of pressure resulting in an essentially vertical or anteriorly tilted orientation of the occipital bone) and the "Oblique" variety (the entire occipital has been flattened and tilted posteriorly).

The cranial remains of only two Swasey individuals (females) could be reconstructed sufficiently to determine presence or absence of shaping. Both show possible signs of pressure from use of a tumpline or head sling (a horizontal depression or flattening in the region where a tumpline might lie), and the lambdoid area of one is also flattened in a manner suggestive of cradleboard use, both examples of unintentional or accidental shaping.

Five Bladen skulls are apparently "normal" in shape or unshaped (two males, two females, one child). Possible "tumpline" shaping is present in one female, and the skull of one subadult is flattened in the region of lambda. The frontal bone of one male shows intentional Tabular flattening, but the skull is too incomplete to determine the type (Table 3.7). Tabular Oblique

Table 3.7 Intentional Cranial Shaping or Dental Decoration

Phase	Sex	Degree[a]	Type[b]	Decoration[c]
Bladen	M	++	T?	0
	M	++	TO	0
	F	0	0	A-1
	M	+++	TO	0
Mamom	F	++	T?	?
	M	+	TE	?
	M	+	TO	?
Chicanel[d]	F	++	TO?	0
	F	0	0	F-4
	M	++	TE	0
	M	+	T?	F-4
	M	0	0	B-2 or B-4
	M	+++	TE	?
Mass Burial I	M	?	?	C-2 or C-6

NOTE: M = male; F = female; 0 = absent; ? = could not be determined; + = present; ++ = moderate; +++ = pronounced; T? = Tabular of uncertain variety; TO = Tabular Oblique; TE = Tabular Erect.

[a] Degree of cranial shaping.

[b] Type of cranial shaping.

[c] Dental decoration type. Romero (1970) categories.

[d] No mass burials.

shaping appears in two males and the most pronounced of the two may be the earliest example of Tabular Oblique shaping in the Maya area (850–750 B.C.).

Six Mamom skulls (males) were definitely not shaped, intentionally or unintentionally. The frontal bone of one female has been flattened, but the type of Tabular shaping cannot be determined. Tabular Oblique and Tabular Erect shaping appear in two males, although not pronounced, and the lambdoid regions of one male and one female are somewhat flattened.

Chicanel cranial shaping is predominantly of the unintentional cradleboard-use lambdoid flattening variety (10 individuals). Two male skulls are examples of Tabular Erect shaping, one female skull has Tabular Oblique shaping, and the frontal bone of one other male is flattened in Tabular fashion, but of unknown variety. The skulls of nine other individuals show neither intentional nor unintentional cranial

shaping. (See also Saul and Saul 1991.) Some Preclassic Altar individuals have possible cradle-board flattening. For Preclassic Seibal individuals, one has Tabular Oblique and one has Tabular Erect shaping.

Dental Decoration

Teeth in the Maya area were "decorated" by filing the incisal edge of incisors (also occasionally canines and premolars), drilling shallow holes for insertion of jadeite or iron pyrite on labial surfaces, engraving labial surfaces, or combinations of the above. The classification system most commonly used in México and Central America was developed by Romero (1970), and is based on location and type of decoration.

The earliest dental decoration to be found at Cuello (and perhaps in the Maya area, so far) appears in an Early Bladen (900–800 B.C.) female (Table 3.7; Fig. 3.5). All four of her max-

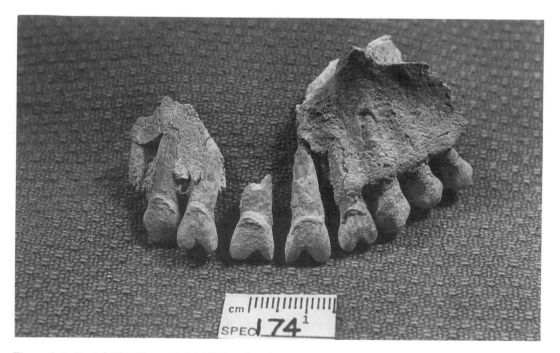

Figure 3.5. Burial 174, Young Adult Bladen female (900–800 B.C.). Anterior view of maxillary incisors showing Romero Type A-1 filing of incisal edges. This may be the earliest example of dental decoration in the Maya area. Note also calculus deposits. Photo by B. Weaver.

illary incisors show central notching (Romero Type A-1).

Only four other Cuello individuals have decorated teeth. Type F-3 or F-4 (asymmetrical filing of both angles of the crowns) was present in the teeth of one male and one female from Chicanel; Type B-2 or B-4 (filing of one of the angles of the crown) in a Chicanel male; and Type C-2 or C-6 (symmetrical filing of both angles of the crown) in one male from the Early Chicanel mass burial.

In only one case were shaping and decoration found together at Cuello: a Chicanel male with Type F-4 decoration and Tabular cranial shaping of unknown variety. The skull of the Early Bladen female with Type A-1 decoration has a normal shape, as does the Chicanel female with F-4 dental decoration and the Chicanel male with B-2 or B-6 decoration. Cranial shape could not be determined for the male in Mass Burial I with C-2 or C-6 decoration. (See also Saul and Saul 1991.) Types A-1, C-2, C-6, F-3, and F-4 were not present at Altar or Seibal during the Preclassic. B-2 and B-4 were present at Preclassic Altar, but not Preclassic Seibal.

Lingual Surface Attrition of the Maxillary Anterior Teeth

Dental attrition, although a dental finding, should perhaps be considered a cultural trait, as it is related to cultural activities such as food preparation, types of foods eaten, use of teeth as tools, and so forth. Marked attrition is very common in the Maya area, owing in large part to the practice of grinding maize and other foods between stones, thus introducing large amounts of stone grit into the diet as the stones grind each other, as well as the food between them. A modern Maya is quoted by Gann (1918:71) as saying that "an old man eats two rubbing stones (*metates*) and six rubbers (*manos*) during his life." Such abrasive foods typically produce a relatively flat (horizontal) wear on the occlusal surfaces of all teeth, particularly molars.

We have noted a curious pattern of tooth wear at Cuello (Saul and Saul 1989, 1991), which we have not seen described elsewhere in the Maya area (Fig. 3.6). It involves heavy diagonal (or oblique) lingual surface attrition of the maxillary anterior teeth, but without corresponding oblique wear of the mandibular anterior teeth. This wear appears to be similar to that described by Irish and Turner (1987) as seen in prehistoric Panamá and by Turner and Machado (1983) in an Archaic Brazilian site. At those sites lingual surface attrition of the anterior maxillary teeth was found in combination with a high incidence of caries, as seems to be the case at Cuello, where 21 dentitions with this type of wear are also carious (although 16 dentitions without caries were present, only 5 of them had 30 or more teeth available for inspection). All but 2 dentitions also had calculus present.

Counting only those adult individuals whose dentitions could be evaluated, this lingual wear pattern is found in 64% (7 of 11) Swasey/Bladen, 100% (11 of 11) Mamom, and 48% (12 of 25) Chicanel individuals. Occurrence in the Early Chicanel mass burial is 67% (6 of 9) and in the Late Chicanel mass burial is 40% (2 of 5) (see Table 3.8).

Although found in both males and females, lingual wear was more common in males during both Swasey/Bladen (86% male, 25% female) and Chicanel times (56% male, 29% female). The single evaluable Mamom female also manifested this pattern, as did all eight evaluable males (100%). Lingual wear persisted over a long period of time and does not appear to be exclusively limited to either sex.

Wear at Cuello is usually most pronounced on central incisors, occasionally produces lingual surfaces worn to a smooth concavity, and sometimes extends to include canines. Lingual wear of the left maxillary incisors of one Young Adult Chicanel male is so extreme that the pulp cavity of the mesial incisor is completely exposed and open, and a pinhole-size opening in

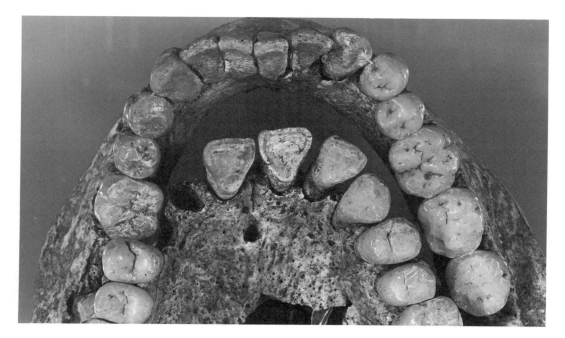

Figure 3.6. Burial 123, Young/Middle Adult Bladen male. View of occlusal surfaces of mandibular teeth (above) and maxillary teeth (below) showing moderate (++) lingual surface attrition of the maxillary anterior teeth on central and left lateral incisors.

Table 3.8 Lingual Surface Attrition of Maxillary Anterior Teeth (Assessable Adults Only)

	Absent			Present			
Phase	M	F	?	M	F	?	n
Swasey/Bladen	1	3	0	6	1	0	11
Mamom	0	0	0	8	1	2	11
Chicanel[a]	7	5	1	9	2	1	25
Mass Burial I	3	0	0	5	0	1	9
Mass Burial II	3	0	0	2	0	0	5
Totals	14	8	1	30	4	4	61

NOTE: M = males; F = females; ? = unknown sex; n = number of individuals.

[a] No mass burials.

the lateral incisor culminates in a large maxillary abscess.

Tooth root resorption is evident on the central maxillary incisors of several individuals with pronounced lingual wear. The affected roots appear "fat" and "stubby." Excessive mechanical or occlusal forces can cause external resorption of permanent tooth roots. The forces involved in producing such severe and angled wear may have been enough to cause resorption, although systemic disturbances that may predispose to root resorption, and "ideopathic" resorption (no obvious cause), are also possible explanations. Modern studies show that there can be destruction or resorption of two-thirds of the apical root without evidence of looseness or other signs of difficulties (Shafer et al. 1974).

Turner and Machado (1983) and Irish and Turner (1987) theorize that use of the upper anterior teeth and tongue to manipulate (much as we eat artichoke leaves) a gritty cariogenic food such as manioc roots may have produced this unusual wear coupled with caries cavities. Sex differences in incidence may indicate more access for males to a particular food item, with perhaps a decreased consumption of this item by Chicanel males. Alternatively, a cultural activity involving use of the teeth as tools, and performed more frequently by males, may be responsible.

We have now noted this type of attrition in 64% (7 of 11) of evaluable Classic dentitions at Río Azul, where it is present in both males and females. It may or may not exist in other Maya populations, as we ourselves only first noticed it in our Cuello people, and were not "looking" for it in earlier studies.

Stature

The measuring of stature or height in the living is subject to variation due to individual measurer's technique as well as increasing intervertebral disc compression during our "upright" hours. Estimating stature from individual bones of unknowns is an even more uncertain process involving selection of an appropriate statistical formula, sex and age adjustments, etc.

At Cuello, the problem was further compounded by the fact that owing to poor preservation only one male femur and one female tibia could be measured directly. We therefore decided to estimate femoral length by comparing landmarks on sufficiently intact femurs with the complete Cuello femur and complete femurs from other Maya samples, thus arriving at statural estimates based on the complete femurs. We did not use Steele's (1970) formulas for incomplete long bones because previous experience had demonstrated that some of his landmarks were difficult to determine with sufficient reliability. This "comparative" approach enabled us to increase our stature sample from one to ten males and one to nine females (Saul and Saul 1991). While in the field in 1992 and 1993 we were able to obtain three head-heel lengths and five long-bone lengths (four tibiae, one radius) from skeletons in the ground, further increasing our total stature sample to 16

males and 11 females. Our precedent for this procedure was Haviland's (1967) landmark study on stature change and social differences at Tikal, which also required *in situ* measurements owing to poor bone preservation.

We are reluctant to draw conclusions from such potentially inadequate data, but stature is important because it is a polygenic and multifactorial trait that may be affected by nutrition and disease within both an ontogenetic (life cycle) and phylogenetic (generation to generation) context. It may also provide clues to gene flow and population change. Previous studies at Altar de Sacrificios (Saul 1972a) suggested a decrease in male (and possibly female) stature over time, from the Preclassic onward, resulting in the very short Maya of modern times.

The mean stature of both males and females at Cuello appears to increase slightly from the Swasey/Bladen phase to the Mamom and then decline sharply for both females and males in the Chicanel if the three possibly intrusive mass burial males are excluded (or slightly for males if they are included; Tables 3.9 and 3.10). The mean (161.7 cm) for the 16 Preclassic Cuello males is less than those for their four Altar and

Table 3.9 Cuello Male Stature in Centimeters

	Mean	Range	n[a]
Swasey/Bladen	161.3	157.0–165.3	3
Mamom	163.8	158.8–167.0	6
Chicanel (all)	160.3	151.0–164.5	7
Minus Mass Burial I[b]	158.5	151.0–164.5	4
Mass Burial I alone	162.6	158.0–164.5	3
Altar de Sacrificios	166.6	163.5–173.0	4
Tikal	164.7	162.0–168.0	6
Cuello (all)	161.7	151.5–167.0	6
Minus Mass Burial I	160.9	151.5–167.0	13
Mass Burial I alone	162.6	158.0–164.5	3

[a] n = number of individuals.

[b] No statures were obtained from Mass Burial II.

Table 3.10 Cuello Female Stature in Centimeters

	Mean	Range	n[a]
Swasey/Bladen	155.9	152.0–159.8	2
Mamom	157.1	151.0–163.3	2
Chicanel (all)	151.5	146.5–159.8	7
Minus Mass Burial I[b]	152.3	146.5–159.8	6
Mass Burial I alone	146.5	146.5	1
Altar de Sacrificios	148.3	147.5–149.0	2
Tikal	147.0	145.0–148.0	4
Cuello (all)	153.3	146.5–163.3	11
Minus Mass Burial I	154.0	146.5–163.3	10
Mass Burial I alone	146.5	146.5	1

[a] n = number of individuals.

[b] No statures were obtained from Mass Burial II.

six Tikal counterparts (166.6 cm and 164.7 cm, respectively) but the 11 Cuello females are taller (153.3 cm) than the two Altar and four Tikal females (148.3 cm and 147.0 cm, respectively).

Status

Two early individuals at Cuello are considered to be of probable "high status," (Hammond et al. 1992). Burial 160, a Mamom (ca. 450 B.C.) Young Adult male, is thought to have been of great importance, perhaps a ruler. He was accompanied by a large assortment of grave goods: two bowls, one "bag-shaped" jar, three small jade beads, three tubular shell beads, a perforated shell, four bone tubes (three carved, one with the *pop* motif, a Classic Maya symbol of authority), a piece of turtle carapace, and on his chest, a bone gorget with a cutout mask design similar to the *ahau* or "lord" Classic period hieroglyph. He was located within a structure, along the east-west axis at the point where it crosses the north-south axis, a prestigious location.

Almost directly beneath Burial 160 was found another Young Adult male, Burial 170, also Mamom phase but slightly earlier (ca. 500 B.C.). Two bowls had been placed in his grave, along with 56 shell beads found on his chest and one shell bead in his mouth (on the occlusal surface of the left mandibular third molar). A small green bead (jade?) had worked its way into the broken shaft of the left femur. He is thought to have perhaps been an "ancestor" of Burial 160.

Both of these males were robust and at the "tall" end of the male range for the Mamom phase, ca. 166 cm. Burial 160 had no signs of possible treponemal disease, his skull was not shaped and his teeth could not be evaluated for decorations or lingual attrition. Present were linear enamel hypoplasia, periodontoclasia, caries, and calculus. The tibiae and fibulae of Burial 170 showed cortical expansion and striations, but no anterior-posterior curvature was evident. Linear enamel hypoplasia, periodontoclasia, and caries were not present. Lingual surface attrition was moderate, his head was unshaped, and his teeth were undecorated.

Although these males may have been "important" when interred, the grave cut for Mamom Burial 161 cut through them both, removing left and right femurs from just above the knee up through the pelvis of Burial 160, and the ankles and feet of Burial 170.

Conclusions

Although poorly preserved, intensive reconstruction and analysis of this unusually large and well-documented sample of Preclassic skeletal remains has enabled us to provide information relating to population composition, health status, and several cultural traits at Cuello.

Cuello's people were fortunate in having access to a wide range of nutritional resources. Archaeological evidence (Hammond 1991) shows that maize was present (and cultivated) at Cuello from the initial phases onward. Other food plants such as beans, chile peppers, avocado, hogplum, and nance were also available, but presumably not cultivated, as the varieties found were in the wild size range. The large quantities of shells of the edible snail *Pomacea flagellata* recovered (with shells of the most "edible" size predominating) are suggestive of controlled selection for consumption. Among the faunal sources of protein were deer and dog, with stable isotope analysis indicating that the dogs also ate maize, presumably table scraps (Norman Hammond, pers. comm. 1995). Fish also made up a part of the Cuello diet, mostly freshwater fish during the Middle Preclassic and shifting to marine types in the Late Preclassic.

This integration of maize with a large variety of other plant and animal food sources, rather than an overreliance on maize to the exclusion of other foodstuffs, may have protected the Preclassic people of Cuello from more severe nutritional difficulties.

Postscript

Throughout this paper, when talking about our population sample, we have made reference to the poor preservation of the Cuello skeletal remains due to a form of "natural selection" involving root damage, animal activity, localized drainage and soil conditions, and so forth. Remains are also subject to differential preservation related to the individual's age and sex (bone size and density) or pathology, as well as subsequent digging activity on the part of later occupants of the site.

It cannot, however, be overemphasized that the sample recovered is determined by the archaeologist in charge and his or her goals. Some choose to excavate only tombs and similar high-status locations. Furthermore, some choose to ignore skeletal remains or otherwise dispose of them in hasty fashion. In the case of Cuello, the sample is as complete as it is because Norman Hammond, the archaeologist in charge, chose to extract every bit of information from every source (including skeletons) in every portion of the site, and he excavated to bedrock.

Aside from the role of the archaeologist, we wish to stress once more the importance of having the physical anthropologist on site in order to conduct the actual excavation of burials so as to insure the recovery of information *in situ* (such as bone length) from remains that may not survive excavation.

One final (and personal) note from FPS, who states that he was fortunate to have begun his career in Maya skeletal research studying the Altar de Sacrificios material (Saul 1972a) excavated by Willey and Smith (1969), who were also "complete" excavators, but perhaps even more fortunate because the Altar remains were in such relatively good condition (which is related to differential preservation due to site location within the Maya area). FPS concedes that he would probably still be working on his Ph.D. dissertation or in another line of work if he had started with Cuello.

4

Height among Prehispanic Maya of the Yucatán Peninsula: A Reconsideration

Lourdes Márquez and Andrés del Ángel

Physical anthropologists have long been interested in the study of height and its variation among populations because of its potential to further understanding of some evolutionary changes and their causes. The influence of the environment and cultural habits, especially the positive or negative effects of the nutritional and sanitary conditions under which a given population lives, on body size is generally acknowledged. Adverse circumstances induce, after a period of time, a differential selection that favors the survival of small-bodied individuals, whose development requires a smaller quantity of nutrients than is required by large-bodied individuals. On the other hand, optimal living conditions are associated with increase in stature, as observed in the so-called secular trend found in industrialized countries (Tanner 1973).

Various researchers have accumulated evidence of a secular trend of stature reduction among populations of Mesoamerica, in particular among Prehispanic Maya and inhabitants of the Basin of México. Some explanatory hypotheses have been offered for this tendency.

Now, some 45 years after Stewart (1949, 1953) first explored the topic, we believe it necessary to reevaluate the evidence from the perspective of advances in the field during the intervening years. In the first place, we must evaluate the widely held conception that the height of both sexes was greater in more ancient skeletal series than it was in more recent ones. In his report on osseous material examined by him at sites in the Guatemalan highlands (San Augustín Acasaguastlán, Kaminaljuyú, Zaculeu, and Huehuetenango), Stewart (1953) compared the estimated heights of a sample of Prehispanic Maya with those of the modern Kaqchikel Maya population of the same region. He found a difference of 5 cm for each sex, the taller being the more ancient populations. The author provided two possible explanations, the first being that the former population of Guatemala was replaced by a more recent, shorter one, and the second being that the size of people in the area somehow diminished through time. He defended the idea that the present-day inhabitants of the Guatemalan highlands are, in fact, the descendants of the Prehispanic Maya and rejected the notion of hot weather having an influence on the height of the population, since, by definition, the highlands have a cold climate. The author argued that nutrition was a major factor in the observed height difference, although he acknowledged that the actual causes were unknown.

Longyear (1952), faced with the same question at Copán, Honduras, suggested that a small-sized Maya group invaded the surrounding regions at some point, later interbreeding with the original, taller population. On the other hand, after analyzing the skeleton morphology of a skeletal sample from Barton Ramie, Belize, Willey (1965) pointed out that stature decreased through an unbroken string of related archaeological periods.

Haviland (1967) reported a diachronic tendency at Tikal, Guatemala, in which a marked decrease in stature occurred toward the Late Classic period in association with general environmental deterioration, which he directly translated into nutritional terms. This tendency appeared only among the male population; apparently women kept the same stature through time at Tikal. However, stature of women elsewhere diminished. The author believed he had found an important difference based on social class structure: the taller individuals were buried in more ostentatious surroundings than were shorter individuals. However, as we will learn, it has not been possible to corroborate this hypothesis.

Saul (1972a) presented a very complete report on the population biology of the ancient inhabitants of Altar de Sacrificios, Guatemala. One of his main objectives was to reconstruct the physical characteristics of Prehispanic Maya of the region, particularly their height. He also intended to provide an explanation for stature diminution toward the Late Classic period. Like his predecessors, he encountered a clear tendency for decreasing stature only among the male population. The picture for females was unclear. Unfortunately, data gathered by Saul do not indicate a particular tendency in the health status of the population, although there were several pathological conditions present. There was not, we believe, a clear association between social class and body size.

Nickens (1976) compiled all available information on northern Mesoamerica, with the intention of formulating a hypothesis on secular stature variation. He found that variation lost statistical significance among samples coming from farther south. He based his perceptions of diachronic change on the studies by Haviland (1967), Saul (1972a), and Stewart (1953), the difference being that he tried to find the causes for the trend toward body-size reduction. He tried to associate this tendency with the health conditions of the population. Lacking access to data other than Saul's (1972a), Nickens relied on cases from contemporary populations from within and outside of the region to explain by analogy the Prehispanic decrease. He stated alternative explanations in explicit terms in asking "whether these secular trends in stature and body size are the result of genetic change or are they the result of human plasticity or adaptability" (Nickens 1976:39). His main thesis, as interpreted by bioanthropologists (Cohen and Armelagos 1984), was that the transition from a nomadic hunter-gatherer to a sedentary agriculturalist way of life affected health conditions by increasing nutritional stress. The overall biological effect may have translated into a general diminishing of body size, which was an adaptive response to more difficult environmental conditions rather than a genetic change among these human groups.

Márquez (1984) analyzed several Maya skeletal collections excavated some time ago, as well as some obtained from recent excavations in the Yucatán Peninsula, in order to understand the trends in height among inhabitants of this region and to further document the findings of the previously cited authors. The objective of the present work is to reevaluate results obtained by Márquez (1984) by surveying more than a dozen Prehispanic Maya skeletal collections. The intention is to find and interpret the causes of the observed changes. It is our opinion that the origins of stature reduction are related to changes in way of life (i.e., in the economic structure and social organization of the Maya groups) which led to precarious living conditions for most of the population during the Classic period. These, among other political and ecological factors, may have provoked morphological changes, which took the form of stature reduction through time, as a way of adapting to prevailing life conditions (Márquez 1984, 1992; Márquez, Benavides, and Schmidt 1982; Márquez, Peraza et al. 1982; Márquez and Schmidt 1984; Peña 1985).

Methodological Problems for Height Determination among Ancient Populations

Researchers of many countries have dedicated energy to constructing tables which allow them to determine the height of ancient people. The tables are based on the knowledge that a living person's stature is proportional to the length of various long bones (Stewart 1979). The tables are based on studies of "reference" populations, which have the problem of not being representative, since they result from previous selection of various sorts. This causes observed patterns to be inaccurate and relative. In the case of México, this type of study has been pursued by Genovés (1964, 1967).

According to Comas (1983), the use of long bones to estimate living stature in Prehispanic populations seems to work well, even though the series on which the formulas were based was not statistically representative of the Mexican population. However, the enormous amount of genetic intermixture among Mexicans makes use of the formulas very complicated, as does the great physical variation among the Prehispanic inhabitants of the region. Nonetheless, Genovés's is the only study done on a sample that is genetically very similar to the autochthonous populations of the country. As a result, it is valid to use the formulas, but adjustments proposed by Andrés del Ángel and Héctor Cisneros (1991) must be incorporated because of an error in the original study (Santiago Genovés, pers. comm. 1991).

Researchers wishing to study height among the Prehispanic Maya face great adversity. Where is it possible to obtain an adequate formula, that is, one that is based upon a population with very little intermixture from other populations? Even if we sampled a contemporary population and obtained the ratio between a long bone and total height through radiographic images, we would not obtain an adequate formula, for there is evidence that both stature and proportions of body parts have changed through time.

Materials and Methods

The present study is based upon metric data from collections of skeletons from Prehispanic Maya populations of México (Márquez 1984), data published by Saul (1972a), and analysis of the Xcaret series (Márquez 1993). All bones whose preservation allowed maximum length measures to be taken were selected. The skeletal series studied by Márquez are from Cancún, Cenote Sagrado (Chichén Itzá), Chiapa de Corzo, Cozumel, Dzibilchaltún, El Meco, Jaina, Komchén, Palenque, Playa del Carmen, Río Bec, Xcaret, and Xcan. Chronologically, they

Table 4.1 Samples from Each Site by Size and Sex

| Site | Chronology[a] | Sample Size | | Reference |
		Males	Females	
Altar de Sacrificios	I, II, III	12	8	Saul (1972a)
Cancún	III	10	11	Márquez (1984)
Cenote Sagrado	III	6	6	Márquez (1984)
Chiapa de Corzo	I, II	9	2	Márquez (1984)
Cozumel	III	8	2	Márquez (1984)
Dzibichaltún	I	2	–	Márquez (1984)
El Meco	III	1	2	Márquez (1984)
Jaina	II	18	11	Márquez (1984)
Komchén	I, II	4	–	Márquez (1984)
Palenque	II	3	2	Márquez (1984)
Playa del Carmen	III	36	9	Márquez, Peraza et al. (1982)
Río Bec	II	1	–	Márquez (1984)
Xcan	II	3	1	Márquez, Benavides et al. (1982)
Xcaret	II, III	14	7	This paper
Modern		4	4	Márquez (1984)
Total		129	66	

[a] I = Preclassic, II = Classic, III = Postclassic.

come from the Preclassic, Classic, and Post-classic cultural periods. There is also a sample from the cemetery of the city of Mérida, Yucatán. Height and length data obtained by other researchers are from Chiapa de Corzo (Jaén 1968), Altar de Sacrificios (Saul 1972a), and Jaina (Pijoan and Salas 1980).

These collections are end products of archaeological excavations of the past 30 years, although none of the excavations had as a primary goal the collection of skeletal materials for this study. However, archaeological explorations have resulted in very rich and complete skeletal samples from the populations of México, which made it possible to study Maya samples which corresponded to each cultural period. Generally speaking, the quality and quantity of each of the osseous collections from throughout the Maya area are very heterogeneous. In some cases we are speaking of large samples with 60 to 90 skeletons, but in others the numbers are smaller. However, what is almost a constant is the poor state

of preservation, which constitutes a major factor, since only a small number of skeletons contribute measurement data (Tables 4.1 and 4.2).

The osteometric techniques employed were based on those proposed by Stewart (1979). All measurements were of maximum length, except for the tibia, where measurement of length excluded the intercondylar tubercles. The legs were selected for stature estimation, since the tibia and femur, especially, give more accurate results than do arms (Genovés 1964). The data were subjected to descriptive statistical analysis. Information was registered on cards listing long-bone lengths of each of the measured individuals, the individual's catalog number, and the cultural period to which the individual belonged. We decided to use the formula proposed by Genovés for stature estimation and for comparing the maximum lengths of femurs and tibiae between sites and chronological periods, in order to detect variations in length through time and the relationships of these

Table 4.2   Studies of Stature of the Ancient Maya

Site	Periods	Number of Individuals		Method of Estimation	Author
		Males	Females		
Guatemalan highlands	Classic and Postclassic	19	7	Pearson's formula	Stewart (1949, 1953)
Copán	Early Classic	3	–	Measured *in situ* and Pearson's formula for femurs	Longyear (1952)
	Late Classic	1	1		
Tikal	Preclassic	6	4	Measured *in situ* and Trotter and Gleser (1958)	Haviland (1967)
	Early Classic	9	3		
	Late Classic	21	11		
	Postclassic	–	1		
Altar de Sacrificios	Preclassic	4	2	Genovés (1967); Trotter and Gleser (1958)	Saul (1972a)
	Early Classic	4	1		
	Late Classic	2	2		
	Classic/Postclassic	1	2		
	Postclassic	1	1		

variations to those occurring in body segment proportions and total size.

Results

Average values for the maximum lengths of the femur, tibia, humerus, and ulna for males are greatest for the Preclassic period (Table 4.3). During the Classic, the number of individuals is greater, but all average values drop, especially for the femur. In the Postclassic, the average lengths of the femur and ulna increase slightly, although they do not reach the sizes recorded for the Preclassic period. The present-day sample generally has the lowest measures of all cultural periods (Márquez 1984).

The number of female individuals from the Preclassic in the sample is very low. The average value for the femur is slightly greater than the values recorded for subsequent periods. This is not the case for the ulna and tibia, whose average lengths remain almost unchanged through-

out the four time periods. The mean values for the Classic are a bit greater than ones for samples from other cultural periods, with the smallest values occurring during the Postclassic.

The arithmetic mean of male height varies somewhat, depending upon the particular bone used for calculations (Table 4.4; Fig. 4.1). In the case of the tibia, stature estimates are greatest during the Preclassic and progressively drop in more recent populations. On the other hand, for the femur the highest values also occur during the Preclassic, but there is a clear decrease during the Classic period, followed by a partial recovery during the Postclassic.

The mean value for female height has only very insignificant differences between the Preclassic and Classic periods (Table 4.4; Fig. 4.1). Between the Classic and Postclassic, however, mean stature decreases by more than 2 cm. During the Postclassic, the tallest individuals, from in the Cenote Sagrado series, stood 144.25 to 156.25 cm tall, based on humerus, ulna, and radius length, or 145.25 to 153.50 cm tall,

Table 4.3 Descriptive Statistics of Measured Maya Skeletons for Maximum Length of Long Bones

Bone	Preclassic			Classic			Postclassic			Modern		
	n	Mean	sd	n	Mean	sd	n	Mean	sd	n	Mean	sd
Males												
Femur	11	43.51	2.79	22	41.62	1.94	29	42.87	2.51	4	41.80	1.96
Tibia	7	37.33	1.62	22	36.16	1.93	25	35.88	2.28	4	35.13	1.87
Humerus	7	31.26	1.54	20	30.09	1.12	22	30.65	1.52	4	29.75	2.06
Ulna	5	26.72	1.36	17	25.64	1.35	19	26.33	1.61	4	24.58	1.13
Females												
Femur	3	39.13	.29	17	38.99	2.27	11	38.20	1.48	4	39.13	2.31
Tibia	2	33.05	.92	14	33.26	1.87	5	32.02	2.47	3	32.93	1.57
Humerus	–	–	–	11	28.19	1.33	13	27.02	1.09	4	27.43	1.29
Ulna	1	24.10	–	9	24.17	1.44	17	22.99	1.08	4	22.90	1.21

NOTE: See Table 4.1 regarding sources of data. All dimensions in centimeters; n = number of individuals; sd = standard deviation.

Table 4.4 Descriptive Statistics of Measured Maya Skeletons for Stature Estimates

Bone	Preclassic			Classic			Postclassic			Modern		
	n	Mean	sd	n	Mean	sd	n	Mean	sd	n	Mean	sd
Males												
Femur	11	162.31	6.30	22	158.03	4.39	29	160.85	5.67	4	158.44	4.44
Tibia	7	164.35	3.16	22	162.06	3.78	25	161.51	4.47	4	160.03	3.66
Females												
Femur	3	148.52	.75	17	148.14	5.88	11	146.10	3.84	4	148.49	5.97
Tibia	2	151.19	2.50	14	151.77	5.08	5	148.38	6.72	3	150.87	4.27

NOTE: See Table 4.1 regarding sources of data. All dimensions in centimeters; n = number of individuals; sd = standard deviation.

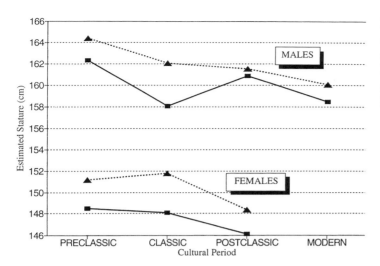

Figure 4.1. Changes in estimated stature of males and females through time. Rectangles and solid line, femur; triangles and dotted line, tibia.

based on femur, tibia, and fibula length (Márquez 1984). In the present-day sample, the average values for height are 150.87 cm (tibia) and 148.49 cm (femur).

To summarize, bone lengths and heights of both males and females from each period show some differences. Through these differences, we can observe a trend toward stature reduction after the Preclassic period. Even though there are some discrepancies, depending on the bone from which the calculation is made, based on tibia length it is possible to distinguish an average height of 164.35 cm for Preclassic males; 162.06 cm for Classic males; 161.51 cm for Postclassic males; and 160.03 cm for present-day males. For women, the average values obtained from femur length are 148.52 for the Preclassic, 148.14 cm for the Classic, 146.10 cm for the Postclassic, and 148.49 for the present.

Analysis of the mean lengths of the various bones by cultural period indicates to us that there was a reduction of every bone between the Preclassic and Classic. The femur and humerus were the most greatly affected elements, followed by the tibia and ulna. This is very important, since there are specific growth periods for the different body segments. The proximal portions of the limbs undergo growth and de-

velopment first. During this first growth stage, the nutritional requirements of a person increase. If these requirements are not met, the body parts which will be most affected are precisely those with higher nutritional needs at that time. If nutritional requirements are not met during this growth stage through several generations, the likely result will be shorter individuals because of leg bone reduction. We also consider that disproportions of height to arm length and height to leg length are very likely to appear.

The metric change between the Classic and Postclassic periods is of a smaller magnitude. The only body part which continues to decrease is the femur. The tibia does not show significant changes, while there are small increases in the lengths of the fibula, ulna, and radius, and a slightly greater increase in the size of the humerus (Márquez 1984; Table 4.3; Figs. 4.2 and 4.3).

We interpret the reduction of the length of long bones that we find during the transition from the Preclassic to the Classic to mean that the ancient inhabitants of the Yucatán Peninsula were not only taller than those who live there today, but also had a different ratio of arm length to leg length. During the Postclas-

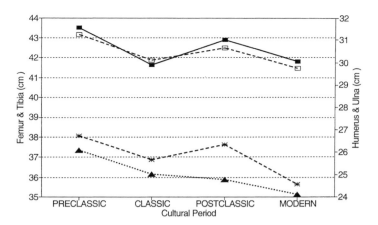

Figure 4.2. Changes in maximum length of long bones in males through time. Closed rectangles and solid line, femur; triangles and dotted line, tibia; open rectangle and dashed line, humerus; asterisk and dashed line, ulna.

sic, although we encounter a slight recovery of total height, the tendency toward decreased length for the femur continues. The disproportion between lower and upper extremities has become a trait which characterizes modern Maya groups. According to Steggerda (1932), Maya are "individuals of small height . . . with long arms as compared to their size." From the analysis of Altar skeletons (Saul 1972a) it appears that the Maya of the Preclassic had shorter arms in comparison to their legs; however it is a very small sample (n = 3) and the results could be misleading. The slightly greater maximum length of some bones during the Preclassic could be due to better life conditions during this period. In comparison to later peri-

ods, the work burden may have been lighter, with people involved in subsistence agriculture, and distribution may have been more equitable.

The interpretation of data is very complex because factors such as differential preservation for the various samples and heterogeneous deterioration of individual bones makes a definitive analysis difficult. Therefore, we only point out the possible direction the trend in variation in proportions may have taken. The Postclassic series are generally the largest and are usually in better condition. Other factors to be taken into consideration are environmental differences between the archaeological sites in which these burials were found. Many of the Postclassic series came from coastal sites such

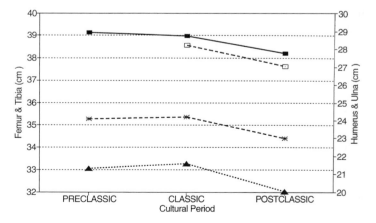

Figure 4.3. Changes in maximum length of long bones in females through time. Closed rectangles and solid line, femur; triangles and dotted line, tibia; open rectangle and dashed line, humerus; asterisk and dashed line, ulna.

as Cancún, Playa del Carmen, and Xcaret. We assume that the nutritional resources coastal populations had available included seafood as well as terrestrial foods, and that their diet was a more balanced one (Márquez 1992). Finally, migrations of other ethnic groups to the Yucatán Peninsula is a possibility.

Health and Nutritional Conditions

Because of the influence of nutrition on stature, it is necessary to elaborate somewhat on Maya diet. We especially must mention the relationship between the nutrients an organism requires for its reproduction and the nutritional sources available, as well as the technology required to obtain, store, and consume food. Finally, there are the effects of age, gender, socioeconomic status, work burden, and technological development, among others, in relation to the natural resources available.

Through recent studies by multidisciplinary teams, paleoenvironmental reconstructions are being developed that describe what kinds of plants and animals there were and what the climate was like (Barrera 1979; Harrison and Turner 1978; B. Turner 1979). Archaeologists delimit the sites, make population calculations for different periods of settlement, and uncover the state of technological development for these periods. Bioanthropologists analyze, through paleodemographic and paleoepidemiologic methodologies, diseases that remain identifiable in the skeletal records and that have any relation to the inhabitants' eating habits (Goodman et al. 1984; Márquez 1992; Márquez, Benavides et al. 1982; Márquez, Peraza et al. 1982; Márquez and Schmidt 1984; Saul 1972a).

Protein for the Maya, according to ethnohistoric documents (Cogolludo 1955; Garza 1983; Landa 1978), was obtained by hunting animals such as deer, wild boar, jaguar, lynx, cougar,

badger, and armadillo, among others. A considerable portion of the Maya area is surrounded by seas, and various regions have a wide variety of fish and mollusks, most with high nutritional qualities. Fish, preserved with salt and by sun drying, was taken inland by traders. Fishing and hunting had religious aspects, including the rite of giving part of the catch to the lords as tribute. Although these nutritional resources seem to have been abundant, it is likely that they were consumed only during festivals and ceremonies.

The vegetables consumed were some roots, legumes, leaves, and even certain flowers. Several kinds of pumpkins, *yuca*, cucumber, pinto beans, *jícamas, camote,* and *chaya* were also widely consumed.

This ethnohistoric information corresponds to a specific historical moment, the period at which Europeans met Maya. However, it is known that habits in general and particularly eating habits undergo modifications only over very long time periods. The stability of eating habits enables us to assume that the ethnohistoric information holds for preceding time periods.

By using skeletal records and studying in them health and nutritional indicators, bioarchaeologists have begun to establish the state of nutrition among the ancient Maya. The frequency and types of diseases among different sex and social status groups are being taken into account, which is part of the epidemiologic approach.

The results obtained to date suggest the existence of various nutritional deficiencies. Among the Altar de Sacrificios collection, 32 out of the 36 persons in the sample showed evidence of having suffered from anemia. Twenty-four of 36 Maya skeletons analyzed at the Peabody Museum and 52 of 54 skeletons at the National Museum of Anthropology in México have been diagnosed with iron deficiency anemia (Saul 1974).

Studies of skeletal materials from infants from Chichén Itzá revealed high percentages of scurvy, directly related to vitamin C deficiency. There were high frequencies of cribra orbitalia and spongy hyperostosis, which are associated with anemia (Márquez and Schmidt 1984). At Tancah, on the Quintana Roo coast, in a small skeletal sample of 11 individuals, 4 of them had evidence of anemia (Saul and Saul 1985). Near Tancah, at Playa del Carmen, of 28 skeletons 33.33% had spongy hyperostosis, 40.00% had cribra orbitalia, and 11.76% had enamel hypoplasia (Márquez, Peraza et al. 1982). In the Jaina collection, evidence of anemia, vitamin deficiencies, periodontal degeneration, and periostitis is very common (Pijoan and Salas 1984).

Discussion

The overall results agree with what has been noted in other osteological studies of Maya collections: that height diminishes in the more recent skeletal series. In our series, the major stature differences are between the Preclassic and the Classic. The magnitude of stature differences becomes smaller between Classic, Postclassic, and present-day series. The trend in stature is not very clear for females, as there are not many skeletons from the Preclassic. Average heights from the Postclassic and present-day samples are not significantly different.

Possible causes of stature change include the process of biological adaptation to the environment, change of activities, dietary variations, population fluctuations, and excessive work burdens. The presence of high frequencies of nutritional diseases is supported by lesions on the Prehispanic skeletal materials. Archaeological evidence of population growth occurring during the Classic, along with increasing size and number of Maya settlements, implies a major work burden, specialization in the production and distribution of foods and services, an increase of mortality rates in general, espe-

cially infant mortality, and increased morbidity. These circumstances may have led to selection of those individuals whose smaller sized bodies allowed them to survive with a smaller quantity of nutrients until they reached the age of reproduction. Through time, biological and social selection of the physical type adapted to these life conditions took place, which acted as a barrier to full development of genetic potential.

Bioanthropological research on the living and into the health conditions of ancient populations lead us to a conclusion relating to the impact of the change from a hunter-gatherer lifestyle to a sedentary way of life. It is proposed that the hunter-gatherers, because of their social organization, daily activities, and nutrition, among other factors, enjoyed better health than agriculturists. This hypothesis is based on dependency on maize agriculture and the increase of infectious disease within sedentary populations, among other factors (Cohen and Armelagos 1984).

We believe that the explanation for the biological impact detected through stature variation within the Maya population must be multifactorial in nature. Various interacting causes must have triggered this microevolutionary process. The social and economic organization of Maya groups had great complexity and underwent a long cultural development throughout the Classic. The number of people involved in manufacturing consumer goods and in constructing buildings must have been enormous. The amount of food available may not have been sufficient to supply the nourishment necessary to support such a growing population, which would have caused a reduction of individual food consumption. On the other hand, the work burden must have increased. These factors would have acted against the optimal development of individuals.

In addition, we believe it necessary to take into account other factors. Although the quantity and quality of natural resources were more than sufficient for the Maya during some time periods, either because nature itself provided the resources or because social organization and technological development allowed the Maya to obtain the nourishment they required, this is no guarantee that these resources were consumed equally by everyone in the communities. It may well be that, as the social organization became more complex, the population had to meet more and greater demands, thereby reducing the possibility of satisfying the needs of the whole community. Another factor may have been the climate and its relationship to morphological and structural changes, taking into account that the Maya appeared as a linguistic group around 2000 B.C. In addition, migration movements and the relationship between the Maya and other cultural groups in Mesoamerica must not be overlooked when dealing with the Maya as either a homogeneous or a heterogeneous group. Comas (1966) pointed out the lack of sufficient evidence with which to explain the question of homogeneity, by which he fundamentally meant the absence of skeletons in a fair state of preservation. These would allow the application of specific multivariate analyses of genetic distances through dental patterns and craniometric and morphometric features. There has been considerable discussion of the hypothetical arrival of human groups from different geographic areas, with cultural and physical traits distinct from those of the Maya. Up to this moment we do not know for sure whether or not this arrival led to political or cultural domination or genetic interchange. However, the available data seem to indicate that between the Classic and the Postclassic there was a physical interchange between the inhabitants of the central regions of the Yucatán Peninsula and the people from coastline sites such as Playa del Carmen, Tulum, and Cozumel.

The extreme complexity of Maya civilization brought upon the people conditions that were detrimental to their physical development and which were precisely recorded as biological deterioration. This contrasts with the cultural splendor achieved during this period, of which the monumental constructions, magnificent roads, and ceramic figures are ample evidence.

We interpret the slight increase in length of some body segments during the Postclassic, detected in the coastal groups of this period, as being the result of an economic and social organization which allowed the Maya better physical development. This is not to imply that tallness is intrinsically preferable to shortness. Rather, it is known that under optimal conditions the organism tends to develop fully to its genetic potential. Predominantly precarious conditions through many generations will induce a species to adapt to the available amounts and quality of nourishment.

At this time, compilation of existing osteological information about Maya groups and submission of proposals for additional research would be of great utility. To this end, the objective of this work has been to increase the amount of information on Prehispanic Maya stature fluctuation by publishing new data on the subject. In the review and analysis of the material, we were faced with the problem of largely fragmentary data, so the partial conclusions we have reached have a provisional character and new studies on the topic are anticipated.

It is expected that the impetus given to archaeological explorations in the Maya area today will allow further delineation and clarification of stature trends. From an osteological perspective, the existing samples are deteriorated and quite small, have incomplete background information, and come from distinct cultural periods. These force us to be cautious and prudent in our present observations and interpretations.

5

A Maya Skull Pit from the Terminal Classic Period, Colha, Belize

Virginia K. Massey and D. Gentry Steele

Excavation during the 1980 field season at Colha, Belize, uncovered a remarkable collection of human remains (Eaton 1980, 1982; Massey 1989, 1994; Massey and Steele 1982; Steele et al. 1980). Next to the staircase on a monumental structure's second terrace, a pit had been dug to receive the heads of 30 decapitated victims. The pit, about 110 cm long, 80 cm wide, and 20 cm deep, contained skulls, arranged in two layers and separated from one another by fragments of Late to Terminal Classic pottery (Hester et al. 1980, 1982, 1983, 1994; Hester and Shafer 1984; Roemer 1984; Shafer and Hester 1983, 1986).

The goals of the osteological study of these remains were to discover the innate biological status of the individuals, the cultural modifications to which their crania had been subjected, and the culturally prescribed ways their remains were handled after death.

Methods

Detailed discussions of the osteological methods considered for the Colha skull pit analysis and of the related literature may be found in Massey (1989). In general, osteological analyses followed Bass (1971), Krogman (1962), Steele and Bramblett (1988), and Stewart (1979), and diagnosis of pathological conditions followed Ortner and Putschar (1985) and Steinbock (1976).

Sex assessment was limited to adult remains, because traits that distinguish males are discernible only in mature crania. The sample was too highly comminuted to assign sex by metric analysis, but visible features of the skull were informative. Male skulls were generally more robust and female skulls were generally smaller, smoother, and retained more prominently the juvenile parietal and frontal eminences.

It was possible to classify adult skulls into three general age groups. A young adult was considered to be one in whom a third molar had erupted but showed little or no wear. An adult had a full set of permanent dentition and had not yet experienced extreme wear on the teeth or extensive tooth loss with alveolar resorption. An old adult had suffered either of these conditions. Further indicators of old age included fusion of cranial sutures and arthritic deterioration of the temporomandibular joint.

Tooth wear was ranked using Hinton's modification of Murphy's (1959) classification as seen in Smith (1984). (See Hinton 1981 for an earlier version of this ranking scheme.) The ordinal categories of tooth wear range from Stage 1 to Stage 8 based on increasing exposure of dentin and increasing erosion of enamel. Stage 1 designates teeth showing no dentin and either no wear at all or a light polishing of the enamel. Stage 8 indicates a complete loss of crown with no enamel remaining. Comparing individuals on the basis of their average tooth wear added to the qualitative information about the sample but was not used to assign age in years.

The age of subadults was primarily estimated from the development of their teeth, following Schour and Massler (1941, 1944). In some instances age was also indicated by the absence of fusion between centers of ossification in a bone such as the occipital or one of the cervical vertebrae.

Dental disorders observed included caries, alveolar abscesses, enamel hypoplasia and other malformations of the teeth, calculus, periodontal disease, and antemortem tooth loss. Other malformations noted included notching on the edges of the incisors and tooth fusion or gemination.

Dentitions were ranked from 0 to 3 for relative degrees of carious destruction. Rank 0 was given to dentitions that were free from decay. Rank 1 indicated that any of the teeth may have had one or several small, pinhole-sized lesions and no more than one larger cavity. When larger areas of caries were present, but no more than one tooth surface was nearly obliterated by decay, the dentition was given Rank 2. Rank 3 indicated extensive damage to larger areas with near obliteration of more than one surface.

Bone disorders and common Maya cultural traits that left evidence on the skeleton, such as intentional cranial modeling and tooth filing were noted. In the skull pit material where

the modeling could be seen, it was classified in Dembo and Imbelloni's (1938) categories of Tabular Erect, Tabular Oblique, and Annular (as presented in Comas and Marquer 1969). Tooth filing was noted and its style classified according to Romero's (1970) categories, which are based on alteration of the crown contour.

Results

The skull pit skeletal material comprised the remains of 30 individuals, 28 of whom are represented, at least in fragments, by cranium and mandible. (Of these, 22 have associated cervical vertebrae or vertebral fragments as well, and 2 individuals are represented by cranium, mandible, cervical vertebrae, and hyoid. A 29th person is represented by facial bones, the mandible, and one vertebra, but no bones of the skull vault, and the 30th individual is represented only by a mandibular fragment).

The 10 juveniles represented in the sample (Table 5.1) ranged in age from about 6 months to 6 or 7 years. Five juveniles were under 3 years of age, four were between 3 and 5, and

Table 5.1 Sex and Age-at-Death of Individuals Represented in Colha Skull Pit Skeletal Collection

	Males	Females	Unknown Sex
Old adults	1	3	
Adults	5	6	2
Young adults	2	1	
Subadults			
6–7 years			1
4–5 years			1
3–5 years			1
3–4 years			2
1.5–2.5 years			2
1.5–2 years			1
7–11 months			1
6 months			1

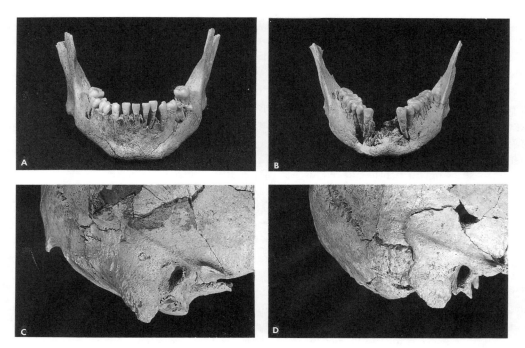

Figure 5.1. Sexual dimorphism in adult skulls: *A*, male mandible (Skull G); *B*, female mandible (Skull H); *C*, lateral view of male skull (Skull G); *D*, lateral view of female skull (Skull M). Photos courtesy of Colha Project.

one was 6 or 7. Of the 20 adult skulls, 10 were female, 8 were male, and the sex of 2 could not be determined; 3 were considered young adult, 13 were classified simply as adult, and 4 were categorized as old adult.

The skull pit population exhibited a great deal of individual variation in robusticity. Sexual dimorphism at its most distinct is shown in Figure 5.1. Much of the Colha material was more ambiguous. Some males had larger mastoid processes; some females had small ones; but many of both sexes had mastoid processes that were moderately large. Both sexes tended to have long zygomatic crests that extended back past the ears, although on some males this crest was more sharply marked. Determining the sex of the more ambiguous individuals finally rested on one characteristic that seemed reliable for this population: the mandibular body height was greater for males than for females.

No tooth wear difference between the sexes was observed (Table 5.2). Individual variation was pronounced, with the general category "Adult" including average tooth wear ranging from Stage 1 through Stage 4. However, no young adult showed greater wear than Stage 2 and only old adults showed average wear as advanced as Stage 5. These findings confirm the assumptions that tooth wear increases with age but cannot be used to give precise age estimates in this sample.

The most prevalent pathological state in adult dentition, affecting 19 individuals, was calculus deposits. Next in frequency was caries, which afflicted 15 adults. Of these, 11 were rated for caries severity at Rank 3, the most severe, one was ranked at 2, and three were ranked at 1. Eleven individuals lost teeth before death, and one more had either just lost teeth or was in the process of losing them at

Table 5.2 Tooth Wear Stages Observed on Colha Skull Pit Adults by Sex and Age Classification

	Wear Stage[a]				
	1	2	3	4	5
Young adults					
Male	1	1			
Female		1			
Unknown					
Adults					
Male	1	1	2	1	
Female		1	2	3	
Unknown		1		1	
Old adults					
Male				1	
Female				1	2
Unknown					

[a] Wear stages follow Smith (1984).

time of death. Seven individuals showed signs of enamel hypoplasia. Alveolar abscess afflicted six adults, and periodontal disease affected two or possibly three. These two conditions are more likely to be underestimated than the other dental disorders because the fragile alveolar margins, which retain evidence of these lesions, are less likely to be preserved in this material than sturdier bone or teeth. Examples of adult dental disorders, some associated with alveolar infection, are shown in Figure 5.2. In addition, each of three skulls exhibited one of the following infrequent, atypical dental traits: rotation of premolars out of normal position, unusual occlusion and attrition, and impaction of a third molar.

Seven of the juvenile skulls showed evidence of dental caries (Table 5.3). Of the three (EE, F, GG) that were free from caries, one had no

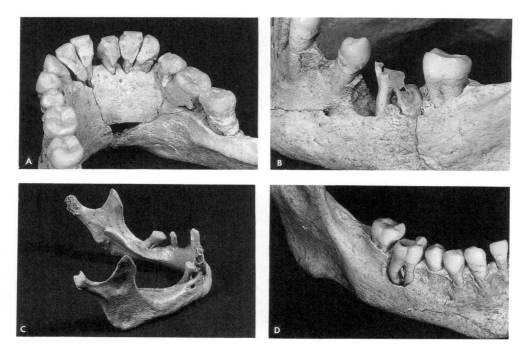

Figure 5.2. Dental disorders in adult remains: *A*, calculus (Skull Q); *B*, carious destruction of crown (Skull G); *C*, antemortem tooth loss (Skull M) *D*, carious lesion with associated alveolar abscess (Skull G). Photos courtesy of Colha Project.

Table 5.3 Dental Disorders in Colha Skull
Pit Children Listed by Caries Rank

Catalog Letter	Age	Caries Rank[a]	Enamel Hypoplasia	Malformation
GG	6 months	0		
EE	7–11 months	0		
F	1.5–2 years	0		
Z	1.5–2.5 years	1	+	
C	1.5–2.5 years	2		
W	3–4 years	2		+
Y	4–5 years	2	+	
CC	6–7 years	2		
I	3–4 years	3		
D	3–5 years	3	Possible	+

NOTE: + = Present.

[a] See text for explanation.

erupted teeth preserved, so its actual dental health is unknown. The other two had estimated ages of 7 months to 2 years and probably had not been weaned before death (see Pagden 1975). Skulls C and Z, however, are considered to be the same age as Skull F or just slightly older and probably were not weaned either, but they have caries ratings of 2 and 1, respectively. No doubt other foods had been added to these older babies' milk diet, yet it seems surprising that an unweaned child would already have tooth decay. Four children had a caries rating of 2: one child was 1.5 to 2.5, two were around 4 years of age, and one was 6 or 7. The two children with the worst teeth, rated as 3, were approximately the same age, 3 to 4 years old and 3 to 5 years old. (Figure 5.3A depicts the carious damage observed in Skull D, representing a child between 3 and 5 years of age at time of death.) Much of these dentitions had been destroyed. Several of their lower premolars, for example, had only enamel outlines left surrounding their occlusal surfaces. Furthermore, the skull pit children probably had even more caries than is recorded here, as not all teeth were preserved. Several of these missing teeth probably had varying degrees of decay.

Some of the children's skulls exhibited other dental disorders in addition to caries: enamel hypoplasia, unusual notching of incisors, and tooth fusion or gemination. Skull Y and Skull Z showed definite evidence of enamel hypoplasia. Their age-at-death ranged from 1.5 to 5 years of age. In each, the insult to enamel development occurred early in life: at the age of 6 to 9 months for Skull Y, and at about 9 months for Skull Z. Figure 5.3B shows horizontal hypoplastic grooves on the tooth bud for Skull Y's lower right first permanent molar. Skull D possibly may have had hypoplasia on some of the anterior deciduous teeth stemming from arrested enamel development before birth or shortly thereafter. These teeth have extensive carious lesions, some of them transverse.

Two of the juvenile skulls (D and W) show an unusual form of shallow notching on one or more incisors or incisor buds. Congenital syphilis often produces a more pronounced notching, but at least one worker (Pindborg 1970) attributes shallow notching to syphilis as well. However, both skulls have normally shaped incisors, too, and since treponemal infection typically affects the shape of several teeth, it is probably not implicated here. Skull D's notched permanent mandibular incisor bud is shown in Figure 5.3C.

Skull W also presented unusual lower deciduous incisors (Fig. 5.3D) which are quite broad and have a central notch on the incisal surface continuous with a deep lingual groove. Light-microscope inspection revealed no sharp edges to the grooves or other signs of cultural modification. One of these teeth fit quite well into the partial alveolus for the right lateral deciduous incisor. If the mandible were reconstructed with these teeth in the lateral incisor position, a small diastema would separate them. Tooth fusion or tooth gemination (partial splitting of a tooth crown) would account for the shape of these teeth. The number of teeth and their spacing here suggest that the incisors were fused, not geminated. However, the roots appear to

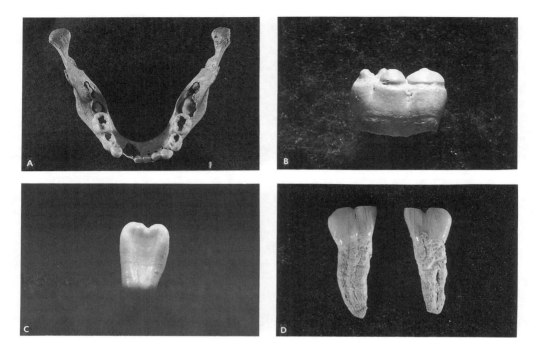

Figure 5.3. Dental disorders in juvenile remains: *A*, mandible with dental caries (Skull D); *B*, enamel hypoplasia in M_1 (Skull Y); *C*, notched permanent incisor bud (Skull D); *D*, fused or geminated incisors (Skull W). Photos courtesy of Colha Project.

be single, so gemination is a possibility. Both of these conditions are most often seen in mandibular deciduous incisors (Colby et al. 1971).

One dental condition needs additional discussion because it may have implications of disease epidemics or nutritional stress. This condition is enamel hypoplasia, the insufficient production of enamel during a period of tooth growth, which indicates the presence of severe physical stress at that time. It is common in the skull pit sample, being positively identified in nine dentitions and possibly indicated in one more. Figure 5.3B shows a child's hypoplastic lower right first permanent molar bud which has two horizontal lines reflecting at least two discrete periods of stress.

Hypoplasia was evenly distributed in this sample. Two old adults, one male, one female, showed evidence of hypoplasia. Four adults, one male, two female, and one of unknown sex, also had these lesions. In addition, one young

female adult and two children suffered this disorder, and one other child possibly had the condition. Apparently there was no sex difference in susceptibility and no change through time in the physical stress having impact on younger members of the population.

One might expect the hypoplasia and bone disorders to occur in the same individuals under certain kinds of stressful conditions. For example, severe malnutrition or serious disease might be expected to leave signs on both teeth and bone. Such a coincidence did not occur in this sample. Of the nine individuals with definite hypoplastic teeth, two also had definite bone disorders and two others had possible bone lesions. Yet, only one of these lesions, possible cribra orbitalia in a child's skull, might conceivably have resulted from anemia produced by the same agent that caused hypoplasia. The other three lesions, a possibly infected palate, a small developmental anomaly, and

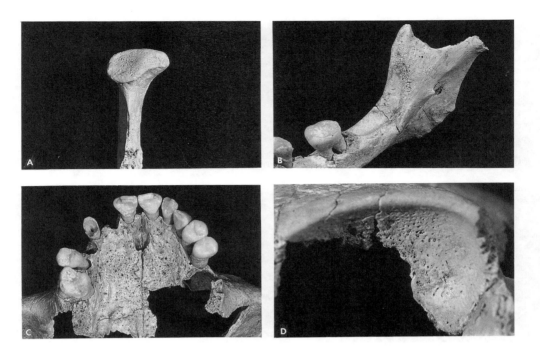

Figure 5.4. Bone disorders in adult and juvenile crania: *A,* deformation of mandibular condyle (Skull V); *B,* infected bone on mandibular ramus, probably secondary to evulsion of M_3 (Skull DD); *C,* unusual roughness of palatal bone (Skull II); *D,* cribra orbitalia in child (Skull I). Photos courtesy of Colha Project.

deformation of the temporomandibular joint, could not reasonably be connected with hypoplasia. These findings leave hypoplasia in this sample as the single remaining evidence of physical stress in early childhood.

Bone disorders in adults included infection of bone, joint deformation, developmental anomalies, and cribra orbitalia. In addition, some unusual conditions of bone were found whose pathological status was difficult to assign.

Three adult skulls had evidence of bone infection. One (Skull M) showed signs of infection (porosity and signs of osteoblastic and osteoclastic activity) on the inner table of the occipital. Two other skulls (DD, II) appear to have had porous subperiosteal bone deposited on the medial aspects of the mandibular rami up to the coronoid processes, as seen in Figure 5.4B. The infectious bone seemed to be continuous with that in the gumline and probably was contemporaneous with an infec-

tion that accompanied the loss of mandibular molars.

Skull V had a marked disorder of the right temporomandibular joint. The mandibular condyle's lateral portion was flattened superiorly, hypertrophied, and porous (Fig. 5.4A). The right glenoid fossa was greatly expanded anteriorly and showed evidence of osteoblastic and osteoclastic activity near the articular eminence. It is possible that the primary deformation was in the glenoid fossa, and that the mandibular condyle became deformed through articulation with it. The left temporomandibular joint was not observable.

A developmental anomaly was seen in Skull M. On the inner surface of the frontal of the left orbit, a fine crack traversed a small tuberosity and continued out to demarcate the temporal crest for a distance of about 1 cm. There, the crack resembled a fold in the bone. No signs of trauma were present.

A more extreme developmental aberration was premature fusion of the cranial sutures in Skull E. Although the lambdoidal and squamosal sutures appeared normal in the portions of the Skull E cranium that were recovered, the coronal suture was completely fused and obliterated, and the sagittal suture was about half fused and obliterated. Even at the age of death, this individual would have been young to exhibit such advanced fusion (see McKern and Stewart 1957), but Skull E had fused many years before. The cranial bone was thinner than that of other adults in the collection, and impressions from the cerebrum, unusual in adult bone, remained on large parts of the frontal and parietals. Both of these conditions indicate premature synostosis, or fusion, of the cranial suture. This developmental disorder causes the cranial bones to unite, preventing further expansion of cranial capacity, before the brain has completed its growth. The bone thinning here is not extreme (it is thicker than that of the oldest juvenile in the sample) and the cranium does not show extreme distortion, so the fusion probably began not long before the brain ceased growing. It is not known whether or not premature synostosis was harmful to this particular individual's health. Problems that may result from craniostenosis include protopsis, visual disturbances, and impaired growth and development of the brain (Beighton 1978).

Another disorder observed in this bone is cribra orbitalia. Although often considered to indicate anemia, here it is plausible to think it may have been caused by the pressure exerted on the cranial bones by the growing brain. An additional unusual feature is the gracility of the skull, seen especially in the relative smoothness of the external occipital and in the small size of the mastoid processes. Gracility is usually considered a female characteristic and contrasts strikingly here with the robusticity and extremely large size of the mandible. It seems reasonable that premature synostosis could produce a smoother surface in the cranium, but it

is not known if the size of the mastoid process can be influenced by the disorder.

Four individuals exhibited an unusual roughness of the palate which is illustrated in Figure 5.4C. It is not known if the roughness is the result, in one instance, of palatal fracture, of severe periodontal disease with infection of the palate, or if it is merely a normal variation in palatal surface texture.

Bone disorders in children were limited to cribra orbitalia (Fig. 5.4D). Two skulls (I and Y) showed signs of mild cribra orbitalia in one orbit. The other orbits are missing in these skulls. Because few orbits are present in this poorly preserved sample, the actual frequency of this disorder is unknown.

No signs of treponemal infection were found in the sample in adults or juveniles. The absence of lesions suggests that the notching of incisors in Skull D and W may not be due to congenital syphilis or other treponemal infection.

Intentional cranial modeling was found in this sample as in many other Maya skeletal collections. Eight skulls were unmistakably deliberately shaped (Table 5.4). Two other individuals, both children, showed ambiguous signs of possible antemortem cultural shaping. (These are not included in the following discussion.) Nine crania were definitely not modeled and

Table 5.4 Characteristics of Skull Pit Crania that Show Intentional Cranial Modeling

Catalog Letter	Sex	Age	Enamel Hypoplasia	Filed Teeth
A	F	Old adult		+
B	F	Adult	+	
J	M	Old adult	+	
K	M	Adult		+
P	M	Adult		
T	M	Young adult		
W	U	3–4 years		
AA	M	Adult		+

NOTE: F = female; M = male; U = unknown sex; + = present.

the others could not be assessed. Two of the individuals with modified cranial shape were adult females, five were adult males, and one was a child of 3 or 4 years. Three of the adults with deformed skulls also had filed teeth, and four adults did not. Two individuals with culturally modified crania had enamel hypoplasia, indicating some kind of physical stress at an early age, but the other six did not. None of the modeled crania with a preserved occipital exhibited the lesion in the suprainion region

which Holliday (1993) attributed to the use of cradle boards and which McCormick (1994) associated with cranial modeling. It seems that the practice of cranial modeling in this sample was independent of sex, age, severe physical stress in early childhood, or other cultural modification.

Two styles of cranial modeling are represented in the skull pit sample. Five skulls were shaped in the Tabular Erect style, illustrated in Figure 5.5, and at least one was molded in the

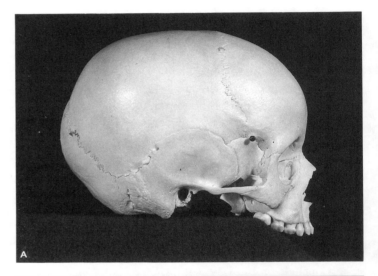

Figure 5.5. Cranial deformation: *A,* normal child's skull; *B,* artificially deformed child's skull (Skull W), style is Tabular Erect. Photos courtesy of Colha Project.

Tabular Oblique form. For two other skulls it was not possible to discern the shape of the back of the head, from which the style is named. These two crania exhibited abnormally sloping foreheads, though, and are classified as intentionally deformed.

Filed teeth were found in the dentitions of nine individuals, all adults, in the skull pit collection. These individuals exhibit various styles of tooth modification (Table 5.5). Two old adult females, four males, one adult female, and two adults of unknown sex all had filed teeth. None of the three young adults had teeth which had been culturally shaped.

Of those individuals with filed teeth, all had upper central incisors modified in Romero's B-4 shape, where a square is removed from the distal corners. Other anterior teeth were more variable in filed shape than the upper central incisors. Three skulls had teeth in the C-3 shape, where both mesial and distal corners were removed, leaving a rectangle of tooth projecting from the center of the incisal edge. A fourth individual's teeth could be classed only to Type C, indicating that both mesial and distal corners had been modified in some way. Two crania had teeth with a "V" shape removed from the middle of the incisive edge (Type A-1) and two had teeth filed straight across (Type A-4). Two dentitions had teeth filed so that the distal corner of the tooth was removed, but the edge filed in from the distal side slanted closer to the cemento-enamel junction (Type B-7). The various styles are illustrated in Figure 5.6.

Although dentitions varied in filing shapes, it seemed that tooth position limited the styles in this collection. All filed maxillary central incisors conformed to the B-4 style. One skull had maxillary canines in the B-4 style as well, but no other teeth exhibited this shape. B-7 filing was seen only on maxillary canines, and A-1 filing was found only on lower incisors. The C-3 style, on the other hand, appeared on upper and lower lateral incisors and canines. The A-4 style shaped upper lateral incisors and canines.

There is no evidence either that men and women had their teeth filed differently or that there was a short-term change through time in filing styles, as would be suggested by a difference in styles between the old adults and the younger individuals. An interesting question is whether or not the prevalence of tooth filing was changing through time. About one-half of the old adults and adults in the sample had filed teeth, but none of the young adults did. Unfortunately, the small sample size makes it impossible to judge whether the absence of filing in the younger group indicates that it was performed later in life, represents a change in cultural practice, or results merely from the vagaries of sampling.

Table 5.5   List of Skull Pit Crania with Filed Teeth

Catalog Letter	Sex[a]	Age	Style[b]	Tooth[c]
A	F	Old adult	B-4	I^1
			C	I^2, C^-
G	M	Adult	B-4	I^1
			C-3	I^2, C^-
K	M	Adult	B-4	I^1, C^-
M	F	Old adult	B-4	I^1
			A-1	I_2
Q	F	Adult	B-4	I^1
			A-4	I^2, ?C^-
V	U	Adult	B-4	I^1
			B-7	C^-
			A-1	I_1, I_2
AA	M	Adult	B-4	I^1
			B-7	C^-
			C-3	I_2, C_-
DD	U	Adult	B-4	I^1
			A-4	I^2, C^-
II	M	Adult	B-4	I^1
			C-3	I^2

[a] F = female; M = male; U = unknown sex.

[b] Styles follow Romero (1970).

[c] Incisor and canine positions.

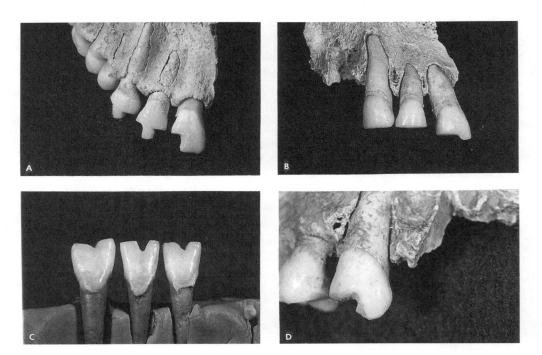

Figure 5.6. Filed teeth in Colha skull pit dentitions: *A*, Type B-4 in I^1, Type C-3 in I^2 and C (Skull G); *B*, Type B-4 in I^1, Type A-4 in I^2 and C (Skull DD); *C*, Type A-1 in I$_1$ and I$_2$ (Skull V); *D*, Type B-7 in C (Skull AA). Photos courtesy of Colha Project.

The most unusual feature of the skull pit skeletal material, one that makes the sample unique among Maya collections, is that the bone exhibited numerous cut marks. The literature (Pagden 1975) chronicles flaying of sacrificial victims, but this sample is the first to document the practice in skeletal evidence. The cut marks could be found on 20 of the 30 skulls (see Figs. 5.7 and 5.8). The other 10 did not show the marks but had such damaged or encrusted surfaces that the skulls could not be adequately examined for cuts.

Figures 5.9 and 5.10 are composite drawings of the cut marks observed on 17 cleaned skulls. Four other cleaned skulls did not exhibit cut marks, but one of these was burned and the other three were badly eroded. The few marks that could be observed on the uncleaned skulls were not included in the composite. No single skull presented all the marks illustrated in the drawings; the average number per skull of cut marks visible in frontal view, for example, was 17. Nevertheless, the composite view may more accurately reflect the skulls' condition shortly after death than do the discernible cut marks remaining on the poorly preserved bone surface.

Many, perhaps all, of the marks could have been made during the process of removing the skin. These include long cuts around the skull vault and shorter marks around the orbital rims and the external nasal aperture. Other marks appear on the inside of the mandibular ramus, on the lower edge of the zygomatic, and on the lower edge of the mandible. Possibly these marks were made during the removal of soft tissue other than skin. However the marks occurred, it is clear that the skulls, mandibles, and cervical vertebrae were not disarticulated,

Virginia K. Massey and D. Gentry Steele

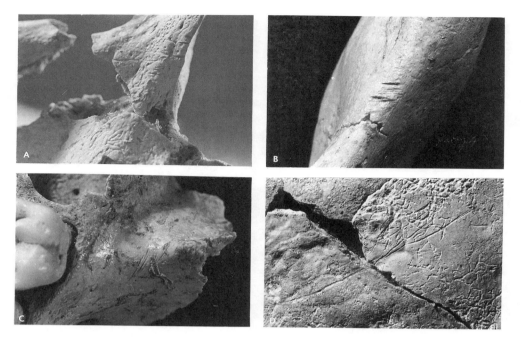

Figure 5.7. Cut marks on skulls: *A*, around external nasal aperture (Skull CC); *B*, on inferior surface of mandible (Skull I); *C*, on inferior surface of maxillary zygomatic process (Skull I); *D*, on occipital squama (Skull W). Photos courtesy of Colha Project.

because they were found in close anatomical association.

Deeper cuts were found on fragments of two cervical vertebrae. These seem to represent unsuccessful efforts to decapitate the victim. Both of these vertebrae were found associated with infant Skull GG, but they belonged to two individuals.

One of the skulls (BB) was badly burned and two others had portions that were charred. All three were buried in the lower layer. As noted in the preliminary report (Steele et al. 1980), it is unlikely that the burning took place in the pit, because there was no charcoal or other evidence of fire. The destruction of the building apparently was accompanied by fire, and it seems to have occurred shortly after the skull burial. The post-burial fire, though, could not have charred only a skull on the lower layer,

left the upper layer unburned, and left no sign of fire other than burned bone. The burning of Skull BB, then, must have been a separate event prior to burial.

Table 5.6 shows the age and sex distribution and the frequencies of cranial modeling and tooth filing within each of the two layers which constituted the skull pit burial. Skull II, whose provenience within the pit is not known, has been excluded from the table and the following discussion. There were 13 individuals in the upper level and 16 in the lower. The table reveals only one major difference: the greater number of older individuals in the upper level and the greater number of younger ones in the lower layer. All four of the old adults in the sample were buried in the upper level, all three of the young adults were placed in the lower level, and each level had six adults who were

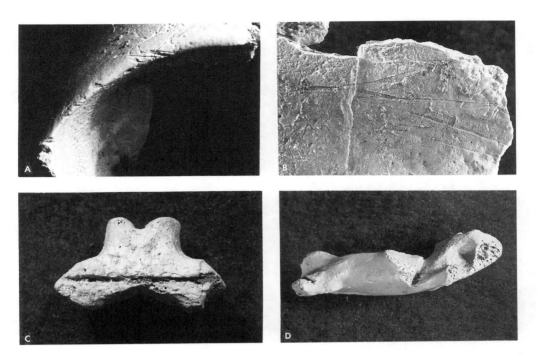

Figure 5.8. Cut marks on crania and cervical vertebrae: *A*, on orbital rim (Skull Z); *B*, on cranial vault (Skull C); *C*, on fused neural arch of child's axis vertebra (Skull GG); *D*, on child's cervical vertebra (Skull GG). Photos courtesy of Colha Project.

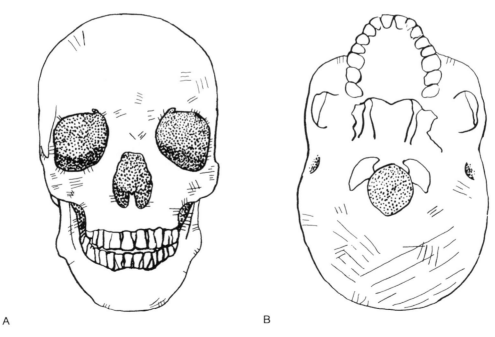

Figure 5.9. Composite cut marks on skulls: *A*, frontal view; *B*, inferior view.

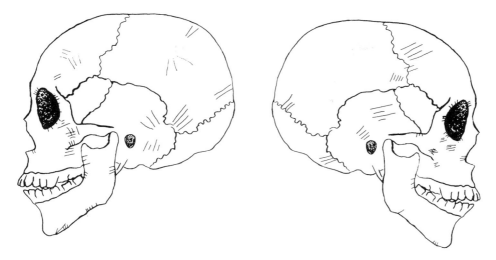

Figure 5.10. Composite cut marks in left and right lateral views.

neither young nor old. There were only three subadults in the upper layer as contrasted with seven in the lower.

The different frequencies of females in the two levels may be misleading. According to the remaining skeletal evidence, the upper level

Table 5.6 Characteristics of Skulls in Each Burial Level (n = 29)

	Upper Level	Lower Level
Old adults		
Male	1	
Female	3	
Adults		
Male	2	2
Female	4	2
Unknown sex		2
Young adults		
Male		2
Female		1
Subadults	3	7
With intentially		
modeled crania	5	3
With filed teeth	4	4

NOTE: Skull II has no provenience and is excluded; n = number of individuals.

had seven females while the lower level had only three. However, two adults and all of the subadults are of unknown sex, so it is possible that the sex ratios in each layer were similar.

The cultural characteristics, cranial modeling and tooth filing, are about evenly distributed between the two layers. Five individuals in the upper level and three in the lower showed definite cranial modeling. Two children in the lower level showed ambiguous signs of modeling and are excluded from the category. If they had been included, cranial modeling would seem to have been equally prevalent in the two layers. The other cultural trait examined, tooth filing, appeared in four individuals in each layer, again suggesting no difference between the levels.

Summary and Implications

The results of our investigation give an overall picture of the sample and document some of the circumstances surrounding the death and burial of the victims. The Colha skull pit contained the cranial remains of 20 adults, of both sexes and a wide range of ages, and 10 young children. The absence of children and teenagers between the ages of 6 or 7 and 18 suggests that the group of skulls did not constitute the remains of actual nuclear families. This is the only age group not represented. However, the nearly equal numbers of adult males, adult females, and children suggest a symbolic meaning to the demographic composition of the burial.

Osteological examination of the skeletal material revealed no signs of widespread serious disease or malnutrition. The frequency of tooth decay, though, was high, even among young children. Adult dentitions had a great deal of calculus and antemortem tooth loss, findings not unexpected in an agricultural population lacking modern dentistry. Definitive evidence of syphilis or other treponemal infection was not found either in adults or children, although inconclusive signs of congenital treponemal disease were found in the juvenile dentition.

Synchronous variation in cultural modification of the skeleton proved to be considerable. Some crania were molded in the Tabular Erect style, some in the Tabular Oblique manner, and some were not deformed. Several adults and old adults of both sexes had filed teeth, but the styles varied somewhat, and several adults did not have their teeth artificially shaped. None of the three young adults had filed teeth. Perhaps the practice was dying out, or perhaps it was the custom to have teeth filed at some time after the young adult period. Possibly, the young adults in the skull pit were not representative of the greater Maya population of young adults.

The other question of great interest is, why were these individuals killed? They did not die of natural causes but, rather, were killed at approximately the same time, decapitated, and the heads then flayed and buried together next to the stairway of a monumental structure. The best guesses for the reason they were killed are first, that they were sacrificed for religious reasons; second, that they represented a ruling class or an elite lineage that was violently deposed; or third, that they were political victims

treated with ritual violence (Mock 1994). Reasonable arguments can be constructed in favor of each scenario.

The following observations support the idea that the burial represented religious sacrifice. First, the demographic composition of the sample resembles a group of nuclear families, yet they are probably not actual or complete nuclear families, as indicated by the absence of older children and teenagers. Therefore, the significance of the group's composition must lie in the symbolism of the pattern. Symbolic behavior is an essential aspect of religious ceremony and would be expected in a sacrifice. Second, the remains of the victims were handled in a manner compatible with Maya sacrifice. They were decapitated, skinned or butchered, possibly displayed on ceramic bowls or plates, and buried in a location that probably had religious or political significance. Landa (Pagden 1975) described flaying as part of his account of Maya human sacrifice. Third, the layers of skulls within the burial may show a pattern based on deference and respect. All of the old adults were in the upper layer; all of the young adults were in the lower layer. Landa reported that "The young people greatly revered the old. . . . The old were so highly esteemed that the young people had no contact with them except when such contact was unavoidable . . ." (Pagden 1975:87). One might argue that the arrangement of adult skulls with respect to age actually was random, and that inferences from the arrangement are inappropriate. On the other hand, if the victims' remains were handled with the same respect that was accorded the living, then the burial does not likely indicate that they represented a hated ruling class or a foreign enemy. Last, one of the skulls was extensively burned and two others were partially burned. Fire has no known association with human sacrifice among the Maya, but Landa (Pagden 1975) noted that it was used in mortuary practices for certain high-status persons,

Virginia K. Massey and D. Gentry Steele

where both burning and cutting of human remains was a way of showing respect. Thus, these practices would not be inappropriate in treating the remains of religious human sacrifice.

While it seems that there are several reasons to believe the burial represents religious sacrifice rather than political upheaval, equally reasonable points can be made to support the latter view. First, there is archaeological evidence that shortly after the skull pit burial, the structure with which it was associated burned and fell. In field notes, the excavator indicated that the fill within the pit was the same as that above the terrace floor, suggesting that the skulls were not deliberately buried. However, they were not disturbed by scavengers as they would have been if the pit had been exposed. The accidental covering of the pit by the falling structure above must have occurred almost immediately after placing the skulls in the pit. The structure was not rebuilt. Second, Classic Maya culture at Colha came to an abrupt end shortly after the skull pit burial (Eaton 1980). The population was much smaller than in Late Classic times and monumental building ceased. The Postclassic occupants may have been Maya, but their culture was quite distinct from an archaeological perspective compared with that of the Late Classic residents. Third, the skinning or flaying of the skulls may not have been reverential. Rather, the skulls may have served as war trophies for invaders. Landa's observations about sacrificial victims are compatible with the notion of processed skulls as trophies: "If they were slaves captured in war, their lord would carry off the bones to use them as a fetish in their dances as a sign of victory" (Pagden 1975:84). Also, "After the victory they removed the jawbones of the dead men and wore them stripped of flesh on their arms" (Pagden 1975:86). Last, the burning of Skull BB and charring of other skulls may not have been a gesture of respect. It may rather have been a spontaneous expression of contempt for a deposed ruling class.

A final interpretation is of a political coup, conducted in a ritual context and having spiritual overtones. Mock (1994) argues that facial mutilation or flaying of facial skin literally strips the victim of power and personality. If the flayed skin is then worn as a mask, the power is transferred to the wearer. The "defacement" of the skull pit victims is parallel to the defacement of monumental art at other Mesoamerican sites. It marks the complete termination of their effect on the Maya world.

It is clear that we cannot positively identify the reason for the skull pit deaths. It may have been religious sacrifice; it may have been political defeat; it may have been both. Speculations about the motivations for behavior that occurred centuries ago are difficult to confirm. Nevertheless, if other Maya skull caches are found and analyzed, perhaps patterns will emerge that will shed light on the skull pit origins.

Acknowledgments

The authors' orginal photographs are reprinted through the courtesy of the Colha Project. The Colha Project is a collaborative effort involving The University of Texas at Austin, Texas A&M University, The University of Texas at San Antonio, and the Centro Studi Ricerche Ligabue, Venice.

6

Archaeology and Osteology of the Tipu Site

Mark N. Cohen, Kathleen O'Connor,
Marie Elaine Danforth, Keith P. Jacobi,
and Carl Armstrong

According to ethnohistorical documents (Graham et al. 1989; Jones 1989; Jones and Kautz 1981a,b; Jones et al. 1986) the town of Tipu (in what is now Belize) was the site of a Spanish *visita* mission at the edge of the Spanish colonial empire in the 16th century. The site was on a frontier in a no-man's-land between areas under Spanish control in Yucatán and areas of the Petén controlled by Itzá Maya. The town maintained political independence; Maya lifestyles and religion persisted in combination with Spanish influence. Eye-witness testimony indicates that pagan rituals continued alongside Christianity. Tipu acted as a refuge for Yucatec Maya fleeing Spanish control, so the population at the site was a mixture of several Maya groups. The town was a center for the cacao trade for much of the Petén. Yucatec elites at Tipu apparently used wealth generated by the trade to encourage rebellion among the Maya.

The documents suggest that Tipu was inhabited solely or almost solely by Maya. The *visita* mission would have been served by a circuit-riding Spanish priest assisted by local Maya personnel. According to a census in 1618, Tipu had approximately 100 *vecinos*, suggesting that the community consisted of 300 to 500 people (Danforth 1989; Jones 1989). However, the population seems to have fluctuated widely. In 1622 there may have been as few as 30 people. In the 1640s the population reached 1000 people or more, but by 1680 the population had dropped to 700 and by 1697 it had dropped further to about 400 (Jones 1989).

The Spanish almost certainly had a significant impact on the Tipu community before there was direct contact. They brought epidemic diseases into Yucatán as early as 1517 and the population of Yucatán was seriously reduced, to about one-third of its former size, before 1544 (Graham et al. 1989). We also know that both Yucatán and Guatemala were visited by famines and epidemics repeatedly during the 16th and 17th centuries (Farriss 1984; Lovell 1982; Veblen 1982)

Documentary evidence provides good temporal definition for the Tipu site. Direct Spanish influence at Tipu began in 1544 following a "violent, vicious" *entrada* (Jones 1989). However this early contact may not have resulted in significant reorganization of the Tipu community (Graham et al. 1989). In 1567 and 1568, the Spanish used Tipu as a base, resulting in a more profound restructuring of the community. In 1638, the Maya of Tipu overthrew Spanish civil and ecclesiastical control and they then remained largely independent for a period of 50 years. However, in the 1690s Tipu made contact again with the Spanish at Mérida, introducing a period of peace and reestablishing Christianity in the region. From 1695 and 1697, the Maya of Tipu cooperated with attempts by the Spanish to conquer the Itzá and capture Tayasal. However, after the conquest of the Itzá in 1697, Tipu lost its importance. The population was forcibly removed to the Petén in 1707.

Archaeology of the Site

In 1978, Grant Jones located Tipu at the site of contemporary Negroman on the west bank of the Macal River south of modern San Ignacio. Jones and Robert Kautz identified the foundation of the Spanish mission at the site and found the Colonial cemetery in 1980. Mark Cohen and Sharon Bennett excavated the skeletal population in its entirety between 1982 and 1987 while Elizabeth Graham continued excavation of the architectural features.

Archaeological remains suggest that Tipu may originally have been settled as early as the Late Preclassic period (ca. 300 B.C.). The occupation extended through the Historic period. Tipu was apparently a significant community at the time of initial Spanish contact in 1544. The archaeological refuse confirms that Spanish trade continued during the period of mission activity. In fact, compared to other contemporary sites, Tipu apparently enjoyed relatively privileged access to Spanish trade goods (Graham et al. 1989). However the same wares were also found in typically "pagan" Postclas-

sic architectural features indicating that a non-Christian population, or at least non-Christian activities, continued during the period of Spanish trade.

The archaeological refuse also indicates, however, that Tipu was part of the Itzá economic sphere, interacting with the Petén in trade which included not only Spanish wares, iron, and cacao, but also marine fauna, ceramic wares from the Petén, and copper. The refuse suggests, in fact, that the Spanish had relatively little impact on Maya material culture at Tipu. Graham et al. (1989) point out that the food refuse from the site indicates continuity in subsistence rather than serious restructuring of agriculture to meet Spanish tribute demands. This may be a reflection of Tipu's isolation. Maize and squash continued as major crops and the community continued to exploit a wide range of fauna, including birds and fish. The Tipu community, enjoying relative independence, fared better than the forcibly restationed Colonial period population at nearby Lamanai.

Although the utilization of the church (and the deposition of most of the skeletal population) is clearly bounded by the dates 1544 and 1707, it is not clear what portion of that time period is represented. There may have been more than one Christian church built between 1544 and 1638. The Tipu church design is probably of the 16th, rather than the 17th, century. However, Spanish pottery has been found incorporated in the walls of the church, and the church walls were built over the corner of a Precolumbian building (a building which had already been modified in the Colonial period). It appears, therefore, that the church does not date to the very earliest period of Spanish influence. Graham et al. (1989) believe that use of the church cemetery probably began during the period of renewed Spanish influence in 1567 to 1568.

The ending date for the church and the cemetery is also in question. Excavations in the nave of the church have revealed an intrusive structure in pagan Maya style that appears to have resulted from an act of willful desecration of the church. Stylistic elements suggest that the structure was created during the historically documented rebellion of 1638. It therefore seems to provide a firm ending date for the use of the church. However, Graham's excavations have revealed one structure built over a collapsed portion of the church, a structure which in turn contains intrusive Christian burials. Apparently, some Christian burial continued after the desecration of the church. The cemetery population may, therefore, represent a period as narrowly bounded as 1567 to 1638 (71 years), or it could represent the period 1544 to 1707, a span of 163 years. We also do not know whether the cemetery represents the entire Tipu community during the period it was in use, inasmuch as the mission apparently did not embrace the entire community (or at least did not represent all of its religious activity).

The Skeletal Population

The total skeletal population numbers more than 600 people buried in the nave of the church and in the surrounding churchyard. (O'Connor [1995] has recently identified 631 separate individuals in the process of generating an age-at-death profile for the site.) Much of the cemetery, particularly in the nave, was reused repeatedly. Individuals were interred in the same location at different times. In many places two or three bodies are buried directly beneath one another (generally separated by several centimeters of soil) and a substantial proportion of the sample was accidentally disturbed, redeposited, and sometimes scattered by subsequent burials, complicating our attempts to determine the number of individuals present and reducing the effective size of the population for many types of analysis. Only 270 individuals are complete, articulated, primary burials and an additional

106 are primary, articulated burials with some portion of the body cut off by later intrusion. The remaining individuals are redeposited and mixed together. Of the intact primary burials, 253 are Colonial period burials associated with the *visita* mission. The disturbed individuals are overwhelmingly of the same period. The few remaining burials are associated with Maya houses excavated by Graham in the immediate vicinity or they are Maya-style burials (flexed or seated, with grave goods) found on the fringes of the Christian burial area.

The Christian burials conform to a pattern. The bodies are supine. Heads are oriented to the west and arms are folded across the chest or pelvis. Most appear to have been buried in shrouds, as evidenced by the presence of shroud pins and the cramped position of the feet. The oldest man in the sample was buried in a coffin in the front and center of the nave. In keeping with Christian practice, individuals were not, as a rule, buried with ceremonial offerings. The primary exception is a single individual (a relatively young female [?] adult) who was buried holding a censer of Christian, European style but of Maya manufacture. Otherwise burial furnishings consist only of the shroud pins or relatively simple personal jewelry which was most often found with children. Adherence to Christian doctrine may also be reflected in the fact that we found no worked or burned human bone, in the fact that few teeth were inlaid or filed in the Maya manner, and in the fact that with one possible exception, there are no signs of deformation of skulls.

The quality of skeletal preservation is uneven but it is excellent by standards for the Maya region. Teeth are very well preserved. Long-bone preservation is generally good. Skull vaults are generally less well preserved (and many are broken) and facial bones are only rarely preserved. (An attempt to assess cranial metric and non-metric traits proved futile.) We have been able to age 128 adult individuals by examination of the auricular surface of the pelvis. On the other hand, only 29 pubic symphyses are available for analysis and some of these are partially eroded. Only 33 vertebral columns are sufficiently preserved to permit age assessment by vertebral osteophytosis or evaluation of spinal diseases.

Physical Anthropology

The historically documented pattern of migration and differential status, plus the common Christian practice of giving elite individuals preferred burial inside the church near the altar, led us to search for class or ethnic distinctions in burial placement. The spacing of burials and the placement of the coffin suggest that burial in the front of the nave may have been a privilege. We also found some preferential burial of adults, particularly men, inside the church. However we found no significant distinctions in rates of pathology or nutritional indicators to suggest differential economic status associated with burial location. Jacobi (this volume) found no evidence of ethnic distinctions within the cemetery so we were not able to establish either ethnic stratification or the presence of separate migrant groups. However, he was able to demonstrate the existence of some family plots (confirming our sense that the vertical placement of bodies resulted from repeated use of the same plot, not from the stacking of bodies in mass burial) and he was able to demonstrate that all individuals, including the individual buried in the coffin and the individual with the censer, were probably Maya.

Demography

We have identified 173 men, 119 women, 47 unsexed adults, and 249 children which represent the Colonial period. Of these 588 Colonial period burials only 547 individuals are preserved well enough for skeletal age-at-death estimation. (This number has increased since our

previous publication [Cohen et al. 1994] because O'Connor [1995] has added additional estimates based on tooth wear to her earlier work.) Age estimation of children was based on tooth development and eruption, epiphyseal formation and union, and diaphyseal length. Adult age-at-death was estimated utilizing metamorphosis of the auricular surface and the pubic symphysis, dental attrition, ectocranial and endocranial suture closure, and degree of vertebral osteophytosis. In addition, Wright (1989) aged a small sample of the population using cementum annulation. Multivariate summary age estimates (Lovejoy et al. 1985) were generated for each of the individuals and an age-at-death distribution was generated (O'Connor 1991, 1995).

Mortality appears low at 0 to 1 years of age, and then increases in the first few years of life. We suspect that individuals in these age categories are underrepresented. This may reflect the pattern of poor preservation of the very young common to archaeological sites. The pattern may also reflect the *visita* nature of the Tipu mission. Spanish priests were rarely present and, as unbaptized infants were unlikely to be buried in the church cemetery, it is probable that many of those dying as infants were buried elsewhere.

It is well known that changes in fertility can have a much larger impact on population age structure in a cemetery than changes in mortality (Coale 1972). Consequently, paleodemography must consider the contributions of both mortality and fertility on observed age-at-death structures. If population is close to stationarity, or if death rates are constant and at a minimum, then fertility can be estimated by: average age at death = 1/B, where B is the birthrate (Johansson and Horowitz 1988; Sattenspiel and Harpending 1983). For the case of Tipu, the population is clearly not stationary and the death rates are not likely to be either constant or at a minimum. Consequently, fertility cannot be estimated for Tipu. A reliable life expectancy at birth cannot be estimated, either, given the likely nonstationarity (Sattenspiel and Harpending 1983). Given the ethnohistoric information, it would be expected, however, that the low average age-at-death of Tipu is largely a result of high mortality rather than high fertility.

With these caveats, estimates of "life expectancy" at birth for the population (for comparison to other cemetery profiles) range from 15 to 18 years (depending on what assumption is made about the growth rate of the population). This figure is low even in comparison to that of other skeletal samples (Cohen 1989; Cohen and Armelagos 1984; Lovejoy et al. 1977). The proportion of individuals dying before the age of 15 years (50%) is reasonably in accordance with the range observed in the best-preserved skeletal samples and in historical populations. However, given the suspected infant underenumeration this percentage is probably an underestimate. "Life expectancy" for individuals who reached age 15 (10 to 15 additional years, again depending on the assumption made about the growth rate of the population) is at the low end of the range observed for skeletal samples.

Individuals in the oldest age categories seem to be underrepresented; only nine individuals 45 years of age or older were identified, and no one survived past age 50. It is possible that conservative elderly individuals would not have been buried in a newly established church cemetery, but given the 70- to 160-year span during which the cemetery was used, we would expect young converts to have grown old and been buried in the church.

Documented patterns of frontier immigration are also likely to have involved disproportionately high percentages of young individuals, which may bias the cemetery sample. Again we would expect young immigrants to grow old.

Poor preservation and recovery of elderly remains and the underestimation of skeletal ages may also lead to an apparent lack of older individuals. However when we aged other Maya populations by the same methods, we found them to have older age distributions. It is also possible that individuals died at relatively young ages from epidemic diseases. The early- and mid-adult years are indeed characterized by an apparently high level of mortality, a pattern which may, in part, reflect epidemic disease. If so, however, there should have been more elderly individuals found as some would have been elderly when the epidemics struck. Moreover, the placement of individuals in the cemetery does not indicate hasty or mass burial which might occur under epidemic conditions.

Pathology

Armstrong (1989) reviewed long-bone pathology (trauma and infection or periosteal reaction). He found that 457 individuals could be scored for these pathological conditions. Identifiable trauma was infrequent. Of 275 adult individuals, 24 (8.7%) displayed trauma on at least one bone. This included 16 of 154 men (10.1%) and 8 of 116 women (6.9%). Only one child displayed long-bone trauma. Men were slightly more likely to have leg trauma than women. Women were more likely to have a fracture of the ulna or radius, but the differences are not significant. Three fractures of the arm were classified as parry fractures. However, most fractures appear to have been accidental and the frequency of trauma increases gradually with age, suggesting accidental accretion. One adult individual did display crushing of the left zygomatic arch of the skull which may reflect violence, one individual had a possible entry wound on the tibia, and one child displayed multiple cranial perforations. With the exception of one possible cut mark on a frontal bone, no bones displayed trauma which distinctively implicates Spanish weapons.

Overall, the pattern of trauma in the Tipu

population suggests random but not systematic violence which probably was domestic rather than political in origin. The nature and frequency of the trauma does not appear to match the expected picture of rebellion and violence on the colonial frontier. Moreover, normal economic activities apparently did not pose a high risk of physical injury.

Periosteal reactions of long bones, usually considered to result from infection, were also comparatively rare. Of 159 males, 36 (22.6%) displayed some reaction on at least one bone; 16 of 116 females (13.8%) and 4 of 182 juvenile individuals (2.2%) displayed some reaction.

Systemic infection (which we define as the presence of reaction on two or more limbs or on other areas of the skeleton) was found in 9.9% of men, 7.5% of women, and only 1.1% of children. Overall, 19 of 457 coded individuals (4.2%) displayed systemic infection by this definition. Most changes were of a relatively minor order.

Tibiae were the most commonly afflicted bone. However, the slight nature of most lesions, the fact that both tibiae were only rarely affected, and the absence of lesions on other bones such as the frontal bone of the skull, suggests to us that treponemal infection did not afflict the Tipu population. However, paleopathologist Israel Hershkovitz, who has examined a portion of the population, believes that treponemal infection was present and is undertaking histological analysis to confirm his suspicions. Despite Jacobi's thorough analysis of teeth, we found no signs of congenital treponemal infection. Similarly, (although the preserved sample of affected bones is much smaller) we saw no evidence of tuberculosis or smallpox.

Cohen (Cohen et al. 1989) has undertaken an analysis of linear enamel hypoplasia in 180 individuals using a low-power binocular microscope. Low-grade hypoplasias were very common, but most could not have been scored by eye alone. Severe hypoplasias were relatively rare. Of 138 incisors coded, 95 (69%) had at least one hypoplastic lesion. Of 146 canines, 132 (90.4%) had some hypoplasia; 100 of 105 individuals who could be scored for both teeth had hypoplasia on one or both. However, severe hypoplasias occurred only on 2.2% of incisors and on 10.3% of canines. Only 2 of 105 individuals (1.9%) who could be scored for both teeth had severe lesions on both. Hypoplasias on the incisor teeth suggest that stress was most common between the ages of 2.5 and 3 years. Lesions on the canine display a similar peak but suggest a second peak between 4 and 4.5 years. Only 30 individuals displayed three or more hypoplasias of the canine. Of these, only 12 appeared to display rhythmic spacing. Apparently, regular seasonal stresses accounted for only a small portion of the stress experienced.

Danforth (1989, this volume) concluded that the Colonial Tipu population did not display patterns of enamel defects suggesting high levels of stress associated with epidemic or enzootic infections or with severe nutritional deprivation. Instead, she considered the pattern of dental defects to be consistent with a generally healthy, even privileged population. She also suggested that signs of severe prenatal stress were relatively rare, suggesting that the population did not suffer severe maternal malnutrition. The Tipu sample was found to display sexual differentiation in the frequency of enamel defects. Significantly higher rates of Wilson bands and hypoplasias were found among men, a pattern not found in any of the Late Classic sites. The pattern of sexual differences in hypoplasias has been confirmed by Cohen on a sample of adult incisors and canines from 56 male individuals and 36 female individuals. He found (Cohen et al. 1989) an average of 1.56 hypoplasias on adult male central incisors vs. 1.15 for adult women; and 1.92 hypoplasias per mandibular canine for men vs. 1.47 for women (the differences are not significant). Men are significantly more likely than women to display three or more hypoplasias: 16 of 56 male individuals (28.6%) vs. 3 of 36 female individuals (8.3%; $\chi^2 = 5.4$, p < .05).

Danforth (1991) has also undertaken an analysis of Harris lines in 58 femurs and 44 tibiae from individuals of various ages in the Tipu population. She concluded that Harris lines were rare. Women displayed fewer lines than men. Stress episodes appear to have been scattered through childhood, showing no apparent age peak. Several men displayed multiple lines, suggesting that they were subject to cyclical stresses.

Danforth concluded that childhood at Tipu was relatively healthy. She argued that the small number of Harris lines probably cannot be attributed to erasure by subsequent bone turnover because the adult individuals were quite young, and because adult men and women display frequencies of lines similar to those of children. She also concluded that line formation was not depressed by protein-calorie malnutrition since cortical bone growth and maintenance appear healthy.

Danforth, Bennett et al. (1985a) analyzed femoral cortical involution in a sample of 127 adult individuals and 37 children. They found osteoporosis in only 3% of adult individuals, suggesting that bone was maintained by relatively good calcium:phosphorous ratios in the diet. (However, the sample consisted of relatively young adults, making the appearance of osteoporosis unlikely.) They also reported that juvenile cortical bone area and femoral diaphyseal length increased regularly with age. Tipu children showed slight but steady gains in bone length and cortical thickness through childhood, suggesting that severe protein-calorie malnutrition was not present (cf. Huss-Ashmore et al. 1982). A follow-up study by Dina Casey and Sharon Bennett (Cohen et al. 1989) on 96 juvenile skeletons produced similar results.

Adult statures at Tipu are average by Maya standards and do not suggest significant economic deprivation relative to Precolonial populations. Adult male individuals in the Tipu sample (n = 149) have an average stature of 160.3 cm calculated by Genovés's (1967) formulas; 106 adult female individuals have an average stature of 148.3 cm. The mean male stature at Tipu is less than that of the Preclassic and Early Classic populations from Altar de Sacrificios and Tikal, but it is comparable to or greater than statures for the Late Classic and Postclassic populations from these sites (Haviland 1967; Saul 1972a).

Cribra orbitalia could be scored in one or both orbits of 214 individuals. Remodeled lesions (all grades) occurred in 49 of the 214 (22.9%). Moderate lesions occurred in 39 (13.6%) of all individuals, afflicting 15.5% of adult individuals and 42.4% of juvenile individuals. Remodeled severe lesions occurred in 8.8% of adult men, 5.4% of adult women, and 30.5% of children.

Porotic hyperostosis was scored on at least one region of the skull of 304 individuals. Of these, 16 cases (5.3%) displayed active lesions, 61 (20.1%) displayed remodeled severe lesions, and 168 (55.3%) were scored positive at at least one location on the skull vault for porosity of any grade. Among children, 15 of 106 (14.1%) displayed active porotic hyperostosis, 23 of 106 (21.7%) displayed severe (but remodeled) porosity, and 42.5% displayed remodeled porosity of any grade. Active anemia was found in 10 of 37 children (27.0%) age nine or older but in only 5 of 69 children (7.2%) age eight and younger. Remodeled severe lesions were found in 15 of 37 children (40.5%) age nine and older but in only 8 of 69 children (11.6%) of younger ages. Anemia therefore seems to have been more common in older children than in younger children among those in our sample. These rates are no worse than moderate in comparison to other Maya populations we studied (Harvard University collections from Seibal, Barton Ramie, and Copán) or in comparison to other reported Maya populations (cf. Hooton 1940; Saul 1972a, 1982; White 1986).

We found no correlation between cribra orbitalia or porotic hyperostosis and the presence of systemic infection. Of 193 individuals who could be coded for cribra and infection, 15 had systemic infection and 44 had cribra, but only 1 individual displayed both symptoms. Similarly, 237 individuals could be coded for porotic hyperostosis and any infection. Of these 16 had infection of at least one bone and 81 had porotic hyperostosis, but only 6 displayed both conditions. The lack of correlation may reflect the fact that almost all of the infection observable in the population occurred among adults, but the results suggest that infection of the type visible in the skeleton did not play a significant role in the etiology of childhood anemia.

The presence of anemia may have had some effect on adult stature. Both men and women who displayed porosity on the skull averaged about .5 cm shorter than their counterparts without porosity. Women with severe lesions averaged about 2 cm shorter than women without, and men with severe lesions averaged 2.5 cm less than those without. The results are consistent, but none of the contrasts is statistically significant.

Among adults there is no association between cribra and mean age-at-death. However, porotic hyperostosis of the parietal is significantly correlated with reduced lifespan. Adults with any sign of porotic hyperostosis had an average age-at-death of about 25.4 years, compared to 28 years for other individuals who could be coded. Adults with more severe indications had an average age-at-death of 23.9 years, compared to 27.3 years for the remainder of

the population. However, the meaning of the result is ambiguous; it may reflect either the reduced life expectancy of once-afflicted individuals, or the shorter period of time for remodeling of porotic hyperostosis to occur in individuals dying at younger ages. Among children there is no relationship between anemia and reduced diaphyseal length, cortical area, or percent cortical area.

Because of the prominence of Saul's (1972a) hypothesis about scurvy among the Maya, Cohen et al. (1987) attempted to determine whether the scurvy syndrome as described by Saul was present at Tipu. Saul used the combination of antemortem tooth loss and periosteal reactions ("subperiosteal hemorrhages") as the basis for diagnosing scurvy. We reasoned that if he were correct the two symptoms (as well as other symptoms associated with scurvy such as porotic hyperostosis) should co-occur in our sample. Small sample size limits the certainty of our conclusion, but we found that, at Tipu, antemortem tooth loss and periosteal reactions occurred together no more often than they would by chance, suggesting that the two are not part of a single syndrome. The low frequency of periosteal lesions in the population also counters the hypothesis that they result from dietary deficiency.

Danforth (1989, this volume), recording hypoplasias in deciduous canines, concluded that individuals who experienced growth disruption in months immediately following birth were less likely to survive the weaning period than their unaffected counterparts, a pattern confirmed also by Apmann (in Cohen et al. 1989). Apmann found 11 individuals with deciduous hypoplasias had an average age-at-death of 2 years while 42 individuals without hypoplasias had an average age-at-death of 2.8 years. Cohen (Cohen et al. 1989) also found that individuals with permanent teeth dying as children had significantly higher rates of hypoplasias on the permanent canine (2.50 per tooth, n = 26) than either adult men (1.92, n = 56) or adult women (1.47, n = 36), supporting the hypothesis that higher frequencies of growth disturbance in childhood contributed to an increased probability of dying in childhood. Moreover, high frequency of hypoplasias (three or more on the same tooth) seems to be significantly correlated with the probability of dying in childhood, as 11 of 26 children (42.3%) with adult teeth had three or more hypoplasias on the same tooth whereas only 19 of 92 adult individuals (20.7%), including 16 of 56 men who could be scored (28.6%) and 3 of 36 women who could be scored (8.3%), had as many hypoplasias per tooth (χ^2 = 5.04, p < .05). Cohen also found that the presence of three or more hypoplasias on the canine had no significant effect on male or female stature. However, a one-tailed separate-variance t-test showed that male individuals with at least one severe hypoplasia (mean = 155.9 cm, n = 5) were significantly shorter on average than the rest of the adult male population (mean = 160.6 cm, n = 45; t = −3.08, p = .0125).

Summation

The Tipu cemetery represents a Christian Maya population on a colonial frontier in intermittent contact with Spanish colonial rulers between 1544 and 1707. The population postdates the first wave of epidemics in Yucatán but was contemporary with a significant number of epidemics and famines recorded in adjoining regions.

The population displays few signs of violent trauma despite the political unrest which is supposed to have characterized the frontier during the period in question. It also displays rates of other pathological conditions (accidental trauma, infection, growth disruption, and porotic hyperostosis) which are low or moderate by the standards of Precolonial Maya groups or of prehistoric populations elsewhere, a pattern which seems at odds with the time and place and known frontier situation of the site. (However, we do not know whether the church cemetery represents the entire community.)

This apparent good health might reflect the deaths of individuals from epidemics before their bodies had time to register insults in the skeleton (see Wood et al. 1992). However, even under these conditions, one would expect skeletons of those who died in the epidemics to reflect the pre-epidemic burden of malnutrition and chronic infection felt by the community. One would also expect the survivors of such epidemics to display high rates of enamel hypoplasia and other signs of severe growth disruption as well as more chronic stresses resulting from social dislocation following epidemics. The Tipu skeletons show few signs of such stresses.

The cemetery does not appear to be complete. Very few infants and very few individuals more than 40 years of age have been recovered. The cemetery has produced an extremely young age-at-death distribution. Estimated "life expectancy" at birth (15 to 18 years) and from age 15 (10 to 15 additional years) are low even by paleodemographic standards. Whether this pattern reflects death in epidemic conditions, paleodemographic techniques, or some principle of selective burial is not clear; however, the treatment of the dead does not suggest mass or hurried burial and the population does not display the high frequency of severe growth disruption which should be expected in survivors of epidemics.

Acknowledgments

We wish to acknowledge the support of National Science Foundation grants BNS 83-03693 and BNS 85-06785.

PART 3

Dental Studies

7

Late Postclassic Tooth Filing at Chau Hiix and Tipu, Belize

Lorena M. Havill, Diane M. Warren,
Keith P. Jacobi, Karen D. Gettelman,
Della Collins Cook, and K. Anne Pyburn

An old and fascinating human practice, body ornamentation can be achieved through a variety of means including clothing, piercings, tattooing, and scarification, among others. Another such method, artificial dental modification, is found in many areas of the world but is perhaps best known in Mesoamerica. (For a comprehensive list of sources see Milner and Larsen 1991.) Modification is usually limited to the anterior, maxillary dentition (Fastlicht 1962). This supports the interpretation that Mesoamerican dental modification was ornamentation, these teeth being the most visible. Modification of other teeth is rare. However, when other teeth are modified, the next most visible areas, maxillary premolars or the anterior dentition of the mandible, are generally used (Fastlicht 1962; Linné 1940).

Artificial dental modification can take several forms including inlaying or "filling," ablation, filing, or a combination of these. As with other body ornamentation, it is very possible that dental modification has significance be-

yond aesthetics; however, it is generally agreed that these techniques were not restorative, but instead purely decorative or perhaps ritually significant (Fastlicht 1962).

Rubín de la Borbolla (1940) and Romero (1970) have each developed a system for classification of artificial dental modification (Figs. 7.1, 7.2). Rubín de la Borbolla's system involves 24 types of tooth modification designated as A through X. This system is based on varieties he found in collections at the Department of Physical Anthropology at the Museo Nacional de Antropología, México. Romero (1970) examined a collection of 1212 modified teeth from the Instituto Nacional de Antropología e Historia in México and grouped them into seven basic types (A through G). He further divided each of these types into several variants, recognizing a total of 59 types or variants. Neither Romero nor Rubín de la Borbolla observed ablation in Mesoamerica.

These systems of classification involve tooth filing and inlaying, both of which were practiced

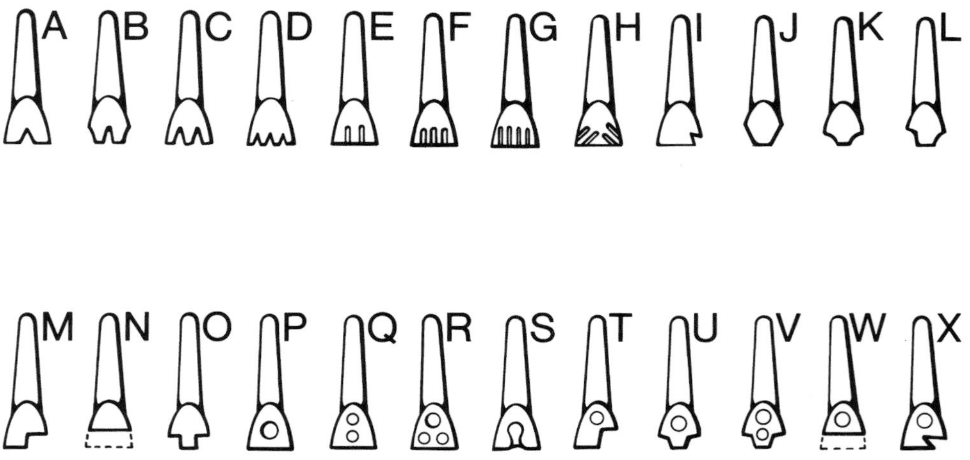

Figure 7.1. Rubín de la Borbolla's system of classification for artificially modified teeth. Adapted with permission from Rubín de la Borbolla (1940:353, Fig. 1).

by the Maya (Fastlicht 1962). Linné (1940) hypothesized that the tradition began with filing, progressed to inlaying (or a combination of both) and then back to filing alone. According to Romero (1970), tooth filing among the Maya came into practice in the Preclassic (1400–600 B.C.). In the Early Classic (100 B.C.–A.D. 300), inlaying takes hold as the predominant practice. The Late Classic (A.D. 700–900) is a period of elaborate combinations of filing and inlaying. During the Postclassic (A.D. 1000–1500) filing is again predominant.

Filing is the practice with which we are primarily concerned. Romero (1970) suggests that filing is not limited to males or to females, but it appears to be more common among one sex or the other in different time periods. For example, during the Early Postclassic, filing seems to be more common in females. He provides no quantitative data to illustrate these trends. Linné (1940) notes that more research is needed to determine any sex-specific nature of artificial dental modification.

The relationship between dental filing and social status is also unclear. Joyce (1914) mentions that tooth filing was practiced among Aztec women of high status, but Romero (1958) finds no apparent association between tooth filing and social status. Saville (1913) notes that in Precolumbian Ecuador, the "principal" individuals in some villages wore gold inlays. The relationship between social status and tooth filing among the Maya in particular has not been discussed.

Although many studies involve description and classification of artificially modified teeth, few examine the method by which artificial modification was achieved. Some methods of filing are suggested. For example, Fastlicht (1962) translates Landa's reference to filing teeth with stones and water. Stewart (1942), citing Conzemius's report of another method practiced by the Sumu of Central America that involves chipping the teeth with a dull knife, suggests that the "filed" teeth from Mesoamerica could not have been chipped, but must have been filed, and associates chipping with recently introduced African practices. Dembo and Imbelloni (1938) review experimental studies showing that the Mesoamerican filing patterns

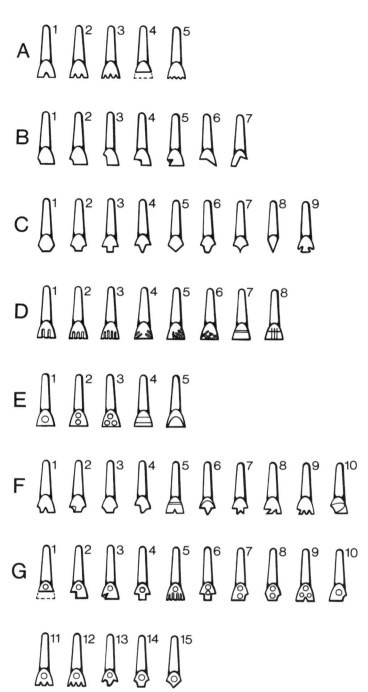

Figure 7.2. Romero's system of classification for artificially modified teeth. Adapted with permission from Romero (1970:51, Fig. 1).

could have been produced with prismatic flint blades. Romero (1958) suggests that an assemblage of worked bone, pyrites, and jade found by Ricketson with Burial 15 at Baking Pot, Belize, may have been a tool kit for making dental inlays. Specific tool types for dental filing remain unknown and may have varied temporally and geographically.

Gwinnett and Gorelick (1979) used scanning electron microscopy (SEM) to describe cavity preparation in a single skull with multiple inlays. They conclude that the inlays were done at different times and that a wooden, circular drill with sand abrasive was the likely instrument. Although dental inlays have received some attention, little research has been done on dental filing in Mesoamerica since the work of Romero (1970) and Fastlicht (1976), and SEM analysis of filed teeth does not seem to have been attempted. The Maya sites of Chau Hiix, a Late Postclassic residential center, and Tipu, a Colonial period site, have each yielded filed teeth. Scanning electron microscopy was used to evaluate the method by which they were filed.

Sites

Chau Hiix

Chau Hiix is a medium-sized residential center located in northern Belize approximately halfway between Lamanai and Altun Ha. Preliminary excavations have demonstrated that the site was occupied continuously from 1500 B.C. until the 15th century A.D., and possibly later. A dense Postclassic settlement is evident, although specific density figures are not yet available. The site center includes a main platform and associated structures located at the edge of a seasonally flooded lagoon. Outlying settlements are connected to the site center by *sacbes* (causeways). This surrounding settlement area is at least 5 km long, and is concentrated into a strip along the edge of the lagoon. The settle-

ment area is a more or less continuous scattering of platform groups and small mounds. In at least four areas there are clusters of much larger buildings on secondary platforms. The edges of the lagoon show evidence of extensive raised field agriculture in the region.

Most burials recovered from Chau Hiix to date are from the Postclassic period. The majority consist of shallow, extended graves in house mounds. Preservation is generally poor. During the first field season in 1993, 31 burials and many isolated bones were recovered. Anterior dentition was recovered for 12 individuals. Four of these have filed teeth. Three of the individuals with unfiled teeth are juveniles, thus dental modification might not yet be expected (Fastlicht 1948; Rubín de la Borbolla 1940). Hence, four of nine adults have filed teeth.

Tipu

The Colonial *visita* mission church at Tipu, Belize, dating from 1544 to 1638, has yielded the remains of more than 600 individuals (Graham et al. 1989). However, individuals under the age of two and older adults are underrepresented (Cohen et al. 1994). These Maya were buried in and around the church following the traditional Spanish Catholic mortuary practice of burial in the extended position with feet oriented toward an altar.

Unlike those at Chau Hiix, skeletal remains at Tipu are generally very well preserved. Nearly 90% of the burials include teeth. These teeth exhibit little dental wear. Of the 10 burials thought to date to the Postclassic period because they reflect interment procedures characteristic of prehistoric Maya, none have modified teeth. However, eight Maya from the Colonial period do exhibit dental modification. These burials include three females, three males, and two adults of unknown sex ranging in age from 18 to 40 years. In all cases, modification is found in the anterior dentition and involves the maxillary or mandibular central incisors. Two

Table 7.1 Chau Hiix Individuals with Artificial Dental Modification

	Right								Left							
ID, Sex, Age	M3	M2	M1	P2	P1	C	I2	I1	I1	I2	C	P1	P2	M1	M2	M3
CH 0557, unknown, adult																
Maxilla	–	–	–	–	–	–	–	–	xM	–	–	–	–	–	–	–
Mandible	–	–	–	–	–	–	–	–	–	–	–	–	–	–	–	–
CH 0561, male, adult																
Maxilla	x	–	–	–	–	–	–	xM	–	x	–	–	–	–	–	–
Mandible	–	–	–	–	–	–	–	–	–	–	–	–	–	–	–	–
CHT 0813, male, adult																
Maxilla	–	–	–	–	–	–	–	–	xM	xM	xM	–	–	–	–	–
Mandible	–	–	–	–	–	–	–	–	–	–	–	–	–	–	–	–
CHT 0651, unknown, adult																
Maxilla	x	x	–	–	x	xM	xM	xM	xM	xM	xM	x	–	x	–	–
Mandible	–	x	x	x	x	x	–	x	x	x	x	x	x	x	x	x

NOTE: x = tooth present; M = tooth modified.

Materials

Chau Hiix

The filed teeth discovered at Chau Hiix during the 1993 field season belong to two adult males and two adults of unknown sex. None of the filing is associated with caries or abscesses. For two of the individuals, only one tooth was recovered. However, one individual is represented by three filed teeth and another by six. Tooth preservation is generally good with some postmortem breakage primarily involving the roots. Both filed surfaces and ordinary occlusal wear planes at Chau Hiix are generally highly polished. The teeth from Chau Hiix fit nicely into the classification systems of both Rubín de la Borbolla and Romero. An inventory of filed teeth from Chau Hiix appears in Table 7.1.

CH 0557 (ISOLATED TOOTH). This specimen consists of an isolated left maxillary central incisor. Wear indicates that this was an adult. The sex of the individual is not known. The occlusal one-third of the distal one-half of the tooth crown has been removed, producing a right-angled groove. The apical border of the groove is approximately parallel to the occlusal surface of the tooth. Moderate attrition has resulted in exposure of the dentin. There is a small postmortem fracture of the enamel on the lingual surface of the unfiled occlusal portion. This filing pattern is Rubín de la Borbolla's Type M and Romero's Type B-4.

CH 0561 (BURIAL 26). Burial 26, an adult male, includes a filed right maxillary central incisor. The occlusal one-fourth of the mesial two-thirds of the crown has been removed. The resultant groove is shallow and curved rather than right-angled as described for CH 0557. This may be due to more extensive occlusal wear in this individual. Enamel surfaces are rounded and highly polished with exposure of secondary dentin on the occlusal surface. Wear on the lingual surface extends to the exposed portion of the root. Two linear enamel hypoplasias are visible on the labial surface. Grooving of the mesial surface instead of the

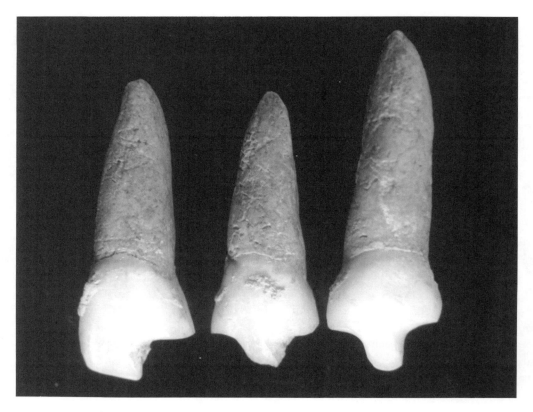

Figure 7.3. Artificially modified left maxillary incisors and canine of CHT 0813.

distal one makes this the inverse of Rubín de la Borbolla's Type M and Romero's Type B-4.

CHT 0813 (BURIAL 23). Burial 23 is that of an adult male. A shallow ceramic vessel associated with this burial is Middle to Late Postclassic. The three teeth present are all filed and consist of a left maxillary central incisor, lateral incisor, and canine. The central incisor is grooved in a manner almost identical to that of CH 0557, in keeping with Rubín de la Borbolla's Type M and Romero's B-4 (Fig. 7.3). The occlusal one-half of the mesial and distal corners has been removed from the lateral incisor and the canine, leaving a central occlusal projection approximately one-third the width of the tooth. Both the mesial and distal grooves are right-angled and have apical borders paral-

lel to the occlusal surface. These teeth correspond to Rubín de la Borbolla's Type O and Romero's Type C-3.

Small striations are visible on the labial surface of the canine extending mesially and apically from the distal groove. Wear on these teeth is minimal with almost no dentin exposure except in the filed areas. Exposed dentin surfaces on both incisors show labiolingual striations indicating the direction of filing. The tip of the central occlusal projection of the lateral incisor has been broken off postmortem.

CHT 0651 (BURIAL 9). Burial 9 is an adult of unknown sex. The maxillary incisors and canines have been modified in a manner similar to that of Burial 23. The corners of the grooves are more rounded in this individual. This is especially apparent on the canines and the right lateral incisor. Again, this may be the effect of greater attrition. However, filed surfaces on the canines are slanted labially upward, and labiolingual striations are visible. Dentin is exposed on all occlusal surfaces. The central projections of the lateral incisors are somewhat narrower in width than those of Burial 23. The occlusal part of the central projection of the left lateral incisor was fractured during life. Several linear enamel hypoplasias are visible on the labial surface of the canines. As with Burial 23, the central incisors are of Rubín de la Borbolla's Type M and Romero's Type B-4. Lateral incisors and canines are of Rubín de la Borbolla's Type O and Romero's Type C-3. The remainder

of the available dentition is unmodified. Again, the lingual surfaces of the anterior teeth are very polished.

Tipu

In contrast to the style of modification seen at Chau Hiix, most teeth from Tipu exhibit very narrow, V-shaped grooves cut into the occlusal surface (Fig. 7.4). These grooves are single in most cases, but occasionally double on larger teeth, such as the maxillary incisors. The mesial and distal corners of the occlusal surface are filed off of the canines and some lateral incisors, producing an obtuse point. Rubín de la Borbolla's Types A, B, C, J, and K and Romero's A-1, A-2, C-2, C-5, and C-9 are represented.

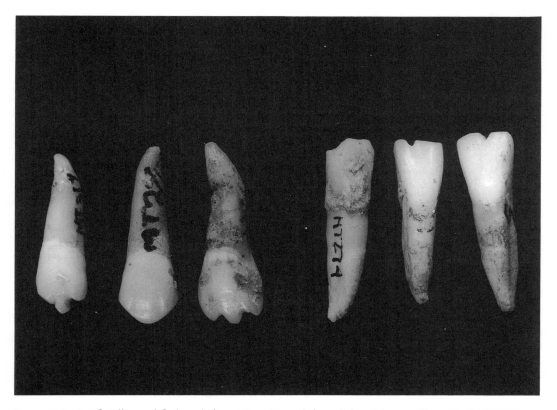

Figure 7.4. Artificially modified teeth from Tipu. From left to right: right maxillary I2 of MT 317, maxillary canine of MT 253 (unmodified), right maxillary I2 of MT 4, right mandibular I1 of MT 279, right mandibular I1 from MT 67B, left mandibular I2 of MT 4.

Table 7.2 Tipu Individuals with Artificial Dental Modification

ID, Sex, Age (Years)	Right								Left							
	M3	M2	M1	P2	P1	C	I2	I1	I1	I2	C	P1	P2	M1	M2	M3
MT 4, female, 35–45																
Maxilla	x	x	x	–	–	–	xM	xM	xM	xM	x	–	–	–	–	–
Mandible	–	–	–	x	x	x	xM	xM	xM	xM	–	–	x	–	–	–
MT 67B, unknown, 15–20																
Maxilla	x	x	x	x	x	x	x	x	x	x	x	x	x	x	x	x
Mandible	x	x	x	x	x	x	x	xM	xM	x	x	x	x	x	x	x
MT 81, male, 18–22																
Maxilla	x	x	x	x	x	x	–	x	x	x	x	x	x	x	x	x
Mandible	x	x	x	x	x	x	x	xM	xM	x	x	x	x	x	x	x
MT 124, unknown, 18–25																
Maxilla	–	x	x	x	x	x	–	xM	xM	xM	x	x	x	x	x	x
Mandible	x	x	x	x	x	x	x	xM	xM	xM	xM	–	x	–	x	–
MT 141, female, 25–35																
Maxilla	x	x	x	–	x	xM	xM	xM	xM	xM	–	x	x	x	–	x
Mandible	–	x	x	x	x	x	xM	xM	xM	xM	xM	x	x	–	–	–
MT 174, female, 25–35																
Maxilla	x	–	x	x	x	x	x	x	x	x	x	x	x	x	x	x
Mandible	x	x	x	x	x	x	x	x	xM	x	x	x	x	x	–	x
MT 279, male, 18–25																
Maxilla	–	–	–	–	–	–	–	–	–	–	–	–	–	–	–	–
Mandible	x	–	x	x	x	x	x	xM	x	x	x	x	x	x	–	x
MT 317, male, 25–35																
Maxilla	x	x	x	x	x	x	xM	xM	xM	xM	x	x	x	x	–	x
Mandible	x	–	x	x	x	x	xM	x	x	xM	x	x	x	x	x	x

NOTE: x = tooth present; M = tooth modified.

Gross descriptions below do not include all filed teeth from Tipu, but only those available for study. Table 7.2 provides an inventory of all individuals from Tipu with filed teeth.

MT 141. This individual (Fig. 7.5) is an adult female aged 25 to 35 years. The maxillary central incisors each display two shallow occlusal grooves corresponding to Rubín de la Borbolla's Type C and Romero's Type A-2. The labial margins of these grooves are rounded and the labial surfaces are highly polished. The maxillary lateral incisors are pegged and very reduced in size. There are single, shallow, occlusal, V-shaped grooves in both, correspond-ing to Rubín de la Borbolla's Type A and Romero's Type A-1. The left lateral incisor is also filed diagonally on the mesial and distal corners, corresponding to Rubín de la Borbolla's Type B. Romero does not provide a designation for this filing pattern. All four mandibular incisors exhibit single, shallow occlusal grooves (Rubín de la Borbolla's Type A and Romero's A-1). The intersection of two filing planes results in pointed maxillary and mandibular canines corresponding to Rubín de la Borbolla's Type J and Romero's C-5. The direction of filing is visible in all cases, and the resultant surfaces are remarkably flat and consistently labiolingual in orientation. The edges of these

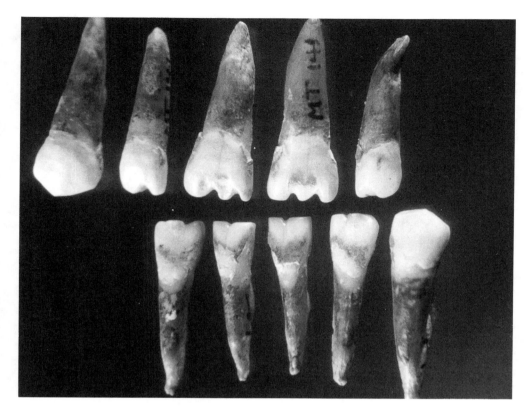

Figure 7.5. Dental arcade of MT 141.

surfaces are sharply defined, in contrast to the rounded edges of the V-shaped grooves in the occlusal surfaces of the incisors.

MT 4. This is an adult female of approximately 35 to 45 years of age whose right maxillary lateral and central incisors show two V-shaped grooves in the occlusal surface consistent with Rubín de la Borbolla's Type C and Romero's A-2. The mandibular incisors show single occlusal grooves as seen in Rubín de la Borbolla's Type A and Romero's A-1.

MT 67B. A single right mandibular central incisor from this 15- to 20-year-old of unknown sex shows a 1 mm × 1 mm V-shaped groove that has been cut into the distal half of the oc-

clusal surface. The other mandibular central incisor is also modified but was not available for study. Several linear enamel hypoplasias are grossly visible on the apical half of the crown and wear is moderate. This style closely resembles Rubín de la Borbolla's Type A and Romero's A-1, except that the groove is distal to the tooth midline.

MT 279. This is an adult male aged 18 to 25. The right mandibular central incisor, the only tooth recorded as modified in this individual, was available for study. The mesial and distal corners of this tooth have been chipped away. Consistent surface coloration indicates that the chipping is not postmortem. This is included in Rubín de la Borbolla's system as Type K and in

Romero's as C-2. There is also a very shallow groove on the labial margin of the midocclusal surface which may or may not be an intentional modification. If it is intentional, then the pattern is Rubín de la Borbolla's Type B except that the occlusal groove is much shallower than would be expected. Romero does not provide a classification for this type. However, a combination of his A-1 and C-2 would yield a similar result.

MT 317. This right maxillary pegged lateral incisor is one of six modified teeth from an adult male aged 25 to 35. Wear on this tooth is minimal. It is modified in a manner similar to that of the canine in CHT 0813 except that the central occlusal projection is achieved by V-shaped grooves in the occlusal surface on either side instead of angled grooves removing the mesial and distal corners as in CHT 0813. This pattern corresponds to Romero's C-9, but is not represented by any of Rubín de la Borbolla's types.

SEM Methods and Results

Filed teeth from two Chau Hiix individuals (CH 0557 and CHT 0813) and three Tipu individuals (MT 4, MT 67B, and MT 279) were examined by scanning electron microscopy to evaluate the method by which they were filed. We examined the left maxillary central incisor of CH 0557, the left maxillary canine of CHT 0813, the right maxillary lateral incisor and left mandibular lateral incisor of MT 4, the right mandibular central incisor of MT 67B, and the right mandibular central incisor of MT 279. These specific teeth were chosen based on good surface preservation and minimal attrition. Visibility of striations on the labial surface of the canine from CHT 0813 was also important in its selection for SEM examination because the striations are closely associated with the distal groove and possibly resulted

from the filing procedure. The Chau Hiix teeth were cleaned ultrasonically in water only. Teeth from Tipu were cleaned with water using a soft toothbrush.

CH 0557. SEM examination of this specimen was unremarkable. Striations in the modified area are labiolingual in direction. Edges are rounded, perhaps as a result of subsequent wear. There is no evidence of chipping or fracture of the tooth prior to filing.

CHT 0813 (BURIAL 23). SEM study of the canine from this individual was enlightening (Fig. 7.6). The mesial and distal grooves are rounded in profile. All filed surfaces show fine labiolingual striations that diverge toward the labial margin of the groove, indicating the principal movements of the filing instrument. Small, natural facets on the labial and mesial surfaces of the tooth retain perikymata seen as small areas of prominent circumferential striations. Flatter facets with fine vertical striations appear on the labial margin of the mesial groove and on the lingual margin of the distal groove. These facets may represent careful chamfering to modify any sharp edges resulting from the two principal grooves. While some postmortem pitting is visible, there is no evidence of chipping or fracture of the tooth margins as an initial stage in filing.

MT 4. SEM analysis of the right maxillary lateral incisor and the left mandibular lateral incisor from this individual showed a simple labiolingual abrasion pattern resulting in a polished surface within the grooves (Fig. 7.7). Intraoral wear may have contributed to the polished appearance.

MT 67B. SEM analysis of this tooth was unremarkable. As with CH 0557, filed edges are rounded and there is no evidence of chipping or fracture before filing (Fig. 7.8).

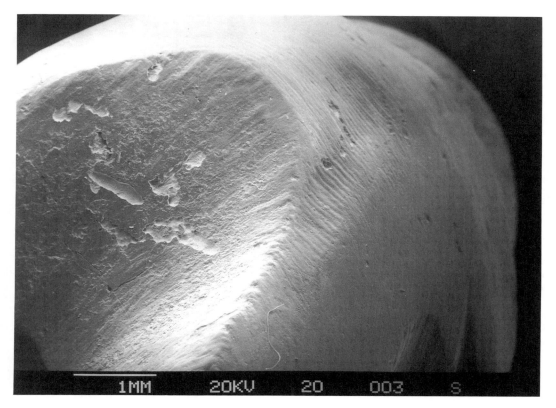

Figure 7.6. Scanning electron micrograph of left maxillary canine of CHT 0813 showing chamfered edges of mesial groove. Labial surface of tooth occupies right half of micrograph.

MT 279. The scanning electron micrograph of this tooth (Fig. 7.9) shows clearly the irregular surface where the mesial corner has been chipped away. Some wear is evident on this surface, but it appears very "fresh" relative to the edges of the groove. The labial margin of the groove is smoothed, as is consistent with the margins of artificial grooves in the other teeth (Fig. 7.10). However, the other margins have not been smoothed. Whether this tooth has been intentionally modified or accidentally chipped remains unclear.

Discussion

The diversity of styles in both these small data sets is striking. While the manner in which the modifications were produced seems fairly uniform and consistent with Landa's (Tozzer 1941) account of the use of stone abraders, the variety of appearances speaks to aesthetic or idiosyncratic factors in the choice of styles. Further, our evidence indicates that both notching and filing of teeth to a point (in Stewart's 1942 terms a wedge-shaped point) were part of both Preconquest and Colonial Maya practice.

SEM analysis of some teeth yields more specific information about filing technique. For example, the fine labiolingual striations in the grooves on the incisors of MT 4 and the shape of the groove itself indicate that an abrader with a sharp, narrow edge being moved from front to back would have been necessary for their production. Chau Hiix grooves could have

Figure 7.7. Scanning electron micrograph of left mandibular I2 of MT 4. Labial surface of tooth occupies lower right corner of micrograph.

been produced with a similar instrument or with something a bit larger. The left canine of CHT 0813 shows that great care was taken to finish the edges of this tooth after the original grooving was completed. Also, one can see the direction of the filing action as the labiolingual striations within the grooves diverge toward the labial surface. None of the teeth shows antemortem fracturing associated with the filed surfaces as would be expected if the tooth was first chipped and then filed to complete the modification.

The right mandibular central incisor of MT 279 presents an interesting problem. The tooth was apparently chipped during life because, although the surface of the chipped area is still

very irregular, it has been slightly worn. If this is intentional modification, it is unusual in that the combination of chipping and filing as a method of modification is not common in Mesoamerica. In fact, Stewart (1942) states that chipping was not used prior to contact with Africans. Interpretation of the filing method is difficult in the absence of other SEM studies of similarly modified teeth. The complexity of the pattern and the fact that the chipping off of the tooth corners is bilateral suggests an intentional modification. This interpretation, however, is problematic. As previously described, the chipping looks very fresh relative to the smoothing of the groove's edges. Perhaps this is an indication that a tooth that was originally filed was

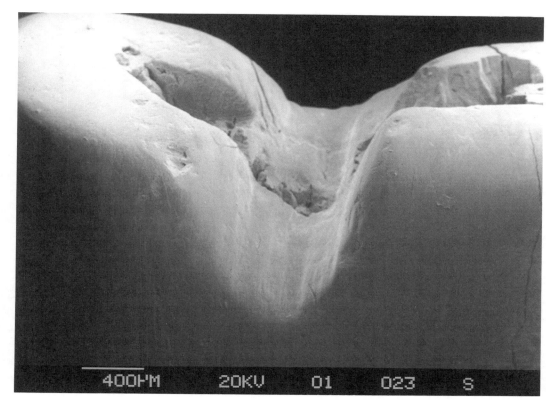

Figure 7.8. Scanning electron micrograph of right mandibular I1 of MT 67B. Labial surface of tooth occupies lower half of micrograph.

later accidently chipped. The presence of the shallow occlusal groove at the tooth midline presents another problem for interpretation. This groove is much shallower than those found on the other modified teeth. In fact, it is barely noticeable macroscopically. Is this actually part of a complex modification or is it simply another, earlier, accidental chip? It should be noted that if this is truly intentional modification, then it is the only modified mandibular tooth from this individual (the maxillary dentition was not recovered). Also, he would be the only individual in which the central mandibular incisor is the only artificially modified tooth.

Social status seems unimportant in both of our data sets. All of the Chau Hiix burials with

modified teeth are from house mounds. Some of these may have been of not inconsequential status in the sense that the house mounds are Postclassic residences built within the core of a medium-sized residential center. However, none of the burials is specially marked. Similarly, the burials with filed teeth at Tipu received no special attention.

There is no clear association between sex and tooth filing at Chau Hiix or Tipu. Although two of the four Chau Hiix individuals are male, the others are of unknown sex. Three of the eight Tipu individuals with filed teeth are female, three are male, and two are of unknown sex.

All of the individuals with filed teeth are adults, consistent with previous suggestions

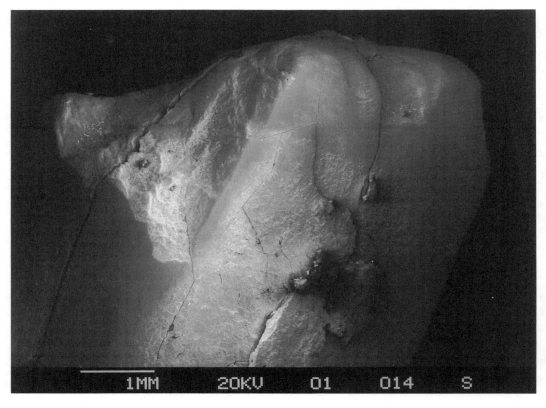

Figure 7.9. Scanning electron micrograph of mesial groove on right mandibular I1 of MT 279. Labial surface of tooth occupies right two-thirds of micrograph. Note difference in smoothing between groove's surface and groove's labial edge.

that filing is not usually performed before adolescence (Fastlicht 1948; Romero 1958; Rubín de la Borbolla 1940). As previously mentioned, the canines of MT 141 display sharply defined edges whereas the incisors show more rounded edges. This may indicate that the Type C-5 modification was carried out later in life than either the Type A-1 or A-2 modification. Perhaps the aim was to refurbish these decorations as the original ones were lost to occlusal wear. However, another possible explanation is differential wear between the canines and incisors.

Just under half of the adult burials at Chau Hiix with anterior teeth display filing, whereas modified teeth are rare at Tipu. We know that filing persisted into the Colonial period, both from

Landa's 16th century description and from 18th century and even 19th century accounts (Hamy 1882, 1883). We also know that the styles of dental modification we report here were shared widely throughout Mesoamerica. We can only speculate as to the roles that acculturation and active suppression of traditional body ornamentation practices may have played in these disparate frequencies.

It is interesting to note that at Tipu, dental modifications were found in 6 of the 195 individuals buried inside the church but in only 2 of the 313 individuals buried outside the church. Those buried within the church were probably among the earliest converts to die at the site, since it was common practice to bury

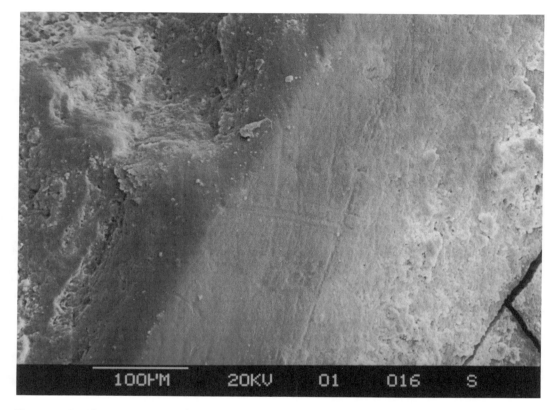

Figure 7.10. Close-up scanning electron micrograph of labial portion of mesial groove of right mandibular I1 of MT 279 emphasizing the difference in appearance between groove's surface and groove's labial edge. Surface of groove occupies approximately the left third of micrograph while labial edge of groove runs up and to the right in middle of field of view. Labial surface of tooth can be seen in right third of micrograph.

within the church first and then move to other areas. The higher frequency of individuals with filed teeth buried inside vs. outside of the church suggests that dental modification was more common among the individuals who died first, leading us to conclude tentatively that tooth filing became less frequent over time among the Maya at Tipu. However, questions about the extent to which the Tipu mortuary population represents the actual population must be answered before any definitive conclusions can be made (Cohen et al. 1994).

This finding is similar to that of Handler et al. (1982), who used archaeological and eth-nohistorical data to infer that dental modification was more frequent among African-born slaves in Barbados than among their descendents born in the New World. These authors suggest several possible reasons for this decline, including changing aesthetic values, the potential use of permanent body markers such as filed teeth and scarification in tracing runaways, and the lack of "positive inducements" from slavemasters to continue the practice.

Further discussion of frequency differences is hampered by the virtual absence of frequency data in the copious literature on tooth filing. Romero's (1958) exhaustive catalogue includes frequency data from only a few previous publications, for example Thompson's (1939) report of 20% of burials with inlays at San José.

The presence of complete anterior maxillary dentitions at both Chau Hiix and Tipu allows for examination of the complete pattern and desired effect of tooth filing. Examination of the teeth from Burial 09 at Chau Hiix shows that the two central incisors come together to form what looks like a "T." Because the filing on the recovered central incisors of the other individuals is similar, it can be assumed that these individuals also displayed bilateral filing resulting in the "T" appearance. Linné (1940) discusses this pattern of filing and its resemblance to that of the Sun God. He goes on to speculate that this "T" motif is similar to the Maya glyph *Ik,* one of the day-glyphs from the 260-day almanac (Morley and Brainerd 1983). Romero (1958) dicusses the same pattern as an aspect of the Rain God in the Dresden Codex, and of Cosijo in the Zapotec region.

Our rather preliminary look at Maya tooth modification practices suggests that SEM analysis may provide technical and processual dimensions that have escaped a more typological approach. We hope that further inquiry into the distribution of tooth modification practices through time and space can shed some light on their meaning in the past.

Acknowledgments

The Chau Hiix project was funded by a grant from the National Science Foundation (SBR 92-23103). We thank the Department of Archaeology in Belize and Acting Commissioner Alan Moore. Special thanks to the people of Crooked Tree Village and the Crooked Tree Village Council for their cooperation and enthusiasm regarding the project. We also thank M. N. Cohen for access to filed teeth from Tipu (project funded by NSF grants BNS 83-03693 and BNS 85-06785). Further, we are grateful to the Department of Biology at Indiana University, Bloomington for access to and assistance with the scanning electron microscope. This SEM facility was purchased with a grant from the National Science Foundation (PCM 82-12660).

8

Cultural Odontology: Dental Alterations from Petén, Guatemala

Nora M. López Olivares

From the archaeological perspective, especially in the Petén region of the Maya lowlands, during the recovery of human skeletal remains one should consider all relevant factors. In addition to the primary process of burial, social and cultural factors should be considered, such as the past act of burying and the ritual that accompanied it, that is, the burning of copal or treatment of the cadaver. Additionally, one should consider cultural processes after interment, natural factors such as rain and animal disturbance, recent human activities such as excavations or looting, and other factors that occur before the remains come into the hands of archaeologists.

Human remains are delicate materials subject to rapid alteration by the factors mentioned above. The remains most commonly present are dental fragments, which are valuable from the biological and sociocultural point of view, and are well suited for bioarchaeological and anthropological analyses.

This chapter is translated from the Spanish by Scott Zeléznik.

The dental samples presented here come from several Petén sites. Between 1983 and 1985, 45 Uaxactún burials were found, although only half have dental fragments. Other samples presented here come from the southeastern Petén sites of Ixtontón, Ixcol, and Yaltutú, which were excavated through 1993. Sixty-three burials were recovered, but not all have dental remains. Most of the human remains are products of archaeological excavation. A few samples are remnants of looted burials where systematic excavations were subsequently performed and yielded dental fragments. Although pathological lesions have been detected in the dental samples, in this paper I only focus on dental alteration as a product of cultural activities.

Provenience

Northern Petén

Uaxactún

This site has been well known from investigations made since the first part of the century. It is situated in northeastern Petén close to Tikal, in a region composed of limestone hills that slope down toward the east. Uaxactún was investigated by the Carnegie Institution until 1937; afterward, between 1983 and 1985, it was investigated by Guatemalan archaeologists from the Proyecto Nacional Tikal.

Uaxactún is composed of various architectural groups, including A, B, E, and H. These groups are filled with carved stelae, astronomical complexes, causeways, and multiroom palaces with vaulted roofs. The site is best characterized as a nucleated settlement with human occupation that increased from the Preclassic through the Early Classic and into the Late Classic period.

The objectives of the 1983–1985 project were not necessarily carried out for the recovery of human skeletal material. Human remains were recovered in the process of excavations designed to understand the site. The most significant structures were not excavated, and the human remains recovered are from diverse contexts. The burials come mostly from plazas, platforms, transects, and stairs, and a few of them come from formal structures.

Dolores Valley of Southeastern Petén

The southeastern mountain zone is composed of various geographic features. Mountain passes allow for communication between the plains of the middle Mopán River and the valleys that are toward Belize, Izabal, and Alta Verapaz. These geographical features must have influenced how exchange relationships developed and interactions among neighboring groups (Laporte 1992). Dolores, one of the largest valleys in the southwestern Maya Mountains, contains sites hierarchically composed of ceremonial areas and large, complex habitation zones.

As a part of the activities of the Archaeological Atlas of Guatemala Project, new sites in the Dolores Valley of the southeastern Petén have been reported, among them are Ixtontón, Ixcol, and Yaltutú.

Ixtontón

Ixtontón is the principal center of the Dolores Valley and covers a 7-km^2 area with imprecise limits fixed only by physiographic conditions. To the north and to the east is the Mopán River, to the south are savanna and pine forests, and toward the west are karstic limestone hills with archaeological sites on their summits.

The central zone contains all that one anticipates from an important lowland Maya center, including large plaza groups, ball courts, causeways, and architectural groups with specialized functions, for example, buildings of a religious character on basal platforms in two plazas. In the East Plaza is an astronomical complex, and in the West Plaza is a pyramidal structure on the south side.

Many stelae were stolen before the site had been reported, and only two remain. Three causeways lie to the north, west, and south. Two ball courts are located in its ceremonial area and approximately 120 residential groups are integrated into a dispersed settlement pattern, with vacant zones that could have been used for cultivated crops.

The ceramic materials indicate that settlement occurred at the beginning of the Late Preclassic period, with a smaller occupation during the Early Classic, and a major occupation during the Late Classic and Terminal Classic (Laporte 1992).

Ixcol

Ixcol is a large settlement which includes the present-day town of Dolores and occupies a central place in the valley. It adjoins Ixtontón to the southeast, Sukché to the southwest, Ixek to the west, Yaltutú to the northwest, and El Tzic to the north.

The definition of Ixcol as a center distinct from Ixtontón, though possibly a subordinate one, is based on the presence of an astronomical complex in the central sector of the site. Seventy-two associated archaeological groups are known in an area of 8.8 km^2. Ixcol has a high settlement concentration without causeways or monuments. In general, the groups located on the hills of the Ixcol area integrate plazas, some on top of basal platforms. A number of the hills have terraces, one of the agricultural systems employed at Ixcol more than at other sites.

Because of its dimensions and complexity, Ixcol is considered a middle-range site. According to Laporte (1992), middle-range sites demonstrated their ancestral position by means of astronomical complexes and by reserving highly ceremonial aspects like ball-game activities, the erection of stelae, and causeways for themselves.

A different situation is observed for the northern Petén centers where the distance between sites is greater. Possibly as a result of sociopolitical conditions, a nucleated settlement pattern developed in northern sites during the Late Classic. In contrast, the Dolores Valley sites appear to have been less centralized, with nuclear families or lineages occupying powerful positions in middle- and lower-range sites.

Therefore, the dental samples come from regions with different settlement patterns. Settlements in the north are more nucleated, while groups in the southeast are more dispersed and interdependent. The samples come from one site from the north and three sites of different sizes from the south. Even though the samples come from sites with different characteristics, they have similar patterns of dental alteration.

Dental Alteration

Types

Dental mutilations for the Maya area involve purposeful cuts on the teeth, supposedly carried out as part of religious practices. Probably, tooth alteration was a rite of initiation or "rite of passage" when a person reached the age to receive some charge or office, or a supernatural bequest for certain people. These possible ex-

planations have been inferred from studies of teeth that were not worked for ornamentation, such as premolars and molars, as well as similarities with the representations in art of the dentitions of gods (e.g., the *Ik* glyph). No final conclusion has been reached. In this study, samples with mutilation or inlaying come from different types of ceremonial structures, as well as common residential areas.

Dental mutilation techniques include sharpening, cutting, filing, and inlaying. It is also known that dental extraction was practiced. Mexican investigator Romero (1958, 1986) published a valuable catalogue of dental mutilation. In it he identified seven types, categorized as either filing or inlaying (see Fig. 7.2). For Mesoamerica he eliminated the "fracture" and cut categories that several authors have described for Africa. His classification includes:

1. Modification of the edge
   A. On the incisal edge
   B. On only one angle of the crown
   C. On both angles
2. Modification of the anterior face
   D. Lines
   E. Inlays or partial wearing away of the enamel
3. Mixed modifications, edge and anterior face
   F. On the incisal edge with lines on the anterior face or on the occlusal edge with partial removal of the enamel
   G. On the incisal edge or on one or both angles and inlays.

The descriptions of samples in this paper are based on this classification.

Temporal Features

Before describing the dental patterns and characteristics, we must consider, in addition to the location, different cultural phases. It is necessary to relate patterns in each area to each cultural phase in order to compare differences and similarities in technique and type of material that develop through time.

EARLY AND MIDDLE PRECLASSIC. According to Romero, during the Preclassic in the Maya region, the three most common patterns of mutilation correspond to Type A, in which the upper incisors are worked on their cutting edge. However, frequency of alteration is low. Probably, during this period, dental mutilation was mainly limited to upper incisors, although there are some cases of mutilation similar to Type A in the lower teeth, generally characterized by undulations or small peaks.

LATE PRECLASSIC. The commonly recorded type is the one already described, but additional types such as D are frequently found in the upper incisors. Crisscrossed lines on the labial surface of the incisors and upper canines, and undulations on the lower edge of the upper teeth also are present. Filing continues to be common, but some inlaying also appears. A new technique is found in the southeastern Petén as early as this period and will be described below.

EARLY CLASSIC. From the earliest part of this period, a high level of skill is evident in the execution and application of the distinct variants. Diverse patterns of mutilation, such as combinations of filing and inlaying, are found.

CLASSIC. Based on evidence from these and other areas, it can be concluded that filing was a technique for alteration in all time periods. However, during the Classic the frequency of filing decreased while the frequency of inlaying increased. In several cases the techniques were combined, and it is in them that dental alteration reaches the highest development.

Outstanding for the Classic period are the diversity of Type G forms (filing and inlaying in the same tooth) and the profusion of combinations, such as the repeated presence together of the simple forms B-4 and B-5 and the mixed forms G-2 and G-3, which appear on the central

upper incisors more than on other teeth. However, for some samples it is difficult to determine if a combination really represents a pattern or could be incomplete or interrupted work.

After this cultural period, in other areas, the use of inlaying declines and filing again becomes the dominant form of alteration (Romero 1986). However, for the two areas of the Petén in this study, up to now the most recent burials excavated have been from the Terminal Classic in the southeast.

Analysis of the frequency of the patterns is interesting, but one should not lose sight of the intensity with which sites or regions have been investigated, as well as the location and forms of exploration (i.e., general survey or transects). In the case of the two areas, Uaxactún in the northern lowlands and Ixtontón, Ixcol, and Yaltutú in the southeastern Petén, the intensity in the exploration has been approximately the same, but coverage and investigation objectives differ. Different environments, settlement patterns, architectural arrangements, ways of living, probably sociopolitical systems, and maybe ethnic differences also existed. Nevertheless mutilation and filing are present in the samples from these two regions.

Analysis of Samples

Uaxactún (1983–1985 Seasons)

LATE PRECLASSIC (CHICANEL PHASE). For this period at Uaxactún only 25 of the 45 burials had tooth fragments. Five cases exhibited dental alterations (Tables 8.1 and 8.2). Three of them, burials No. 200, 201, and 241 have Type A alterations. No. 200 has Type A-1 alteration of lower incisors, as does No. 241 to an upper incisor. No. 201 has Type A-4 alteration of incisors and canines. In burial No. 196 Type F-4 alteration is found in the upper incisors. Burial No. 228, a female with cranial deformation, exhibits the common Type B-5 alteration.

Table 8.1   Burials with Dental Alterations from Uaxactún, 1983–1985

Burial	Position	Provenience	Grave Offerings	Notes
Late Preclassic (Chicanel phase)				
196	Extended, lying on back	Center of residential structure of Group D under stucco floor	Plate inverted over skull and shells	
200	Extended, lying on back	North plaza of Group E	None	
201	Flexed on left side	Under Floor 6, near bedrock next to corner of Building C	Plate inverted over skull with jade bead in mouth	
228	Flexed on left side	Outside of plaza to north of Structure XII of Group D	None	Tabular Oblique deformation of skull
241	Flexed on right side	Center of residential structure	None	
Early Classic (Tzakol phase)[a]				
191	Extended, lying on back	Under stucco floor in central room of Temple E-X, Group E (oldest group)	Shell, lithics, sting ray spines	Skull with Tabular Erect deformation
Late Classic (Tepeu phase)[b]				
195	Flexed on right side	Under floor of Room 4 of Structure A-XII	None	
202	Probably flexed	Near central staircase of Palace A-XVIII	Lithics	Poorly preserved
209	Extended on back	Under upper platform and near center of Structure B-IV	Diverse offerings	In tomb of small stones covered with flat slabs

[a] Other burials from this period were without dental mutilation.

[b] The other 10 burials from this period had no dental alteration.

EARLY CLASSIC (TZAKOL PHASE). For this time period, three types of dental mutilation were observed in one adult female with peculiar burial characteristics, sex being determined from pelvic remains and the presence of Derry's preauricular groove. She was found in the principal room of Group E at Uaxactún, had Tabular Erect cranial deformation, and was buried with an offering of sting ray spines, commonly associated with high offices held by males. In this woman two upper incisors have Type C-7 alteration, four lower incisors have Type C-1, and a canine has the common Type B-4.

LATE CLASSIC (TEPEU PHASE). For this period, four different dental patterns were iden-

Table 8.2 Uaxactún Dental Mutilation Types

Burial	Type[a]	Age[b]	Sex	Tooth
Late Preclassic				
(Chicanel phase)				
196	F-4	MA	Indeterminate	Upper incisors
200	A-1	MA	Male?	Lower incisors
201	A-4	MA	Indeterminate	Incisors and canines
228	B-5	YA	Female	Incisor and canine
241	A-1	OA	Indeterminate	Upper incisor
Early Classic				
(Tzakol phase)				
191	C-7	MA	Female	2 upper incisors
	C-1			4 lower incisors
	B-4			Canine
Late Classic				
(Tepeu phase)				
195	F-4	OA	Male	Canine
202	E-1	MA	Male?	Lower incisor with pyrite and 4 canines without material *in situ*
209	G-2	A	Indeterminate	Upper central incisor
	G-1			Upper lateral incisor

[a] Types follow Romero (1970).

[b] YA = young adult (21–35); MA = middle-aged adult (36–55); OA = old adult (55+); A = adult.

tified in three individuals. Only burial No. 195 could with certainty be determined to be an adult male. He was found below four floors of Structure A-XII, one of the more important architectural groups at the site. One canine has Type F-4 alteration. Burial No. 202 from Group A-XVIII has Type E-1 alteration with pyrite in one lower incisor and without the material in place in four canines. Type G-2 alteration occurs on a central upper incisor and Type G-1 on an upper lateral incisor of burial No. 209 from Group B-IV.

At Uaxactún, Type F alteration is found in different cultural phases, and Type C is also frequently found.

Southeastern Petén Sites of Ixtontón, Ixcol, and Yaltutú

Even though these sites are adjacent to one another in the same area, each one developed its own pattern. Nearly 50% of the 63 burials analyzed from this region have dental fragments

and, although some have complete sets of teeth, most of them are incomplete. Only 10 of the approximately 30 burials with teeth display dental mutilation. However, the general frequency of its occurrence can not be defined with precision, since a part of this material was recovered from looters' pits and only some was the product of systematic excavations in different places within this area.

LATE PRECLASSIC. For the Late Preclassic various cases of dental mutilation were discovered (Tables 8.3 and 8.4). From the Yaltutú multiple burial PSP-017 came an individual with Type G-1 alteration of a canine and Type A-2 filing of four upper incisors.

Another individual in the same burial has a type of alteration of an incisor not recorded in the catalogue of Romero (Fig. 8.1). It consists of four circular inlays of pyrite and an angular cut. The first flat circular inlay is approximately .5 mm in diameter, the second is .3 mm, the

Table 8.3 Burials with Dental Alterations from Southeastern Petén (Ixtontón, Ixcol, and Yaltutú)

Burial	Position	Provenience	Grave Offerings	Notes
Late Preclassic				
Yaltutú PSP-017	Probably extended	Funerary precinct in south plaza—Mound 5	Looted	Two adults and one infant
Ixcol PSP-038	Flexed, lying on left side	Test pit along axis of room of Structure 7	Obsidian blades, polishers, and shell fragments	
Late Classic				
Ixtontón PSP-013	Partially extended, lying on back	Looters' pit in Mound 4	Miniature vases, green stone earring fragments, thousands of small shell beads, obsidian blades, bone discs, mother-of-pearl discs	Two individuals
Terminal Late Classic				
Ixtontón PSP-025	Extended	Structure 5 of southeastern group	Ceramic vase, tripod plate and obsidian blade	
Ixtontón PSP-042	Extended, lying on back	In pit along central axis of west structure	Tripod plate	Left ear exostosis
Ixtontón PSP-051	Extended, lying on back	In pit on axis of east structure	Plate and vase	A mandible and maxilla fragment with mutilation and one jade inlay
Ixtontón PSP-062	Extended, lying on back	In pit on central axis of north structure	Tripod plate, vase, and two obsidian blades	
Terminal Classic				
Ixtontón PSP-031	Extended, lying on back	North Structure 12	Plate fragment, vase, bowl, and figurine remains	
Ixcol PSP-037	Secondary burial	Inside steps of north staircase of Structure 6	None	
Ixcol PSP-045	Possibly extended, lying on back	East structure of another group	Vase, plate, and ceramic sherd	

third is .25 mm (without the inlay material), and the smallest is .02 mm. Three of the holes retain their inlay material. X-rays of the sample show the healthy state of the tooth, which indicates the high level of knowledge and technique reached in early periods in the region. More evidence of this is the presence of Type G-1 alteration, a pattern uncommon for other regions, including Uaxactún, for early periods.

On the other hand, Type A alteration is one

Table 8.4 Southeastern Petén (Ixtontón, Ixcol, and Yaltutú) Dental Mutilation Types

Site	Burial	Type[a]	Age[b]	Sex	Tooth
Late Preclassic					
Yaltutú	PSP-017	G-1	MA	Male	Canine
		A-2			4 upper incisors
		New	MA	Male?	Upper incisor with pyrite
Ixcol	PSP-038	A-1	A	Indeterminate	Incisor
Late Classic					
Ixtontón	PSP-013	E-3	MA	Male	Incisors, without material *in situ*
Terminal Late Classic					
Ixtontón	PSP-025	G-1	MA	Indeterminate	Canine
	PSP-042	B-5	MA	Female?	Incisor
		C-6			Canine
	PSP-051	G-3	MA	Indeterminate	Canine
		E-1			Incisor with jade
	PSP-062[c]	E-1	OA	Indeterminate	Upper premolars with pyrite
Terminal Classic					
Ixtontón	PSP-031	B-2	A	Indeterminate	Upper incisor
Ixcol	PSP-037	E-1	A	Indeterminate	Canine
	PSP-045	B-2	A	Indeterminate	Incisor

[a] Types follow Romero (1970).

[b] MA = middle-aged adult (36–55); OA = old adult (55+); A = adult.

[c] Poorly preserved skeleton.

of the initial filing techniques for the Maya area in general and also is present in teeth from burials PSP-017 and PSP-038. Thus, we can see that both filing and inlaying techniques are present in the same early cultural period in the southeastern Petén.

LATE CLASSIC. In this time period, the sample with dental alteration comes from one burial. An Ixtontón male, burial PSP-013, has Type E-3 alteration of the incisors; the three holes lack inlay material. This pattern is similar to the one mentioned above, which may be evidence of a certain preference for this pattern.

TERMINAL LATE CLASSIC. In burial PSP-051, a middle-aged adult of indeterminate sex, Type G-3 alteration of a canine and Type E-1 alteration of an incisor were observed. In the

incisor one hole contained a very small jade inlay. According to specialists, this is evidence of the level of skill reached in performing the alterations. Because the perforation is of small size, the work would have been more difficult, especially when it is considered that electric drills were not available at that time. Solares (1990) suggests that in the Petén the work of jade inlaying was much more careful, and that inlays of large size were not employed, in contrast to other regions, such as Alta Verapaz, Guatemala.

From Ixtontón, a probable female (burial PSP-042) has Type B-5 alteration of an incisor, a common pattern for other regions during the Classic, and Type C-6 alteration of a canine. Burial PSP-025, an Ixtontón individual of indeterminate sex, exhibits Type G-1 alteration of a canine. A curious case is burial PSP-062, an old adult of indeterminate sex from Ixtontón, in

Figure 8.1. Incisor from Yaltutú burial PSP-017 with a new Type G pattern of alteration. Drawing by Jorge Chocon.

which Type E-1 inlaying with pyrite occurred on the buccal surface of the upper premolars.

TERMINAL CLASSIC. For this cultural phase Type B alteration continues. In burial PSP-031 from Ixtontón an upper incisor exhibits Type B-2 alteration. Burial PSP-045 from Ixcol also has this pattern on an incisor. Another pattern is also present in the Terminal Classic. From nearby Ixcol, Type E-1 alteration of a canine was found in burial PSP-037.

In general, according to this analysis, in the southeastern Petén Type G alteration is common and appears early; Type C is not common.

Sex of Individuals in the Samples

Many of the burial samples were too poorly preserved for sex determination, particularly those from Uaxactún. Others, such as those from looted or disturbed contexts, were too incomplete. Sex determinations that could be made are included in Tables 8.2 and 8.4. The cases at Uaxactún clearly defined as female individuals with dental mutilation are No. 191 for the Early Classic and No. 228 for the Late Preclassic. Sexes in the southeastern region are not clearly defined, but PSP-042 from the Terminal Late Classic period is considered to be female.

Age of Individuals in the Samples

To answer the question of at what age operations were commonly practiced, the dental growth cycle must be considered. The dental enamel that covers the crown has variable thickness, to a maximum of 2.5 mm. The enamel does not increase once the crown is completed, but its level of mineralization increases with age, as does its fragility. The thickness of the adjacent dental tissue, dentin, increases with age because of the continuous formation of an odontoblast layer. Dentin's increased thickness occurs at the expense of the pulp cavity, and the dental pulp found in the pulp cavity reduces its size proportionately with age. This means that the distance between the tooth surface and the dental pulp increases with the age of the person.

Considering the tooth growth cycle, it is not possible to apply dental alteration to very young individuals because of the extent of the pulp cavity, nor to mutilate the teeth of individuals so old that mineralization of the enamel will not permit work. If we take into account that enamel increases in fragility with age, while dentin expands and pulp diminishes with age, then there exists a restricted period of life that should present adequate conditions for the execution of dental alteration.

In addition, if mutilation and its various forms were related to certain life events, such as installation into an office, then presence of mutilation might correlate with age. It is certain that the earliest age for mutilation and in-laying would have been after adolescence (i.e., 13 to 17 years of age). Romero (1986) mentions that some specimens he studied were young adults or juvenile adults (21 to 35 years old), some were middle-aged adults (36 to 55 years old), and some were old adults (over 50 years old) at time of death. However, it is unclear at what age the mutilation occurred. For the samples discussed here, the youngest individual is Uaxactún burial No. 228, who was 25 to 35 years old.

Comparative Summary

The Late Preclassic at Uaxactún has 5 of 13 burials (38%) with dental alteration (Table 8.5). Although there is evidence for a Middle Preclassic population, the burials recovered during 1983 to 1985, dated to this period, do not show any evidence of dental mutilation.

In contrast, in the southeastern Petén there is no recorded early population, but for the Late Preclassic there is a small population. In the four burials that were recovered, two (50%) show different mutilation patterns. It might be

Table 8.5 Comparison of Dental Mutilation Types for Southeastern Petén and Uaxactún

Site	Type[a]
Late Preclassic	
Uaxactún	F-4
	A-1
	A-4
	A-1
	B-5
Yaltutú	G-1
	A-2
	New
Ixcol	A-1
Early Classic	
Uaxactún	C-7
	C-1
	B-4
Late Classic	
Uaxactún	F-4
	E-1
	G-2
	G-1
Ixtontón	E-3
Terminal Late Classic	
Ixtontón	G-1
	B-5
	C-6
	G-3
	E-1
Terminal Classic	
Ixtontón	B-2
Ixcol	E-1
	B-2

[a] Types follow Romero (1970).

that the frequency of alteration is higher in the southeast.

For the Late Preclassic at Uaxactún, there was common use of Type A filing. In contrast for the southeastern Petén, in spite of pieces that show Type A filing, we also find combinations of inlaying and filing: Type G alteration. We can see this in the previously mentioned incisor with a new pattern that could be catalogued under Type G, and in a canine defined as Type G-1.

For the Early Classic at Uaxactún, only one individual of 11 (9%) had mutilation (burial No. 191). In the southeastern Petén, none of the few burials that were recorded for this period showed any dental alteration.

By the Late Classic the situation is different. Of 12 individuals from Uaxactún, 3 (25%) have four different types of mutilation: F-4, E-1, G-1, and G-2. However, by the Terminal Classic no burials display these categories. In the southeastern Petén the majority of the burials recovered are dated to the Late Classic or Terminal Late Classic. There is evidence of diverse techniques, including simple patterns such as Type B and complex patterns such as C, E, representing inlaying, and G, involving a combination of filing and inlaying.

Environmental characteristics could be an influence on the regional differences. To the north in the Terminal Classic there is no evidence of a large population and everything indicates that it diminishes in size. In the southeastern Petén, however, probably owing to environmental conditions such as fertile ground, abundant water, and dispersed settlements, a larger population could be maintained during this period. This is reflected in the number of burials recorded for this period in the area.

What can be seen from the Uaxactún samples is the use of Type F-4 alteration in the Preclassic and Late Classic, a pattern that does not appear in any of the samples from the southeastern Petén. In contrast, in this zone Types B, E, and G appear with greater frequency and in a certain balance. Additionally, in the southeastern Petén the mutilations are observed in individuals recovered from simple structures or other contexts not necessarily associated with elite architecture.

Conclusions

Probably people living at each site or place had a style preference. This may have reflected the availability of specialists, knowledge of only some of the possible patterns, or the ease of access to different inlay materials, as in the case of pyrite, which appears with high frequency in the southeastern Petén instead of jade, perhaps owing to proximity to deposits of this material. Although differences in the practice of cultural dental alterations can be detected between the sites of the north and those of the southeastern Petén, it is evident that the practice occurred in both regions.

Even if the age at which individuals were subjected to dental alterations cannot be clearly established at this time, we can, at least, establish the age-at-death of the individuals. Probably in the future we will be able to approximate the age at which dental alteration was executed on this basis.

In archaeological investigations, the discovery of human remains constitutes an important source of information that complements other data. However, this is only the beginning of what can be a new phase of investigation. The use of screening is necessary after removing the burial, as human remains in the Maya region, especially teeth, are commonly found incomplete, encrusted in the dirt, or scattered by the actions of animals or other factors. The extra effort is worthwhile because dental remains are recovered in a better state of preservation than the postcranial skeleton and allow us, through their analysis, to understand biological, cultural, and social aspects of the inhabitants of the Maya area.

9

Individual Frailty, Children of Privilege, and Stress in Late Classic Copán

Rebecca Storey

One of the important skeletal samples available from the Late Classic period (A.D. 700–1000) for the important Maya center at Copán, Honduras, was recovered from a large elite compound, 9N-8, in the residential *barrio* of Sepulturas. This densely populated *barrio* is just to the east of the ceremonial and political center of the site, the Acropolis, and contained a variety of compounds. The 9N-8 compound, the "House of the Bacabs" (Webster 1989b), was the largest in Sepulturas, containing 12 adjoining patio groups with more than 50 structures housing around 200 individuals. The compound is believed to have been occupied by families belonging to a prominent noble lineage and possibly a few retainers serving the nobles. The power and importance of the lineage are revealed by the elaborate hieroglyphic bench and sculptured building occupied by the head of the lineage (see Webster 1989b), the high quality of the architecture of the patios, and the large number of individuals integrated into the functioning of the residential group.

Mortuary characteristics varied within the compound, from tombs with various offerings that included exotic shell and jade or serpentine objects to simple earth pits with no offerings. Thus, there was probably a range of status within the compound, and only some individuals may have had a recognized noble rank. However, the compound's patios all exhibit similar domestic functions and evidence of cooperation and integration as one elite social group (see Hendon 1992). Thus, all individuals residing in the compound probably benefited from the obvious wealth and power of their lord and enjoyed as high a standard of living as a group as it was possible to enjoy in Late Classic Copán society, better than that available to most of the society.

Copán, as was common with other Maya lowland centers of the Classic Maya civilization, declined rapidly in population size after the florescence of the Late Classic period, and the valley was eventually abandoned by A.D. 1200 (Webster and Freter 1990b). This "Classic Maya collapse" has long been of interest to archaeologists (Culbert 1988); the antecedents of this phenomenon should be visible in the lifestyles of the people during the period before abandonment. Thus, the Late Classic skeletons available from the society should hold important information about the processes leading to societal decline.

A variety of information can be deduced from a skeleton, but the main information desired is age-at-death and the presence of pathological conditions, so that some indications of possible demographic characteristics and general health can be added to information from archaeology to reconstruct life during Late Classic period Copán. This paper will begin to examine the age-at-death and pathological lesions of subadults from the 9N-8 elite compound as a first step to demographic analysis and life way reconstruction.

Developmental defects of dental enamel are of interest to anthropologists because of their potential as nonspecific paleopathological indicators to inform about the occurrence of physiological stress as a result of health, nutritional status, and living conditions during childhood (e.g., Goodman and Rose 1991). The defects include hypoplasias, deficiencies in the thickness of enamel, and hypocalcifications, opacities and discolorations resulting from impaired enamel mineralization and maturation. The advantages of studying such defects are that they can be observed macroscopically, as well as histologically, that once formed they are permanently recorded in a tooth, and that the age of occurrence of hypoplastic defects can be determined from their location on a crown. Although many studies have proved them useful in indicating situations of both ubiquitous and rare stress during childhood in past and present populations (e.g., Goodman and Capasso 1992), there have been recent questions over methodology, such as how to determine age of occurrence (e.g., Skinner and Goodman 1992)

and how to interpret them as nonspecific stress indicators (Wood et al. 1992). However, recent work on contemporary populations has also supported the linkage of socioeconomic status and poverty to hypoplasias (Lukacs and Joshi 1992; Goodman, Pelto et al. 1992) and has shown the sensitivity of hypoplasias to undernutrition (May et al. 1993).

A recent article questions the interpretation of skeletal lesions, such as dental defects, on skeletal series as health indicators of past populations, because the interpretation is confounded by demographic nonstationarity, selective mortality, and individual frailty (Wood et al. 1992). Especially important to this position is that skeletons represent a biased mortality sample of individuals that died at a certain age and thus are no guide to those that survived those ages. In other words, the dead, and by extension, the skeletal sample, should obviously appear sicker and in poorer health than the living population. On top of this selective mortality bias are the effects of hidden heterogeneity, or the differences in individual frailty, the individual's susceptibility to disease and dying. Because individuals vary in their frailty, population-aggregate mortality patterns cannot tell us what any one individual's risk of death was. Thus, "inferences from paleodemographic life tables to the health status of individuals in prehistoric populations are, to say the least, problematic" (Wood et al. 1992:349). Various mortality risks in the past can create the same pattern of deaths seen in the individuals of a skeletal series, and the pattern of dental defects in the dead is likely to be different from that in the living population; this is what complicates interpretation.

The criticisms of osteological analysis in that article deserve hard thought, but there are several issues here, not all of which are adequately addressed by Wood et al. For example, osteologists are aware of the selective mortality underlying skeletal series and often address it in their interpretations (see Goodman 1993). Demographers have long recognized an *individual* and a *population* level of analysis, both intended for very different research questions (Riley 1993). Wood et al. are correct that aggregate patterns of mortality do not reveal individual risks of death from different causes. Yet, demographers do not ignore aggregate patterns as being devoid of information. On the contrary,

> Morbidity and mortality are also structural phenomena, which is to say that, considered for a sizable number of people, they display certain regularities. The most important of these relate to age and appear as curves or schedules when morbidity and mortality are arranged by age (Riley 1993:230).

In his criticism of the Wood et al. article, Goodman (1993) pointed out the importance of cultural context, the "regularities," in interpreting mortality information. The importance of such context can be illustrated using Wood and Milner's (1994) own reply to Goodman and others. They wish to illustrate the effects of individual susceptibility to death and the selective mortality issues by use of an example of one of them, with high serum cholesterol, keeling over suddenly from a heart attack. Such an individual is no guide to what will happen to the other authors and to the general health of U.S. academics. True, but were the skeleton to be analyzed by an osteologist, sexed as male, aged to between 40 and 65 years of age and determined to come from a probable privileged member of the society, the osteologist, *knowing the cultural context of overeating and lack of exercise in the late 20th century United States,* especially among the upper-middle class, might guess that the individual died of a heart attack, the leading cause of death for such individuals (see Howell 1993).

Similarly, many children in developing countries die from interactions of malnutrition and infection that are directly related to features of their environment that expose them to these causes (Millard 1994). While it is not possible to *predict* which child will die beforehand, the *reasons* for the deaths of children and the ages at which they are most susceptible to various types of causes can be understood, and some important information about the health and lifestyles of that society also gained. The dead children of a skeletal series contain information in their age-at-death and in evidence of their exposure to malnutrition and infection as to the risks in their environment. The population level of analysis is used to understand the interaction of biological and socioeconomic factors influencing death and survival of individuals (Millard 1994).

Morbidity is ill health or sickness, a demographic entity much more ambiguous than mortality for several reasons. One, the definition of ill health is subjective and culturally influenced, so that there is a problem defining a consistent measure (Riley 1993). Also, it can be measured several ways, by incidence of ill health during a period or by duration of episodes of ill health, for example (Riley 1993). Further, there is no simple relationship of morbidity to mortality, in that more illness does not necessarily lead to more mortality (Alter and Riley 1989). Dental defects indicate episodes of morbidity serious enough to impede normal enamel development, morbidity that is often due to problems in the child's environment, the effects of malnutrition or infection (Goodman and Rose 1991). While skeletons do not preserve evidence of every episode of morbidity in a child's life, dental defects provide evidence of the incidence of serious morbidity and can be compared to the age-at-death.

Individuals that die in childhood in a skeletal series definitely have been selected against in the population and are victims of premature mortality, as they did not reach adulthood. These children would be expected to differ from those that survived into adulthood, as one would expect them to have suffered more morbidity. *One way to study the possible effects of* individual frailty and the effects of morbidity upon mortality is to follow individuals through childhood, comparing defects of the deciduous and permanent dentitions and the age-at-death. Continuing the individual level of analysis that is possible from a skeletal series, other skeletal pathoses and any status information from the mortuary context can also be compared among the children. Although such a study will represent only a limited portion of the life span, a few months prenatally to 9 years old, the number of stressful episodes strong enough to be recorded on bone plus the age-at-death will provide evidence of the amount of morbidity that eventually resulted in death for each individual, and thus for each age. These children will provide insight into stress and mortality, and through the dental defects the cultural environment they lived in, but certainly not answer all questions about population health and nutrition.

The Sample

Out of the 264 individuals in the Late Classic sample from the 9N-8 compound, 122 were subadults. This sample certainly does not represent a complete set of the deaths in the compound over a time span of about 300 years, but it does contain individuals of all ages and both sexes. The size of the sample is directly attributable to the importance placed by the project directors, Dr. William T. Sanders and Dr. David Webster of The Pennsylvania State University, on recovering as many skeletons as possible in order to be able to make some demographic and paleopathological inferences about the population of the compound. Thus, although some infant underrepresentation is present, which has no effect on the work presented here, it is the only sample from Copán in which the number of subadults even approaches half of the skeletons recovered and has enough individuals to look for populational patterns of mortality and morbidity during the crucial childhood years. That is why this sample is the focus of investi-

gation here. The 9N-8 sample is evidence that recovering a sufficient number of more delicate subadult skeletons during archaeological excavation in the Maya area requires a concerted effort to locate and excavate them.

Out of the 122 subadults in the compound sample, 60 children had at least some of both the deciduous and permanent dentitions. Here, only a few ages can be sampled and investigated in depth: ages 1 and 2, as these are generally ages of high risk in prehistory and in poorer countries today (Goodman and Rose 1991), and ages 5, 8, and 9, older children whose risk of death is usually quite low. Thus, the contrast will be between ages of high risk and those of low risk in a population. A total of 32 individuals are studied.

Age-at-death for individuals in the 9N-8 sample was determined on the basis of tooth formation standards, which are felt to be the most accurate aging technique for juveniles (Saunders and Hoppa 1993), plus eruption standards (El-Nofely and İşcan 1989), and a seriation of all subadults based on size (see Storey 1992c). As always, the methodological problem of aging subadults accurately, given individual variation and variation in the standards available (Saunders and Hoppa 1993), means that there might be errors in the age-at-death assigned to individual juveniles. The individual juveniles discussed here have been aged at two different times, with the three indicators agreeing for all but six individuals. These were then aged by agreement of two indicators. Thus, it cannot be guaranteed that individuals aged 1 year at death were actually chronologically that age, but they do form groupings with the same skeletal ages for this population.

Scoring of Dental Enamel Defects

Scoring of hypoplasias and hypocalcifications generally follows that of the International Dental Federation (see Skinner and Goodman 1992) and are described in Table 9.1. The most sus-

Table 9.1 Dental Defects Scored

Hypoplastic defects	
LEH	Linear enamel hypoplasia, a horizontal groove across most of buccal/labial surface
Pit	Found as a single pit into enamel or as a horizontal line of discontinuous pits
Missing enamel	An area where enamel apparently never formed and underlying dentin is visible
LHPC	Localized hypoplasia of primary canine (Skinner and Hung 1989), commonly in the form of a patch of missing or thinner enamel caused by a combination of nutritional factors and minor trauma
Cracked	On a developing crown, a horizontal line where the enamel has cracks and commonly a gap of missing enamel
Indent	On a developing crown, a clear horizontal line commonly indicates the beginning of a ring of thinner enamel that continues to crown edge. This could be an LEH in development when the individual died
Rough	A patch or band of uneven, pitted enamel. Contrasts with smooth enamel around it. Similar to a pit patch (Goodman, Martin et al. 1992), it is found on molars as well
Hypocalcification defects	
Band	A linear band of opacity, either white or yellow-brown, with demarcated edges. Difference in color may be due to differences in etiology (Suga 1992)
Blotches	Opacities that are patchy in their occurrence over the buccal/labial surface with diffuse edges. A single blotch or several over the surface can be white or yellow-brown
Circular caries	Caries on buccal/labial or lingual surfaces that commonly have eaten bands or large areas of enamel that tend to be associated with bands of demarcated hypocalcifications (Duray 1992). Not counted as separate defects, but as the result of a defect

ceptible teeth (Goodman and Rose 1991) are the upper central incisor and the mandibular canine but all available teeth were scored for defects. Hypoplastic defects are the result of disturbance of secretory ameloblasts, and the age of the individual at the time of the defect can be determined, with some error (Skinner and Goodman 1992). Hypocalcifications are the result of disturbance of the maturation of enamel, and thus cannot be aged with any certainty, although they also are the result of systemic disturbance (Suga 1992). Because all possible dental defects for an individual needed to be counted, incomplete crowns, which are usually not studied, were also scored. The number of different defects present on the deciduous and permanent teeth of an individual were summed, as a crude index of the amount of morbidity suffered before death. A high number should reflect either the severity of a single stress episode, such that it was recorded in many teeth as two or three kinds of hypocalcifications or as linear enamel hypoplasias (LEH) and

pits, or else indicates several different episodes of morbidity. Whether the result of one severe episode or several lesser ones, higher numbers of total defects should indicate more overall stress was survived to be recorded in the teeth.

An earlier study of the 83 deciduous dentitions present in this sample had already indicated the ubiquity of defects among these children and the complexity of the pattern of defects present on individual teeth (Storey 1992c). Hypocalcifications are the more common defect on the deciduous dentition, but the permanent dentition is characterized by more hypoplastic defects, although hypocalcifications are also fairly common. Because of the ages of crown formation, defects in deciduous teeth indicate stress during the perinatal and early infancy months, while the permanent teeth reflect more stress during ages 2 to 5 (Skinner and Goodman 1992).

Besides the dental defects, evidence of porotic hyperostosis, a skeletal lesion due to iron deficiency anemia, and periosteal reactions, a bony response to infectious disease, are also scored. These paleopathological indicators would be further evidence of morbidity affecting a child, and also reflect problems in the environment with nutrition or infection. The base mortuary pattern for children in the compound was a simple earthen pit with no offerings. The presence of offerings or a more elaborate grave, indicating a higher status, will be noted. The status information is another environmental variable that could affect individual frailty, by perhaps buffering a higher status individual somewhat from malnutrition and disease. The dental defects, because of their permanency and other characteristics, serve as the best measure of morbidity, with the other indicators and status as contributing factors. The goal is to look at the variability in possible individual frailty within one age and see if there is any visible population pattern by age.

Morbidity in 1-Year-Olds

As would be expected, individual variability is high, and each life course had its own bouts of stress reflected in the deciduous and permanent dentition. Figure 9.1 has the number of differ-

ent defects for each individual. As an example of how defects were totaled, Burial 16-20, the individual with the most defects, had white bands, brown bands, white and brown blotches of hypocalcification, a localized hypoplasia of the primary canine (LHPC) and an area of missing enamel on the deciduous dentition, a line of cracked enamel, a white band, and an indentation forming at the bottom of a crown on the permanent dentition. On the other hand, Burial 17-28 had brown bands and brown blotches of hypocalcification on the deciduous dentition but nothing on the permanent (although the more sensitive teeth were not recovered). As can be seen in Figure 9.1, these individuals have more defects on the deciduous teeth, but only a few permanent crowns are developing at this age. The average number of defects is 4.4, with a standard deviation of 1.73. The individuals with fewer defects, or morbid episodes survived, might be considered frailer individuals, and those with more than the average might be seen as sturdier individuals, with more episodes survived before succumbing.

In these individuals, dying during their second year of life, morbidity severe enough to cause dental defects during the prenatal period or early infancy is common, along with at least

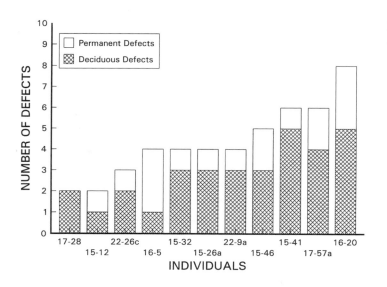

Figure 9.1. Number of dental defects per individual aged 1 year at time of death.

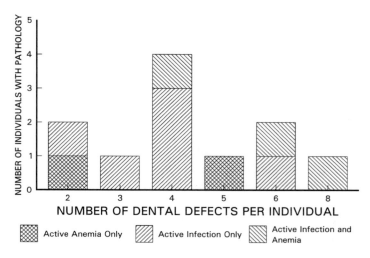

Figure 9.2. Other pathological lesions present in 1-year-olds according to number of defects present per individual.

one episode reflected in the immature permanent teeth. As for other factors affecting the individual, status may play a minor part among this age group, although only three individuals were buried in more than an earthen pit. Two of these individuals, 15-26a and 22-9a, had four defects, and as they are part of a multiple interment with older individuals, it is not certain that the cobble cyst graves and one offering each were intended for them. Burial 16-20, the individual with eight defects, had a ceramic earspool but an earthen pit. The individuals with fewer than four defects all had just earthen pits, but so did three out of the four individuals with more than four defects. It is possible that Burial 16-20 may have been "sturdier," because he or she was from a higher ranked family, but status certainly did not buffer this individual from morbidity.

All of these individuals had another pathological indicator that was active at time of death, and death was probably related to the ongoing stress. Figure 9.2 has the incidence of porotic hyperostosis and periosteal reactions per individual according to the number of dental defects. While the individuals with two defects have either anemia or infection, a trend of having both indicators with more defects is

weakly present. These are, in general, sick children that have already survived some morbidity.

Morbidity of 2-Year-Olds

Figure 9.3 has the distribution of defects for the 15 individuals who died during their third year of life. The range is wider than for the younger children, although the majority of individuals here have more than five defects. This could indicate that there are fewer "frail" individuals and more "sturdy" ones dying at this age. The average is 5.5 and the standard deviation is 2.25. Thus, there is about one more defect per individual, but wider variation. Individuals also tend to have defects on both the deciduous and permanent teeth, not surprisingly with more development of the latter. Status is also a possible factor here, as of the eight individuals with more than five defects, five have offerings or a capstone. Burial 16-26, the individual with nine defects, had a capstone but no offering, for example. Only two out of the seven individuals with five defects or fewer have an offering or a capstone. However, even if status helped these children survive episodes of morbidity, they certainly were not being

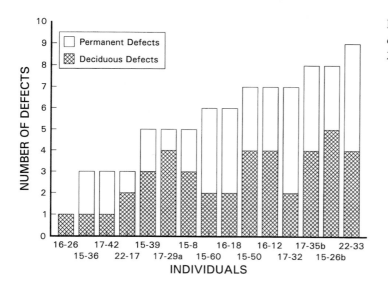

Figure 9.3. Number of dental defects per individual aged 2 years at time of death.

buffered from suffering stress strong enough to cause dental defects.

Of these 15 individuals, 3 were definitely too fragmentary and 2 more possibly too incomplete to be able to score either porotic hyperostosis or periosteal reactions. Figure 9.4 contains the information for the other 10 individuals. Only one had no pathological indicators at all, and one had only healed periosteal reactions. Eight individuals then had an active lesion at

time of death, so that these children were not uniformly as sick as the 1-year-olds. Both of the individuals that could be scored for these other pathological conditions, but that had no active lesions, had only three defects, placing them with the "frailer" individuals. Seven out of the eight children with more than five defects had been sick for some time before death and had already survived significant morbidity.

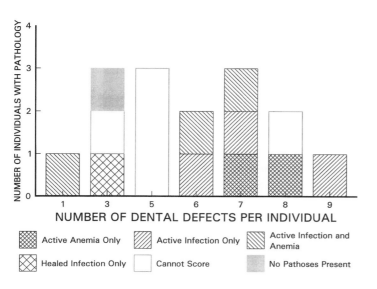

Figure 9.4. Other pathological lesions present in 2-year-olds according to number of defects present per individual.

Morbidity among Older Children

There are only six children in this group, three dying at 5 years of age, two at 8 years, and one at 9 years. Childhood mortality occurs overwhelmingly in children less than 5 years old, so one should not expect to find many individuals in these ages. Because most individuals who survive to 5 years of age would be expected to survive into adulthood, the characteristics of these individuals are of interest. Figure 9.5 has the number of defects for each of these individuals. Most have high numbers of defects, except for two. All, however, have few defects in the deciduous teeth and, thus, less evidence of morbidity in the prenatal period or early infancy than the younger children, but more defects in the permanent teeth, indicating more morbidity at ages 2 to 5. Four of these had only an earthen pit. One, Burial 8-7, was probably the highest ranking juvenile in the compound sample, being from Plaza A, the residence of the lineage head (Webster 1989b). He or she had a cobble cyst grave, and was accompanied by two ceramic whistles, one piece of jade, and four faunal bones. This individual had only three defects. The 9-year-old, Burial 16-13a, had a capstone and two ceramic vessels but was buried with an adult, who might have been the real recipient of the offering. Thus, most of these individuals seem to have survived quite a bit of morbidity without any particular status buffering.

All these individuals also have another pathological indicator, but one individual, 15-45 with nine defects, only has a healed slight infection on a long bone. This individual has fragmentary postcranial bones, so it is possible that he or she could have had an active infection that has not been preserved. The other five individuals had an active lesion. The most serious case of porotic hyperostosis, Burial 22-4, and the most extensive active infection, Burial 16-13a, in the childhood sample are here. Burial 17-43 had no porotic hyperostosis, but had

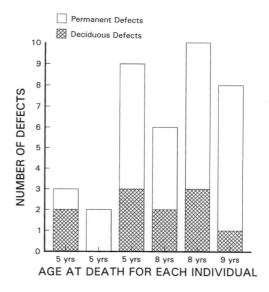

Figure 9.5. Number of dental defects per individual aged 5, 8, and 9 years at time of death.

an active infection on the cranium, as well as a healed localized infection on the legs. Burial 16-11 had active incipient porotic hyperostosis and small healing areas of infection on the legs. Again, most of these individuals were sick for a time before death, but also had to survive generally more episodes of morbidity than the younger age groups discussed above.

Summary Observations and Future Work

A few patterns are visible in the children studied here. No individuals have no defects at all, and few have no defects on either the permanent or deciduous dentitions. Most individuals in this sample had experienced morbidity during development of both the deciduous and permanent dentitions. Not surprisingly, the more serious and extensive defects in the deciduous dentition were present in the younger children, while the more serious defects in the permanent dentition were found in the older children.

Circular caries is a complication of the weakened enamel of hypocalcification (Duray 1992). The exact cause of the band of hypocalcification during very early infancy is unclear, but it is common in children dying before 6 years of age in other skeletal series (Cook 1990). The carious lesions are often extensive and may make a child more susceptible to infection entering the body through the pulp chamber of the tooth. Three of the 1-year-olds, nine of the 2-year-olds, and one 8-year-old in this sample had circular caries. Three could not be scored well for other pathological lesions, but six of the remaining ten had active infections and the other four had active porotic hyperostosis. This lesion is probably an example of how morbidity earlier in life can lead to mortality later.

In terms of individual frailty, frail individuals would be those with few defects compared to others, while sturdy individuals would be those with more defects per age-at-death. Both types are present at each age, but no child in this sample, all victims of premature mortality, died without first surviving some earlier episode(s) of morbidity that caused enamel defects. Thus, environmental factors, malnutrition or infection, were responsible for the morbidity, and most children had been ill for some time before death, because skeletal involvement in terms of porotic hyperostosis and periosteal reactions is present. There is also a trend of increasing average number of defects from 4.4 in the 1-year-olds, to 5.5 in the 2-year-olds, to 6.3 for the older children. While individual constitutional factors probably affected how much morbidity a child could survive and status differences may have provided more strength to some individuals, the environment in Late Classic Copán put these children at risk.

The importance of individual frailty and selective mortality is that with high mortality, high-risk frail individuals are removed from the population early so that, with increasing age, the aggregate hazard of death falls because, increasingly, only sturdy individuals are left (Wood et al. 1992). As the 9N-8 data show,

more sturdy individuals are represented in each ascending age, in that on average they must survive more morbidity to survive one more year or to older childhood. The pattern at 9N-8 seems to be one where frailty is best modeled not as some constant or one specific risk but as an insult accumulation, "in which all individual experiences of sickness increase the risks of both morbidity and mortality later in life" (Alter and Riley 1989:26). The environment in 9N-8 was putting these children in harm's way.

However, individuals do vary greatly in the morbidity, that measurable from skeletal lesions anyway, suffered before death. But are these individuals really differing in a meaningful way in terms of frailty, or were they mostly just unlucky in being subject to some strong stressor at the wrong time when they happened to be somewhat malnourished with their immune function temporarily impaired, whether they were 1 year old or 5 years old? "Infectious diseases are known to be highly selective, especially with respect to nutritional status and immune function" (Wood and Milner 1994:634). The important conclusion is that morbidity, which conditions mortality, is caused by the environment and the cultural context, and yes, as Wood et al. (1992) and the 9N-8 data show, individual risks are variable depending on both constitutional and life experience factors. Does that then mean that nothing can be said of the health conditions, or is it precisely the fact that environment affects morbidity and mortality for children in this population that gives an important insight into this past society? Wood et al. are correct that these children are no guide to those that survived or to overall levels of population health, but as many demographers and public health researchers know, the deaths and survival of children can often be explained by quite definite links of biological characteristics of malnutrition and disease with the differential distribution of basic necessities of life, that is, socioeconomic factors (Millard 1994). Where individual differences in susceptibility to death or morbidity, frailty, have important environmental components, as they usually do, understanding the cultural context of a population allows the making of inferences about the dynamics affecting individuals and populations. The hypothetical heart-attack victim discussed above and the individual children from 9N-8 do not represent the living, but their deaths are certainly understandable and give valuable insight into their societies. Is that not what osteological analysis is attempting to do?

The multiple stress episodes suffered by most individuals in this population, in spite of their supposed privileged living conditions, indicate that the environment of these children was not buffering them very well, although perhaps it was possible for them to survive more episodes of morbidity than children in nonnoble households. The repeated periods of morbidity do not seem to indicate that most of these children were somehow "frail," but that socioeconomic conditions were such that eventually each child's constitution could not pull him or her through another episode. The implication is that there was trouble in providing the basic necessities of life for children even in wealthier compounds, and the society was probably losing too many of its individuals prematurely during childhood. The archaeological evidence that this was a society on the verge of decline means these children provide probable evidence of nutritional and disease problems in Late Classic Copán that affected the long-term viability of this culture.

Other information and future analysis needed to test this frailty hypothesis include: whether or not the other pathological indicators (i.e., porotic hyperostosis, infections, etc.) are related to certain types of dental defects; a better index of morbidity from dental defects that includes an estimate of the timing of defects and its pattern among these children; and the pattern of dental defects of adults in this population, because if the number of defects and morbidity are generally lower among individuals surviving to adulthood in this compound (preliminary analysis indicates this is true) or the overall number of defects is higher in individuals of lower ranking compounds, then the socioeconomic factors and individual risk factors at work in this population will be clarified. Also, an attempt must be made to study paleodemographically the mortality in this population, although this is difficult as Wood et al. indicate, to see if there is excess childhood mortality. This paper represents only a preliminary step in the analysis of mortality and pathology in the Copán skeletal series, but the ability through osteological analysis to look at both the individual and the aggregate level, plus knowledge of how the cultural context affects morbidity and mortality, are what allow researchers to make meaningful inferences about the past.

Acknowledgments

The Copán osteological study is conducted with the permission of the Instituto Hondureño de Antropología e Historia and has been supported by the Government of Honduras, the Fulbright Program, and the University of Houston.

10

Late Classic Maya Health Patterns: Evidence from Enamel Microdefects

Marie Elaine Danforth

Most well-known models of the Classic Maya collapse (e.g., Culbert 1988; Lowe 1985; Santley et al. 1986; Willey and Shimkin 1973) incorporate a number of factors, including increased warfare, ecological devastation, and overpopulation, that would have had disastrous effects on the health of those living in the Petén at that time. Many of the consequent disease and nutritional conditions, such as anemia, infection, growth disruptions, and trauma, would be expected to leave bony lesions. Through analysis of patterns of these lesions, the skeletal record would thus appear to offer a valuable independent means of testing archaeological models. Surprisingly, however, few studies have attempted to so do, primarily because of the poor bone preservation in the lateritic soils of the tropical rainforest.

The osteological evidence cited in the collapse models is primarily based on changes in metric and pathological markers from the Preclassic to the Postclassic periods. At Barton Ramie, a reduction in long-bone dimensions was noted (Willey et al. 1965), and at Tikal, Haviland (1967) observed a decrease in male stature. Both changes were attributed to nutritional inadequacy. The most extensive osteological data, however, came from Altar de Sacrificios, where not only was there a similar decrease in stature, but also high frequencies of lesions suggestive of anemia, growth disruption, infection, and possibly scurvy.

Although data from only three sites are considered in these studies, most models discuss the decline in health associated with the collapse as more or less uniformly affecting inhabitants of the Petén. The specific impact of site size on Late Classic disease and nutritional patterns has only at times been debated. For instance, Sanders (1973) has suggested that smaller, more rural sites might be more adversely affected because of increasing social stratification over time. Others (e.g., Culbert 1988) propose dramatically increased competition between regional centers, which conceivably may have placed greater tribute and labor demands on sites lower in the political hierarchy.

Although these political factors undoubtedly had enormous impact on the lives of the inhabitants of Petén centers, it seems likely that their influence on health would have been more sporadic than those associated with population size and density. Although the Maya did not share the same infectious disease load of their Old World counterparts, they still had a number of health conditions, most notably respiratory infections, whose spread would have been facilitated by higher population densities. Based on demographic analysis at Teotihuacán, Storey (1985) has also effectively argued that New World urban centers experienced problems of public sanitation and hygiene. Water shortages were a recurrent problem in the Petén even though the region is generally swampy. Thus, certain large sites, such as Tikal, had to arrange for effective reservoir storage as well as sewage control. The tropical environment also provided a potential home for a number of endemic diseases and parasitic infections whose health effects on humans would have been potentially exacerbated by higher population densities (Shimkin 1973). Furthermore, it might also be argued that inhabitants of larger settlements would have less access to diet supplements through foraging during times of shortage compared to those residing at smaller sites.

In attempts to analyze the health status of the Late Classic Maya, most studies thus far have been of skeletal series from individual sites, usually with a diachronic approach. Other than Saul (e.g., 1973, 1975b), Saul and Saul (1984), and Wright (1994), relatively little work has been done to compare indicators synchronically across sites, even though it would allow testing of hypotheses such as the relationship between population level and health. One primary explanation for the paucity of these studies might be the problem of small sample size associated with poor preservation. For this reason, comparison of dental indicators perhaps holds the most promise. Teeth also provide a permanent chronological record of growth disruptions occurring during childhood, which is one of the most sensitive markers of a population's adaptive success. Thus, the present study considers patterns of formation of various enamel defects in Late Classic samples from three Petén sites that differ markedly in size and political importance.

The sample came from Tikal, Seibal, and Barton Ramie. Tikal was one of the very largest Maya centers, with a Late Classic population of nearly 60,000 (Culbert et al. 1990). Only a few other sites, such as Palenque and Copán, could rival its importance. The generally high population density of the region is reflected in the preponderance of structures being multiple dwellings (Ford and Fedick 1992). In contrast, Seibal had about 8000 inhabitants by A.D. 900 (Tourtellot 1990b). Although some consider it to have been only one of several important centers in Pasión Valley, analysis of monument counts lead others to suggest that it was the premier power in the region during the Late Classic (Willey 1990). Barton Ramie was the smallest of the three sites evaluated in this study. It was at most a minor center in the Belize River Valley, which had a total of perhaps 18,000 residents during the Late Classic (Ford 1990). Although the overall density of the valley was nearly as high as that of the Tikal region, the population was more evenly spread over the landscape, as reflected in the majority of structures being single dwellings (Ford and Fedick 1992).

The three sites do share several similarities important for comparison of health patterns. First, their ecosystems would have posed some of the same general challenges and opportunities for subsistence and disease. All were inland sites in quasi-rainforest settings that were either within or relatively close to swampy regions (Culbert 1973). The local land was generally quite fertile, and they enjoyed good water supply by virtue of being located on rivers or in areas where reservoirs could be constructed. Second, all three sites reached their pinnacles of political importance and population density during the Late Classic period before being largely abandoned by A.D. 1000 (Culbert et al. 1990; Ford 1990; Tourtellot 1990b). Thus, none appears to have escaped the collapse. Finally, all have skeletal samples composed of individuals of relatively modest social status. Most burials at the three sites were recovered in simple graves in nonceremonial locations with usually unimpressive accompaniments (Tourtellot 1990b; Willey et al. 1965). In a direct comparison of burial goods for all time periods at the three sites, Welsh (1988) found that individuals at Tikal appear to be somewhat wealthier than those at Barton Ramie or Seibal. The elite burials at Tikal, however, date mostly to the Preclassic and Early Classic periods; the Late Classic sample is overwhelmingly middle and lower class (Haviland, pers. comm. 1985). As will be discussed later, an additional factor that also decreased the likelihood of elites being included in the sample was the lack of decorated teeth, often taken to be a sign of high status.

In order to provide a comparative context for the Late Classic sample in general, dental markers were also evaluated in a Colonial Maya population from Tipu, Belize. Although a Postclassic skeletal series would have been preferable, none was available. Tipu, however, may be considered to be a good substitute, as there seems to have been extensive cultural continuity from the Postclassic into the early contact period for those Maya residing on the Spanish frontier where the site was located (Graham et al. 1989). At Lamanai, Wright (1990) observed an increase in enamel microdefects from the Postclassic to Historic periods, which she suggested might be related to introduction of malaria. Although it is possible that those buried in the Tipu cemetery may have died in epidemics from introduced diseases, no evidence thus far has

been uncovered to support such a conclusion (Cohen et al. 1994). Furthermore, the site is a bit more isolated than Lamanai, which may have offered it further protection against extensive exposure to epidemic diseases.

Materials and Methods

Permanent lower mandibular canines were chosen for study because they have been found to be among the teeth most susceptible for enamel defect formation (Goodman and Armelagos 1985). Teeth with no filing or jewel inlays were pulled from burials dating to A.D. 650–900. Sex for the individuals in the Barton Ramie and Seibal series was determined using standard cranial and pelvic indicators (Bass 1971) when possible. As many of the remains were fragmentary, bone robusticity was also used. Individuals were aged as adult or juvenile on the basis of third molar eruption. For the Tikal sample, age and sex assignments provided by Haviland (pers. comm. 1985) were used.

A total of 85 canines were collected for the Late Classic sample. Although subsamples from the three sites were of roughly equal size, the sex and age distributions did vary somewhat (Table 10.1). As the sample sizes were small for each site, it is not surprising that they are not a representative sample of the population (Weiss 1973). Juveniles are underrepresented, and males outnumber females five to one. The Colonial sample of 130 canines had a higher proportion of females and juveniles, but nonetheless there again is doubt as to whether those in the Tipu cemetery are representative of the living population (Cohen et al. 1994).

Three enamel defects were observed. The first was striae of Retzius, which are areas of hypomineralization that occur when there is an interruption in the daily maturation of enamel (Gustafson 1959). They appear as brownish stripes running obliquely from the dentino-

Table 10.1 Canine Tooth Distribution by Site

	Tikal	Seibal	Barton Ramie	Late Classic Totals	Colonial Tipu
Deciduous canines	5	1	3	9	34
Permanent canines					
Juveniles	8	1	6	15	40
Adults	18	28	25	71	129
Males	10	24	16	50	52
Females	4	3	4	11	43
Undetermined sex	4	1	5	10	34

enamel junction to the tooth's outer surface. Those striae associated with a more severe health disturbance may appear darker or wider (Rose 1973). A second microdefect, called Wilson or pathological bands, is a subset of striae in which a linear distortion of enamel prism arrangement is seen. The distortion can take several forms, but commonly it appears as a bending or other disjuncture of the otherwise straight, parallel-appearing prism rows (Rose 1977; Wilson and Schroff 1970). The third defect scored, enamel hypoplasias, results from premature cessation of enamel matrix formation, which leaves transverse furrows of depressed or pitted enamel on the tooth's surface. It has been suggested that those episodes resulting from severe disruptions may be deeper (Suckling 1989; Suckling et al. 1986) or broader (Blakey and Armelagos 1985; Hutchinson and Larsen 1985). The three microdefects each have different mechanisms of causation, but all are nonspecific stress indicators that have been associated with a range of health conditions from nutrition to infectious disease (Goodman and Rose 1990; Hillson 1986; Pindborg 1982). Condon (1981), however, has suggested that Wilson bands may result from a more short-term stressor of perhaps one to five days' duration whereas enamel hypoplasias form only after a few weeks of exposure.

In order to score the enamel microdefects, each tooth was sectioned bucco-lingually through the center. It was then thinned, polished, and etched in weak hydrochloric acid. Thin sections were observed using a transmitted light polarizing microscope that had been fitted with a micrometer ruled to .01 mm. Location of defects was scored using the procedure developed by Cook (1981). Under 40× magnification, the buccal side of the dentino-enamel junction was divided into 1-mm sections beginning at the tip of the cusp if no dentin was exposed. If heavier wear was present, measurement began at the cemento-enamel junction, which was assigned to the tenth millimeter zone as this was the modal number of zones on unworn teeth in both sexes.

Within each millimeter section, striae of Retzius were recorded as present if they had demarcations on both the buccal and dentino-enamel margins and could be followed entirely through the enamel. Polarization was used at times to enhance appearance. Stria width and color were each scored on a five-point ordinal scale. Individual striae were then checked at 400× magnification for presence of a Wilson band. As before, the defect had to be present throughout the entire length of the stria. Stria and Wilson band locations were assigned to the millimeter unit of the dentino-enamel junction from which they emanated. A maximum of 10 units, or developmental zones, was possible.

Using 40× magnification, enamel hypoplasias were identified when the tooth's profile dipped below the expected surface. Depth and width of each episode were measured using the micrometer; these measurements were then reclassified on an eight-point ordinal scale. Episode location was similarly recorded by millimeter unit using associated striae. For this defect, a maximum of only six units, or developmental zones, was evaluated since the first four were usually associated with buried, rather than surface, enamel (Hillson 1986).

Age-at-formation for each microdefect was determined using the developmental zones. Each zone was assigned an age range based on patterns of enamel formation in modern populations (Fanning and Brown 1971). Though this particular standard suggests that permanent canines develop between ages 6 months and about 5 years, other standards suggest that development may routinely continue as late as 6 years (Massler et al. 1941).

The statistical tests used were chosen for their applicability to small samples. Comparisons involving mean frequencies, such as number of defects per unit of enamel, were evaluated using the nonparametric Mann-Whitney U tests. Those comparisons involving distributions, such as defect frequencies by age-at-formation, were evaluated using Komolgorov-Smirnov tests, which are also nonparametric. All other comparisons, such as presence/absence of defects or color differences, were tested using chi-square tests of association. As sample sizes were small and results at best can be considered preliminary, p-values were set at .10.

Results

In initial analysis of results, the Late Classic samples were checked for differences by age and sex. Unfortunately, as so few females and juveniles were present, it was nearly impossible to consider each site separately. When males and females from all three sites were compared, none of the three developmental defects showed statistically significant differences. Thus, a small leap of faith was made, and the sexes were combined into a single adult sample for each site. In contrast, patterns of defect formation in the combined site sample did vary by age. Those dying as children (under age 18) had significantly higher rates of striae of Retzius in three of the ten developmental zones, and significantly higher rates of hypoplasias in one of six zones. Wilson band formation was also higher, although the differences were nonsignificant. Consequently, only adults were included in further analysis.

Overall, a common pattern of age-specific morbidity emerged in the samples from all three sites. Microdefect formation in the permanent canines suggests that the period from 6 months to 2 years was generally healthy, but after that, the number of growth disruptions experienced rose dramatically (Figs. 10.1, 10.2). Both Wilson bands and striae reached their greatest levels between ages 1.5 and 3. The highest period of hypoplasia formation, however, occurred between ages 3 and 5. Spacing of episodes did not suggest a regularly occurring growth disruption, such as might be associated with annual famines.

When enamel defect formation was compared among the three sites, a complex pattern emerged. The mean number of striae per millimeter of enamel did not significantly differ by site (Table 10.2), and similarly, chi-square analysis showed no significant differences among the sites in color or width of striae. The distribution of striae by age-at-formation did vary, however. Barton Ramie and Seibal generally peaked about one year apart whereas Tikal had a flatter pattern of frequencies by age-at-formation (Fig. 10.1). When mean frequencies by each developmental zone were compared between Tikal and Seibal, only one was statistically significant, that occurring between ages

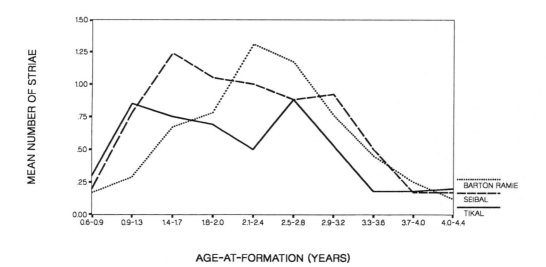

AGE-AT-FORMATION (YEARS)

TIKAL: N=18   SEIBAL: N=24   BARTON RAMIE: N=30

Figure 10.1. Mean frequency of striae of Retzius per developmental zone by Late Classic site.

2.9 and 3.2 years. In contrast, differences in mean frequencies between Tikal and Barton Ramie for the three zones between ages 2.5 and 3.6 were statistically significant. None of the frequencies by millimeter unit showed significant differences between Seibal and Barton Ramie.

Frequencies of Wilson bands by developmental zone were not calculated for each individual site as the defects were relatively rare. When the percentage of striae containing Wilson bands was considered, Tikal again had the lowest rate (Table 10.2). Levels of formation at Seibal and Barton Ramie, however, were only

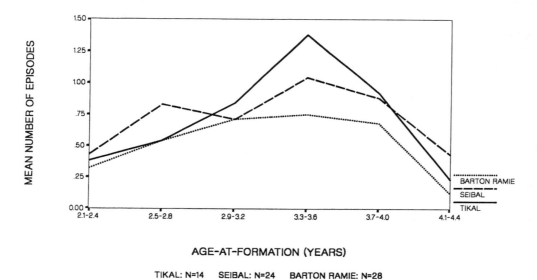

AGE-AT-FORMATION (YEARS)

TIKAL: N=14   SEIBAL: N=24   BARTON RAMIE: N=28

Figure 10.2. Mean frequency of linear enamel hypoplasias per developmental zone by Late Classic site.

Table 10.2 Mean Frequencies of Defect Formation per Millimeter of Enamel

Defect	Barton Ramie	Seibal	Tikal	Late Classic	Colonial Tipu
Mean striae/mm of enamel	.65	.70	.52	.65	.70
Mean hypoplasias/mm of enamel	.54	.73	.72	.54	.37
% striae with Wilson bands	6	9	8	8 *	5 *

*Difference significant at p < .05.

slightly higher, and comparisons among the three sites showed no statistical differences.

In analysis of linear enamel hypoplasia formation, Barton Ramie had the lowest mean frequency of enamel hypoplasias per millimeter of enamel (Table 10.2), although it was not statistically different from values at the other sites. Some of the differences by distribution of age-at-formation were, however (Fig. 10.2). Compared to Seibal, Barton Ramie had significantly fewer episodes form in two of six zones (ages 2.5 to 2.8 and ages 4.1 to 4.4). One zone, ages 3.3 to 3.6, was significantly different between Tikal and Barton Ramie. No units between Tikal and Seibal were significantly different. Episode width and depth were similar among all three sites.

When the health of the Late Classic Maya, as indicated by enamel defects formation, was compared with that of the Colonial Maya, a conflicting pattern was seen. In stria formation, the two samples had very similar mean rates per millimeter of enamel (Table 10.2). When age-at-formation was considered, however, differences emerged (Fig. 10.3). Although the marked peak of the Colonial sample might

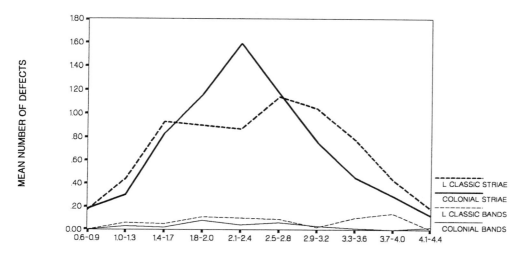

Figure 10.3. Mean frequency of striae of Retzius and Wilson bands per developmental zone by time period.

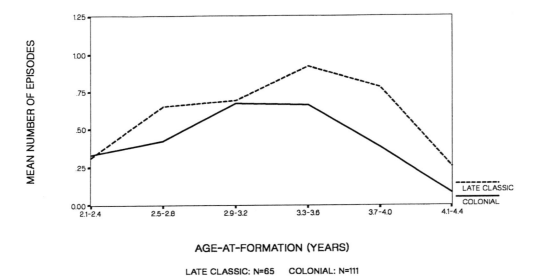

AGE–AT–FORMATION (YEARS)

LATE CLASSIC: N=65   COLONIAL: N=111

Figure 10.4. Mean frequency of linear enamel hypoplasias per developmental zone by time period.

have suggested otherwise, only one zone, ages 3.3 to 3.6, showed a significantly different mean and, surprisingly, the Late Classic group had more defects. The striae were also significantly darker, although not wider, in the Late Classic group. Rates of Wilson band formation were also consistently higher in individuals from the earlier time period (Fig. 10.3) in the distribution by age-at-formation, and the percentage of striae containing enamel prism disruptions was significantly higher compared to Colonial values.

When enamel hypoplasia formation was considered, the pattern reversed. The Late Classic sample had significantly more episodes in five of the six developmental zones (Fig. 10.4), as was also reflected in the mean number of episodes per millimeter of enamel (Table 10.2). Interestingly, hypoplasias in the Colonial sample were significantly wider on average, but most were very shallow. Perhaps the most telling difference in hypoplasia formation between the two time periods was a subset of hypoplasias in which a deep V-shaped episode was associated with a dark stria that nearly always contained

a Wilson band. This co-occurrence most likely represents a severe acute rather than chronic growth disturbance. Although by no means common in the Late Classic sample, such enamel disruptions were virtually absent in the Colonial group.

When defect interaction was considered, fewer than half of the striae of Retzius scored were associated with hypoplasias in all of the subsamples evaluated. However, there was a consistent statistically significant association between darker striae and hypoplasias in the Late Classic and Colonial samples. Similarly, broader and darker striae were also significantly more likely to contain Wilson bands in both groups. In the Late Classic group, Wilson bands were more than twice as likely to occur in conjunction with hypoplasias than were nonband striae, this difference being statistically significant. The same pattern was not seen in the Colonial group.

In summary, Tikal, the largest site, had the lowest level of short-term health disruptions, as indicated by striae of Retzius, whereas Barton Ramie, the smallest site, had the lowest level of longer term disruptions, as indicated by enamel hypoplasias. It needs to be emphasized, however, that these patterns were very weak, reaching statistical significance in only a few developmental zone comparisons. When Late Classic and Colonial samples were compared, the later sample had somewhat higher rates of stria formation, but the differences were again mostly not statistically significant. In contrast, however, the linear enamel hypoplasia and Wilson band differences were consistently statistically significant, and the patterns seen strongly support the interpretation that health was better in the Colonial group.

Discussion

Before discussing the results of the microdefect analysis, several caveats must be presented. First, this is obviously an imperfect sample with which to explore the complex interaction between the variables involved in the collapse and their effects on health. As previously mentioned, the low number of females and juveniles precludes the sample from being representative of the living population (Weiss 1973). Even if these segments constituted a greater proportion, the sample size still is very small. As Tourtellot (1990a) noted, the Seibal skeletal series includes only 1 in 200 people who had resided at the site. Thus, it is impossible to say that the health experiences seen in this study are necessarily characteristic of the general Late Classic population.

Even if the samples were larger, we still have no guarantee that individuals were buried at the site where they grew up as children. Considering the massive monumental construction and military encounters that were common during this period, it is possible that residents of the Petén, especially males, may have been moved many places during their lifetimes. Since Maya society was highly patrilineal, with kin

relationships being integral to subsistence activities (Haviland 1972), however, it does not seem that individuals usually would have been buried away from their families. Some individuals may not have been buried in their natal region if they belonged to populations that were shifted during food shortages (Santley et al. 1986).

Although some noteworthy differences were present in the comparison of enamel defect formation among the various samples, overall the similarity of results to those found in other investigations of Maya populations is striking. First, most other studies involving developmental enamel defects have reported no marked differences between the sexes in terms of percentage affected (Danforth et al. 1991; Whittington 1992). Even though small sample size would make statistical significance difficult to reach, the values are actually quite similar for males and females in most populations. In his study of individuals at Copán, Whittington (1992) concluded that such a pattern indicates that female children were not being neglected. It would seem that if no preferential treatment were occurring, however, the health of young males would have been worse than that of their sisters, especially during the difficult conditions of the Late Classic period. Many investigations have supported the presence of biological buffering against stress, especially during early childhood (Stini 1969; Stinson 1985; Stuart-Macadam 1994). Thus, Maya boys may have indeed enjoyed somewhat greater access to resources, which would be consistent with cultural practices in many patrilineal societies.

The age of peak rate-of-formation for the three defects is also similar among most studies. Striae of Retzius have not been analyzed in the Maya before, but Wright (1990) did examine Wilson band frequencies in a Postclassic and a Historic population from Lamanai in northern Belize. Although her sample size was small, she similarly found a peak rate of formation occurring around ages 2 to 3. Her frequencies of Wilson bands were higher than those seen in the present study, but direct comparison of microdefect data is not recommended because of the likelihood of interobserver differences in scoring.

Nearly all studies of hypoplasias in Maya populations have also noted peak formation around ages 3 to 4 (e.g., Saul 1972a; Whittington 1992). Saul (1972a) and most others have attributed this pattern to stresses associated with weaning. Ethnohistorical information reported by Landa (Tozzer 1941) supports such a conclusion. An additional factor that might be affecting ages of peak formation, however, is tooth architecture, which may result in certain areas of the enamel being more susceptible to formation of specific developmental defects. Condon and Rose (1992) have suggested that cuspal enamel is less likely to form Wilson bands. Cook (1981) has proposed that hypoplasias may be most common in cervical regions of the tooth because ameloblasts there are older and perhaps weaker. These effects, however, are rarely addressed in interpreting microdefect results. Thus, the timing of the major increase in defect frequencies may not reflect cultural homogeneity in age-at-weaning as it might at first seem.

When differences in enamel defect formation among the three Late Classic samples in the present study are considered, a very complex picture is seen. Hypoplasia results very much conform to expectations in that the largest site, Tikal, had the highest frequencies whereas the smallest, Barton Ramie, had the lowest. Although the patterning of striae is more varied among sites, the only consistent period of differences between Tikal and Barton Ramie occurred at the same ages as when hypoplasia frequencies were peaking. With striae, however, the smallest site had the highest rates of the defect. Enamel microdefects are nonspecific, so inhabitants of both sizes of site might have in-

curred high levels of growth disruption, but from different causes. This is especially likely since co-occurrence of defects was rather low. Considering that hypoplasias most likely represent more long-term health disruptions compared to those causing striae, it may indeed indicate that the stressors at Barton Ramie had less of a severe impact on the health of the Late Classic residents.

Unfortunately, few other health data exist that might help us understand the nature of the stressors at the three sites. Within this particular sample from Barton Ramie, some 22% had porotic hyperostosis, a condition usually thought to result from childhood anemia (Stuart-Macadam 1985), as compared to the Seibal sample in which 41% were affected (Cohen et al. 1989). Thus, individuals at the smaller site may have enjoyed a more adequate diet or experienced fewer infections (Mensforth et al. 1978), both of which accord with expectations for more advantageous health conditions at smaller sites. Stature, which is a cumulative indicator of childhood growth disruptions (Falkner and Tanner 1986), also supports such a difference in disease and nutritional experiences between Tikal and Barton Ramie. When calculated from femoral length using the Genovés (1967) formula, Late Classic males at Barton Ramie (n = 17) average 156.6 cm (n = 10) as compared to about 155 cm (recalculated from Haviland 1967) for their nonelite counterparts at Tikal (n unknown; cf. Danforth 1994). Males at Seibal (n = 21) were the tallest, with a mean height of 158.8 cm. Female sample sizes for stature were too small for any meaningful comparison.

In considering these data, it must be remembered that the differences in levels of enamel microdefects between the largest and smallest sites are relatively meager, and it is easy to overinterpret their meaning. Furthermore, the stature and porotic hyperostosis analyses presented above involve small sample sizes and the values do not differ significantly among the sites. Although some recent skeletal analyses also have found worsening health associated with the Late Classic (Storey 1985, 1992a; Whittington 1989, 1992), others have not (Glassman 1994). In fact, White et al. (1994) observed more nutritional pathological lesions in the Postclassic and Historic Maya at Lamanai than in their earlier counterparts. Thus, the results seen are at most a preliminary confirmation in the Late Classic Maya of the ill effects of population aggregation on health, a pattern which has been observed in many other parts of the world (Cohen 1989; Storey 1985).

The results of the microdefect analysis do more strongly confirm another long-held assumption, that the health of Late Classic Maya was worse than that of their descendants. Daily life for the Postclassic and frontier Colonial Maya, with their lower population densities and less complex political systems, theoretically would not have included the nutritional challenges or political instability commonly associated with the collapse. As with Late Classic site comparisons, the hypoplasia, and this time also the Wilson band, results support initial hypotheses, but again the stria results do not. Thus, many of the same patterns concerning types and intensities of stress seen at sites of different sizes during the Late Classic may apply to the Colonial period as well. This should not be surprising as population levels in the later period were similarly lower. The general lack of dark striae containing Wilson bands and associated with deep hypoplasias also supports the conclusion that introduced infectious diseases did not have a significant impact on the childhood health of those in the Colonial sample, which has been supported by other health and archaeological evidence as well (Cohen et al. 1994).

Conclusions

In summary, this study attempted to look across sites to examine health patterns during the Late Classic period. Hypoplasia results weakly suggest that residents at larger sites had incurred more health disruptions during childhood compared to their more rural counterparts. Similarly, hypoplasia and Wilson band frequencies were also significantly higher than during later periods, which also conforms to hypotheses of increased stressors preceding the collapse.

Those who study Maya skeletal remains will always be plagued with the problem of small sample size related to poor preservation. Given this circumstance, it is only through continued aggregation of information from a number of sites, regardless of whether the sample size is 10 or 1000 and whether one or many disease and nutrition indicators are observed, that we can begin to test the broad statements concerning health that are so much a part of the models of the Late Classic collapse.

Acknowledgments

I would like to thank Mark Cohen (SUNY-Plattsburgh), William Haviland (Vermont), and the Peabody Museum at Harvard University for permission to use the skeletal series. I would also like to express appreciation to the editors for their helpful comments on drafts of this manuscript. The study was funded in part by a grant from Sigma Xi.

11

Dental Genetic Structuring of a Colonial Maya Cemetery, Tipu, Belize

Keith P. Jacobi

Teeth are not everlasting but they come close. Natural elements only slowly break down enamel, the hardest substance in the human body. For this reason, teeth provide an excellent source of information about burials recovered from an archaeological context. At Tipu, Belize, the remains of more than 600 individuals were found beneath and surrounding a colonial *visita* mission (Fig. 11.1; Cohen et al. 1989, 1994). The primary and extensive use of the burial area at the Tipu mission was between A.D. 1568 and 1638, the latter year marking the Maya rebellion against the Spanish (Graham et al. 1989; Jones 1989). The burials at the mission are believed to be Maya and are the largest number excavated to date from contact times in a single cemetery. The dental remains from these individuals were examined and the results were used to attempt to reconstruct the burial pattern or mortuary strategy employed at the church. The teeth were used to compare this population to other prehistoric, historic, and modern Maya and to explore the extent of Spanish influence on the Tipu Maya. The analysis utilized both the morphological and metric variation of the teeth from this archaeologically derived Maya population from historic times.

Nonmetric and metric skeletal traits observed on the skull, axial skeleton, and appendicular skeleton are often used in the study of human morphological variation (Buikstra 1976; Conner 1984, 1990; Droessler 1981; Hauser and De Stefano 1989). The traits are used to show relationships between or among population groups. Teeth are analyzed for morphometric information as well. Both metric and nonmetric traits are heritable, and the results of analyses of both kinds of traits are highly correlated (Cheverud et al. 1979; Cheverud and Buikstra 1982). Metric and nonmetric traits express variation. Metric traits are on a continuous scale of measurable variation (e.g., tooth length and width are measurable traits). Nonmetric traits are landmarks such as cusps, ridges, and grooves that are present on the crown and root of a tooth. These traits can be either discontinuous or partially continuous and are difficult to measure (Hillson 1986).

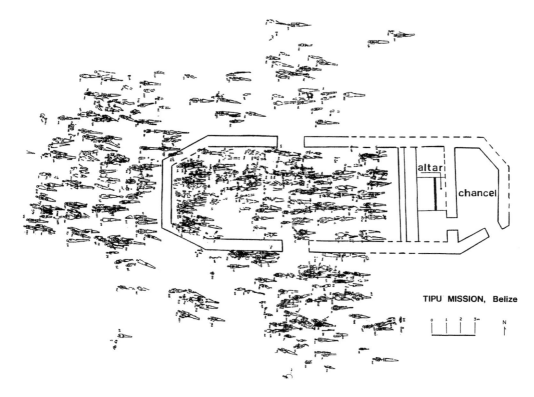

Figure 11.1. Tipu church with burials.

Previous investigations have recorded dental nonmetric and metric characteristics of populations over large geographic areas (Dahlberg 1951; Kieser 1990; Moorrees 1957; Turner 1985). Populations have been subdivided into single geographic areas or regional populations in studies such as Lukacs and Hemphill's (1991) temporal investigation of Baluchistan or Harris and Bailit's (1987) work on individuals in the Solomon Islands and Oceania. Some morphometric analysis has involved further subdivisions of populations such as the investigations of Barksdale (1972) and Boyd (1972) of the different village populations included in the Kainantu Language Family in the Eastern Highlands of New Guinea (Littlewood 1972). The dental genetic structure of a population has been subdivided even further to involve the extended family or immediate family (Harris and Weeks 1973). The dental remains from Tipu

were analyzed to determine the geographical/regional, temporal, and family influences on the Tipuan genetic makeup.

The nonmetric and metric data recorded from the dental remains at Tipu were used to create a complex of Maya dental traits indicative of that population. Through the analysis it was determined whether or not it was possible to discern influxes of Maya refugees to Tipu as ethnohistorical documents suggest happened (Jones 1989). It was also determined whether or not Spanish individuals were interred at the site and the degree of Spanish admixture at Tipu. In addition, it was hoped that nonmetric traits might identify family groups or relations within the cemetery and offer information on traditional Spanish Catholic burial practices.

At Tipu two cultures met: the Maya with a long-standing complex of their own religious beliefs and the Spanish with an agenda of religious conversion. The first Spanish emissaries were friars of the Catholic Church who were charged with the mission of converting the Maya to Catholicism. Do the Tipu church and the individuals buried there give evidence that the friars met some of their goals of conversion, including adoption of Spanish Catholic burial practices? Do the burials resemble the pattern of Spanish influence found at another settlement, Tancah, Quintana Roo? Miller and Farriss (1979) describe the Tancah site as having burials within the church and its surroundings. At Tancah, there is evidence of sex segregation in burial placement, a practice that parallels the Spanish custom of segregation in worship. Did this take place at Tipu, too, or does the Tipuan mortuary record reflect what Douglass (1969) found in a Spanish Basque village? There parishioners were buried in *sepultures,* which are burial plots in the church floor designated for specific households. Family worshippers sat

above these burial plots during a religious service. Finally, does the Tipu burial program merely show Maya tolerance of the visiting friars' presence rather than espousal of portions of their Catholic theology? Such tolerance could have resulted in the Maya simply adapting their Precolonial practice of burying dead below household floors and temples to burying them beneath the Catholic church. In addition to considering various models such as those above, the Tipuan mortuary record was examined for evidence of migrant population groupings, familial and temporal units, and Spanish individuals, including friars.

The Tipu cemetery was divided into five areas by the skeletal analysis team at the State University of New York (SUNY) at Plattsburgh: inside church front, inside church back, north of church, west of church, and south of church. No burials were found to the east of the church. Figure 11.2 shows the breakdown

TOTAL BURIALS BY LOCATION

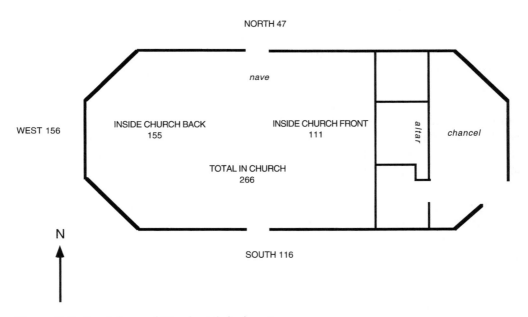

Figure 11.2. Breakdown of Tipu burials by location.

SEX BY LOCATION

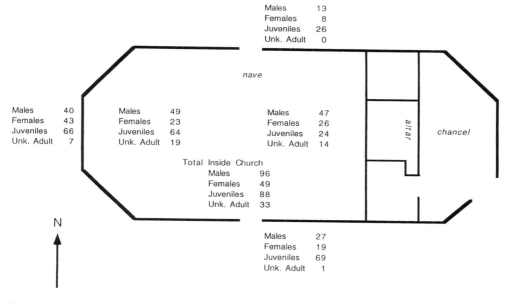

Figure 11.3. Distribution of burials by sex and location.

of the Tipu burials by location. There are a good number of individuals buried within the church. More burials are present, virtually crammed, in the back of the church than in the front. There are more burials outside the church than inside, and the outside burials are primarily in the western and southern areas surrounding the church. The burial remains are in extended position with their feet facing the altar, a Catholic tradition.

Using age and sex data provided by the Osteology Lab at SUNY at Plattsburgh, the burials had this distribution by sex: 176 males, 119 females, 249 juveniles, and 41 adults of unknown sex, for a total of 585 historic burials. In addition, there were 19 non-Colonial burials which were not the primary focus of this study. The distribution of burials by sex and location is illustrated in Figure 11.3. Some sex stratification is evident in burial location; significantly more males than females were buried inside the church ($\chi^2 = 5.077$, p = .0242). This

number might even be more significant if the burial site included the 80 males who left Tipu with Father Delgado in 1624 to help convert the Itzá. These men were massacred, decapitated, and had their hearts torn out by the Itzá at Tayasal in what is now Guatemala (Fancourt 1854; Jones 1989; Villagutierre 1983).

Examining the numbers of adults inside and outside the church vs. juveniles, we find significantly more adults than juveniles buried within the church ($\chi^2 = 17.938$, p =.0001). If this figure is broken down further into front vs. back of the church, we find significantly more adults than juveniles buried in the front ($\chi^2 = 11.303$, p = .0008).

Of the nearly 600 burials at Tipu, 518 had some dental remains that could be examined for nonmetric and metric traits. The teeth were measured and scored for nonmetric traits using the Arizona State University dental plaques and scoring procedures developed by Christy Turner and colleagues (Turner et al. 1991).

A complex of traits that is indicative of the Maya was revealed through examination of the Tipu nonmetric dental traits. In the maxillary dentition, the Tipu Maya exhibit high frequencies of the following: shoveling of the central incisor (98%, n = 225), double shoveling of the central incisor (63%, n = 254), Carabelli's cusp of the first molar (46%, n = 305), hypocone cusp or fourth cusp on the upper molars (M1 = 99%, n = 335; M2 = 83%, n = 260; M3 = 47%, n = 146), and canine distal accessory ridge (46%, n = 143). High-frequency mandibular traits include: presence of the canine distal accessory ridge (44%, n = 179), anterior fovea on the first molar (82%, n = 231), groove pattern sequence of Y X X on the first through third molars respectively (M1-Y = 90%, n = 267; M2-X = 53%, n =235; M3-X = 79%, n = 124), and deflecting wrinkle on the first lower molar (40%, n = 238).

More moderate nonmetric maxillary trait frequencies include: interruption groove on the lateral incisor (21%, n = 215), tuberculum dentale on the central and lateral incisors and canine (I1 = 21%, n = 219; I2 = 28%, n = 227; C = 28%, n = 205), labial curvature on the central incisor (19%, n = 272), and enamel extensions on the second molar (23%, n = 203). The mandibular dentition exhibits the following traits at moderate frequency: cusp six on the first molar (17%, n = 281), Tome's root on the first premolar (28%, n = 149), protostylid on the molars (M1 = 16%, n = 302; M2 = 25%, n = 240; M3 = 22%, n = 134), and congenital absence of the third molar (15%, n = 206).

Maxillary nonmetric traits found at low frequency include: winging of the central incisors (13%, n = 70), cusp five on the first molar (7%, n = 321), parastyle on the third molar (4%, n = 151), peg lateral incisors and third molars (I2 = 12%, n = 276; M3 = 12%, n = 165), labial groove on the central and lateral incisors (I1 = 5%, n = 222; I2 = 2%, n = 225), and congenital absence of the third molar (6%, n = 187). Discussion of the labial groove is rare in the literature. Brin and Ben-Bassat (1989) have noticed what they call a labiogingival notch on the permanent maxillary central incisors among primary school children in Jerusalem. The labial groove found at Tipu (Fig. 11.4) may be within the range of expression of the labiogingival notch, but it could be a distinct trait (Dahlberg, pers. comm. 1988). This groove also is found on the labial aspect of the maxillary lateral incisor and the canine. Very rare maxillary traits found at Tipu such as odontomes on premolars (Fig. 11.5), palatal

Figure 11.4. Variations in labial groove trait.

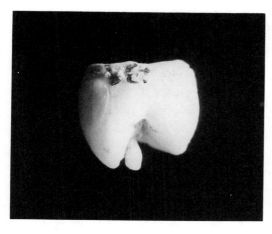

Figure 11.5. Odontome on maxillary premolar.

measured in mesiodistal and buccolingual dimensions using a Mitutoyo sliding caliper with sharpened tips calibrated to .02 mm. Discriminant function analysis was used to determine the morphometric similarity between two sample populations, such as individuals from specific burial locations at Tipu. It was hoped that this analysis would allocate the Tipu individuals into one of these four groups: indigenous historic Maya; historic Maya from somewhere else, possibly the Yucatán; historic Spanish; or prehistoric Maya.

In order to maximize the number of complete adult cases used in the discriminant function, it was necessary to replace a missing measurement on one side of the mouth with its antimere measurement from the other side of the mouth, which means that the issue of dental asymmetry among the Tipuans had to be addressed. The results of 32 t-tests to compare the statistical means of the two independent samples show that throughout the Tipu population there is little significant difference between the mesiodistal and buccolingual measurements from the left and right sides of the mouth (Jacobi 1996). The similarity between

canines (Fig. 11.6), and enamel pearls (Fig. 11.7) are at frequencies of 1% or less.

Mandibular traits at low frequency include: presence of the seventh cusp on the first molar (6%, n = 305) and odontomes on the second premolar (3%, n = 265). The occurrence of three roots on the first molar is rare (less than 1%; Fig. 11.8).

Metric variation also was examined in the Tipuan dental remains. The tooth crowns were

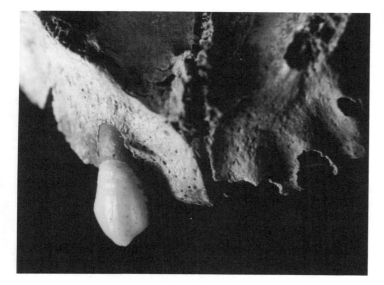

Figure 11.6. Palatal canine.

Figure 11.7. Enamel pearls.

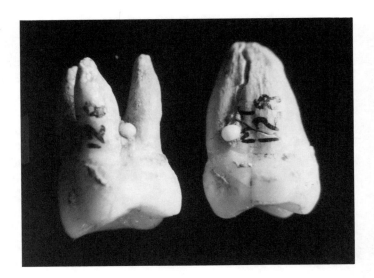

the right and left side measurements is sufficient to allow the replacement process to be used. Similarly, statistical correlations between right and left teeth of the same type are high, as one would expect. The similarity between the sides as revealed through these statistical tests validates the replacement process.

To maximize further the number of cases used in discriminant function analysis, all the burials inside the church were combined into one group, as were the burials outside the church. The focus was to discriminate status differences between individuals inside and outside the church, based on the fact that in the

Catholic Church it is most desirable to be buried beneath the church and as close to the altar as possible. The individuals were then examined separately by maxillary mesiodistal and buccolingual measurements as well as by mandibular mesiodistal and buccolingual measurements. Segregating the measurements in this manner reflected the variation between maxillary and mandibular dentitions and facilitated management of the massive Tipu data set.

Discriminant function analysis was performed on the measurements using the SPSSX-II statistical package (SPSS 1988). This test describes the maximum difference between two or more

Figure 11.8. Three-rooted mandibular first molars.

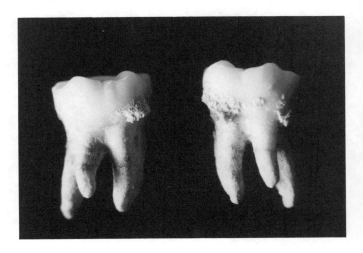

Table 11.1 Discriminant Function Analysis of Tipu Burials by Burial Location

	n (X/Y)[a]	Number of Variables in Function	p	Canonical Correlation	Percent of "Grouped" Cases Correctly Classified
Maxillary mesiodistal	34/65	3	.1845	.222	55.4
Maxillary buccolingual	31/50	1	.0108	.282	49.8
Mandibular mesiodistal	40/57	3	.0125	.331	60.4
Mandibular buccolingual	39/20	4	.0031	.502	71.2

NOTE: n = number of individuals; X = inside church; Y = outside church; p = p-value.

[a] Includes individuals of unknown sex.

groups in terms of several variables (Klecka 1982; Reyment et al. 1984). In this case the groups are the historic Tipu remains from inside and outside the church. The variables are the mesiodistal and buccolingual measurements of the maxillary and mandibular teeth. There is some significance at the .05 level in maxillary buccolingual, mandibular mesiodistal, and mandibular buccolingual measure-ments in the discriminant function analysis of the Tipu data (Table 11.1). The maxilla contributes only one variable, the maxillary first molar buccolingual measurement (MAXM1BL), to the function. The variable is significant but with a low canonical correlation. Canonical correlation is an indicator of the relatedness of the groups, so a high correlation is desirable (Klecka 1982). The mandible contributes seven variables with low canonical correlations: MDP2MD, MDM3MD,

MDM2MD, MDM3BL, MDM1BL, MDM2BL, and MDI1BL. There is almost no sign of discrimination between inside and outside the church when examining the maxillary mesiodistal and buccolingual measurements. There are no significant differences between most mandibular mesiodistal and buccolingual measurements, either. Mandibular buccolingual measurements (MDM3BL, MDM1BL, MDM2BL, and MDI1BL) account for 50% of the variance and mandibular mesiodistal measurements (MDP2MD, MDM3MD, and MDM2MD) account for 33% of the variance in the discriminant function. Thus, the difference in tooth measurements between those buried inside and outside the church proves to be slight, and most variation is in the mandible.

Another discriminant analysis was done for the entire population grouped by sex (Table 11.2).

Table 11.2 Discriminant Function Analysis of Tipu Burials by Sex

	n (X/Y)	Number of Variables in Function	p	Canonical Correlation	Percent of "Grouped" Cases Correctly Classified
Maxillary mesiodistal	57/32	4	.0005	.457	66.2
Maxillary buccolingual	47/28	1	.0001	.430	63.6
Mandibular mesiodistal	59/31	4	.0000	.523	72.1
Mandibular buccolingual	34/19	2	.1282	.281	65.4

NOTE: n = number of individuals; X = males; Y = females; p = p-value.

Table 11.3   Discriminant Function Analysis of Tipu Burials by Sex and Burial Location

	n (X/Y)	Number of Variables in Function	p	Canonical Correlation	Percent of "Grouped" Cases Correctly Classified
Males					
Maxillary mesiodistal	18/39	3	.0462	.373	62.8
Maxillary buccolingual	18/29	2	.2088	.262	53.5
Mandibular mesiodistal	24/35	3	.0508	.362	57.8
Mandibular buccolingual	25/9	2	.1371	.347	68.0
Females					
Maxillary mesiodistal	9/23	4	.0622	.524	73.1
Maxillary buccolingual	8/20	2	.1980	.349	69.7
Mandibular mesiodistal	10/21	2	.2608	.303	66.7
Mandibular buccolingual	9/10	3	.0422	.641	67.6

NOTE: n = number of individuals; X = inside church; Y = outside church; p = p-value.

Tooth measurements are different between the sexes, as one would expect, with some maxillary mesiodistal, maxillary buccolingual, and mandibular mesiodistal measurements significant and, thus, contributed to the function. The variables are MAXP2MD, MAXCMD, MAXM1MD, MAXM2MD, MAXM2BL, MDCMD, MDI1MD, MDM1MD, and MDM2MD. Again canonical correlations are low. The most highly significant variables involve the maxillary and mandibular canines and maxillary first and second molars.

In a discriminant analysis calculated on the burials grouped by sex and location (inside vs. outside the church; Table 11.3), some measurements are significant for males (MAXP1MD, MAXM3MD, MAXI2MD, MDP2MD, MDM3MD, and MDI2MD) and others for females (MDM3BL, MDM2BL, and MDM1BL). Canonical correlations are low. The highest level of significance is in mandibular measurements in the buccolingual direction of female molars.

In summary, because of sample size the only comparison of burial location that can be made is inside vs. outside the church. Differences in some measurements of teeth from different burial locations are statistically significant, but canonical correlations are low. Basically, dental measurements of individuals inside the church are similar to measurements of those outside the church. Nearly 100% of the individuals have shovel-shaped incisors, a Mongoloid trait. In a Spanish population one would not find such a high frequency of this trait. Therefore, all of the individuals buried at the Tipu cemetery are similar and appear to be Maya.

To test the inside vs. outside discriminant function results with a different body of data, more than 150 chi-square tests of nonmetric traits were run. Only eight of the tests are significant at the .05 level (n = 153, 5.23%) which is what can be expected by chance in a series of tests this large. The eight significant traits are maxillary shoveling of the central incisor, maxillary canine distal accessory ridge, enamel extension on the maxillary second molar, anterior fovea on the mandibular first molar, Y groove pattern on the mandibular first molar, + groove pattern on the mandibular third molar, and cusp number six on the mandibular third molar. Therefore, the chi-square results support the conclusion drawn from discriminant function analysis that the individuals buried inside the church are similar to those buried outside.

The Tipu population as a whole is homogeneous, but on a more specific level, family relationships may be seen. For example, the labial groove on the maxillary central and lateral incisors is a low-frequency trait that could isolate individuals who are related within the cemetery. Out of the 11 Colonial Maya individuals with the labial groove trait on the central incisor, 6 are within the church, 3 in the front and 3 in the back. Two individuals buried outside and to the west and three persons buried south of the church have the labial groove. The three burials in the front of the church, an adult female, an adult of unknown sex, and a juvenile, are in close proximity to one another. An examination of shared dental traits and the extent of their expression points to the very good possibility that two of the three individuals, the female and the juvenile, buried in the front of the church were related. These individuals share similar lower molar groove patterns, expressions of the sixth cusp on the lower first molar, and enamel extensions. The three buri-

als in the back of the church, a female and two juveniles, are in close proximity to one another as well. These individuals have a greater number of affinities than the other three. They share the presence and expression of a deflecting wrinkle, Carabelli's cusp, lower molar groove pattern, enamel extensions on the lower second molar, presence of enamel pearls on the upper second molars, and presence of protostylids on the lower molars.

One individual (MT 232 buried to the west of the church) with a labial groove is unique in her dental morphology and any relationship to other individuals would have been obvious. This adult female has her maxillary canine and lateral incisor in rotated positions (Fig. 11.9). The lateral incisor is peg shaped and the canine protrudes from the palate anteriorly. She has stubby roots for both central incisors, low-grade Carabelli's cusp on her first molar, Tome's root on her mandibular first premolar, an enamel extension on her lower second molar, and three-rooted first molars. She appears to be unrelated to anyone else in the cemetery.

In one instance burial placement appears to indicate a family relationship. Two females

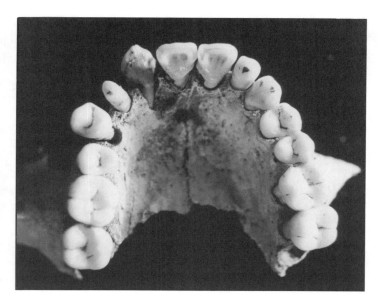

Figure 11.9. Adult male with maxillary canine and lateral peg incisor in rotated positions.

Figure 11.10. Two females who appear to be holding hands.

(MT 169 and MT 171; Fig. 11.10), the former aged 30 to 35 and the latter 25 to 35, were found in what appeared to be a common grave and looked like they were holding hands. Were these individuals related? This does not seem to be the case. One individual (MT 169) exhibits heavy shoveling and double shoveling of the maxillary incisors, an interruption groove, a large tuberculum dentale, and an enamel pearl on a molar. The other individual (MT 171) has low expression of shoveling, no double shoveling, and none of the other features. The only trait they share is a low-grade expression of Carabelli's cusp on the first molar. Perhaps they were good friends.

Analysis of the dental remains from Tipu provides no evidence of Spanish individuals at the site, which lends credence to the theory (Graham et al. 1989) that none of the 600 burials was Spanish. Two individuals were investigated as being possible Spaniards because their burial treatment was different from the rest of the population. One (MT 78) was buried in a coffin in the front of the church and the other (MT 96) was buried with a church censer.

The individual buried in the coffin was between 40 and 50 years of age and was probably a higher status male. His placement within a coffin and burial in the front of the church are consistent with the treatment of important individuals buried at other Spanish Catholic churches such as Tancah in the northern Yucatán Peninsula (Miller and Farriss 1979; Saul 1982), but he did not have any religious paraphernalia such as a cross associated with him. His teeth, including the central incisors, were heavily worn, which made it impossible to code for shovel-shaped incisors, a Mongoloid trait. The nonmetric traits are not revealing owing to occlusal wear, although a large tuberculum dentale on the maxillary lateral incisor and minor expression of a Tome's root on the mandibular first premolar were evident. Some teeth had been lost and the bone resorbed. The dental metrics of the teeth of this individual are consistent with the statistical means of the entire Tipu male population.

Studies of modern populations have shown that Spaniards are generally taller than Maya. Mean height for Spanish males ranges from 159.80 cm to 164.50 cm (n = 18,646) and mean height for Spanish females is 153.05 cm (n = 111) (Aranzandi and Hoyos 1894; Deniker 1907; Oloriz y Aguilera 1896; Williams 1931). Williams (1931) reported mean statures

of 155.24 cm (n = 100) for modern Maya males and 141.52 cm (n = 25) for females. Steggerda (1941) reported similar values of 155.41 cm (n = 128) for males and 141.84 cm (n = 94) for females. The Tipu male in question was 162.20 cm tall, within the range of modern Spanish male stature. However, the mean height for Tipu males is 160.30 cm (n = 149), so he certainly would not have towered above the rest of the population. He and his fellow Tipuans were tall in comparison with modern Maya, and other researchers have found a decrease in stature in some Maya populations between Preclassic and modern times (Nickens 1976; Stewart 1949).

The individual buried with the censer was a female aged 16 to 21 years (Fig. 11.11). The presence of the censer may indicate some special religious function, probably akin to that of

Figure 11.11. Female buried with censer.

an altar boy. Her dental measurements are consistent with the statistical means for the rest of the Tipu females. Nonmetric traits include shoveling of maxillary incisors, an interruption groove on maxillary incisors, and low-grade expression of a tuberculum dentale on the incisors. She has low-grade expression of Carabelli's cusp on the first molar and enamel extensions on the maxillary third molar. On the mandibular teeth she has low-grade expression of Tome's root on the first premolar, a deflecting wrinkle on the first molar, and low-grade expression of the protostylid on the second molar. These traits are all included in the Maya dental complex established above and the woman was most likely Maya. Her stature of 147.50 cm was comparable to the mean for Tipu females (148.30 cm, n = 106), but taller than the mean for modern Maya females. Once again, there is some evidence that Maya stature has declined over time.

Nonmetric traits also were used to understand the relationship of the Tipu Maya to other Maya populations. A Standardized Mean Measure of Divergence (SMMD) was calculated from data derived from the following populations: Tipu (A.D. 1568–1638; Jacobi 1996), Early Seibal (800 B.C.–A.D. 800; Austin 1978), Late Seibal (A.D. 800–900; Austin 1970, 1978), Early Altar de Sacrificios (800 B.C.–A.D. 750; Austin 1970, 1978), Late Altar de Sacrificios (A.D. 750–900; Austin 1970, 1978), Lubaantun (A.D. 650–900; Saul 1975a), Tzeltal (modern Maya; Ángel et al. 1993), Postclassic Lamanai (A.D. 950–1544; Lang 1990; White et al. 1994), Historic Lamanai (A.D. 1544–1641; Lang 1990; White et al. 1994), and Chichén Itzá (A.D. 900–Conquest; Pompa y Padilla 1990). Because the Chichén Itzá data did not include the traits that all the other populations had in common, it was compared to four of the other populations in a separate SMMD calculation. A cautionary note must preface the results: It is problematic to compare data compiled by different observers with varying scoring standards. In addition, with the exception of Tipu and Tzeltal, the sample sizes are small. Nevertheless, bearing these problems in mind, the scant data were used to compare these populations to one another.

Frequencies of five genetically independent traits were derived from all the sources with the exception of Chichén Itzá. The five nonmetric dental traits are: 1) shoveling of the maxillary central incisor, 2) Carabelli's trait on the maxillary first molar, 3) presence of the hypocone on the maxillary second molar, 4) presence of the Y groove pattern on the mandibular second molar, and 5) presence of the sixth cusp on the mandibular first molar. It is preferable to use more that five traits for a study such as this but these were the only traits that all the populations had in common.

The Mean Measure of Divergence (MMD) is calculated using the formula developed by C. A. B. Smith and employed by Berry and Berry (1967, 1972), Buikstra (1976), Green and Suchey (1976), and Johnson and Lovell (1994) among others. To correct for varying sample size, a Standardized Mean Measure of Divergence (SMMD) was calculated by dividing the raw MMD result by its standard deviation (Johnson and Lovell 1994; Sofaer et al. 1986). A SMMD value greater than 2.00 indicates a significant difference at the .05 level (Johnson and Lovell 1994; Sjøvold 1973).

In the results (Table 11.4) it can be seen that there is a significant divergence between Tipu and Late Seibal, Lubaantun, Postclassic Lamanai, and Historic Lamanai. The comparison of Tipu and Tzeltal results in a value of 2.00, which just misses the criterion for significance. There is a significant divergence between Lubaantun and all populations except Early Seibal. This could be due to a number of factors. The archaeological site of Lubaantun is somewhat isolated south of the Maya Mountains in

Table 11.4 Standardized Mean Measure of Divergence of Maya Samples

	Early Seibal	Late Seibal	Early Altar	Late Altar	Tzeltal	Lubaantun	Post-classic Lamanai	Historic Lamanai
Tipu	1.08	2.54*	1.17	1.83	2.00	3.61*	3.61*	3.85*
Early Seibal		1.27	.73	.36	1.64	1.17	1.06	3.52*
Late Seibal			.80	1.00	1.78	3.55*	2.60*	2.00
Early Altar				.89	.67	3.10*	1.54	.80
Late Altar					1.17	2.90*	1.53	.71
Tzeltal						3.71*	2.56*	2.04*
Lubaantun							2.76*	3.32*
Postclassic Lamanai								.31

* Significant at $p < .05$.

Belize and the population may in fact be exhibiting a unique dental morphology. Alternately, we may be seeing the impact of the small sample and a different dental trait scoring methodology. The nearly significant divergence of Tipu from Tzeltal also might be explained by geography. The modern Tzeltal Maya are in the distant highlands of Chiapas in southeastern México. The significant divergence between Tipu and Late Seibal could be explained by an influx of migrants to Seibal as proposed by Marcus (1973) and discussed by Austin (1978) and, more recently, Tourtellot (1990a). These hypothetical immigrants compose a distinct subsample, the Bayal phase, of the Late Seibal skeletal series. (Tourtellot 1990a). However, divergence between Tipu and Late Seibal may again reflect the small sample size from Late Seibal.

Postclassic Lamanai significantly diverges from Tipu, Late Seibal, Tzeltal, and Lubaantun. Historic Lamanai significantly diverges from Tipu, Early Seibal, Tzeltal, and Lubaantun. Lang's (1990) chi-square tests also indicate a significant difference between the Historic Lamanai and Historic Tipu samples. These findings are surprising because Lamanai is close to Tipu geographically and one would expect the populations to be similar. There are several

possible explanations for the divergence. One is that there was a greater amount of admixture of Maya individuals from the northern Yucatán Peninsula at Lamanai than at Tipu. Another is that more refugees from the northern Yucatán Peninsula fleeing Spanish domination found refuge at Lamanai than at Tipu.

Another possible explanation is alluded to by Miller and Farriss (1979) and Saul (1982) concerning Tancah in the northern Yucatán. They believe that there is evidence at Tancah of extended Maya and Spanish coexistence. Miller and Farriss (1979) explain that, although the chapel was only partially tested archaeologically, there is a good possibility that the inside of the church is "crammed" with burials. The burials that they did excavate reflect a Spanish-Maya or *mestizo* population. The Historic Lamanai sample might include *mestizos* whereas the Tipu population does not. Lang's (1990) chi-square results support this conclusion, as there is a difference between the ancestral Postclassic Lamanai and the Historic Lamanai samples. However, the SMMD does not indicate a significant divergence.

In order to include the Chichén Itzá dental material in this study, a second SMMD was calculated using a different set of nonmetric traits (Table 11.5). It would be most informa-

Table 11.5 Standardized Mean Measure of Divergence of Maya Samples Including Chichén Itzá

	Postclassic Lamanai	Historic Lamanai	Chichén Itzá	Tzeltal
Tipu	6.58 *	7.08 *	2.86*	3.75 *
Postclassic Lamanai		1.00	4.58 *	4.21 *
Historic Lamanai			3.69 *	3.56 *
Chichén Itzá				1.25

* Significant at p < .05.

tive to use a historic population from the northern Yucatán for comparison because it is from this region that Maya are said to have fled Spanish control and taken refuge in the Tipu area (Jones 1989). Unfortunately, there is no dental morphology information for such a population, but there is for prehistoric Chichén Itzá (Pompa y Padilla 1990). The traits included in this SMMD were the same as in the previous analysis except for exclusion of shoveling of the maxillary central incisor and addition of the protostylid on the mandibular first molar. The dental samples included are from Tipu, Postclassic Lamanai, Historic Lamanai, modern Tzeltal, and Chichén Itzá. All samples are significantly divergent from one another except for Historic Lamanai compared with Postclassic Lamanai, and Chichén Itzá compared with modern Tzeltal.

Interpretation of these results requires caution. Although the SMMD calculation was designed to correct for varying sample sizes, spuriously significant values might result from comparing small samples to the large Tipu sample and from the limited number of common traits that the observers recorded. Interobserver error is a potential problem as well, and could involve something as simple as misidentification of first vs. second vs. third molars.

The amount of observer experience influences the ability to recognize nonmetric traits regardless of presence of wear, and scoring discrepancies can result. Nichol and Turner (1986) conducted a study on intra- and interobserver concordance and found that certain traits have higher agreement in identification within and between observers than do other traits. Three dental traits recognized by Nichol and Turner as being problematic were used in the comparison of Tipu to other sites: Carabelli's cusp, groove pattern of the lower molar, and protostylid. Even with a good dental cast system such as that offered by Dahlberg (1956) or Turner et al. (1991), consistent standardized use or understanding of the cast by observers cannot be assumed. Cook (pers. comm. 1988) has noted the misidentification in textbooks and other publications of the Y-5 pattern in lower molars. This type of error perpetuates spurious results.

In conclusion, this study has provided a profile of the historic Maya of Tipu. All individuals buried at Tipu are with good probability Maya. There is no evidence to indicate that there were friars or other Spanish individuals buried at the site. There was probably very little or no Spanish-Maya admixture at Tipu.

Immigrant groups of Maya may have been incorporated into the indigenous Tipu population, as historical documents suggest, but based on the nonmetric and metric traits analyzed, the historic Tipu population probably represents successive migrations of the Itzá people over time. During the Postclassic the Itzá migrated into the northern Yucatán and then into the Tipu area. Later, upon contact with the Spanish, the Itzá elite fled from the northern Yucatán to the Tipu area and beyond. In addition, ethnohistorical documents suggest that there were successive *reducciones,* or forced resettlements, of Maya from outlying areas into a compact community at Tipu. This process did not do anything to increase the differences in dental genetic variation. Perhaps recruitment was focused consistently on the same groups of Maya.

The historic Tipu population looks homogeneous and probably was composed of only indigenous individuals. No discriminant analysis could be done on the Postclassic Tipu burials because the sample is too small, so we do not know how they compare to the historic Maya. Future excavations at outlying portions of Tipu may yield a larger sample of prehistoric burials.

There is no difference in either nonmetric or metric traits between the individuals buried inside and outside the church. This is consistent with the findings from a preliminary study by Danforth, Light et al. (1985) using a mix of cranial, dental, and postcranial traits.

When comparing the Tipu population with other Maya using the SMMD, there is significant divergence from Late Seibal, Lubaantun, Postclassic Lamanai, Historic Lamanai, and Chichén Itzá. It should be noted that this comparison might be problematic because of the varying sample sizes, the small number of traits employed in the analysis, and interobserver error.

Future comparisons between Maya populations would be facilitated by more emphasis on dental metric and nonmetric analyses by researchers. Standardization of morphological trait analysis is critical to making meaningful comparisons between populations. Dental morphology casts created by Dahlberg (1956) and Turner et al. (1991) provide a good basis for evaluation and discussion of nonmetric traits.

Acknowledgments

Excavation and analysis of the Tipu material was supported by grants BNS 83-03693 and BNS 85-06785 from the National Science Foundation. I would like to thank Mark Cohen for use of the collection and permission to use certain photos and figures included in the paper. Bruce Hardy provided photographic assistance. I am indebted to Lori Jacobi and Marie Danforth for comments on earlier versions of this paper. Thanks to Kathryn Propst and Paul Jamison for computer assistance.

PART 4

Stable Isotope and DNA Studies

12

Commoner Diet at Copán: Insights from Stable Isotopes and Porotic Hyperostosis

Stephen L. Whittington
and David M. Reed

Archaeological excavations, even when directed by someone sensitive to the value of human skeletal remains for helping answer important questions about Maya civilization, do not always result in large, well-preserved, well-provenienced, or statistically representative samples. Whether or not a collection of human bone from the Maya area has characteristics approaching some ideal, however, it is worthy of analysis because it contains data concerning ancient diseases, causes of death, and population structure. Osteologists have the responsibility of describing relevant cultural, temporal, geographic, and statistical characteristics for a sample and presenting data on pathology and demography within these contexts. In what follows, we attempt to live up to this responsibility as we describe results of our analysis of commoner skeletons from Copán, Honduras.

The population of Copán, a major center of Maya civilization, was affected by the processes that caused Classic civilization to collapse at many sites throughout the southern lowlands.

Dated monuments ceased to be erected at Copán in the early 9th century A.D. (Schele and Freidel 1990), at which time centralized political authority is assumed to have disappeared, but the valley continued to be populated until the early 13th century (Webster and Freter 1990a). There is evidence from pollen cores that environmental degradation was associated with the collapse (Abrams and Rue 1988; Rue 1987).

We studied human skeletons from the low-status segment of Copán's population in order to learn about health and diet around the time of the collapse. We considered individuals buried in Type 1 and Type 2 sites as defined by Willey and Leventhal (1979), Aggregate sites as defined by Webster and Freter (1990a), or various types of nonmound sites to be commoners. Type 1 and Aggregate sites are similar in their small size and structural simplicity, so we grouped them together under the heading "Type 1" for this analysis. Except for nonmound sites, commoners came from small residential compounds with between two and eight structures, usually organized around one or two plazas. We considered individuals from larger, more complex Type 3 and Type 4 sites to be high-status or elite. In all, 163 skeletons excavated in the Copán Valley during the 1970s and 1980s fit the definition of low status (Table 12.1).

Whittington subjected the skeletal remains of 145 low-status individuals to detailed osteological analysis and 3 to cursory examinations. This produced data on pathological bone and tooth lesions, age-at-death, and sex used in this study. Reed performed stable carbon and nitrogen isotope analysis on 22 of the 148, on an additional 3 commoners, and on 57 elite individuals. Rebecca Storey (pers. comm. 1991) determined age and sex for the elite and the additional low-status individuals. Reed chose materials for isotopic analysis to represent all social, political, and demographic spectra and to assess expected dietary variability. In all, he analyzed 82 humans, 5 deer, and 1 jaguar.

Skeletons of low-status people came from both urban and rural locations. The density of structures in the Main Group and surrounding crowded residential areas is 1484/km^2. Outside of this area structure density decreases to between 30/km^2 and 139/km^2 (Webster and Freter 1990a).

Skeletons in the sample were from three archaeological phases as defined by Webster and Freter (1990a). The Acbi phase (A.D. 400–700) was a time of population growth and the development of Copán's political power. The early Coner phase (A.D. 700–800) was just before the collapse of Copán's political power, when the population growth rate reached its maximum and population size approached its peak. The late Coner phase (post–A.D. 800) was after the collapse of centralized political power, when population size began to decline (Webster et al. 1992). Coner phase skeletons lacking contextual indications of being from the early part of the phase were assigned to the late Coner phase by default.

Table 12.1 Characteristics of Copán Low-Status Skeletons (n = 163)

Skeleton From	n[a]
Site type	
Type 1 or Aggregate	54
Type 2	97
Nonmound or unknown	12
Site location	
Rural	47
Urban	116
Phase	
Acbi	13
Early Coner	17
Late Coner	114
Unknown	19
Sex	
Male	42
Female	47
Unknown	74

[a]n = number of individuals.

Various problems complicated analysis of the low-status skeletal sample at Copán. Poor preservation of bone was the major obstacle, interfering with determination of age and sex and forcing us to deemphasize negative evidence of lesions in reconstructing disease processes. Small sample size was another problem, because high variance in small samples allows spurious and contradictory data patterns to arise. There is evidence, especially in terms of infant underrepresentation, that the distribution of age-at-death derived from the sample of skeletons at Copán may not accurately reflect the structure of the living population. Finally, some basic archaeological data for the burials could not be determined with desired precision.

Methods

Whittington recorded state of preservation and evidence of pathology, including size of lesions and whether they were active or healed, for all bone fragments. A bone was considered to be free of a particular lesion only when more than 50% of the part usually affected was preserved and no lesion was present. It was considered to have missing data if less than 50% was preserved and no lesion was present.

Sex was determined through osteological analysis and multivariate statistics. When possible, physical traits of the pelvis and cranium (Bass 1971) were used to sex individuals. When visual sexing was impossible, discriminant functions similar to those created by Giles (1970) and Ditch and Rose (1972), but tailored to this population, were applied to bone and tooth measurements to increase the number of sexed individuals.

A calculation of "exact" age-at-death for each individual was used to answer questions concerning age patterning of morbidity and mortality. The complex methodology involved in the calculation has been described elsewhere (Whittington 1992).

Bone specimens for stable isotope analysis were preferentially taken from ribs when available. Otherwise, several grams of miscellaneous bone fragments were removed from the skeleton. Differences in the isotopic composition of collagen extracted from different skeletal elements are insignificant (DeNiro and Schoeniger 1983).

A protocol for collagen preparation was developed based on the widely used hydrochloric acid and sodium hydroxide procedure (Ambrose 1990; DeNiro and Weiner 1988; Schoeninger and DeNiro 1984). The protocol used is further detailed in Reed (1994). Only well-preserved specimens were used for isotopic analysis.

Stable Isotopes

Stable isotope ratios of carbon and nitrogen in bone collagen can be used to infer diet (DeNiro and Epstein 1978, 1981). Extensive reviews and critiques of the process have been published by various authors (Ambrose 1993; De-Niro 1987; Katzenberg 1992; Keegan 1989; Schoeninger and Moore 1992; Schwarcz and Schoeninger 1991; van der Merwe 1982).

The measurement of the isotopic composition of a material is expressed in per mil (‰) as the deviation of the heavy to light isotope ratio in the sample from the ratio in a standard reference. The notation for carbon is $\delta^{13}C_{PDB}$ and the reference is the rostrum from the Cretaceous Pee Dee Belemnite formation (PDB). The notation for nitrogen is $\delta^{15}N_{AIR}$ and the reference is ambient air (AIR).

Isotopic ratios can be related to either terrestrial plant or marine sources (DeNiro 1987). Terrestrial plants can be divided into three photosynthetic types: Calvin (C_3), Hatch-Slack (C_4) or Crassulacean Acid Metabolism (CAM). Typically, C_3 plants have a $\delta^{13}C_{PDB}$ value of -27‰, C_4 plants show a mean $\delta^{13}C_{PDB}$ value of -12.5‰, and CAM plants have $\delta^{13}C_{PDB}$ values between -10‰ and -28‰ (Coleman and Fry 1991). Nitrogen isotopes can be used to distinguish between marine animals ($\delta^{15}N_{AIR} > 12$‰) and terrestrial plant sources ($\delta^{15}N_{AIR} < 10$‰). DeNiro (1987) also used them to distinguish between legumes ($\delta^{15}N_{AIR} = 1$‰), all of which are also C_3-based, and nonlegumes ($\delta^{15}N_{AIR} = 9$‰). These isotopic signatures, along with paleobotanical, paleopathological, and social interpretations of the archaeological record, provide a direct method for assessing diet.

Figure 12.1 shows the relationship between the faunal and human specimens of all social levels. From these values we conclude that humans had a diet rich in C_4 plants, supplemented by small amounts of food from other sources. Current evidence supports the identification of maize as the only source for ^{13}C enrichment at Copán. Deer, the most likely meat source, were clearly feeding on C_3 plants and were not con-

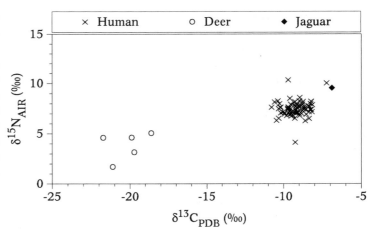

Figure 12.1. Isotopic values for humans at Copán reflect a diet rich in maize, a C_4 plant. Values for deer, which fed on C_3 plants, are very different than those for humans, meaning that deer did not contribute significantly to human diet. The diet of the jaguar included animals eating C_4 plants.

tributing to the enriched signal measured for humans. If deer were a major food source for humans, then the isotopic values for humans would be much closer to those of deer. The jaguar had a diet that included animals eating C_4 plants.

From t-tests, which test equality of group means, we infer that the central tendencies for both the carbon and nitrogen isotope measures of the elite and commoners are essentially equal (Table 12.2). The values of t, df, and p in our tables are based on independent, separate variances t-tests, without any assumption of equal variances (Wilkinson et al. 1992). The range of carbon isotope values for the elite is greater than that for commoners (Fig. 12.2). The inference is that elite diet was more varied than commoner diet. The range difference appears not to be related to meat consumption, because the nitrogen isotope values for individuals with ^{13}C enrichment are the same as the values for the rest of the adults. Lentz (1991) interpreted evidence from paleobotany as indicating that high-status individuals had access to a wider variety of plants than did low-status individuals.

When t-tests are calculated, the null hypothesis of equal carbon and nitrogen means cannot be rejected within the low-status segment of the population for groups based on site type, location of burial, or phase (Table 12.2). Although not statistically significant, the patterns are worth describing.

For type and location, the only difference between groups is in the range of carbon values. Lower status individuals, from Type 1 sites, have a more restricted range of carbon values (Fig. 12.3). The inference is that they had access to fewer food choices than did people in Type 2 sites. Carbon values have a greater range in the urban area than in the rural area (Fig. 12.4). We interpret this to mean that urban individuals had access to a wider variety of foods.

Based on carbon and nitrogen values, we suggest that diet was more restricted and higher in maize content during the Acbi and early Coner phases, a period of growth, than during the late Coner phase, a period of decline (Fig. 12.5). This means that diet became more diverse at the same time that the political situation and environment at Copán were degenerating.

For groups divided by sex, t-tests result in rejection of the null hypothesis of equal means for nitrogen but not for carbon. However, two males have extreme carbon isotope values and a female has an extreme nitrogen isotope value (Fig. 12.6). If they are excluded from the analyses, then t-tests result in highly significant differences between means for males and females.

Table 12.2   Isotopic Differences by Subpopulation

Group	n	Mean	sd	t	df	p
$\delta^{13}C_{PDB}$						
Commoners	23	−9.29	.45	−.80	61.7	.427
Elite	43	−9.17	.70			
Type 1/Aggregate site	9	−9.37	.35	−.75	2.9	.460
Type 2 site	14	−9.24	.51			
Rural	9	−9.41	.36	1.07	2.7	.296
Urban	14	−9.21	.50			
Acbi/early Coner	5	−9.06	.33	−1.61	9.0	.141
Late Coner	18	−9.35	.47			
Male with outliers	12	−9.17	.52	−1.33	19.1	.198
Female	11	−9.42	.34			
Male without outliers	10	−8.96	.19	−3.84	15.8	.001
Female	11	−9.42	.34			
$\delta^{15}N_{AIR}$						
Commoners	23	7.60	.51	1.22	42.7	.228
Elite	43	7.45	.48			
Type 1/Aggregate site	9	7.49	.52	−.84	17.3	.411
Type 2 site	14	7.68	.52			
Rural	9	7.54	.64	.47	12.7	.650
Urban	14	7.65	.43			
Acbi/early Coner	5	7.41	.49	.98	6.7	.363
Late Coner	18	7.66	.52			
Male	12	7.82	.41	−2.27	19.0	.035
Female with outlier	11	7.37	.53			
Male	12	7.82	.41	−3.32	19.7	.003
Female without outlier	10	7.26	.39			

NOTE: n = number of specimens; sd = standard deviation; t = t-test statistic; df = degrees of freedom; p = p-value.

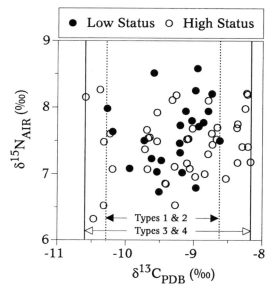

Figure 12.2. Isotopic values for social statuses. The range of carbon values is greater for the elite than for commoners.

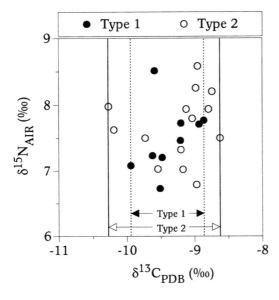

Figure 12.3. Isotopic values for site types. The range of carbon values is greater for larger, more complex sites.

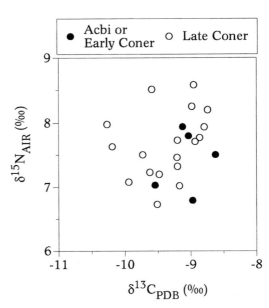

Figure 12.5. Isotopic values for phases. Both carbon and nitrogen values are more restricted for period of population growth.

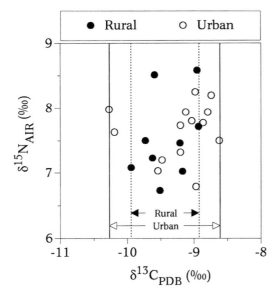

Figure 12.4. Isotopic values for burial locations. The range of carbon values is greater in the most densely populated part of the Copán Valley.

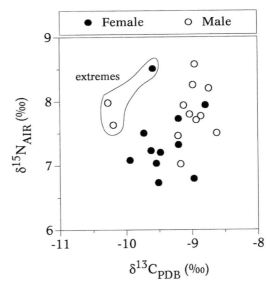

Figure 12.6. Isotopic values for sexes. If outliers are excluded, carbon and nitrogen values tend to form separate clusters for each sex.

Males are typically enriched in the less common isotopes. There was a distinct difference between low-status male and female diets, with males more often eating meals composed of a higher proportion of maize. Similar differences between the sexes have been reported for other groups of ancient tropical agriculturalists in Belize and lower Central America (Norr 1991; White et al. 1993), but with greater shifts in mean values.

Porotic Hyperostosis

Porotic hyperostosis is a pathological condition that has been noted in skeletal series from many locations and times. The cranial lesions of porotic hyperostosis are characterized by expansion of the cancellous part, or diploë, and thinning of the outer table to the extent that small holes pierce the cortex and communicate with the underlying cancellous bone (El-Najjar and Robertson 1976; Hooton 1930;

Ortner and Putschar 1985; Roberts 1987). Osteoporotic pitting and spongy hyperostosis are other names for the lesions found on the frontal, parietals, or occipital in areas where muscles do not attach (El-Najjar et al. 1976). Lesions in the roofs of the eye orbits are called cribra orbitalia. Ortner and Putschar (1985) commented that both cribra and porotic hyperostosis may be found in a single skull, but each may occur separately.

Saul (1977) distinguished between active and healed porotic hyperostosis. Active lesions have significant diploic expansion and sharp-edged, raw-looking holes in the cortex and demonstrate the presence of disease at the time of death (Fig. 12.7). Healed lesions also involve thickened diploë, but the holes may be partially filled in, smaller, and have rounded edges owing to bone remodeling (Fig. 12.8). Healed lesions demonstrate that a pathological state was survived sometime before death occurred (Stuart-Macadam 1985).

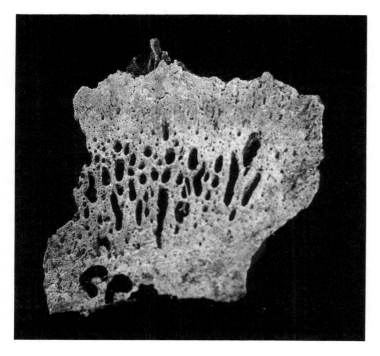

Figure 12.7. Porotic hyperostosis on cranium of a Coner phase 7-year-old from an urban Type 2 site. Vault lesions have sharp edges characteristic of cases that were active at time of death.

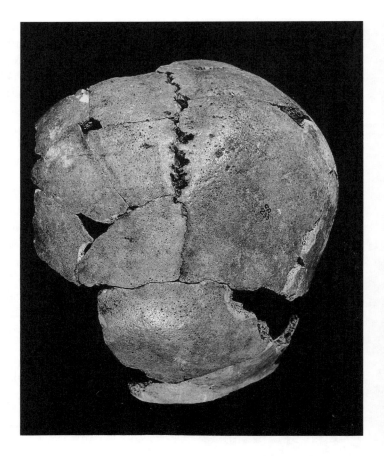

Figure 12.8. Porotic hyperostosis on cranium of a Coner phase 30- to 34-year-old male from a rural Type 1 site. Healed vault lesions have rounded edges due to remodeling.

Steinbock (1976) concluded that nearly all porotic hyperostosis in the Prehispanic New World was caused by iron deficiency anemia. The frequency of lesions of porotic hyperostosis in a sample of skeletons represents a minimum estimate of iron deficiency anemia in the population because bone changes in modern cases of anemia are rare (Ortner and Putschar 1985). Duration, rather than severity, apparently is the critical factor (Perou 1964).

Iron deficiency anemia can have a variety of causes. It is more often the result of poor absorption and heavy iron losses than of diets with deficient iron content (Wing and Brown 1979). Iron in vegetables is much less readily absorbed than that in meat (Baker and Mathan 1975) and maize contains phytates, chemicals that interfere with iron absorption (Fleming 1977). Diseases of the digestive system may be accompanied by internal blood loss and impaired iron absorption (Layrisse and Roche 1964). Some helminthic intestinal infections occurred in the Maya area before European contact, including those caused by *Ancylostoma*, the variety of hookworm that results in the greatest blood loss (Shattuck 1938). Chronic diarrhea related to parasitic infection can cause further iron absorption problems (Saul 1972a). Anemia and infection have a synergistic relationship, one aspect of which is that infection depresses appetite and causes iron to be diverted from the plasma to the liver and other organs (Lallo et al. 1977; Scrimshaw and Tejada 1970; Wing and Brown 1979).

Cribra orbitalia or porotic hyperostosis appeared on 44 out of 157 skeletons of nonfetal low-status individuals at Copán. Many of the skulls lacking evidence were poorly preserved and did not have enough of the ectocranial surface or orbits present for evaluation, so 28% is a minimum estimate of the frequency of lesions. A more realistic estimate can be obtained by controlling for preservation. For individuals possessing more than 50% of parts of the cranium normally affected by both cribra orbitalia and porotic hyperostosis, 14 out of 22, or 64%, had some evidence of anemia.

Table 12.3 shows the breakdown of the evidence for anemia by type of lesion and divides the population between subadults (i.e., those younger than 20 years of age) and adults. For subadults, 59% showed evidence of vault lesions and 38% cribra, while for adults, 60% had vault lesions and 21% cribra.

In comparison with published frequencies from other archaeological sites (Corruccini 1983; El-Najjar and Robertson 1976; Stuart-Macadam 1987), the observed frequencies of cribra in subadults and adults at Copán are above average. The frequency of porotic hyperostosis in adults is remarkable in absolute terms, relative to the frequency of porotic hyperostosis in subadults, and relative to the fre-

Table 12.3 Cases of Anemia by Age-at-Death

Group	Porotic Hyperostosis[a]		Cribra Orbitalia[b]	
	Absent	Present	Absent	Present
Adults	12	18	22	6
Subadults	7	10	5	3

[a] More than 50% of ectocranial surface present.

[b] More than 50% of orbital surfaces present.

quency of cribra. A high overall frequency of porotic hyperostosis and a relatively high frequency of porotic hyperostosis among adults are patterns that have been found in some other studies of Maya populations, including Altar de Sacrificios (Saul 1972a), Chichén Itzá (Hooton 1930, 1940), and Playa del Carmen (Márquez, Peraza et al. 1982).

The relationship between mean age-at-death and anemia is shown in Table 12.4. Even poorly preserved crania with lesions are included to maximize the number of individuals upon which

Table 12.4 Differences in Age-at-Death by Presence of Anemia

Group	n	Mean	sd	t	df	p
Adults						
Vault lesions absent[a]	12	45.08	8.97	2.98	19.7	.007
Vault lesions present[b]	26	36.02	8.13			
Cribra absent[c]	22	38.43	1.06	−.41	18.0	.685
Cribra present[d]	10	39.98	9.77			
Subadults						
Vault lesions absent[a]	7	3.34	5.50	−.68	11.4	.509
Vault lesions present[b]	14	5.05	5.17			
Cribra absent[c]	5	5.23	5.60	.05	6.7	.965
Cribra present[d]	4	5.07	5.41			

NOTE: n = number of individuals; sd = standard deviation; t = t-test statistic; df = degrees of freedom; p = p-value.

[a] More than 50% of ectocranial surface present.

[b] Any amount of ectocranial surface present.

[c] More than 50% of orbital surfaces present.

[d] Any amount of orbital surfaces present.

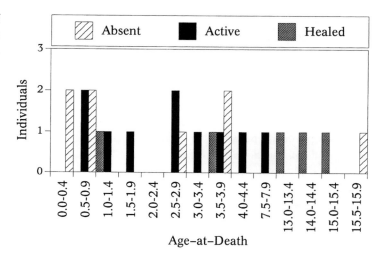

Figure 12.9. Lesions of anemia by age-at-death in subadults.

mean age is based. The t-test results may be interpreted as indicating that adults with healed porotic hyperostosis had a significantly lower mean age-at-death than did adults without lesions, the implications of which will be discussed below.

Only subadults had evidence of active vault lesions or cribra at time of death, and healed lesions became more common with increasing age. Figure 12.9 shows the cases of anemia in subadults by age-at-death. Active cases occurred between the ages of 6 months and 7.5 years, with the earliest healed case in a 1.25-year-old. This healed case must have been active some months prior to death, probably during the latter half of the first year of life. We interpret the fact that anemia appears only in infants more than 6 months old to mean that babies were not born with insufficient iron reserves, but had insufficient dietary iron intakes after their uterine iron stores were depleted (Stuart-Macadam 1987). The data are too sparse to draw stronger conclusions about the relationship of age to incidence of anemia.

Table 12.5 can be divided into four separate four-factor contingency tables based on the variables in the "Group" column: site type, location, phase, and sex. The four factors in each contingency table are subpopulation (e.g., Type 1

Table 12.5 Cases of Anemia by Subpopulation

Group	Porotic Hyperostosis[a] Absent	Porotic Hyperostosis[a] Present	Cribra Orbitalia[b] Absent	Cribra Orbitalia[b] Present
Adults				
Type 1/				
Aggregate site	5	9	10	4
Type 2 site	7	7	11	2
Rural	3	11	9	3
Urban	9	7	13	3
Acbi	0	1	2	0
Early Coner	1	2	5	1
Late Coner	10	15	15	5
Male	5	8	14	1
Female	6	9	8	4
Subadults				
Type 1/				
Aggregate site	2	3	2	3
Type 2 site	5	7	3	0
Rural	2	1	1	1
Urban	5	9	4	2
Acbi	1	1	0	0
Early Coner	0	1	1	1
Late Coner	6	8	4	2
Male	0	1	1	0
Female	1	2	2	1

[a] More than 50% of ectocranial surface present.

[b] More than 50% of orbital surfaces present.

vs. Type 2), age (adults vs. subadults), lesion type (porotic hyperostosis vs. cribra orbitalia), and presence of lesions (present vs. absent). One way to analyze a multiway contingency table so that the relationships between the variables can be described is by using log-linear models of independence (Knoke and Burke 1980). Log-linear modeling of subsets of data in Table 12.5 yields no significant interactions between presence of lesions and subpopulations of individuals based on phase, sex, location, or site type (Whittington 1989).

Although subpopulation differences are not statistically significant, they are worth noting. Evidence of anemia is most common among late Coner individuals and least common among Acbi individuals. The rural frequency of lesions of anemia is higher than the urban frequency. Evidence of anemia is slightly more common in Type 1 sites than in Type 2 sites. Females have more evidence of anemia than do males.

Discussion

Wood et al. (1992) have demonstrated the inherent difficulty with extrapolating from pathological lesions on individual skeletons to population mortality levels. They have shown that the relative health status of two populations may be counterintuitive, with high prevalence of lesions and low average age-at-death actually pointing to the healthier population. If these problems are true for well-preserved skeletons in samples that are accurate reflections of the age distribution of the living population, how much more so must they be true for samples such as this one?

Lesions of anemia appear in a high proportion of low-status skeletons from Copán. There certainly were one or more stresses in the environment causing these lesions. The proportion of skeletons with lesions is high in comparison with other populations, but whether we are dealing with an especially unhealthy population or one composed of robust individuals able to survive the stresses long enough for bone lesions to form is unclear. The proportions of adults and subadults with porotic hyperostosis are nearly equal, supporting the latter interpretation. Assuming it is driven by mortality, the significantly lower average age-at-death for adults with porotic hyperostosis would seem to contradict this. These contradictory results do not help us to understand the implications of porotic hyperostosis at Copán.

Sattenspiel and Harpending (1983) have shown that average age-at-death is more strongly influenced by fertility than by mortality. The group with porotic hyperostosis, therefore, may have had much higher fertility than the group without lesions. If true, this would support the interpretation that the population was robust. Such an unlikely situation could arise because of hidden heterogeneity within the low-status population, producing relatively advantaged and relatively disadvantaged groups.

We explored potential sources of heterogeneity with log-linear models, but no subpopulation differences in presence of lesions were statistically significant. Unless some other factor caused heterogeneity, there is no support for equating low average age-at-death and high fertility in the low-status population. It would be dangerous to try to interpret the nonsignificant patterns, as they could be due to small sample size, related to synergism, or caused by some other factor.

Stable isotope ratios have been tied experimentally to diet in living organisms and their interpretation in skeletal populations is potentially less fraught with difficulty than interpretation of pathological lesions. From stable isotope ratios we know that maize made up a great proportion of the diet and that deer meat contributed relatively little. A direct relationship between presence of anemia and stable isotope ratios would provide us with additional

Table 12.6 Isotopic Differences by Pathology

Group	n	Mean	sd	t	df	p
$\delta^{13}C_{PDB}$						
Anemia absent[a]	4	−9.39	.59	.32	5.2	.976
Anemia present[b]	9	−9.40	.52			
Infection absent[c]	9	−9.41	.51	−2.79	7.1	.026
Infection present[d]	2	−8.85	.15			
$\delta^{15}N_{AIR}$						
Anemia absent[a]	4	7.33	.43	−1.77	6.5	.122
Anemia present[b]	9	7.81	.50			
Infection absent[c]	9	7.49	.48	−3.63	2.8	.041
Infection present[d]	2	8.39	.27			

NOTE: n = number of specimens; sd = standard deviation; t = t-test statistic; df = degrees of freedom; p = p-value.

[a] More than 50% of ectocranial and orbital surfaces present.

[b] Any amount of ectocranial or orbital surface present.

[c] More than 50% of ectocranial surface present.

[d] Any amount of ectocranial surface present.

insights into the effects of a high-maize diet on the health status of the population. This tantalizing possibility remains unproven for Copán.

No significant differences between groups with and without healed lesions appeared in t-tests run on carbon and nitrogen isotope values in adults divided into groups based on presence of evidence of anemia (Table 12.6). Lack of significant differences in these adults may relate to the fact that healed lesions reflect anemia occurring many years before death, but isotope values reflect diet closer to time of death. However, it may relate to the complex patterns introduced by the synergism between diet and infection.

Significant differences between groups appeared in t-tests run on groups based on presence or absence of active periosteal reactions, evidence of active infection at time of death (Fig. 12.10). Whatever diseases were causing the active infections probably also influenced or reflected the afflicted person's eating habits. Unlike the case of healed lesions of anemia, active lesions of infection and isotope values represent two relatively contemporaneous aspects of life.

Group differences in stable isotopes at Copán appear to be on the order of .5‰ when central tendencies are examined. Most differences are not statistically significant and may be due to small sample size, the confounding effects of synergism, the range of dietary choices or some other factor. Only the differences between males and females are significant and safe to interpret. Males had more restricted diets and ate a higher proportion of maize than did females. It is not intuitively clear whether a restricted, high-maize diet was healthy, reflecting access to staple crops, or unhealthy, reflecting lack of food options.

In the overall picture of low-status people at Copán, we interpret available evidence as meaning that it was relatively unimportant whether individuals were buried in Type 1 or Type 2 sites, died before or after the political collapse, or were buried in rural or urban sections of the Copán Valley. Most subpopulation differences in stable isotopes and frequencies of anemia are not statistically significant. With

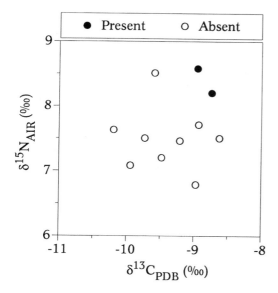

Figure 12.10. Isotopic values for individuals with and without active cranial infections at time of death. Carbon and nitrogen values form separate clusters for each group.

recover small, delicate remains, might help to reduce subadult underrepresentation. More obsidian hydration dates and a more fine-grained ceramic typology would increase the chances of assigning each burial to a narrow range of dates and controlling for temporal changes in site type due to internal population growth.

Osteologists undertaking similar projects at Copán and other Maya sites in years to come can work to change the ways in which archaeologists gather some data and the priorities of excavators, but must accept the limitations imposed by poor preservation and confront them in creative ways. For example, new isotopic and chemical techniques add data to support or refute conclusions derived by other means. Statistical techniques allow significant patterns to be separated from merely tantalizing ones.

Considering cultural, demographic, chemical, and pathological data together in a sophisticated paleoepidemiological approach is critical to interpretation in Maya osteology. The patterns that emerge from individual osteological studies utilizing this approach can be fit together into a coherent picture which, when combined with patterns from archaeological, epigraphic, paleobotanical, and other types of studies, can help in constructing models of Maya civilization and the complex processes surrounding its Classic collapse in the southern lowlands.

the exception of sex, it does not matter to which subpopulations low-status individuals belonged, as all experienced a similar lifestyle.

Representativeness and Interpretation in Maya Osteology

Wood et al. (1992) suggested what can be done to improve interpretation of skeletons left behind by a culture. We would like to add our own suggestions for Mayanists, particularly those working at Copán and similar sites, based on the degree of representativeness of the sample of low-status skeletons. Excavations of more small sites, including both the earliest and latest ones, would produce a larger skeletal sample, which would decrease variance and increase the likelihood of uncovering significant subpopulation differences. More careful excavations, including extensive use of screening to

Acknowledgments

The osteological and isotopic analyses described were performed while we were graduate students in the Department of Anthropology at The Pennsylvania State University (PSU), University Park Campus. David Reed performed the isotopic analyses in the Department of Geosciences Mass Spectroscopy of Minerals Laboratory at PSU, under the supervision of Peter Deines. We appreciate the guidance of Peter Dienes (Department of Geosciences), James Hatch, Robert Eckhardt, George Milner, David Webster, Henry Harpending, William Sanders (Department of Anthropology), the late Clifford Clogg (Departments of Sociology and Statistics), and Rebecca Storey (Department of Anthropology, University of Houston). Research funds for isotopic analyses were provided to David Reed by the National Institutes of Health through a Biomedical Research Support Grant, by the Hill Foundation Fund through the Department of Anthropology, PSU, and by the College of Liberal Arts, PSU. Additional funds for equipment were provided to Peter Deines by the National Science Foundation (EAR 85-11549). Funding for osteological analysis was provided to Stephen Whittington by the National Science Foundation through a Dissertation Improvement Grant (BNS 83-14234) and by a Hill Foundation Fellowship. Excavations, laboratory research, and removal of bone specimens for analysis were undertaken with the kind permission of the Instituto Hondureño de Antropología e Historia.

13

Ancient Diet at Lamanai and Pacbitun: Implications for the Ecological Model of Collapse

Christine D. White

Mayanists in archaeology and physical anthropology have been preoccupied with unravelling the mystery of the so-called "collapse" of Maya civilization for years. The current prevailing explanatory theory, the ecological model, happens to be one that physical anthropologists, particularly, are able to test. The ecological model has existed for over 20 years, but was recently revived in one of its more extreme forms by Santley et al. (1986). It attributes the downfall of Maya society to overexploitation of the environment brought about by attempts to sustain a maize staple in a fragile environment, under conditions of population pressure. As part and parcel of this process, malnutrition, infection, and demographic collapse are believed to be associated with agricultural intensification, monocropping, and environmental degradation. By reconstructing diet and analyzing pathology, physical anthropologists can provide good indirect data which address the relationships between maize consumption, disease, and agricultural intensification resulting from population pressure. It is my contention, however, that the ecological model of collapse should be clearly distinguished from any general nutritional model. It is also my belief that the evidence for an ecological model that is inclusive of a nutritional model, and is based on pathology data alone, will be equivocal. The argument for discrete ecological and nutritional models of collapse is presented here from a theoretical perspective, focusing primarily on the ancient Maya food experience at Lamanai, Belize, with some comparison from Pacbitun. The focus of the data will be on dental pathology as it relates to isotopic measurements ($^{13}C/^{12}C$ and $^{15}N/^{14}N$) in bone collagen from previous studies (White et al. 1993; White and Schwarcz 1989).

Three long-held assumptions have helped to sustain the ecological/nutritional model. The first is the "myth of the *milpa*," the belief that slash-and-burn horticulture was the only subsistence practice in Mayadom. This belief was based on two lines of evidence: it was the only technique observed by Spanish *conquistadores* upon their arrival, and it was the only system used since. *Milpa,* or "dryland outfield" production, and monocropping result in the kind of massive soil depletion that would result in ecological degradation and ultimately fail to support the high population densities existing at most Maya sites. However, it is now known that the Preconquest Maya were sophisticated in their subsistence practices and had developed highly intensive, highly productive agrotechnologies involving crop combinations and water control techniques which were more ecologically sound than *milpa,* such as raised fields and terraces (Turner and Harrison 1983). However, even destroying the myth of the *milpa* cannot completely negate the ecological model. For example, recent evidence from Pacbitun suggests that the development of intensive agriculture seems to coincide with increasing population density (White et al. 1993). Therefore, it is still possible that, in spite of efforts to improve production, the agricultural carrying capacity of the environment was overreached in this area, and possibly in others.

The second assumption was that maize was the staple food throughout Maya history. Not only does it appear frequently in iconography and codices, but the Spanish describe its paramount social and religious importance (e.g., Landa 1566, in Tozzer 1941). However, because the physiography of the Maya region is so diverse, the dietary dominance of maize has been challenged by models which reflect alternate resource potential. In addition to maize, both root crops (*Manihot esculenta;* Bronson 1966) and ramón nuts (*Brosimum alicastrum;* Puleston 1982) have been proposed as staples. Resource diversity models include backyard (kitchen) gardening, the "artificial rain forest" (Wiseman 1973), and multispecies horticulture (Harris 1978; Marcus 1982; Sanders and Price 1968; Wilkin 1971). Notably all of these models are based on C_3 plants and suggest that dependency on maize (a C_4 plant) was reduced by combining it with a number of other plants (e.g., beans, cucurbits, peppers, tomatoes, etc.). To date, there has been no good evidence to support such models on any large or long-term scale in the past. Both palynological data and carbon isotopes from human bone collagen are interpreted to suggest that maize was the dominant food plant from Preclassic times on, and in spite of the varied resource potential of the area, most archaeologists accept maize as the staple in Maya diet. However, recent chemical studies indicate a considerable degree of temporal and regional diversity in the relative amounts of maize in the diet reflecting the variable physiography of the Maya area (Reed 1992; White et al. 1993; White and Schwarcz 1989; Wright 1994). Clearly we need to reassess traditional notions of dietary and cultural conformity among the Maya.

The third assumption forms the basis for the nutritional model. It arises from the belief that skeletal and dental pathology are correlated with high maize consumption (Danforth, Bennett et al. 1985b; Hooton 1940; Kennedy 1983; Saul 1972a; Storey 1992a; Whittington 1989), a phenomenon observed in modern contemporary populations (Scrimshaw and Tejada 1970). While there is little doubt that nutritional, infectious, and parasitic disease can lead to demographic instability and the eventual collapse of a culture, Santley et al. (1986) imply that these conditions are attributable to an increase in maize production, which, in turn, is an indicator of environmental stress. In particular, anemia, which is commonly found in Maya skeletal material, is given a maize-based etiology (Béhar 1968; Scrimshaw and Tejada 1970; Shattuck 1938). As modern research indicates, maize-dependent diets are iron and protein deficient, even when processed with alkali to maximize nutritional yield (Katz et al. 1974). Hooton (1940) was the first to suggest a nutritional cause for collapse, based on the high frequency of iron deficiency he found at Chichén Itzá, but there are two problems in using anemia as a correlate of the Maya downfall. First of all, under conditions of ecological stress and increasing population density, maize should be harder to produce. One would expect to see efforts to intensify agriculture, but the increasing value placed on maize should also show up as a reduction in the amount of maize being consumed by the common population and more extreme status differences in diet. In the absence of outright starvation, a reduction in maize consumption implies a shift to other kinds of foods, and should result in less maize-based malnutrition. It does not follow that those substituted foods will also be iron poor. Certainly, ethnohistorical documents refer to the substitution of wild foods in times of environmental stress (Marcus 1982). These "starvation" foods were less preferred for taste and cultural reasons and would not have yielded as many calories as maize, but were probably qualitatively more nutritional. A shift away from any staple could have either the advantage of creating a greater dietary diversity which is also usually healthier, or the disadvantage of supporting fewer people. Although a drop in the consumption of maize could result in demographic instability, it would not necessarily result in maize-based nutritional problems such as anemia and protein deficiency. Thus, our interpretations can turn on several important questions: Was maize at its peak consumption rate at the time of collapse? Did protein consumption change just prior to collapse? Is there a quantifiable association between diet and nonspecific stress indicators? Santley et al. (1986) note that anemia can be caused by parasites as well as nutritional iron deficiency, and suggest that an increasing parasitic- and infectious-disease burden might have contributed to collapse. The endemic load of parasites in the prehistoric Maya is yet undetermined, but hypothesized to be quite heavy (Podo-Ledezma 1985). Evidence from Lamanai, however, suggests that parasitic infection might have been a greater problem *after* the Conquest

(White et al. 1994). In order to support a model in which nutritional poverty is equated with ecological collapse, we really need to have good skeletal evidence of malnutriton and starvation. At present, this does not exist.

Previous chemical analysis at Lamanai is interpreted to attest to the importance of maize in ancient Maya diet from the Preclassic (ca. 1500 B.C.) to Historic (A.C. 1670) periods, but significant dietary fluctuations also appear to be associated with cultural change (White and Schwarcz 1989). Notably, when maize consumption was at its lowest point during the Terminal Classic, the site was far from collapse. In fact, it was experiencing a revitalization.

In theory, chemical reconstruction of diet and nutritional and dental pathology should create congruent lines of evidence. At Lamanai, for example, there is an association, from the Preclassic to the Postclassic period, between maize consumption (measured chemically) and malnutrition (measured by the skeletal manifestation of iron deficiency anemia; Fig. 13.1). Maize consumption can also be measured by gross pathology in the dentition. The two best preserved measures of dental pathology from Lamanai are caries and enamel hypoplasia.

The only other dental study of similar temporal depth for both pathological conditions in the Maya area comes from Altar de Sacrificios (Saul 1972a). At Altar, just prior to its aban-

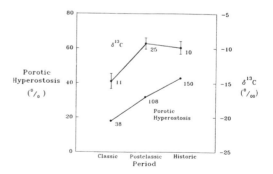

Figure 13.1. Rise in C_4 food consumption associated with porotic hyperostosis at Lamanai.

donment in the Late and Terminal Classic periods, the frequencies of both caries and enamel hypoplasia peak, and the occurrence of enamel hypoplasia appears to coincide with the age of weaning. These relationships have been interpreted as indicating greater infant mortality near the end of the temporal sequence.

Materials and Methods

Lamanai is located in northern Belize on the northwestern shore of the New River Lagoon about 70 km inland from the Caribbean coast. It has a very heterogeneous environment, compared to Pacbitun, which is located further inland in west-central Belize. The skeletal sample from Lamanai represents six time periods: Preclassic (1250 B.C.–A.D. 250), Early Classic (A.D. 250–400), Late Classic (A.D. 650–900), Terminal Classic (A.D. 900–1000), Postclassic (A.D. 1000–1520) and Historic (A.D. 1520–1670). The previously analyzed isotopic sample includes a subset of individuals from each time period (n = 51), but the dental sample constitutes all of the teeth from every individual (n = 167) in the sequence available as of the end of the 1985 field season. Because the research goals of the archaeologist in charge of the excavation (Dr. David Pendergast, Royal Ontario Museum) focused on the ceremonial precinct, most of the skeletal material comes from that area, and is, therefore, assumed to represent individuals of relatively high socioeconomic status. In fact, this may not be a valid assumption, but there is currently no clear evidence to contradict it. The Early Classic is the only time period which has provided a set of very elite tomb burials (one male, one female). These are used in this study to mark possible social contrast in differential access to resources.

The isotopic analysis was meant to determine the relative proportions of maize and other major food resources (in particular, sources of protein). The $^{13}C/^{12}C$ ratios of bone collagen were used to estimate the degree to which the population was dependent on C_4 plants (maize) and C_4 plant-consuming animals. Although it is widely held that maize was the only agricultural C_4 plant used by the Maya in Belize, the isotopic ratios or signatures from the bone collagen of humans cannot validly be interpreted to exclude the possibility that animals who consumed maize (such as dog, deer, and peccary) were not also part of the human diet and contributed substantially to the isotopic signal. Nor is it possible with these data to predict the proportions of C_4-consuming animals to C_4 plants in the diet.

Caries

Of all dental pathology, caries provides the most reliable data because its observability is not highly dependent on preservation. Caries is defined as a focal area of enamel destruction. The development of carious lesions involves complex interactions between many types of infectious organisms, the morphology of the tooth and the integrity of its enamel, and the oral environment. Enamel solubility is enhanced by refined or sticky carbohydrates such as maize. Therefore, the analysis of caries at Lamanai is an important means of confirming dietary shifts in maize consumption interpreted from the chemical data. Although it is not possible from isotopic measurements to discriminate between the consumption of different C_3 plants which make up alternate dietary models for the Maya (e.g., a root crop staple vs. a variety of other plants), analysis of caries does provide a potential for differentiating between the C_3 plants that are sticky carbohydrates (i.e., root crops) and others. In this region, maize is the only C_4 plant of dietary importance (with the possible exception of amaranth and some chenopods, which are not suspected to have been consumed in large quantities).

A carious lesion was identified as any macroscopically observable lytic defect large enough to insert the tip of a dental explorer tool. The total number of carious lesions was calculated per individual as a percent of the observable number of teeth. From these data, a mean percent was calculated per time period, sex, and social status group. The main potential source of error in this study is tooth loss, both pre- and postmortem. Because both caries and periodontal disease are major causes of tooth loss, and because there is a high frequency of periodontal disease in this sample, teeth lost before death cannot be assumed to be carious. As it is not possible to assign the pathological state of caries to unobservable teeth, the number of caries in the sample is probably underestimated. Unavoidably, it must also be assumed that there are no differences in postmortem loss rates between time periods.

Enamel Hypoplasia

Enamel hypoplasia is defined as a defect in tissue growth created by stress and resulting in abnormal metabolism and development of the enamel-forming cells (ameloblasts). It is identified in this study by a macroscopically observable and well-marked transverse line of underdeveloped enamel. The nature and frequency of hypoplastic lesions can be characteristic of several epidemiological problems, including infectious disease and malnutrition. Therefore, this pathology is considered to be nonspecific in etiology. For many agricultural populations, however, lesions seem to be recording stress during the period of weaning. Agricultural diets often lead to protein-calorie malnutrition, iron deficiency anemia, and weanling diarrhea, which are all known to be indirect causes of hypocalcemia, and which, in turn, result in linear hypoplasia (Nikiforuk and Fraser 1981). Although hypoplasia can also be caused by infectious disease, in North America there is a strong nutritional association between its incidence and increasing dependence on maize agriculture (Cook and Buikstra 1979; Rose et al. 1978). Enamel hypoplasia cannot reconstruct diet *per se,* but can be a useful indicator of dietary or physiological stress. In this study,

all teeth were examined macroscopically under strong light for the presence of well-marked linear grooves and occlusal pitting. A mean was calculated from the number of observable teeth for each individual, and then a mean of means ($\mu\bar{x}$) for these individuals was calculated per time period and by sex. Sources of error in quantification include attrition, the cultural practice of tooth filing, and missing teeth.

Results and Discussion

The patterning of enamel hypoplasia at Lamanai suggests physiological or dietary stress precipitated by weaning. Based on enamel formation sequences, this nonspecific stress occurred between the ages of 2 and 4 years throughout the entire time span (Table 13.1). Unlike the phenomenon at Altar de Sacrificios, there is no significant change in its frequency over time (ANOVA, ($df_{5,112}$), F = .501, p < .78), which suggests that infants in all periods suffered equally, in spite of fluctuating dietary change in adults. The period of weaning transition being between ages 2 and 4 years is also supported by age differences in $\delta^{15}N$ (the ratio of $^{15}N/^{14}N$) in bone collagen (Fig. 13.2). Breast-feeding infants in both modern and archaeological populations are enriched in ^{15}N by approximately 2‰ due to a trophic level effect; that is, because they are feeding from their mothers, they are essentially one level higher in the food chain (Prewitt 1988–1989). Only two of the Lamanai juveniles were young enough to be breast-feeding and they are indeed 2‰ more enriched than the older population (11.5 ± .07‰ compared to 9.5 ± .9‰), thus showing the trophic level effect.

Socioeconomic status is a major determinant of diet. Higher status individuals not only have access to more food on a more regular basis, but also to the most socially valued foods. Although all of the burials at Lamanai are assumed to be relatively high-status, the very elite male and a female found in the Early Classic

Table 13.1 Temporal Means of Enamel Hypoplasia, Caries, and Isotopic Values

Cultural Period	Enamel Hypoplasia $\mu\bar{x}$	Enamel Hypoplasia $\sigma\bar{x}$	Caries Mean %	Caries $\sigma\bar{x}$	$\delta^{13}C$ ‰	$\delta^{13}C$ sd	$\delta^{15}N$ ‰	$\delta^{15}N$ sd	n
Lamanai[a]									
Preclassic	.40	.51	20.0	19.9	−12.4	.3	10.2	.6	5
Early Classic[b]	.20	.44	24.5	24.2	−12.3	1.6	10.9	1.5	2
Late Classic	.20	.44	17.1	21.0	−14.2	1.1	10.3	.1	5
Terminal Classic	.44	.52	1.8	3.2	−15.0	1.2	9.9	.4	6
Postclassic	.39	.49	17.6	37.5	−9.3	.8	9.5	.9	50
Historic	.31	.46	20.5	28.5	−9.9	.9	9.7	.6	42
Pacbitun[c]									
Early Classic (Tzul)					−9.2	–	8.1	–	1
Late Classic (Coc)					−8.5	1.3	9.3	.6	3
Terminal Classic (Tzib)					−9.9	1.4	9.2	.6	8

NOTE: $\mu\bar{x}$ = mean of means; $\sigma\bar{x}$ = standard error; sd = standard deviation; n = number of samples.

[a] Enamel hypoplasia and caries are status adjusted, caries is age adjusted.

[b] Values are for nontomb individuals only.

[c] Isotopic data are controlled for status by using crypt and cyst burials only.

tombs provide a source of true social distinction and potential dietary contrast. The two tomb individuals are markedly different from their contemporaries in caries frequency. They experienced no caries at all (the male had 26

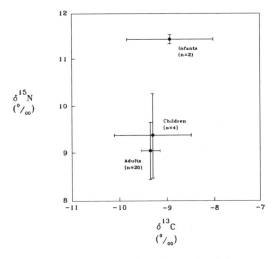

Figure 13.2. Isotopic values of nursing infants compared to adults and older children for Postclassic period at Lamanai.

teeth and the female had 24), whereas the other Early Classic individuals (n = 2) had a mean percent of 24.5 and standard error ($\sigma\bar{x}$) of 24.2. This difference in caries rate is consistent with that found between high-status and lower status Maya at Copán, Honduras (Hodges 1985) and at the nearby site of Tipu (Bennett and Cohen 1985). Both high-status individuals also exhibit lighter $\delta^{13}C$ values than the rest of the population, which strongly suggests that they consumed fewer C_4 (maize) foods (Fig. 13.3). Chemical data from Pacbitun, however, are interpreted to indicate a reverse pattern of C_4 preference in association with status (White et al. 1993; Fig. 13.4).

The social assignment of children to lower status could also create variation in δ values. There is no indication of an age-structured social difference in $\delta^{13}C$ at Lamanai. Juveniles and adults at Lamanai appear to have been consuming much the same proportions of plants and proteins (see Table 13.1; Student's t-test, $p > .05$; $\delta^{13}C$: $t_{(33)} = .92$; $\delta^{15}N$: $t_{(32)} = .87$). Both groups were consuming a dominantly

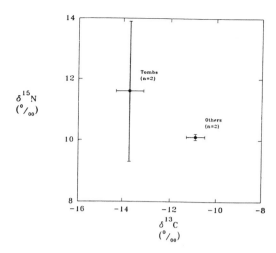

Figure 13.3. Isotopic variation by status at Lamanai.

C$_4$ (maize) diet for this time period, and derived most of their protein resources from plants and terrestrial animals. The lack of variation found here is significant for two reasons: (1) it means that individuals of different ages could be included in the sample used to test temporal trends in δ^{13}C, and (2) it has profound implications for childhood health and nutritional status because children have greater

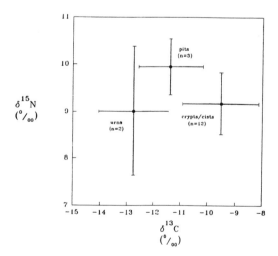

Figure 13.4. Isotopic variation by status at Pacbitun. Urns represent child burials.

protein and iron demands, which might not have been met with a maize staple.

Dietary variation by age does occur, however, at Pacbitun, where children are consuming significantly fewer C$_4$ foods (Fig. 13.4). As C$_4$ consumption and status are well linked at Pacbitun (the higher the status, the more C$_4$ foods), this finding is consistent with the interpretation that children had a lower ascribed status there. Their burial treatment is also different (they are all found in urns). Unfortunately, the bones are not well enough preserved to do pathological analyses.

There is no significant difference in caries frequency between males and females at Lamanai (Student's t-test, $p > .05$, $t_{(90)} = -.64$), although females had a much higher standard error, indicating that they might have had a slightly more variable diet (Table 13.2; mean $\% = 17.82$, $\sigma\bar{x} = 29.61$ for males and mean $\% = 22.33$, $\sigma\bar{x} = 37.57$ for females). This finding is supported by both the high-status couple, who do not differ in their caries frequency, and also the isotopic data which suggest gender equality in plant or protein consumption (Student's t-test, $p > .05$, δ^{13}C: $t_{(27)} = 1.64$; δ^{15}N: $t_{(25)} = 1.20$). Furthermore, an examination of enamel hypoplasia suggests that female children at Lamanai do not appear to suffer any more developmental stresses than males (Student's t-test, $p > .05$, $t_{(109)} = .58$; Table 13.1). We cannot, however, assume a complete lack of dietary inequity by sex within sites. For example, the Early Classic tomb female was not getting the same food that her elite male counterpart was (White and Schwarcz 1989). Nor can we generalize gender equality to other sites. For example, the isotopic data from Pacbitun do indicate significant sex differences in diet (White et al. 1994), where females consumed fewer C$_4$ foods than males (Table 13.2).

Caries is considered an age-dependent pathology. Therefore, only adult teeth were used for quantifying dietary trends over time. Shifts in the frequency of dental caries (Fig. 13.5) and

Table 13.2 Comparisons by Sex and Age for Dietary Measures

Sex and Age	Enamel Hypoplasia			Caries			$\delta^{13}C$			$\delta^{15}N$		
	$\mu\bar{x}$	$\sigma\bar{x}$	n	Mean %	$\sigma\bar{x}$	n	‰	sd	n	‰	sd	n
Lamanai												
Male	.39	.49	61	17.82	29.61	61	−9.6	1.1	16	9.7	.6	16
Female	.34	.48	50	22.33	37.57	50	−9.4	.5	13	9.4	.7	13
Juvenile							−9.2	.6	6	9.8	1.3	6
Adult							−9.3	.8	13	9.4	.7	13
Pacbitun												
Male							−8.9	1.2	8	9.1	.6	8
Female							−10.7	1.3	8	9.5	.7	8
Juvenile							−12.3	1.2	3	8.8	1.0	3
Adult							−9.9	1.4	17	9.3	.7	17

NOTE: $\mu\bar{x}$ = mean of means; $\sigma\bar{x}$ = standard error; n = number of samples; sd = standard deviation.

$\delta^{13}C$ values follow the same trends and indicate marked variability in the amount of maize consumed within the temporal sequence. Notably, $\delta^{15}N$ values have previously indicated that protein resources remained relatively unchanged over the sequence at both Lamanai and Pacbitun (Table 13.1).

Caries incidence in the Preclassic period is high (mean % = 20.0, $\sigma\bar{x}$ = 19.9) and typical

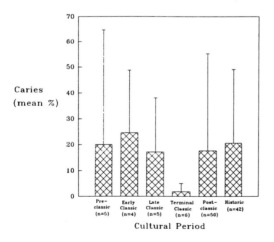

Figure 13.5. Temporal distribution of caries at Lamanai. Thick bars represent mean percent and thin bars represent standard error ($\sigma\bar{x}$).

of populations dependent on high-carbohydrate foods. Similarly, Preclassic levels of C_4 (maize) consumption measured isotopically are even higher than those in North American populations experiencing the later transitional C_4 agricultural stages, as indicated in data from Schwarcz et al. (1985) and Lynott et al. (1986). Thus maize agriculture in the earliest phase of Maya civilization is already full-blown ($\delta^{13}C$ = −12.4‰). The high level of consumption could be a reflection of the increased population density which is hypothesized for the Middle to Late Preclassic period (Weaver 1981).

In the following Early Classic period, both dental and chemical data from the nontomb burials indicate little, if any, change in C_4 food consumption. There are, unfortunately, no samples available for the Middle Classic (A.D. 400–650). During the Late Classic, however, the caries rate drops off and becomes almost nonexistent in the Terminal Classic (mean % = 1.8, $\sigma\bar{x}$ = 3.2). The incidence during the Terminal Classic period is so low, it is actually more characteristic of nonagricultural populations (Sealy and van der Merwe 1988; C. Turner 1979). The chemical data again reflect this pattern where $\delta^{13}C$ values become much lighter

$(\delta^{13}C = -15‰)$. Although the isotopic data cannot clearly indicate whether the C_3 plants being substituted are root crops or represent a mixed plant regime, the dental data suggest that root crops could not have been the main substitution for maize. Given that root crops are starchy carbohydrates with cariogenic properties, it is highly unlikely that they were consumed in significant amounts during this time period without leaving the telltale signs of caries. By process of elimination, and because protein sources appear to be stable throughout the sequence (as indicated by $\delta^{15}N$ values) it appears that the remaining portion of the Terminal Classic diet likely consisted of cultivated, traded, or wild C_3 plants, possibly reflecting a mixed plant model.

Reasons for the dramatic decline in the consumption of maize-based foods at Lamanai are unclear. Similar evidence for reduced maize production in this period has been documented elsewhere and has been used to support the ecological model of collapse (Vaughan et al. 1985; Wiseman 1985). For example, at Pacbitun an association at this time between population increase, agricultural intensification in the form of terracing, and significantly reduced C_4 food consumption also supports an ecological model.

The similarities and differences between these two sites provide a means of differentiating between ecological and nutritional models of collapse, and of illustrating the role played by regional differences in environment and culture. Data from Lamanai do not support an ecological or nutritional model of collapse. Rather, they argue for both physical and cultural health in the face of declining maize-based consumption. Theoretically, shifts in food consumption can be due to changes either in production or in availability of other resources. I would argue that production at Lamanai was affected by cultural, rather than environmental, events. During the 100-year Terminal Classic period, the inhabitants of Lamanai expended vast amounts of energy building monumental architecture. Unlike many of their counterparts in lowland Guatemala, they have left evidence of a cultural fluorescence for a period which represented decline at many other sites. For example, the Terminal Classic phenomenon observed at Lamanai stands in stark contrast with that at Altar de Sacrificios, in the Petén, where caries incidence rises significantly just before the site is abandoned (Saul 1972a). Thus the drop in C_4 consumption which begins in the Late Classic period is not a harbinger of cultural collapse at Lamanai. Instead, this site appears to have been in the process of switching its cultural and trade affinities from the Petén to the Yucatán. The flurry of Terminal Classic construction might have been related to political economy. Such monumental building activity could have created a scarcity of human resources for maintaining maize agriculture. Alternately, changing patterns of trade could have altered diet by making more resources available.

On the other hand, data from Pacbitun are more conducive to ecological explanation. During the Tzib phase (the equivalent of the Terminal Classic at Lamanai), $\delta^{13}C$ values suggest a decline in maize-based consumption in association with an increase in population density and a shift to intensive production (i.e., terracing). Analysis of status differences further supports the notion that maize was a valued food. The higher the status the more maize-based foods were consumed, a phenomenon distinctly contrasted with high-status food preference at Lamanai. Pacbitun, like many other lowland sites, did not survive the Terminal Classic, but Lamanai did. The evidence, to date, certainly implicates an ecological struggle.

At Lamanai, there is an abrupt Postclassic shift to a strongly dominant maize diet. Caries incidence rebounds to levels characteristic of the Preclassic and Early Classic periods (Table 13.1). For the Postclassic, mean % = 17.6 $(\sigma\bar{x} = 37.5)$. This level of pathology is also carried into the Historic period without significant change. Chemical data are again consistent with the dental data. C_4 foods in the Postclassic constitute an even greater proportion of the diet than that found in the earliest stages of the sequence at this site. These high levels of consumption persisted into and throughout the Historic period. In spite of the dietary constancy indicated by both caries and isotopes during the Postclassic to Colonial transition period, anemia (White et al. 1994) and enamel disturbances (Wright 1990) increase significantly. The patterning of these lesions suggests increased physiological stress during the Historic period, particularly in children, as the site experienced a host of newly introduced diseases, both infectious and parasitic. It is interesting to note that these phenomena (which Santley et al. 1986 would predict for the Late Classic), do not occur until the intervention of the Spanish.

The resurgence of maize-based consumption during the Postclassic period supports a growing body of research which challenges previous ideas that the Postclassic was simply a continuation of the "decline, decadence, and depopulation" exhibited at some sites in the Late and Terminal Classic (Chase and Rice 1985; Pendergast 1986). The uniformity of Maya diet at Lamanai throughout the period of the Conquest also provides evidence that the presence of Spaniards in this area had no immediate or significant dietary impact. The ability of the Maya at Lamanai essentially to double their maize-based consumption after the collapse of many other lowland sites, and to maintain this level until driven away by the Spanish, speaks clearly against an ecological model. At Pacbitun, however, archaeological and dietary evidence points to attempts at increasing production in the face of a growing population, and to a greater value being placed on maize just prior to the abandonment of the site, with no appreciable change in protein consumption as indicated by $\delta^{15}N$ values. Being less ecologically heterogeneous, Pacbitun did not have as many production options as Lamanai, and it was more dependent on maize as a staple. The data from Lamanai and Pacbitun would thus support the assertion by Santley et al. (1986) that an ecological model would be less applicable to Maya populations living near the coast, such as those at Lamanai, and that the variable physiography of the Maya lowlands precludes using the ecological model as a generalizing theory. However, the data from both of these sites and a theoretical perspective that separates ecological and nutritional models bring into question what we use as evidence for ecological collapse. High levels of pathology associated with heavy maize consumption do not automatically denote ecological pressure. More convincing evidence for ecological struggle would be found in an increase in status divergence for maize consumption. This would suggest a greater value placed on maize in the face of declining production. To date, we do not have enough skeletal material representing social difference over long enough sequences. Perhaps, as archaeologists come to a better understanding of status in the Maya and continue to design their research to include divergent status groups, we will have a clearer picture of the relationships between Maya diet, disease, culture, and agriculture.

Acknowledgments

I thank Dr. Hermann Helmuth and Dr. Paul Healy, Department of Anthropology, Trent University, for their help with the osteology and archaeology at Lamanai and Pacbitun. Dr. Henry Schwarcz, Department of Geology, McMaster University, provided crucial assistance with the isotopic analysis, as did his technician, Martin Knyf. Dr. David Pendergast, Royal Ontario Museum, graciously provided access to the sample from Lamanai. This research was supported by the Department of Anthropology, Trent University, an Ontario Graduate Scholarship, and a Natural Science and Engineering Research Council Scholarship.

Christine D. White

14

Ecology or Society?
Paleodiet and the Collapse
of the Pasión Maya Lowlands

Lori E. Wright

Over the last few decades, archaeologists have taken great strides in investigating the interaction of ancient cultures with their natural environments. This progress is particularly apparent in study of the lowland Maya, whose rainforest habitat has been under intense scrutiny. We now know that large, socially heterogeneous Maya populations were supported by several forms of intensive agriculture (Harrison and Turner 1978; Siemens and Puleston 1972; Turner 1974) and that they exploited a variety of wild and domestic food resources (Lentz 1991; Pohl 1985a; Wiseman 1983). Maya social adaptations have also been greatly clarified by extensive settlement pattern studies (Ashmore 1981; Puleston 1983; Tourtellot 1988; Willey et al. 1965) and by the decipherment of much of the hieroglyphic writing system (Culbert 1991; Houston 1989).

Yet, the dominant explanation of the collapse of Maya civilization in the southern lowlands around A.D. 900 remains ecological, and fundamentally Malthusian. It is often argued that ancient populations became too large over the course of the Classic period, growing beyond the carrying capacity of the fragile tropical eco-system (Culbert 1988; Sanders 1962, 1963; Santley et al. 1986; Willey and Shimkin 1973). This model proposes that population increase caused the expansion of agricultural systems to utilize all available lands. Soil erosion, grass invasion, and deforestation severely restricted the productivity of Late Classic agriculture (Abrams and Rue 1988; Morley 1946; Sanders 1973). Facing these difficulties, farmers are argued to have concentrated on the monocropping production of highly storable staples, particularly maize (Santley et al. 1986; Wiseman 1985). These agricultural shifts affected the diet consumed by members of the society, and are implicated in the deterioration of nutritional status and health of the population (Haviland 1967; Hooton 1940; Saul 1972a). Ultimately, diet change is linked to demographic instability which brought about the final depopulation of the area (Santley et al. 1986; Willey and Shimkin 1973).

In essence, the model is a biological one, and amenable to testing with biological data from human skeletons. In this paper, I examine three expectations for prehistoric Maya diet that are developed from the ecological model, using bone chemical data from human skeletons from five sites in the Pasión region of the southwestern Petén, Guatemala. The Pasión has seen intensive archaeological work over the last 35 years that has produced sizable skeletal series which span the occupational history of the region. Moreover, epigraphic research in the Pasión provides good historical control of political processes that may also have been involved in the collapse.

The Pasión Region

Located in the southwestern part of the Department of Petén, Guatemala, the Pasión is underlain by Cretaceous Neocomian-Campanian limestones that are faulted into a series of horst plateaus and graben valleys. The Pasión river system traverses the valleys; a number of surface tributaries, such as the Riachuelo Petexbatún, and underground springs flow into the Río de la Pasión, which in turn merges with the Río Salinas to form the Río Usumacinta. Rainfall is heavy during the wet season; runoff causes water levels to fluctuate by as much as 10 m annually. Today much of the region supports a high perennial broadleaf tropical forest, although forest clearance is accelerating owing to recent human reoccupation. The Pasión Valley itself consists of a broad fertile floodplain, with highland-derived alluvium replenished annually. Although raised or drained fields once thought to be visible on airborne radar images (Adams 1983) do not occur, the alluvial plains

and *aguada* sinkholes are fertile niches that supported intensive ancient cultivation. The upland slopes do show relic terracing that indicates a substantial labor investment in the Late Classic agricultural landscape (Dunning and Beach 1994).

This study examines paleodiet at five sites: Altar de Sacrificios, Seibal, Dos Pilas, Aguateca, and Itzán. Altar is located on the Pasión floodplain, near its confluence with the Río Salinas. Excavated by Harvard University in the early 1960s, Altar had a long occupational span, dating from Middle Preclassic through Terminal Classic times (Adams 1971; Willey 1973). Hieroglyphic inscription and monumental construction seem to have ceased at Altar by the end of the Late Classic period, around A.D. 800. However, a substantial population remained at the site through Terminal Classic times, despite the apparently weakened elite authority structure. Seibal, also excavated by Harvard during the 1960s, is located upstream from Altar on the uplifted horst of the west bank of the Río de la Pasión (Tourtellot 1988; Willey 1990). It, too, has a long occupational history, but is distinguished by a Terminal Classic fluorescence of sculptural and architectural construction and a late increase in settlement density. Like Altar, Seibal was abandoned by about A.D. 950.

Recent excavations by Vanderbilt University's Petexbatún Regional Archaeological Project have produced skeletal series from Dos Pilas and Aguateca, two sites that played an important role in the Late Classic Pasión political arena. Dos Pilas lies on the karstic horst plateau south of the Río de la Pasión, midway between the Laguna Petexbatún and the Río Salinas. Aguateca is located to the southeast, on a high escarpment south of the Laguna Petexbatún. Though some limited early remains have been found, both sites date primarily to the Late Classic period, and served as twin capitals of the Petexbatún dynasty, which seems to have originated from Tikal. Epigraphic study documents that Dos Pilas's rulers conducted a campaign of politico-military expansion, gaining control over several nearby sites during the 7th and 8th centuries, including Arroyo de Piedra, Tamarindito, and Seibal (Houston 1993; Houston and Mathews 1985; Mathews and Willey 1991). Dos Pilas was largely abandoned around A.D. 760, perhaps after it was defeated in a battle against Tamarindito in which Dos Pilas's Ruler 3 was killed. Thereafter, the dynasty retired to Aguateca. Excavations demonstrate that Aguateca was, in turn, precipitously abandoned around A.D. 810, presumably as a consequence of warfare (Demarest and Houston, 1989, 1990; Demarest, Inomata et al. 1991, 1992; Inomata 1995; Valdés et al. 1993).

The fifth site, Itzán, is located on a small tributary north of the Río de la Pasión; a small Late Classic burial series has been excavated by Kevin Johnston of Yale University. Like Altar de Sacrificios, Itzán remained politically independent during Late Classic times, albeit linked to Dos Pilas by royal marriage. It may have had stronger political affiliations with Usumacinta Valley sites downstream than with the Pasión/Petexbatún (Johnston 1994).

While the ecological model has dominated discussion of the lowland Maya collapse in the general and theoretical sense, the collapse of the Pasión has often been seen as politically mediated. Early work at Altar de Sacrificios and Seibal brought to light the possibility that invasion by foreigners from the Putún lowlands might have triggered the collapse of these two sites (Sabloff and Willey 1967; Thompson 1970). Changes in Terminal Classic ceramics and sculptural iconography were interpreted as evidence of foreign intrusion, but may simply be local stylistic developments (Stuart 1993). Alternately, "foreign" elements may indicate a local elite strategy that capitalized on the social prestige conferred by long-distance interaction (Helms

1979; Stone 1989). Epigraphic work confirms that the Pasión became the focus of intense political and military competition between local polities toward the end of the Classic period (Houston 1993; Johnston 1985; Mathews and Willey 1991). The Petexbatún dynasty was a key player in this competition, which appears to have led to its demise. After the fall of Dos Pilas and Aguateca, power shifted to the Tamarindito/Arroyo polity for the final years of the 8th century (Demarest and Houston 1989, 1990; Demarest, Inomata et al. 1991, 1992; Valdés et al. 1993). By the Terminal Classic period, Seibal was the only site in the region that continued to erect sculptural monuments of politico-military prowess. With the abandonment of Late Classic centers in the Petexbatún region, remnant populations appear to have gathered at Seibal, boosting its population at this late date (Tourtellot 1988). Although some have argued that this escalated competition was due to agricultural pressures (Adams 1983), this new political information raises the possibility that social (Demarest 1992) rather than ecological factors may have been instrumental in the Terminal Classic transition.

Isotopic Approaches to Ancient Maya Diets

Isotopic analysis of archaeological skeletons provides a new avenue to examine prehistoric subsistence strategies that has enormous potential for investigating the ecological model of collapse. The isotopic composition of foods ingested by all organisms is translated into characteristic signatures in body tissues that are preserved in archaeological remains. Carbon and nitrogen stable isotopes are especially useful for paleodietary analysis because they distinguish between types of plants consumed and between protein sources. Fractionation of the stable isotopes ^{12}C and ^{13}C is distinctive in plants using the C$_3$ (or Benson-Calvin) and C$_4$ (or Hatch-Slack) photosynthetic pathways, owing to the different enzymes employed for carbon dioxide fixation (O'Leary 1988). Using mass spectrometry, stable carbon isotopic ratios, or δ^{13}C, are measured as the ratio of the heavy to the light isotope, ^{13}C/^{12}C, relative to the Pee Dee Belemnite standard. Most leafy plants use the C$_3$ pathway, and have δ^{13}C compositions near -26‰. In contrast, tropical grasses, including the primary Maya cultigen, *Zea mays*, use the C$_4$ pathway, and are enriched in the heavy isotope, ^{13}C, having δ^{13}C near -10‰. Plants using the Crassulacean Acid Metabolism (CAM) photosynthetic pathway may have δ^{13}C similar to C$_4$ plants, but are not abundant in tropical forest environments. As maize is the primary C$_4$ plant consumed by the Maya, δ^{13}C can be considered a measure of maize consumption. Stable nitrogen isotopic ratios, or δ^{15}N, are likewise measured as the ratio ^{15}N/^{14}N relative to the atmospheric nitrogen standard (AIR). Although plants differ in the sources of nitrogen exploited and thus slightly in δ^{15}N, nitrogen isotopic ratios are most useful as indicators of trophic position, because ^{15}N is enriched by isotopic fractionation in mammalian digestive systems. Thus, δ^{15}N can be used to monitor the relative consumption of animal and plant proteins. In this paper, the isotopic composition of bone collagen is used to reconstruct Pasión paleodiet. Although controversy still rages as to the dietary macronutrient source of carbon atoms that are used to synthesize collagen (Sillen et al. 1989), I interpret the isotopic data following the predominant model, which proposes that some routing of dietary protein to collagen occurs (Ambrose and Norr 1993; Krueger and Sullivan 1984; Lee-Thorp et al. 1989; Tieszen and Fagre 1993b).

By analogy with modern Maya peoples (Behár 1968) and from paleobotanical remains excavated at Maya sites (Wiseman 1983) we can assume that ancient Pasión diets emphasized the consumption of maize, which was supplemented with a variety of other cultivated and wild foods that were characterized by C$_3$ isotopic signals. Thus carbon isotopes provide a means to examine the relative contributions of maize versus other plant foods in Pasión Maya diets. In addition to that from plant foods, protein was also obtained from animal sources, such as deer, peccary, agouti, domestic dogs, wild fowl, fish, and freshwater snails. Nitrogen isotopic data can be used to evaluate the consumption of these higher trophic level foods. In their isotopic study of diet at Lamanai, White and Schwarcz (1989) found substantial changes in δ^{13}C from Preclassic through Postclassic times, demonstrating significant shifts in the importance of maize to Lamanai diets over time. Although dietary changes at Lamanai do not necessarily shed light on the process of collapse because Lamanai itself did not collapse, the magnitude of variation observed suggests that changes in resource utilization that might have occurred with the collapse should be recorded in bone isotopic compositions.

As articulated by Culbert (1988), Sanders (1962, 1963, 1973), Santley et al. (1986), and Willey and Shimkin (1973), among others, the model attributes environmental degradation and subsequent health stress to maize agriculture. Hence, the chemical data should demonstrate that Pasión peoples relied heavily on maize as a primary source of nutrition. Secondly, maize reliance is posited to have increased over the span of occupation, with farmers shifting to greater maize cultivation during periods of population pressure. This shift should produce an increase in the δ^{13}C of human bone collagen. Finally, the expansion of agricultural systems to all cultivable land in the Late Classic would have dramatically reduced wild faunal habitats. Together with heavy predation by large human populations, this placed inordinate stress upon faunal populations, so that animal protein supplies were compromised. Chemically, this should be indicated by a decline in $\delta^{15}N$ over time.

Materials and Methods

Skeletal Series

Burial series from Pasión sites differ somewhat in character owing to the varied excavation strategies of the projects that recovered them. Excavations at Altar de Sacrificios focused on ceremonial architecture in the site center, and many burials were recovered from these non-domestic contexts. In contrast, projects at Seibal, Dos Pilas, Aguateca, and Itzán have placed greater emphasis on residential excavations. Accordingly, the social dimensions represented are not necessarily congruent between series, an issue I address through statistical analysis of mortuary variables.

I divide the skeletal series from each site into four chronological periods, following the ceramic dates assigned to the features by each project. I designate "Preclassic" burials as those from the Xe, San Felix, and Plancha phases at Altar de Sacrificios, and the Escoba and Cantutse phases at Seibal. "Early Classic" burials occur only at Altar de Sacrificios, and include those dated to Salinas, Ayn, and Veremos phases. Definition of the "Late Classic" series follows the ceramic chronology of Seibal (Sabloff 1975) and of the Petexbatún (Foias 1993), spanning A.D. 600 to 830. "Late Classic" burials are classified as Tepejilote phase at Seibal, Nacimiento phase in the Petexbatún, and Ixcayao and Ajsac at Itzán (Johnston 1994). For Altar, "Late Classic" burials are those dated to Chixoy, Pasión, and the early facet of the Boca phase only. "Terminal Classic" burials postdate A.D. 830 and are identified as Bayal at Seibal and Sepens in the Petexbatún. For Altar, burials classified as Jimba phase, Boca/Jimba transitional, and those with late facet Boca diagnostic types were considered to be Terminal Classic in date.

Isotopic Sampling

Bone samples were selected for isotopic analysis from all well-preserved adult Pasión skeletons in order to obtain the largest possible series for each site and time period. Samples were preferentially taken from the thick cortical bone of the femoral midshaft. For a few skeletons, samples had to be taken from other long bones such as the humerus or tibia because of poor femoral preservation.

The isotopic compositions of some Maya foods are known from theoretical principles or previous study, but relatively little work has been done on isotopic fractionation in tropical food webs. In order to define the parameters for dietary reconstruction in this ecosystem, local Petexbatún plants and wild fauna were collected. Sample selection was somewhat opportunistic, emphasizing wild plant species available during the dry season in the Petexbatún subregion, but also included important cultigens. Bones of wild animals were obtained from Kekchi hunters in nearby villages. Several animal bones from Petexbatún Project excavations were also analyzed.

Laboratory Procedures and Analytic Methods

The isotopic analyses of archaeological bone samples were conducted in the laboratory of Dr. Margaret Schoeninger at the University of Wisconsin, Madison. The bone chunks were cleaned mechanically and ultrasonically in distilled water, dried and decalcified in .5 M ethylene-diamine-tetra-acetic acid (EDTA) at pH 7.2 and 4°C. Collagen pseudomorphs were rinsed thoroughly with distilled water, treated with .125 M sodium hydroxide (NaOH) to remove humic contaminants, rinsed again, and freeze-dried. The carbon and nitrogen isotopic composition of the collagen pseudomorphs was measured by mass spectrometry. Isotope ratios of modern plants, animal bones, and some human C/N ratios were measured in Dr. Larry

Tieszen's lab at Augustana College. Lipids were removed from modern bone samples with a solution of methanol, chloroform, and water (2:1:.8). These samples were demineralized with .3 M hydrochloric acid at 4°C, treated with NaOH, rinsed, and freeze-dried for mass spectrometry. Plant samples were dried, ground, and loaded directly for mass spectrometry. Snail and fish flesh samples were soaked in chloroform-methanol-water solution, rinsed, dried, and macerated prior to isotopic measurement. C/N ratios of collagen were measured with a Carlo Erba elemental analyzer. Further details of the specimen preparation procedures can be found in Wright (1994).

Dietary Heterogeneity and Mortuary Statistics

It is often hypothesized that diets may have varied substantially among subpopulations within a single Maya site, which was part of a complex stratified society. Differential access to animal protein and plant foods is suggested by ethnohistoric documents (Roys 1972; Tozzer 1941), paleobotanical remains (Lentz 1991), and isotopic data (White et al. 1994; White and Schwarcz 1989). Thus, control over social heterogeneity is crucial to the evaluation of dietary trends. The burial feature constitutes a context rich in symbols of social status that can be used to examine dietary heterogeneity. Although mortuary symbols may be manipulated to distort perception of a social hierarchy (Cannon 1989; Hodder 1982a; Pearson 1982), burial patterns remain one of the better means to examine social dimensions archaeologically.

Social dimensions of funerary ritual were examined by multivariate analysis of the total burial series from each time period at each site (Wright 1994). Binary variables were defined with regard to burial location, grave form, skeletal position, cardinal orientation, and grave goods. Burial data were obtained from Smith (1972), Tourtellot (1990a), and the burial

forms of the Yale Itzán project and the Vanderbilt Petexbatún project. Following the recommendations of Brown (1987) and O'Shea (1984), these data were examined with R-mode principal factor analysis to gain an understanding of the nature of variable interaction in each series. The factoring was conducted on a matrix of *phi* coefficients, with varimax orthogonal rotation, and factors were extracted with eigenvalues ≥ 1. Thereafter, Q-mode cluster analysis was used to identify groups of similar burials in each series. Clusters were defined using the complete linkage method of polythetic agglomerative clustering (Tainter 1975), with Euclidean distance as the measure on which clusters were formed. Isotopic patterning among these burial clusters was used to evaluate social heterogeneity in ancient Pasión diets.

Results

Bone Preservation

Collagen preservation was generally good. Of 121 human samples prepared, only 9 did not yield an organic residue and could not be analyzed isotopically. Atomic C/N ratios and the percent content of C and N were measured to assess collagen integrity. Most Pasión bone has C/N ratios within the expected range for collagen, between 2.9 and 3.6 (DeNiro 1985). A few samples at the high end of the C/N window have somewhat lighter carbon isotope ratios, and may be slightly contaminated by lipids or humic acids. These are mostly Preclassic in date, but as other coeval samples with normal C/N ratios show comparable $\delta^{13}C$, the values may well be dietary, not diagenetic. All contain approximately 45% carbon and 16% nitrogen, which is comparable to bovine tendon collagen, and well above the lower limits of collagen integrity defined by Ambrose (1990). Eight samples were eliminated from statistical analysis because of high C/N ratios or extreme outlying values, bringing the total human isotopic sample size to 104. Details of the isotopic data and measures of collagen integrity can be found in Wright (1994).

An Isotopic Menu for the Pasión

The isotopic composition of ancient Pasión foods is reconstructed in Figure 14.1, which aids in the interpretation of the human data. Isotopic data from which the model is derived can be found in Wright (1994). The box for C_3 plants is obtained from the $\delta^{13}C$ composition of 21 Pasión plant species (32 samples) and the $\delta^{15}N$ composition of 6 samples, including both cultivated and wild species eaten by Kekchi and Ladino inhabitants of the region. The C_4/CAM box is defined by two Pasión maize samples and one sample each of nopal cactus (*Opuntia* sp.) and piñuela (*Bromelia karatas*). The box for herbivore meat is derived from the ranges of 12 modern and 10 archaeological terrestrial herbivore samples, including deer (*Odocoileus virginianus, Mazama americana*), peccary (*Tayassu tajacu, T. pecari*), paca (*Agouti paca*), and armadillo (*Dasypus novemcinctus*). Collagen values were adjusted for the flesh-collagen offset of $-2.4‰$ in $\delta^{13}C$ and $1.7‰$ in $\delta^{15}N$ (DeNiro and Epstein 1978, 1981; van

der Merwe 1982). The values shown for fish and snail meat were directly measured on local fish flesh (*Petenia splendida*) and bones (*Cichlasoma* sp. and *Ictalurus* sp.) and freshwater snail flesh (*Pachychilus* sp.). In the graph, all modern values are shifted by 1.5‰ in $\delta^{13}C$ to counterbalance the recent anthropogenic decline in $\delta^{13}C$ (Tieszen and Fagre 1993a).

The faunal data reveal several critical aspects of dietary reconstruction in the Pasión. For instance, the range of herbivore $\delta^{13}C$ is very broad, a consequence of human impact on the rainforest ecosystem. Most deer, peccaries, and agoutis show the typically light $\delta^{13}C$ of C_3 plant consumers, but two archaeological deer and two modern collared peccaries have much heavier collagen ($\delta^{13}C = -13‰$ to $-18‰$), indicating invasive feeding in maize fields. As the Petexbatún is a frontier area today, and human population density is lower than that hypothesized for the Classic period, this enriched C_4 signature is noteworthy. Assuming a purely herbivorous diet, linear modeling (Schwarcz 1991) estimates that C_4 plants contributed roughly half of the dietary carbon to the peccary with $\delta^{13}C$ of $-13‰$. Conversely, the light C_3-consumer $\delta^{13}C$ of most archaeological herbivores indicates that a sizable amount of

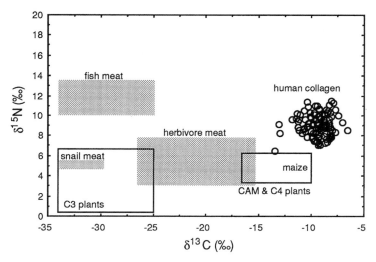

Figure 14.1. Isotopic composition of ancient Pasión foods, reconstructed from analysis of modern plants, and modern and archaeological animal remains collected in the Pasión region.

forest habitat must have remained in this area during the Late Classic. Thus, variability in land use and herbivore consumption may have a significant effect on the interpretation of human $\delta^{13}C$ values.

An interesting result is the extremely light carbon composition of fish from the Laguna Petexbatún. Fish also have heavy $\delta^{15}N$ due to carnivory. Freshwater *jute* or *Pachychilus* snails from Dos Pilas have light meat $\delta^{13}C$ values that are similar to those of the Petexbatún fish, but are lighter in $\delta^{15}N$, since *jutes* are detritivores. Freshwater turtle collagen is more akin to that of terrestrial herbivores but is also somewhat light.

In addition to species consumed by the Maya, carnivore bones were also analyzed to give some indication of $\delta^{13}C$ and $\delta^{15}N$ values that can be anticipated from carnivory in this ecosystem. These include an archaeological puma or jaguar (*Felis* sp.), a modern ocelot (*Felis pardalis*), an archaeological crocodile (*Crocodylus moreletii*), and several modern poisonous snakes (*Micrurus, Porthidium, Bothrops*). Felid collagen is more positive, or heavier, for both C and N ($\delta^{13}C = -14.8‰$; $\delta^{15}N = 11.6‰$) than is herbivore collagen ($\delta^{13}C = -19.6‰$; $\delta^{15}N = 9.8‰$), as expected from trophic enrichment. The crocodile and snakes have somewhat lower $\delta^{13}C$ ($-21‰$ to $-25‰$), probably due to eating frogs or aquatic species that have lighter $\delta^{13}C$ values. It is important to note that carnivores have $\delta^{15}N$ values in the range of Pasión humans. In addition, the archaeological felid ($\delta^{13}C = -14.8‰$) approaches the human values for carbon, demonstrating that it had consumed some C_4-eating prey.

A Culture History of Pasión Diet

The archaeological human collagen is slightly more positive than maize in $\delta^{13}C$, as would be expected if maize were an important dietary staple (Fig. 14.1). Likewise, the heavy $\delta^{13}C$ of prehistoric deer confirms the important role of maize in ancient Pasión agriculture. However, the nitrogen isotopic composition of Pasión humans is fairly heavy, resembling carnivorous signatures more than herbivorous ones. Indeed, the human collagen is about where we would expect trophic enrichment to place consumers of herbivore meat alone, with only slight ^{13}C enrichment beyond that from C_4 plants. Hence, the first expectation of the ecological model is only partially supported. Maize was important to the Pasión Maya, but meat consumption was also important and contributed a substantial amount of dietary protein toward collagen synthesis.

Chronological changes in maize and meat consumption can be evaluated with isotopic data at each site. Summary isotopic data by site, time period, and sex are given in Table 14.1. Statistical significance of the observed dietary patterns is evaluated with the nonparametric Mann-Whitney U-test because of the small sample sizes and nonnormal nature of the distributions (Wright 1994). The assumptions of the ANOVA, often used by paleodiet researchers, are violated in these data by distinct social heterogeneity within the series.

At Altar de Sacrificios, there is a trend toward increasing $\delta^{13}C$ from Preclassic through Late Classic times (Fig. 14.2). The trend is statistically significant between the Preclassic and all later periods at $p \leq .05$, and approaches significance between the Early and Late Classic periods ($p = .06$). In the Terminal Classic period, Altar's residents ceased ceremonial construction and the erection of hieroglyphic monuments, but a large settlement remained at the site. $\delta^{13}C$ dropped slightly, returning to Early Classic levels. Because there is no change in the $\delta^{15}N$ of Altar collagen over time, it is safe to assume that these $\delta^{13}C$ changes are due to shifts in the relative importance of maize.

At Dos Pilas, a small Terminal Classic occupation postdates the withdrawal of the Petexbatún dynasty to Aguateca and the abandonment

Table 14.1 Mean Isotopic Data by Site, Time Period, and Skeletal Sex

Site	Period	Total Sample n[a]	Total Sample Mean	Total Sample sd	Males n	Males Mean	Males sd	Females n	Females Mean	Females sd
$\delta^{13}C$										
Altar	T	16	−9.0	.88	8	−8.8	.87	6	−9.6	.74
	L	7	−8.3	1.03	4	−8.0	1.36	3	−8.6	.42
	E	6	−9.7	1.65	3	−10.3	2.40	3	−9.2	.10
	P	9	−10.7	1.17	7	−10.7	1.34	2	−10.5	.00
Seibal	T	16	−9.4	1.15	10	−8.9	1.07	5	−10.1	.86
	L	11	−9.4	1.34	10	−9.4	1.42	1	−9.0	–
	P	7	−9.6	.95	5	−9.9	.81	2	−8.8	.92
Dos Pilas	T	4	−9.4	.77	2	−8.9	1.06	2	−9.8	.07
	L	14	−9.0	1.03	7	−8.4	1.00	7	−9.5	.92
Aguateca	L	8	−9.6	.69	4	−9.8	.85	4	−9.3	.45
Itzán	L	5	−9.2	.30	2	−9.1	.49	3	−9.2	.21
$\delta^{15}N$										
Altar	T	16	8.8	1.14	8	8.7	1.06	6	9.0	1.42
	L	7	9.0	1.04	4	8.2	.25	3	9.5	.67
	E	6	8.3	.62	3	8.5	.74	3	8.1	.53
	P	9	8.2	.95	7	8.0	.89	2	9.0	.85
Seibal	T	16	8.9	.94	10	8.7	.92	5	8.9	.64
	L	11	9.9	.86	10	10.0	.83	1	8.9	–
	P	7	9.7	.81	5	9.4	.67	2	10.4	.78
Dos Pilas	T	4	8.8	1.21	2	9.2	1.48	2	8.3	1.13
	L	14	9.8	.93	7	10.0	.75	7	9.6	1.16
Aguateca	L	8	9.4	1.16	4	9.8	1.31	3	8.7	.64
Itzán	L	5	8.0	.98	2	8.2	1.06	3	7.8	1.10

NOTE: n = number of specimens; sd = standard deviation; P = Preclassic; E = Early Classic; L = Late Classic; T = Terminal Classic.

[a] Includes adults of unknown sex.

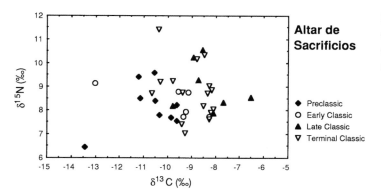

Figure 14.2. Chronological changes in isotopic composition of bone collagen at Altar de Sacrificios.

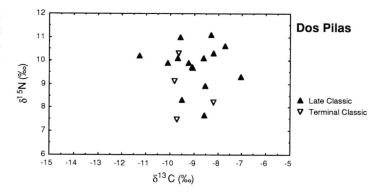

Figure 14.3. Chronological changes in isotopic composition of bone collagen at Dos Pilas.

of most of the site (Foias 1993). Four skeletons from this residual community are lighter in $\delta^{13}C$ than many Late Classic burials from the polity's apogee, although the difference is not statistically significant (Fig. 14.3). Terminal Classic $\delta^{15}N$ values are equivalent to those from the earlier period. This suggests a shift to decreased maize consumption following the collapse of political authority, comparable to that at Altar, but no change in protein procurement systems.

In contrast, Seibal collagen shows no trends in $\delta^{13}C$ over its long occupation span (Fig. 14.4). The small series of Preclassic skeletons has $\delta^{13}C$ values equivalent to those of later residents. These are substantially heavier than at contemporary Preclassic Altar, and could be taken to imply greater maize reliance at Seibal. This intersite difference approaches statistical significance (p = .16), but is not confirmed, probably because of the small sample sizes. In

addition, both Preclassic and Late Classic Seibal collagen is isotopically heavier in $\delta^{15}N$ than that from Altar, differences that are statistically significant at p ≤ .05. This dietary distinction is due either to greater meat consumption at Seibal, which would also raise the $\delta^{13}C$, or to fish eating. As the two sites occupy similar ecological zones, the discrepancy must be due to cultural preferences rather than local environmental determinants. The series differ in that burials are largely from domestic groups at Seibal and from public architecture at Altar, but the distinction does not follow a simplistic model of status-linked meat consumption, on the basis of which we would expect higher $\delta^{15}N$ at Altar than Seibal.

Late and Terminal Classic Seibal bone has equivalent $\delta^{13}C$, hinting at stability in the importance of maize in the Terminal Classic occupation at this site. In contrast, Terminal Classic collagen has a statistically significant decline in

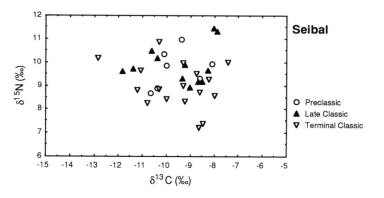

Figure 14.4. Chronological changes in isotopic composition of bone collagen at Seibal.

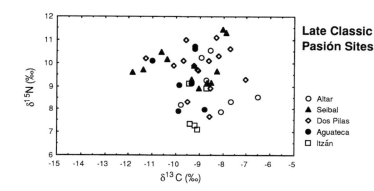

Figure 14.5. Intersite patterns in isotopic composition of bone collagen during the Late Classic period.

δ^{15}N relative to the Late Classic (p = .01). This might reflect a decline in meat consumption in the final occupation, in accord with the expectation of the model. But Late Classic Seibal collagen is the highest in δ^{15}N in the region, being a full per mil higher than Altar or Itzán diets at any period. The Terminal Classic mean of 8.9‰ is sufficiently heavy to imply substantial meat consumption. In view of the composition of Pasión foods (Fig. 14.1), we can hypothesize that this shift reflects a trade-off of protein from ^{15}N-enriched fish to C_3 plants, perhaps beans, in the Terminal Classic, with no change in terrestrial meat or maize consumption at all. This interpretation is bolstered by trace elemental data which show significantly more strontium (Sr) in Late Classic Seibal bones than in Terminal Classic ones, but no difference in barium (Ba). The freshwater ecosystem is characterized by high Sr due to its greater lability than Ba and calcium (Ca) in soil solutions and differential contribution to runoff (Wright 1994). This result confirms the inference that the heavy δ^{15}N of Late Classic Seibal could be due to fish consumption. Regardless, the slight drop in δ^{15}N during the Terminal Classic at Seibal does not imply a critical shortage of animal protein.

Burials from Itzán and Aguateca date only to the Late Classic period, so cannot be used to examine chronological trends, but they contribute to a picture of regional variability during that time (Fig. 14.5). Aguateca collagen is similar in composition to that of Late Classic Dos Pilas. Despite its riverine location, Aguateca δ^{15}N is not so enriched from fish consumption as is that from contemporary Seibal, being lighter, although the difference is not significant. Five burials from nonplatformed or "invisible" domestic groups on the periphery of Itzán have comparable δ^{13}C values, but significantly lighter δ^{15}N values (p = .003). This probably reveals a diet containing relatively little meat, and may be status-related in these semirural burials.

Social Dietary Variation

Clearly, variation in social status is an important factor in comparing diet between sites and time periods. Unfortunately, full details of the mortuary analysis results cannot be included here owing to space limitations; an extended treatment can be found in Wright (1994). The principal factor analyses demonstrate the emergence of a superordinate dimension of redundant pan-Maya funerary symbols during the Late Classic period, indicated by the high eigenvalue of the first factor in the burial series from Altar and Dos Pilas. At the latter site, the two graves responsible for this factor have been identified as that of Ruler 2, and a woman from nearby Cancuén, wife to Ruler 3, on the basis of associated hieroglyphic monuments (Demarest, Escobedo et al. 1991; Wolley and Wright 1990). Thus, we can infer that the variables of this first principal component symbol-

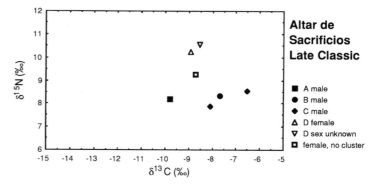

Figure 14.6. Isotopic distinctions among mortuary clusters at Altar de Sacrificios during the Late Classic period.

ize royalty. Indeed, many of these variables have traditionally been recognized as status symbols in Maya archaeology (Hall 1989), such as *Spondylus* shells, jade, large numbers of vessels, elaborate stone crypts, and obsidian debitage. The first principal component does not show these characteristics for the Late Classic series from Aguateca, Itzán, and Seibal, which can be attributed to archaeological sampling error. In contrast, lesser social distinctions are indicated by loose associations among variables that are constituted differently at each site in accord with the local audience of lower status funerals. Because of the nonredundant nature of lower status funerary symbols, it is difficult to rank burials into a simple hierarchy, or to define analogous social groups between sites. Yet, the clusters obtained correspond well with dimensions of variable patterning revealed by the factor analysis at each site. Status distinctions in diet occur in the Late Classic between these clusters. Unfortunately, the small

number of skeletons analyzed isotopically from each cluster prohibits statistical evaluation of the results, although some interesting patterns occur and may be representative of larger trends.

At Altar, the two skeletons of the superordinate or "royal" Cluster D have higher $\delta^{15}N$ than other burials (Burial 88 of indeterminate sex; and Burial 128, female) (Fig. 14.6). The high $\delta^{15}N$ is due to trophic enrichment, indicating greater meat consumption by this group, a distinction associated with high status in many societies. The high $\delta^{15}N$ of Burial 128 contributes to a statistically significant sex difference in $\delta^{15}N$ (p = .03), that may not be representative of the site's population as a whole. Lower status burials may differ among clusters in $\delta^{13}C$, presumably due to variation in maize consumption, but the series are very small.

A somewhat different pattern is found at Dos Pilas (Fig. 14.7). Here, Cluster C contains simple graves with few funerary accompaniments, while the remaining clusters are com-

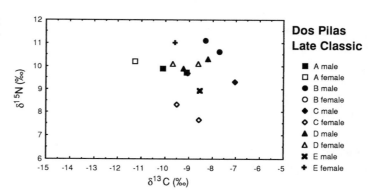

Figure 14.7. Isotopic distinctions among mortuary clusters at Dos Pilas during the Late Classic period.

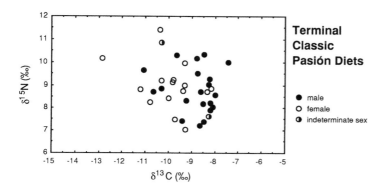

Figure 14.8. Isotopic distinctions between sexes in Terminal Classic burials from Altar de Sacrificios, Seibal, and Dos Pilas.

posed of burials with more complex architecture. The Cluster C burials would typically be interpreted as lower in social status than the crypt graves with funerary accompaniments, and have lower $\delta^{15}N$, implying lesser meat consumption by this group. The two superordinate burials have quite divergent isotopic signatures. Collagen of Dos Pilas's Ruler 2 resembles that of Cluster C simple graves with little furniture, being somewhat depleted in $\delta^{15}N$. That of his daughter-in-law, the Lady from Cancuén, is more like that of crypt burials of Clusters A and D, which may be of intermediate status. Clusters A, B, and D are distinguished by their accompaniments and skeletal positions but are predominantly in crypt graves. The skeletons show general $\delta^{15}N$ homogeneity, but systematic differences in $\delta^{13}C$, indicating social discrepancies in maize consumption. These distinctions are also found in elemental signatures that show cluster-specificity (Wright 1994). Both male and female skeletons occur in each cluster, but there is a slight tendency for males to have higher $\delta^{13}C$, which is statistically significant (p = .05). The enriched $\delta^{13}C$ of Cluster B may be responsible for the statistical result, however, since only males were sampled from this cluster. Systematic sexual differences do not occur in other Late Classic sites. There is some suggestive patterning of diet among mortuary clusters at Aguateca and Itzán, although the series are too small to fully evaluate such trends. The Seibal Late Classic series shows

little partitioning, perhaps due to the sampling biases that are also to blame for its heavy male sex bias. In sum, social distinctions were more significant in defining Late Classic diets than was sex. Moreover, these distinctions seem to have been constituted somewhat differently at each site.

In contrast, mortuary distinctions in diet are absent from the large Terminal Classic series at both Altar and Seibal. The lack of social distinctions in diet parallels a lack of formal structure in the mortuary program at both sites. Instead of social patterning, Terminal Classic diets at Altar and Seibal show a sexual trend, with males having collagen that is isotopically heavier in $\delta^{13}C$ (Fig. 14.8). This distinction is statistically significant for the Seibal series alone (p = .03), approaches significance at Altar (p = .11), and is statistically significant if the two series are pooled (p = .01). Terminal Classic males ate more maize than did females. Together these observations imply a fundamental change in the definition of social status during the Terminal Classic.

Conclusions

Although social patterning was found in Late Classic diets, these distinctions do not entirely negate the chronological and intersite trends noted. For instance at Altar, elimination of the two Cluster D samples would not affect the

δ^{13}C trends, and would have little effect on δ^{15}N stability. Although it could be argued that the Altar series is biased toward higher status burials from monumental architecture, the low mean δ^{15}N at Altar does not support this idea. Instead, the data indicate a fair degree of site-specificity in dietary practices, governed by both environmental and cultural factors during the Late Classic period. Terminal Classic diets do not show social heterogeneity, so there is little reason to suspect their representativeness. Given that the nature of dietary partitioning appears to have changed over the span of Pasión history, it would be impossible to obtain directly parallel samples from each period. With these caveats, I assume that the data do reflect broader trends in Pasión diets.

The three dietary expectations of the ecological model are not fully borne out by the isotopic data. Maize was an important crop in the Pasión, but its consumption did not universally increase with agricultural expansion. If maize consumption is to be blamed for health problems often implicated in the collapse, Terminal Classic declines in δ^{13}C at Altar and perhaps Dos Pilas imply an improvement in health and contradict the ecological model. White et al. (1994) argue that a Terminal Classic decline in δ^{13}C at Pacbitun supports the ecological model, because maize supplies were insufficient. If, however, maize production was expanded to its limits, as they suggest, then ecozones for exploitation of wild C_3 flora would no longer remain, and δ^{13}C should remain high rather than dropping. The nitrogen isotopic data for the Pasión confirm that animal protein supplies were not compromised by increasing population density. Faunal analyses at Seibal and the Petexbatún sites demonstrate continued exploitation of primary forest fauna and, indirectly, the maintenance of these ecozones (Emery 1991; Pohl 1985b). Likewise, Nick Dunning's (pers. comm. 1994) paleoecological studies of the Laguna Tamarindito document minimal Late

Classic soil erosion but substantial quantities of forest tree pollen. Although preliminary, these data imply that deforestation had not reached a critical point in the Petexbatún area. Moreover, the prevalence of enamel hypoplasia, porotic hyperostosis, and periosteal reactions on the human skeletal remains illustrate no deterioration of health over time in the Pasión (Wright 1994). In short, there is no concrete evidence to support an ecological model for the collapse of this region.

It is important to recall that the ecological model arose at a time when the myth of the maize *milpa* dominated perceptions of ancient Maya subsistence. The prevailing perception of ancient agriculture as simple slash-and-burn cultivation of maize was derived from an overly simplistic characterization of Ladinized modern *Peteneros*. We now know that traditional Maya agriculture is complex and exploits microhabitat diversity; this intricate system of "agroforestry" provides a better model for ancient land use and agronomic strategies (Atran 1993; Barrera et al. 1977; Nations and Nigh 1980). We should also be wary of direct analogy that projects modern Mesoamerican diets back into prehistory. In addition to 500 years of Postclassic culture change, the Spanish Conquest initiated substantial changes in Mesoamerican subsistence. For instance, the tortilla became an omnipresent element of Maya meals only recently. As depicted on polychrome ceramics, the Classic Maya primarily consumed maize as tamales, not tortillas (Taube 1989). This dietary shift may have had a significant effect on the role of maize in modern diets. More than dietary preference, today's menu choices are controlled by political inequality in a national economy that bears little resemblance to the Maya past.

Instead, the chemical and mortuary data shed light on changes in the social fabric of Terminal Classic Maya society. Epigraphic and archaeological study is now revealing intense political competition between local Pasión polities at the close of the Classic Period, which implies a dramatic shift in social interaction (Demarest 1992; Demarest and Houston 1989, 1990; Demarest, Inomata et al. 1991, 1992; Valdés et al. 1993). Instead of ecological catastrophe, these sociopolitical transformations are key to unraveling the process of collapse. We can look to the Maya for lessons in tropical ecology, but those lessons are not necessarily negative cautionary tales.

Acknowledgments

This research was conducted in conjunction with Vanderbilt University's Petexbatún Regional Archaeological Project, under the general direction of Dr. A. A. Demarest. Petexbatún excavations have been funded by Vanderbilt University, National Geographic Society, National Endowment for the Humanities, U.S. Agency for International Development, U.S. Institute for Peace, H. F. Guggenheim Foundation, Kerns S. A., Aviateca, and the Swedish International Development Agency. I am grateful to the Peabody Museum of Harvard University and the Instituto de Antropología e Historia de Guatemala for permission to sample skeletons for chemical analysis. I thank Arthur Demarest and Kevin Johnston for the opportunity to study the Petexbatún and Itzán skeletal series. The isotopic analysis of bone samples was funded by a National Science Foundation dissertation improvement grant (BNS 91-12561) and a Wenner-Gren Foundation predoctoral grant (#5447) awarded to Dr. J. E. Buikstra and L. E. Wright. I am grateful to L. Tieszen and M. Chapman at Augustana College, and M. Schoeninger at the University of Wisconsin, Madison, who undertook the laboratory analysis. Fellowship support from the National Science and Engineering Research Council of Canada, the Canadian Federation of University Women, and the University of Chicago was crucial to success of the research. An early version of this paper was presented at the VIII Simposio de Arqueología Guatemalteca in July 1994 and appeared in the Simposio proceedings in Spanish (Wright 1995). Critical comments by Jane Buikstra, Steve Whittington, and Dave Reed improved this manuscript substantially, though I remain culpable for its content.

15

Regional Diversity in Classic Maya Diets

John P. Gerry and Harold W. Krueger

Maize is the dominant staple in the Maya subsistence base. It is prepared in a variety of ways and eaten at every meal, and it accounts for more than 70% of the calories and proteins consumed in modern Maya households (Béhar 1968; Benedict and Steggerda 1937; Katz et al. 1975; Vogt 1990). The Maya also cultivate beans, squash, and a variety of other vegetables, fruits, and herbs, but their relationship with maize is particularly close and longstanding. Historical documents dating as far back as the 16th century record its predominance in the recent past (e.g., Tozzer 1941), and several different kinds of archaeological evidence attest to its importance during the Precolumbian eras (e.g., Healy et al. 1983; Lentz 1991; Taube 1989; Turner and Harrison 1983; Wiseman 1983). The Maya themselves, in the *Popol Vuh*, referred to its role at the very creation of life: The first humans were modeled from corn meal and took their strength from it, thus marking maize literally as "food alone for the human legs and arms" (Tedlock 1985:163–164).

In recent years, with the development of so-phisticated scientific techniques, archaeologists have begun to quantify the role of maize in ancient Maya diets, and to ask questions about patterns of consumption that go beyond simple subsistence issues. Was there any relationship between diet and social status, or between diet and sex? Did levels of maize consumption remain constant through time and space? Can shifts in dietary behavior be tied to political events such as the Classic Maya collapse? Most of this research has been conducted through the analysis of stable isotope ratios preserved in human bone. Site-specific studies have been published for Lamanai (White and Schwarcz 1989), Pacbitun (White et al. 1993) and Copán (Reed 1994), and regional analyses have been completed for the southwestern Petén (Wright, this volume) and for the Belize River Valley, the Copán Pocket, and the northeastern and southwestern Petén combined (Gerry 1993).

Almost all of these analyses have focused on the carbon and nitrogen isotope ratios preserved in *collagen,* the organic bone fraction. The carbon ratios ($\delta^{13}C_{co}$) have been interpreted as an index of overall diet, that is, as a reflection of C_3 vs. C_4 intake from all foods mixed together, and the nitrogen ratios ($\delta^{15}N$) have been interpreted as an index of dietary protein, reflecting relative degrees of herbivory and carnivory, legume consumption, and marine vs. terrestrial distinctions (see Schwarcz and Schoeninger 1991 for a review). To date, the inorganic bone fraction, a crystalline mineral called *apatite,* has usually been ignored because it is prone to diagenesis. However, apatite does contain dietary carbon, and the original isotopic signature of that carbon can be recovered if the bone is chemically pretreated to remove adsorbed carbonates from the crystal surfaces (Krueger 1991). Once done, apatite appears to be the most appropriate tissue for tracking C_3 vs. C_4 carbohydrate intake (Krueger and Sullivan 1984; Lee-Thorp et al. 1989); there is even evidence to suggest that it is better than collagen for tracking whole diet (Ambrose and Norr 1993; Tieszen and Fagre 1993b).

The purpose of this study, therefore, is to add a large set of carbon ratios from apatite ($\delta^{13}C_{ap}$) to the growing corpus of Maya isotope data, and to examine the ways in which they complement or contradict the collagen indexes with regard to patterns of regional diversity. Skeletal samples for the project were drawn from seven Classic period sites: Copán, Seibal, Altar de Sacrificios, Holmul, Uaxactún, Barton Ramie, and Baking Pot. Their isotopic profiles for collagen and for apatite conform to the expected ratios for maize agriculturists, and statistical evaluation of the results indicates that geographic and ecological factors are more significant determinants of maize intake than are social or temporal factors (cf. Gerry 1993).

Theoretical Background

Maize is isotopically distinct among all of the Classic Maya plant foods owing to its carbon composition. The stable carbon isotopes are

^{12}C and ^{13}C. They exist in the atmosphere at a given ratio and are fractionated as a result of chemical reactions that occur during photosynthesis in the plant food web. The degree of fractionation is variable as a function of leaf structure and plant metabolism. Most plants, including all trees, shrubs, and grasses from temperate or shady environments, fixate CO_2 by means of the C_3 photosynthetic pathway, meaning that the CO_2 is metabolized into a three-carbon compound (Calvin and Benson 1948). In contrast, tropical grasses that grow in sunny areas, including maize, fixate CO_2 by means of the C_4 pathway (Hatch and Slack 1966). As a group, C_4 plants have an average $\delta^{13}C$ value of $-12.5‰$; they are isotopically enriched in ^{13}C relative to C_3 plants, which have an average $\delta^{13}C$ value of $-26.5‰$. Succulents follow an entirely different photosynthetic pathway called CAM (Crassulacean Acid Metabolism). Their isotope ratios are intermediate between C_3 and C_4 plants.

The archaeological significance of these isotopic signatures is that they are transferred to body tissues such as skin, hair, muscle, fat, and most importantly, bone, as a result of food consumption and metabolism (DeNiro and Epstein 1978; Tieszen et al. 1983); and because maize was unique in the Maya area as a C_4 cultigen (Gerry 1993), its dietary presence is particularly easy to detect. The most commonly used model for dietary reconstruction holds that carbon isotope ratios in bone collagen are fractionated by an additional $5‰$ relative to overall diet (van der Merwe and Vogel 1978). Accordingly, a pure C_3 diet should yield a $\delta^{13}C_{co}$ value of $-21.5‰$ and a strict C_4 diet should yield a $\delta^{13}C_{co}$ value of $-7.5‰$. A dietary mix of C_3 and C_4 elements should produce values between these two extremes, and because the distribution of $\delta^{13}C$ values for C_3 and C_4 plants is perfectly bimodal (i.e., there is no overlap between the ranges around those means; see van der Merwe 1982), the contribution of each plant type to overall diet can be calculated in

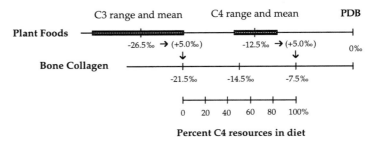

Figure 15.1. Simple model of carbon isotope fractionation between plant food diet and bone collagen.

terms of percentage (Fig. 15.1). White and Schwarcz (1989) used this model in their isotopic analysis of the Lamanai skeletons to demonstrate how temporal fluctuations in maize dependence corresponded to major shifts in political and economic organization.

Despite the simplicity of this model and its apparent utility in studies of maize consumption, it does not always hold true in analyses of animals with diets of known isotopic composition (Lee-Thorp et al. 1989); nor does it withstand testing in feeding experiments with laboratory rats (Ambrose and Norr 1993; Tieszen and Fagre 1993b). Collagen is not a repository for all dietary carbon. It is a protein matrix responsible for bone growth and turnover, and as such its isotopic composition is primarily determined by dietary protein (Krueger and Sullivan 1984). Furthermore, the fractionation of the carbon isotopes between whole diet and bone collagen is not constant at 5‰; it varies according to the dietary mixture and proportions of macronutrients. The trophic step between herbivores and carnivores produces a secondary fractionation, such that carnivore collagen is enriched by a total of 8‰ relative to the plants at the base of the food web, 3‰ more positive than herbivore collagen (Lee-Thorp et al. 1989).

The isotopic composition of bone apatite, in contrast, is a function of energy metabolism (Krueger and Sullivan 1984). For herbivores, plant food carbohydrates are the most important source of energy, and for carnivores lipids and proteins are the most important source of energy. Thus, the routing of dietary nutrients into apatite is not so specific as it is in the case of collagen. The carbonate ions from all dietary macronutrients are scrambled and combined before being incorporated into apatite (Ambrose and Norr 1993). Theoretically, this scrambling should be especially pronounced in the case of omnivorous diets, where energy demands can be met by carbohydrates, lipids, or proteins (Tieszen and Fagre 1993b). The Classic Maya probably met most of their energy requirements with C_4 maize carbohydrates, but they also ate a variety of C_3 plants and animals that would have contributed lipids and proteins for energy metabolism. The net effect of this nutrient scrambling is that the fractionation between whole diet and bone apatite is constant, regardless of trophic level. Lee-Thorp et al. (1989) set the value of this fractionation at 12‰ (Fig. 15.2), based on the isotopic evaluation of herbivores, omnivores, and carnivores in South Africa. Ambrose and Norr (1993) agree that the diet-apatite fractionation is constant, but they set its value at 9.5‰. Their result is based on controlled feeding experiments using laboratory rats.

Because of the fixed fractionation between whole diet and apatite, and the routing of protein into collagen, the spacing between $\delta^{13}C_{ap}$ and $\delta^{13}C_{co}$ has been modeled as an index of meat consumption (Krueger and Sullivan 1984; Lee-Thorp et al. 1989). Herbivore spacing averages about 7‰, omnivore spacing averages about 5‰, and carnivore spacing averages about 3‰ to 4‰. These figures were calculated exclusively from faunal data, but a good example of their relevance to human dietary

John P. Gerry and Harold W. Krueger

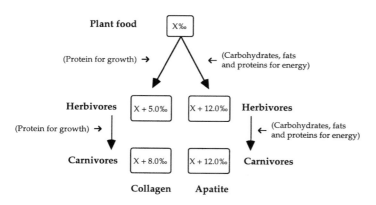

Figure 15.2. Model of carbon isotope fractionation between plant food diet and bone tissues in herbivores and carnivores (after Lee-Thorp et al. 1989; cf. Krueger and Sullivan 1984).

analysis is provided by Roksandic et al. (1988). They found that the collagen-apatite spacings of Jomon hunter-gatherers in southern and central Japan were about 4‰ more positive than those of Ainu populations to the north, indicating significantly greater meat dependency for the Ainu. Nitrogen isotope data are more commonly used as a gauge of meat vs. vegetable intake, but this spacing model illustrates yet another way in which $\delta^{13}C_{ap}$ is an appropriate data set for evaluating prehistoric diet. Perhaps most impressive is the fact that $\delta^{13}C_{ap}$ values actually track overall diet more closely than do $\delta^{13}C_{co}$ values.

The basic model for dietary reconstruction using nitrogen isotopes holds that the $^{15}N/^{14}N$ ratios in collagen (there is no nitrogen in apatite) are enriched by 3‰ to 4‰ relative to diet (Schwarcz and Schoeninger 1991), and that the marine and terrestrial food chains are isotopically distinct (Schoeninger and DeNiro 1984). $\delta^{15}N$ ratios average about 5‰ to 6‰ for terrestrial herbivores and about 8‰ to 9‰ for terrestrial carnivores. The marine food chain is more positive still, with the values of mollusks, fish, and marine mammals ranging from 12‰ to 20‰.

Materials and Methods

We chose 178 Maya individuals for isotopic analysis. The sampling strategy was determined

in large part by skeletal preservation and availability, but was also designed to insure focused and unbiased results. They are all adults, they all date to the Classic period (most of them to the Late Classic), they are of both sexes (50 women, 66 men, 62 unknown), and they were found in a variety of mortuary contexts. As a reflection of social status, not all of them were treated equally in death. Some were found in complex tombs with exotic furnishings and others were found in simple pits with no grave goods whatsoever.

Perhaps the most important of all the sampling criteria is that this study is regional in scope. The sample population is therefore drawn from seven different sites located throughout the Maya area: Uaxactún (Smith 1950), Holmul (Merwin and Vaillant 1932), Seibal (Tourtellot 1990a), and Altar (Smith 1972) in the Petén; Baking Pot (Ricketson 1931) and Barton Ramie (Willey et al. 1965) in the Belize River Valley; and the Main Group of Copán and its satellite settlements in extreme western Honduras (Gordon 1896; Hodges and Leventhal n.d.). They are an appropriate subset of Maya settlements for several reasons. First, they represent the whole spectrum of the Maya site hierarchy. Copán, at one extreme, was a true civic-ceremonial center and it stands as one of the largest and most elaborate of all Maya sites. Barton Ramie, at the other extreme, was a rural settlement of purely domestic nature and not at all complex in terms of architecture. Second, these are all inland sites and most of them are located near rivers that flow year-round; only Uaxactún and Holmul are located in the less-dependably watered *bajo* country. Third, they are all located in similar climatic zones in terms of seasonality, temperature, and rainfall; and all but Copán are lowland sites in terms of elevation above sea level. Finally, each one drew upon a similar floral and faunal resource base (Wing 1981; Wiseman 1983).

As the carbon content of meat is also a determinant of human isotope ratios, several animal species were selected for analysis. Among those most commonly consumed were deer and peccary; their bones are found in abundance at most Maya sites. Dog bones are also commonly found, but as domesticates they might have been valued more as hunting companions or as guardians than they were as food (see Gerry 1993). The total faunal sample consists of 111 individuals, of which 36 were analyzed for $\delta^{13}C_{ap}$: 16 white-tailed deer (*Odocoileus virginianus*), one brocket deer (*Mazama americana*), 11 peccaries (*Tayassu* spp.), five dogs (*Canis* spp.), one paca (*Cuniculus paca*), and two pumas (*Felis cóncolor mayensis*). Most of them were excavated at Copán.

Sampling skeletons for isotopic analysis is a destructive process. A 5-g bone fragment is required for each sample and it is destroyed during the course of chemical treatment. Most of the collagen for this project was prepared at Harvard University according to the protocol outlined by Sealy (1989), whereby the bone samples are not powdered, but are left as chunks so as to promote the formation of collagen pseudomorphs. The chunks are subjected to several phases of surface cleaning, slow demineralization in dilute hydrochloric acid (1% to 2% HCl), and overnight soaking in .1 molar sodium hydroxide (NaOH) in order to remove humic contaminants. After sample combustion and cryogenic purification of the resultant CO_2 and N_2 gases, the stable isotope ratios for each

of the skeletons are determined on a VG Prism 2 mass spectrometer. Diagnostic indexes used to determine the integrity of collagen composition include percent yield calculations and atomic percent carbon to nitrogen ratios (see Ambrose and Norr 1992); any samples with signs of postmortem chemical alteration are discarded. Approximately 85% of the samples chosen for this study yielded reliable isotopic data for collagen. Instrument precision was .2‰ or better based on the analysis of NBS limestone and graphite standards, an acetanalide (C_8H_9NO) standard, and an interlaboratory bovine collagen standard (Merck Gel).

The apatite analyses were conducted at the Geochron Labs in Cambridge, Massachusetts, according to the protocol described by Krueger (1991). Bone samples are cleaned, ground into small chunks, treated with acetic acid (CH_3COOH) to remove surface carbonates (those most likely to exchange isotopically with groundwater and soils), and then reacted under vacuum with HCl so as to liberate the apatite as CO_2 while simultaneously preserving organic residues for future collagen analysis. The liberated CO_2 is cryogenically purified, sealed into Pyrex ampoules, and then admitted to a VG 903 mass spectrometer for determination of isotope ratios.

Faunal Results

The isotopic separation between C_3 and C_4 consumers is most clearly illustrated by the faunal data (Fig. 15.3; Table 15.1). On the collagen axis, the deer, peccaries, and pumas have carbon values that cluster around $-21.5‰$, a strong C_3 signature. Two of the peccaries stand as outliers with values of $-15.7‰$ and $-10.6‰$, and two of the deer have values of $-19.0‰$ and $-18.3‰$. The C_4 protein influence on these animals could either indicate that they were semidomesticated (see Dillon

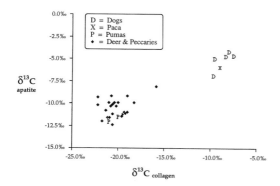

Figure 15.3. Scatterplot illustrating relationship between $\delta^{13}C_{co}$ and $\delta^{13}C_{ap}$ values in herbivores and carnivores with C_3 and C_4 diets.

1988; Pohl 1990) or that they invaded *milpas* for food (see Linares 1976). In either case, maize probably was not a major component of their diets, as the average $\delta^{13}C_{ap}$ value for these species is $-10.6 \pm .9‰$. Presumably, this figure is 12‰ more positive than bulk diet, putting the resources at the base of this food web comfortably within a C_3 range of $-21.7‰$ to $-23.5‰$.

The dogs, as domesticates, all have very positive carbon isotope ratios. The minimum $\delta^{13}C_{co}$ value is $-10.7‰$, the maximum is $-7.5‰$, and the average is $-8.9‰$. Potential C_4 protein sources in their diets include small

prey animals that lived and ate in maize fields, or human fecal matter (cf. White and Schwarcz 1989). Their $\delta^{13}C_{ap}$ values, which average $-5.0‰$, attest further to a heavy dependence on C_4 carbohydrates. In one ethnographic study, Maya dogs were observed to scavenge six to eight tortillas a day (Benedict and Steggerda 1937).

Dogs are accompanied in the C_4 cluster only by one other specimen, the paca. It has a $\delta^{13}C_{co}$ value of $-8.9‰$ and a $\delta^{13}C_{ap}$ value of $-5.9‰$. Pacas are nocturnal rodents and they do eat maize and other cultivated crops, so the positive carbon isotope ratios are not entirely unexpected. However, if this animal did subsist primarily on maize, it seems unusual that the apatite signature is not even more positive. The spacing between the collagen and apatite values is only 3‰, which, according to the model presented above, indicates a carnivorous diet. As a herbivore, the paca gets all of its carbohydrates, fats, and proteins from plant material, and should therefore have collagen to apatite spacing more along the lines of 7‰.

The collagen to apatite spacing model does work well for most of the other animals included in this study. The deer, as herbivores, have an average spacing value of almost 10‰; the peccaries, technically omnivores but pri-

Table 15.1   Summary Statistics for Animals (n = 111)

	$\delta^{13}C_{co}$			$\delta^{13}C_{ap}$			$\delta^{15}N$		
	n	Mean	sd	n	Mean	sd	n	Mean	sd
Odocoileus virginianus	46	−21.1	0.9	16	−10.4	0.8	44	4.4	1.3
Mazama americana	4	−21.7	2.2	1	−9.9	–	2	5.9	1.0
Tayassu pecari and									
Tayassu tajacu	32	−20.6	2.6	11	−10.7	1.3	32	4.1	1.1
Felis cóncolor mayensis	2	−20.5	0.8	2	−11.7	0.4	2	8.3	0.1
Canis familiaris or									
Canis caribaeus	17	−8.9	0.9	5	−5.0	1.0	13	6.2	1.2
Cuniculus paca	1	−8.9	–	1	−5.9	–	1	6.2	–

NOTE: n = number of specimens; sd = standard deviation.

marily herbivores (Gamero 1978), have an average spacing value of 9.3‰; and the dogs, as opportunistic omnivores, have spacing that averages 3.6‰. As dedicated carnivores, the pumas should also have tight spacing, but in this study the distance between their collagen and apatite values is almost 9‰. Their diets were definitely protein rich, but the extra trophic level is not reflected very strongly on the collagen axis.

The $\delta^{15}N$ signatures of these animals do conform to the expected results for herbivores, omnivores, and carnivores. The deer (white-tailed and brocket combined) and the peccaries have average $\delta^{15}N$ values of 4.5‰ and 4.1‰ respectively, perhaps indicating that legumes formed a substantial part of their diets. (Legumes such as peas, peanuts, or beans derive their nitrogen from the air and the soil, and have isotope ratios similar to those found in atmospheric N_2, i.e., $\delta^{15}N = 0‰$; nonlegumes get nitrogen from the soil only and have isotope ratios that are somewhat more positive.) The pumas have an average $\delta^{15}N$ value of 8.3‰, reflecting the trophic level shift of 3‰ to 4‰; and as omnivores, the dogs have $\delta^{15}N$ values that fall in between at 6.2‰.

Human Results

The importance of maize in Classic Maya diets is clearly indicated by the $\delta^{13}C_{co}$ and $\delta^{13}C_{ap}$ signatures for this sample population (Fig. 15.4). The average $\delta^{13}C_{co}$ value, at $-10.2 \pm 1.3‰$, is heavily weighted toward the C_4 side of the scale. Had meat been the primary source of protein, this value would be significantly more negative, in accord with the data discussed above which show that the most commonly utilized Maya meat resources were all C_3 species. The consumption of C_4 dog meat could have produced the more positive collagen values, but this possibility seems unlikely. Dog

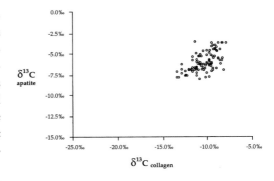

Figure 15.4. Scatterplot illustrating relationship between $\delta^{13}C_{co}$ and $\delta^{13}C_{ap}$ values in human sample population.

bones only account for about 3% of the total number of animals excavated at most Maya sites (Wing 1981). It seems much more likely that protein derived from maize was responsible for the positive collagen values, especially given the modern Maya analogy where maize contributes approximately 70% of the protein diet (Béhar 1968).

The average Maya $\delta^{13}C_{ap}$ value is $-5.9 \pm 1.2‰$. As an index of overall consumption, this figure indicates that Classic Maya diets were typically composed of about 55% maize. This calculation is merely an estimate; it assumes a $\delta^{13}C$ value for maize of $-11‰$ (see Gerry 1993), an average C_3 plant food value of $-26.5‰$, and a fractionation between whole diet and bone apatite of 12‰. The balance of the Maya energy requirements must have been met by C_3 cultigens. Carbohydrates were available in starchy supplements like sweet potatoes, ramon, and manioc, and fats were available in oily plants and plant products like avocados, bottle gourds, and squash seeds. Other published estimates of maize (i.e., C_4) intake at Maya sites are derived from collagen data and range between about 40% and 75%, depending on such factors as time, sex, status, and regional location (White et al. 1993; White and Schwarcz 1989).

The average human $\delta^{15}N$ value produced by this study is 8.7 ± 1.0‰. None of the ratios within this range are positive enough to signal seafood consumption, so the source of variability must lie within the utilization of legumes and other plant proteins as compared to the utilization of animal resources. As a parallel index of meat consumption, the $\delta^{13}C_{ap}$-$\delta^{13}C_{co}$ spacing data average 4.4 ± 1.3‰, skewed somewhat toward the carnivore mean but not beyond the bounds of omnivory. The feeding experiments conducted by Tieszen and Fagre (1993b) indicate that maize diets do tend to produce narrow spacing values, probably as a function of the very strong C_4 protein signal.

Discussion

Although the descriptive statistics listed above provide a composite picture of Maya diet during the Classic period, they do not really provide much more information about subsistence patterning than is available through the traditional archaeological record. However, this sample data can be broken down into meaningful clusters and evaluated more specifically in a variety of ways. At Pacbitun for example, White et al. (1993) looked for and found significant variation along the lines of age, sex, social status, and time. They also examined differences in dietary behavior between Pacbitun and two other sites, Lamanai and Copán, from which isotopic data have been gathered, and concluded that environmental factors were responsible for the observed variation. Regional patterning is the focus of this study as well, but the sample population is much larger, reducing the likelihood of statistical errors. Moreover, the time-, sex-, and status-specific variation within this population has already been analyzed in detail and found to be statistically insignificant in most cases; and in all cases, interaction statistics and F-ratios produced by two-way ANOVA testing indicate that regional variation is highly significant compared to any of the other factors (Gerry 1993).

Site-by-site summary statistics are listed in Table 15.2. A series of two-sample t-tests were

Table 15.2 Summary Statistics for Sites and Regional Groups

	$\delta^{13}C_{co}$			$\delta^{13}C_{ap}$			$\delta^{15}N$		
	n	Mean	sd	n	Mean	sd	n	Mean	sd
Site									
Holmul	14	−9.4	1.3	19	−4.3	0.7	15	9.3	0.8
Uaxactún	6	−10.7	1.1	2	−5.7	0.2	5	9.4	1.0
Barton Ramie	38	−11.2	1.4	30	−7.0	0.5	38	8.8	0.4
Baking Pot	9	−11.0	1.1	4	−6.6	0.6	9	9.2	1.3
Altar de Sacrificios	18	−9.1	0.5	–	–	–	17	8.9	0.7
Seibal	27	−9.5	1.0	26	−6.2	0.8	28	9.5	0.7
Copán	16	−10.0	1.1	9	−5.8	1.3	15	7.6	0.7
Copán satellites	25	−10.3	0.8	27	−5.4	0.9	23	7.5	0.8
Region									
Petén region	65	−9.5	1.0	47	−5.4	1.2	65	9.3	0.8
Belize Valley region	47	−11.2	1.4	34	−7.0	0.6	47	8.9	0.7
Copán region	41	−10.2	0.9	36	−5.5	1.0	38	7.6	0.8

NOTE: n = number of specimens; sd = standard deviation.

Table 15.3 Student's T-test Results Comparing Regional Groups

Regional Comparison	$\delta^{13}C_{co}$			$\delta^{13}C_{ap}$			$\delta^{15}N$		
	p	df	t	p	df	t	p	df	t
Belize vs. Petén	< .01	110	7.672	< .01	79	7.163	< .01	110	2.988
Belize vs. Copán	< .01	86	4.013	< .01	68	7.245	< .01	83	8.172
Petén vs. Copán	< .01	104	3.653	> .50	81	.510	< .01	101	10.840

NOTE: p = p-value; df = degrees of freedom; t = t-test statistic.

used to focus the statistical analysis on specific site pairs, and to determine which of them were most similar and dissimilar. The final results (Tables 15.2 and 15.3) distinguish between three regional clusters: (1) Barton Ramie and Baking Pot; (2) Holmul, Uaxactún, Altar, and Seibal; and (3) the Copán Valley locales. The Petén and Copán groups have one isotopic mean ($\delta^{13}C_{ap}$) in common, but otherwise the differences in regional means are all statistically significant at greater than 99.99% confidence. Schematic illustrations of the isotopic separation between these regional groups are presented in Figures 15.5 and 15.6.

The $\delta^{13}C_{co}$ and $\delta^{15}N$ data, as protein indexes, are plotted in Figure 15.5; Lamanai and

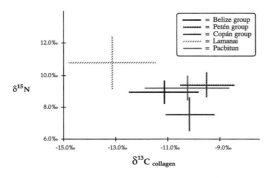

Figure 15.5. Schematic scatterplot showing isotopic separation of regional groups according to bone collagen indices (crossed-line plots represent mean values plus or minus one standard deviation).

Pacbitun have been included for comparison (see White et al. 1993). On the nitrogen axis, Copán and Lamanai are the two extremes, with average $\delta^{15}N$ values of 7.6 ± .8‰ and 10.7 ± 1.7‰ respectively. The other sites and regions all cluster closely together at about 9.0‰. These numbers suggest that the people from Copán had a more purely vegetarian diet, perhaps particularly weighted toward bean (i.e., legume) consumption, than did the rest of the sample population. At Lamanai, proximity to the Caribbean coast and the New River lagoon system seems to have provided site inhabitants with a greater variety of meat and marine resources (cf. White et al. 1993). These results are echoed on the carbon axis, where Lamanai stands again as the most extreme outlier. Its average $\delta^{13}C_{co}$ value of −13.1 ± 1.7‰ stands in sharp contrast to the other sites and regions which range from −9.5 ± 1.0‰ in the Petén to −11.2 ± 1.4‰ in the Belize River Valley. It is interesting to note that all of the most negative ratios occur at the Belizean sites. C₃ resources and maize alternatives must have been more abundant there. In contrast, the Petén and Copán populations relied on maize protein to a significantly greater degree.

The $\delta^{13}C_{co}$ and $\delta^{13}C_{ap}$ data are plotted in Figure 15.6, with the apatite axis providing a picture of overall dietary differences. The Belizean sites of Barton Ramie and Baking Pot are still significantly more negative than any of the

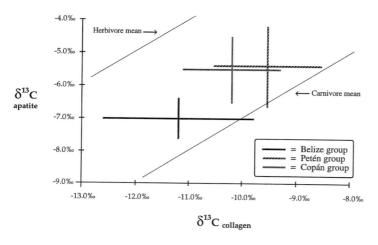

Figure 15.6. Schematic scatterplot showing isotopic separation of regional groups according to $\delta^{13}C$ indices for collagen and apatite (crossed-line plots represent mean values plus or minus one standard deviation).

other locales. Their combined average $\delta^{13}C_{ap}$ value is $-7.0 \pm .6‰$, which translates roughly to 48% C_4 consumption. The Petén and Copán Valley sites, which are significantly different on the $\delta^{13}C_{co}$ axis, actually share an average $\delta^{13}C_{ap}$ value of $-5.4‰$. So despite having different protein regimes, the people from these two areas consumed approximately the same amount of C_4 material, about 59% of bulk diet. The protein differential reflected on the collagen axis is probably the result of eating greater and lesser quantities of meat, with the Copán sample population leaning more toward vegetarianism. Their $\delta^{13}C_{co}$-$\delta^{13}C_{ap}$ spacing is 4.5‰; the people from the Petén sites have an average spacing value of 3.8‰, closer to the carnivore mean.

Again, these spacing values are quite narrow and seem to indicate a heavier dependence on meat resources than was probably the case. During the 16th century at least, meat was a rare component in Maya diets. Roys (1972) reports that tortillas, beans, squash seeds, and other vegetables were eaten at most meals and that game or fish was eaten regularly only by high-status people. Meat-poor diets are also common in modern contexts (Béhar 1968; Vogt 1990). In this light, and considering the fact that

the $\delta^{13}C$ values produced by this study are so positive, it is safe to assume that isotopically enriched maize proteins are responsible for skewing the Classic period spacing data toward the carnivore mean (cf. Tieszen and Fagre 1993b).

Local environment was undoubtedly an important factor in dietary behavior. The Lamanai sample population, for example, had access to a wider variety of aquatic and terrestrial resources than did people who lived further inland, or in drier areas to the west. They took advantage of those resources, and their isotopic profiles stand as a reflection of that behavior; the large standard deviations around their $\delta^{13}C_{co}$ and $\delta^{15}N$ means attest to the diversity of available foodstuffs and to the tailoring of diet to personal taste. Apparently, such extreme deviation from the standard fare was not possible in the other Maya areas. The people from Copán, in particular, appear to have been especially dependent on maize and beans, perhaps as a result of dietary constraints imposed by their upland environment. Still, environment alone is only part of the equation that results in specific dietary adaptations.

Human ecology, the interaction between people and their environment, is also an important consideration. The Copán Valley was a very densely populated area. No matter how diverse the local food base might have been, the urban sprawl and concomitant high demand for resource procurement must have eventually surpassed the renewability of wild resources; thus the dependence on cultivated crops that could be grown intensively and continuously. Assuming that meat resources were scarce around Copán, it is not too surprising that the site inhabitants had such depleted $\delta^{15}N$ values. In fact, the isotopic data produced by this study reveal a gradient in domesticated crop dependence that is proportional to site size and settlement density (cf. Gerry 1993). At the opposite end of the site hierarchy from Copán, the rural Belize Valley sample populations, together with those from Lamanai and Pacbitun, have the most negative $\delta^{13}C_{co}$ and $\delta^{13}C_{ap}$ signatures. They must have had access to the full range of lowland resources, including C_4, C_3, marine, and terrestrial foodstuffs. The rest of the sites, in the more densely settled Petén, also have fairly positive $\delta^{15}N$ profiles, marking meat consumption, but their $\delta^{13}C_{co}$ and $\delta^{13}C_{ap}$ values are relatively enriched, marking a fairly heavy dependence on C_4 proteins and carbohydrates.

Conclusions

Regional differences in dietary behavior are clearly manifest on all three isotope axes. The most outstanding separation occurs between the sites found in the Maya heartland, including Copán, and those found to the east in modern-day Belize. Lamanai stands alone as an isotopic outlier even from the other Belizean sites, but Barton Ramie, Baking Pot, and Pacbitun actually cluster together fairly well. Of course, $\delta^{13}C_{ap}$ values have not yet been generated for Lamanai and Pacbitun samples, so for the time being their isotopic profiles are incomplete.

The real strength of the apatite data as employed in this study is in tracking whole diet and providing reliable estimates of C_3 vs. C_4 consumption. $\delta^{13}C_{co}$ data are unreliable in this respect as they are specifically tied to the protein portion of diet. It is interesting to note that the $\delta^{13}C_{ap}$ data actually serve to bring the Copán and Petén sites into closer accord than is suggested by the $\delta^{13}C_{co}$ data alone. Maize consumption was equally heavy in both areas, but not equally important in terms of protein requirements. The dietary balance between maize, meat, and legume consumption, and between dietary proportions of proteins, fats, and carbohydrates, seems to have fluctuated as a function of settlement density and local environment. These fluctuations would not be visible without the apatite data.

Part of the model for dietary reconstruction that needs adjustment in the Maya case is that which deals with the spacing between $\delta^{13}C_{ap}$ and $\delta^{13}C_{co}$ values. The previously calculated means for herbivores and carnivores do not consistently fit with the faunal data presented here. Most of the animals have spacing values that fall in the neighborhood of the predicted means, but they do not fall along the mean, and the puma and paca spacing values actually stand in direct contradiction to the expected trends. Moreover, the human values are quite narrow in comparison to the expected mean for omnivores, probably because of the isotopically enriched maize proteins that were such an important part of their diets. In order to rectify these problems, more isotopic data should be gathered from the major game species, as well as from small mammals, reptiles, rodents, and freshwater foodstuffs.

Other future studies might focus on a broader spectrum of habitats. The coastal regions, the northern lowlands, the southern highlands, and the transition zones in between are all candidates. None of these areas have been isotopically modeled yet, except for the preliminary work done in the Soconusco region (Blake et al. 1992). Another set of important questions concern the size of local catchment basins, the amount of habitable and usable land as a percentage of total land, and the response of different ecosystems to varying levels of human population pressure. It is of particular importance that all future isotopic studies of Maya dietary behavior include bone apatite as tissue for analysis.

16

Ancient and Contemporary Mitochondrial DNA Variation in the Maya

D. Andrew Merriwether,
David M. Reed, and
Robert E. Ferrell

With the advent of the polymerase chain reaction (PCR) (Saiki et al. 1988) it is now possible to extract DNA from ancient human bone, tissue, teeth, and hair and to amplify the number of copies of DNA to levels which enable molecular genetic analyses. Prior to the invention of PCR, it was not possible to retrieve enough high molecular weight DNA from ancient remains to perform DNA sequencing or restriction fragment length polymorphism (RFLP) analyses. In addition, the advent of PCR has enabled researchers to amplify and analyze DNA from small amounts of blood or plasma from living individuals. In the past ten years these techniques have been applied to the study of the peopling of the New World through the analysis of mitochondrial DNA (mtDNA) variation in ancient and contemporary Native Americans. Wallace et al. (1985) showed that all Native Americans are closely related, and showed evidence for a bottleneck in Amerindian genetic variation compared with modern Asian variation. Schurr et al. (1990) demonstrated that all Native American mtDNA variation can be traced back to just four founding lineages, and that all contemporary Amerindians are descendants of one of these four lineages (termed A, B, C, and D). Merriwether et al. (1994, 1995) and Stone and Stoneking (1994) proved that variants of the four founding lineages were also present in ancient populations.

It is first necessary to present some background about basic genetics, mtDNA, and the methods of data collection, before discussing the data and results. DNA consists of four different components (referred to as nucleotides or bases): adenosine (A), guanine (G), cytosine (C), and thymine (T). There are two primary locations for human genetic material in human cells. Nuclear DNA resides inside the nucleus of cells in the form of chromosomes (22 pairs of autosomes and a pair of sex chromosomes). An individual receives a complete set of 22 autosomes and one sex chromosome from each parent, for a total of 46 chromosomes. The maternally and paternally derived chromosomes exchange portions of their DNA during meiosis. This is called recombination, and leads to each chromosome in the nucleus of the progeny becoming a chimera of maternal and paternal genes. Mitochondrial DNA exists outside the nucleus in an organelle called the mitochondrion. Mitochondrial DNA is a circular molecule, some 16,569 nucleotides (nts) in length (Anderson et al. 1981). Mitochondrial DNA encodes genes which are involved in energy production for the cells, oxidative phosphorylation, and cellular respiration. There are 37 genes in the mtDNA molecule: 13 protein-coding genes, 2 ribosomal RNAs (rRNAs), and 22 transfer RNAs (tRNAs). The protein-encoding genes create subunits of Cytochrome oxidase, NADH dehydrogenase, ATPase, and Cytochrome B. The mtDNA has its own unique tRNAs, and some mtDNA tRNAs code for different amino acids than do the nuclear tRNAs. For example, in mtDNA both AGG and AGA code for protein chain termination, but in nuclear DNA they encode the amino acid arginine. There are approximately 1500 copies of mtDNA in every cell, as there are an average of 2.6 copies of mtDNA per mitochondrion, and an average of 750 mitochondria per cell. This means that there are many more copies of mtDNA than of nuclear DNA in each cell (an important consideration when trying to recover DNA from ancient or suboptimal sources). Mitochondrial DNA is maternally inherited in mammals, meaning that only females pass on their mtDNA to the next generation. Mitochondrial DNA does not undergo recombination, so it is transmitted intact from mother to daughter, generation after generation. The only changes that occur in mtDNA are due to point mutations, insertions, and deletions (with insertions and deletions being rare). Mitochondrial DNA has a mutation rate that is six to ten times higher than that of nuclear DNA, making it an excellent molecule to study when addressing questions involving relatively recently separated individuals, populations, or species. Lastly, the mtDNA from more than 100 individuals has been completely sequenced, making it simple to design primers necessary for the PCR technique, and making it relatively simple to assign the precise location to restriction site cuts.

The data described here were collected by cutting the PCR-amplified mtDNA with restriction enzymes. A restriction enzyme recognizes a specific sequence of four or more bases (nucleotides) and cleaves the DNA strand whenever it detects this "recognition sequence." Restriction enzymes are produced by bacteria as a defense mechanism against invading DNAs from viruses, plasmids, or other bacteria that try to integrate their DNA into the host bacterium's DNA. The name of the restriction enzyme is derived from the host bacterium. For example, Alu I was the first restriction endonuclease derived from the bacterium *Arthrobacter luteus*. The convention for naming restriction endonucleases is to use the first letter from the genus name and the first two letters from the species name (hence, Alu I). If multiple restriction enzymes are derived from a single species, they are numbered with Roman numerals (I, II, III, etc.) in the order in which they were discovered. Alu I, as an example, recognizes the sequence AGCT and cuts the DNA between the G and the C. Alu I would cleave the illustrated (Fig. 16.1) 35-base-pair (bp) sequence into fragments, one 14 bases long and one 21 bases long.

When one loads DNA on an agarose gel and runs current across the gel, the negatively charged DNA molecules move toward the positive electrode. The gel matrix separates the fragments by size. Because the smaller fragments can more easily pass through the matrix,

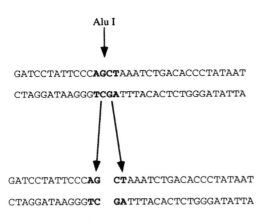

Alu I

GATCCTATTCCC**AGCT**AAATCTGACACCCTATAAT

CTAGGATAAGGG**TCGA**TTTACACTCTGGGATATTA

GATCCTATTCCC**AG**   **CT**AAATCTGACACCCTATAAT

CTAGGATAAGGG**TC**   **GA**TTTACACTCTGGGATATTA

Figure 16.1. Alu I recognizes base sequence AGCT and cuts DNA between G and C.

they move farther through the gel than do the larger fragments in the same time period. It is then easy to tell a 35-bp uncut piece of DNA in one lane from 21-bp and 14-bp DNA fragments in another lane. There are hundreds of restriction enzymes, each recognizing a different specific sequence. It is possible to construct "haplotypes" for different individuals by cutting their DNAs with many different restriction enzymes and compiling a pattern of cuts and lack-of-cuts for each enzyme for each individual. This is how Schurr et al. (1990) discovered that all Native Americans can be traced back to one of four founding haplotypes generated by using 14 restriction enzymes on mtDNA from a large number of individuals. These four founding lineage haplotypes can be defined by three RFLPs and a 9-bp deletion in the mtDNA.

We have collected RFLP data defining the four founding lineage haplogroups in nearly 2000 individuals from 27 contemporary and 3 ancient New World populations (Merriwether 1993; Merriwether et al. 1994, 1995). In addition, more than 30 populations have been reported in the literature (Ginther et al. 1993; Horai et al. 1993; Shields et al. 1992, 1993; Torroni et al. 1992; Torroni, Chen et al. 1994; Torroni, Neel et al. 1994; Torroni, Schurr et al. 1993; Torroni, Sukernik et al. 1993; Ward et al. 1991, 1993).

The lineages can be defined as follows:

Lineage A by the presence of a Hae III cut at nucleotide position (np) 663,
Lineage B by the presence of 9-bp deletion in Region V,
Lineage C by the absence of a Hinc II cut at np 13259 or the presence of an Alu I cut at np 13245,
Lineage D by the absence of an Alu I cut at np 5176.

The Hae III 663 site gain and the 9-bp deletion (defining lineages A and B) are, for all practical purposes, Asian-specific, and only populations of Asian descent (such as Amerindians and Pacific Islanders) tend to possess these mutations. The Hinc II 13259 and Alu I 5176 site losses (defining lineages C and D) are Asian-specific when they are accompanied by Dde I and Alu I site gains at np 10394 and np 10397 respectively. Thus, one can be fairly certain of dealing with Native American (or at least Asian) mtDNAs if they possess these patterns. Torroni et al. (1992) demonstrated this in a phylogenetic tree showing the clustering of the four founding lineages into the "haplogroups" A, B, C, and D.

Materials and Methods

Summaries of New World frequencies of these four founding lineage haplogroups in nearly 70 populations were obtained from the literature and from our own research, for comparison with the data obtained from Maya skeletal remains (ribs) from the Honduran site of Copán. DNA was extracted from rib fragments using the method of Merriwether et al. (1994). Briefly, this method consists of sterilizing the outside surface of the rib fragment with 10% bleach (which destroys DNA) and ultraviolet irradiation (which causes the DNA to cross-link, and therefore be an unamplifiable template for the DNA polymerase in PCR). This initial decontamination step is done to eliminate any "modern" contaminating DNAs deposited on the surface by handling the material. Modern DNA is typically much less degraded than is ancient DNA, and therefore is a better template for the PCR reaction. Thus, a small amount of modern DNA may be preferentially amplified out of a larger amount of ancient (damaged) DNA. After this decontamination step, the bone is heat-sealed in a "seal-a-meal" bag and immersed for 10 minutes in liquid nitrogen to make the bone more brittle. The bag is then removed from the liquid nitrogen, and the bone is crushed to powder inside the bag using a hammer. Once the bone is completely pulverized, the powder is removed from the bag, weighed, and placed in a 15-ml conical polypropylene tube (typically 1 g of pulverized bone is used). Two volumes of an extraction buffer containing 10 mM Tris-HCl (pH 8.0) as a buffer, 2 mM EDTA as a chelating agent, 10 mg/ml dithiothreitol (DTT) and .5 mg/ml Proteinase K to degrade the proteins, and .1% (v/v) sodium dodecyl sulfate (SDS) as a detergent are added. The tubes are then sealed, wrapped in parafilm, and rotated overnight at 37°C. The next day, the DNA is separated from the proteins by extractions using Tris-buffered phenol. One to two volumes of phenol are added directly to each sample, the tubes are resealed and parafilmed, and rotated at 37°C for 10 minutes, centrifuged at 3000 ×G for 10 minutes, and the DNA-containing aqueous (upper) layer is transferred to a new 15-ml conical polypropylene tube. This phenol extraction is repeated on the new tube, and then, after transfer of the aqueous layer to another 15-ml conical polypropylene tube, the sample is extracted

with 24:1 chloroform to isoamyl alcohol. In each extraction, proteins, cell debris, and other contaminants are left behind in the phenol or chloroform phase. The chloroform and isoamyl alcohol remove the phenol from the aqueous layer. The final aqueous layer is centrifuged through a 30,000 molecular weight (MW) cutoff microconcentrator at the manufacturer's recommended speed (this is 3000 ×G for a micron or Centricon 30). This device has a filter which only allows molecules smaller than 30,000 MW to pass through, retaining the larger particles (including the DNA we are trying to retrieve) above the filter. The sample is washed three times with filtered, distilled, deionized water. The DNA is recovered off the filter by inverting the device into a retentate cup and centrifuging at low speed (1000 rpm). The DNA in the retentate cup is then ready as a template for PCR, although it is often necessary to dilute the DNA 100:1 with dH$_2$O prior to amplification. This same method can easily be used to recover DNA from teeth, hair, or tissue (see Merriwether et al. 1994). We recommend that each sample be extracted in duplicate on separate dates to confirm the results. A single tooth, rib fragment, long bone, tissue sample, or hair bulb can serve as a sample. It requires less than a gram of "internal" material to recover DNA from ancient sources. Success ratios vary widely with the quality of the samples and presumably with the soil pH from which the samples were recovered. Alkaline soils preserve DNA much better then do acidic soils. Our success rate in amplifying DNA extracted from ancient remains ranges between 10% and 65% of samples from various sites throughout the New World. New methodologies have increased the success rates and can be expected to improve in the future.

The Copán site itself is described elsewhere in this volume by Whittington and Reed, and by Storey, who were involved in the collection

Table 16.1 Copán Sample Haplotype Data

CP ID[a]	Age (Years)	Sex	Date	Site Type	Lineage Haplotype	Hae III 663	9-bp Deletion	Hinc II 13259	Alu I 13245	Alu I 5176
180	25–29	F	Coner	1	C	–	No	–	+	+
258	30–34	M	Coner/ELC	3	C	–	No	–	+	+
280	35–50	M	LC	4	C	–	No	–	+	+
208	40–45	M	Coner/LC	1	C	*	No	–	+	+
63	20–34	F?	ELC	4	D	–	No	+	–	–
38	50+	F	Coner/LC	1	C	*	*	–	+	+
196	40.8	F	Coner	1	C	–	No	–	+	+
219	38.8	F	Coner	1	C	*	*	*	+	+
240	40–45	F	Coner	3	C	–	No	*	+	+

NOTE: M = male; F = female; F? = probable female; Coner = Coner ceramic phase (A.D. 700–1250); ELC = Early Late Classic; LC = Late Classic; – = absent; + = present; * = individual could not be typed for a particular site. See text for explanation of site types and lineage haplotype data.

[a] Copán Project burial identifier.

and various analyses of the samples prior to the DNA extraction. The descriptions of the samples are listed in Table 16.1. They were all collected during the Proyecto Arqueológico Copán, Segunda Fase.

Results and Discussion

Table 16.1 lists the individual samples that were typed, the approximate skeletal age, sex, period, household type, overall mtDNA haplotype, and the four individual diagnostic site typings. The household site types range from Type 4 (residences of the subroyal elite) and Type 3 (elite sites) to the more numerous Type 2 and Type 1 sites of the commoners. It should be noted that the Type 1 and 2 sites are most likely to contain commoners, but not all burials in the Type 3 and 4 sites may have been members of elite status.

The 9-bp deletion (defining lineage B) has been widely surveyed in New World populations. In Figure 16.2, the populations are arrayed from south to north in the New World through South America, Central America, North Amer-

ica, across the Bering Strait into Siberia, and then they are arrayed north to south from Siberia, down through Asia, Southeast Asia, and out into the Pacific Islands. It is readily apparent that there is a cline in frequency of the 9-bp deletion, with high frequencies in the south (of both the New World and Asia) which declines as one samples farther and farther north, until it is completely absent in Siberia and almost completely absent in Alaska and northern Canada. The exception is the Old Harbor Eskimos, who had the deletion at less than 2%. The deletion frequencies reach 100% in some Pacific Islands and one Chilean Aymara village (the Aymara deletion frequency shown in Figure 16.2 is the average for 11 *altiplano* villages and one coastal population). We believe the deletion arose in northern Asia, Mongolia, or Siberia and spread out in two separate migrations, one south into Asia, Southeast Asia, and the Pacific, and one north across the Bering Land Bridge into Alaska and down into the New World. The deletion could have arisen separately on both continents, but it appears on the same genetic background throughout the New World, Asia, and the Pacific, indicating a common origin.

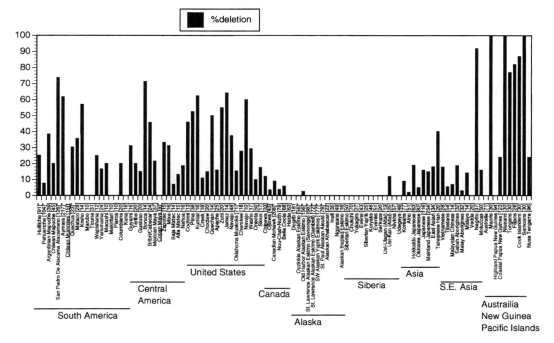

Figure 16.2. Distribution of 9-bp deletion. Samples are arrayed in geographic order from south to north in the New World up through South America, Central America, and North America, across the Bering Strait into Siberia, and then north to south from Siberia, down through Asia, Southeast Asia, and out into the Pacific Islands. Height of black bar indicates deletion frequency. Populations typed by Merriwether and colleagues are followed by an asterisk. Underlined populations are "ancient" DNA populations. Number in brackets following each population on x-axis indicates sample size of that population. Original data and population descriptions can be found in Merriwether et al. (1995).

The distribution of the 9-bp deletion in the New World is displayed on the map in Figure 16.3. Note that the deletion is nearly absent in Alaska and Canada. Only those populations nearest to the Maya are labeled. This figure is a compilation of three figures from Merriwether et al. (1995), and the labels for all the populations can be found there. Note the higher frequencies of the deletion in the southwestern United States and Central America. In particular, note the absence of the deletion in the Copán Maya, and the relatively high frequency in the Mexican Yucatec Maya. These two different frequencies may reflect the fact that these populations probably represent different

Maya linguistic groups, and may be some indication of the level of variation within the Maya civilization. Lastly, we can see that the deletion reaches very high levels in northern Chile, before declining again in southern Chile and Argentina.

The frequencies of the four founding lineages (plus "other" lineages) are displayed in Figure 16.4. Note that in Siberia there are many "other," non-Amerindian haplotypes. In the New World the frequency of "other" types is presumably an indication of Caucasian admixture, as the haplotypes making up the "other" group are often found in Caucasians. We can see that lineage A is predominant in the

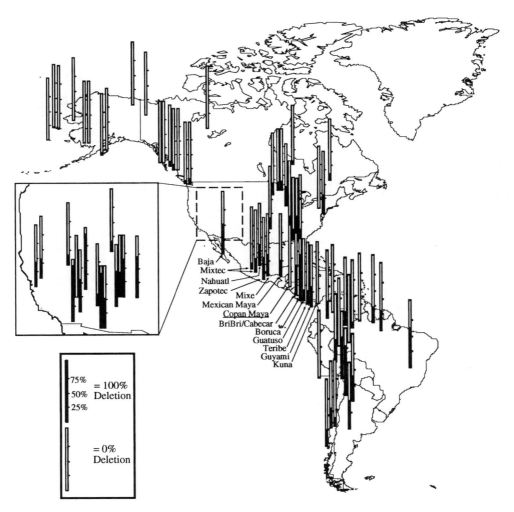

Figure 16.3. Map of distribution of 9-bp deletion in the New World. Height of black bar inside empty bar indicates deletion frequency. Original data and population descriptions can be found in Merriwether et al. (1995).

north, and almost absent in South America, with the reverse trend being true for lineage B (defined by the deletion). Lineages C and D have widely varying frequencies. The contemporary Mexican Maya are predominantly lineages A and B, with lower frequencies of C and D; the ancient Copán Maya that could be completely typed were all lineages C and D. However, when additional preliminary data from individuals that could only be partially typed (not presented here) is included, there are clearly additional individuals who are not C or D (i.e., they lack the Hinc II 13259 site loss or the Alu I 5175 site loss). We therefore would temper discussion of the significance of the haplotype frequencies with a warning that the true frequencies are likely to be different. We did preliminarily identify one individual who

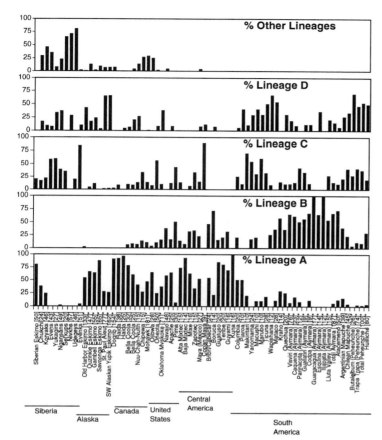

Figure 16.4. Distribution of the four founding lineage haplogroups. Populations are arrayed in geographic order starting in Siberia, across the Bering Strait into Alaska, and then south through Canada, the United States, Central America, and South America. Number in brackets following each population on x-axis indicates sample size of that population. Underlined populations are derived from "ancient" DNA. Populations typed by Merriwether and colleagues are followed by an asterisk. Original data and population descriptions can be found in Merriwether et al. (1995).

was Hae III 663 + (indicating lineage A), who could not be typed for the additional sites. The deletion was not identified in our additional preliminary data.

If the haplotype frequencies for the ancient Maya are correct, this may be an indication of founder effects within the Maya, small sample size of the ancient sample, intra-Maya population differences, or a change in frequencies over time due to drift or selection. The discrepancy in frequencies between ancient and contemporary Maya may also be due to admixture in the contemporary populations with surrounding non-Maya native groups. The contemporary Maya possess all four founding lineage variants, as do many of the surrounding populations. The deletion, which is at very low fre-

quencies in North American Amerindian populations, rises to appreciable levels in Mexican, Panamanian, and Costa Rican populations.

Future Studies of Ancient Maya DNA

Additional ancient Maya populations are now being surveyed (including the highland Maya site of Iximché) to get a better picture of ancient Maya variation. To avoid problems due to small sample size, we are currently typing approximately 150 Maya skeletal remains from Copán and 49 Maya teeth from Iximché (these are some of the preliminary data mentioned above) for the diagnostic founding lineage markers and a subset of these will be sequenced (for the hypervariable portions of the mtDNA control region known as the D-loop or displacement loop). We hope to relate these findings to the health, diet, and burial status data (described elsewhere in this volume by Whittington and Reed and by Storey) to address other questions, such as: Are the ruling and lower classes represented by different mtDNA haplotypes? Do certain lineages persist over time? How are the Maya related to their neighbors? How are the different Maya areas related? Are the same lineages present in the ruling class over time, or is there any indication of change (i.e., new mitochondrial haplotypes)?

Ancient DNA Research Problems and Prospects

In general, one should understand the limitations and advantages of working with ancient DNA. The advantages include being able to sample populations or cultures at different points in time to see how genetic variation changes in conjunction with observed changes in the archaeological and historical records and being able to test for the presence of specific genetic markers to detect the presence of specific lineages, genetic diseases, bacterial and viral infections, and domesticated crops and animals at specific times in the past. DNA can be obtained from floral and faunal remains, including plant seeds, leaves, and pollen; animal bones, tissue, teeth, hair, and feces; and bacteria and viral parasites inhabiting human, animal, and plant remains.

The disadvantages depend on the questions you hope to address. First, it is difficult to obtain true "populations" from ancient assemblages. For example, the Copán Maya sampled in this study, although restricted to the Late Classic period, still represent hundreds of years of occupation, and it is possible that none of these individuals may have been alive at the

same time. Stone and Stoneking's (1994) Oneota population is probably as close to a true population as one could hope to sample, as that site was occupied for less than 100 years.

Second, especially with Native American variation, one needs to examine differences in gene frequency to compare populations, and this requires reasonably large sample sizes (40+). Most population-specific polymorphisms tend to exist at low frequencies in the populations where they are found (Merriwether et al. 1991).

Third, to achieve large population samples, one must also overcome the generally less than 50% success rate in extracting amplifiable DNA from ancient samples. If you can only extract DNA from 33% of the samples, you would need to attempt 120 samples to get the suggested 40+ individuals.

Fourth, when attempting to amplify ancient human DNA, one must be aware of the possibility or even probability of modern DNA contamination when humans are performing the lab work and excavations. Human DNA contamination is usually irrelevant when working on other animal or plant remains. Contamination can be avoided, but it requires extreme caution (Merriwether et al. 1994).

Fifth, owing to the level of damage to ancient DNA, it is usually not possible to amplify larger genes from ancient remains. Most ancient DNA fragments are less than 300 nts in length, thus requiring multiple amplifications and typings to construct higher resolution haplotypes. Additionally, one must be cautious about which samples should be included in analyses of gene frequencies, as the inability to amplify some sites from ancient DNA may bias the observed distribution of haplotypes. In our data, we were able to type only a small number of samples for most of the key sites. However, we have since been able to type a larger number of samples for just one or two sites, and can confirm that the frequencies we observed in the "fully typed" samples are incorrect. This is presumably because of some bias in our ability to amplify the different sites. Some questions may never be addressable by ancient DNA owing to this size restriction. Nonetheless, we would encourage archaeologists and anthropologists to consider the use of ancient DNA as a powerful tool for examining human prehistory.

Acknowledgments

Thanks to Aubrey Watkins for help typing the contemporary samples, Kenneth Weiss for providing the contemporary Maya samples, and the W. M. Keck Foundation for Advanced Training in Computational Biology at the University of Pittsburgh, Carnegie Mellon University, and the Pittsburgh Supercomputing Center for partial support of Merriwether. This research was supported in part by Pittsburgh Supercomputing Center grant NIH 1P41RR06009 and the Wenner-Gren Foundation for Anthropological Research, Inc. Thanks to the Instituto Honureño de Antropología e Historia for providing access and permission to use the samples.

PART 5

Conclusion

17

Jane E. Buikstra

Studying Maya Bioarchaeology

My great desire was to discover an ancient sepulchre, which we had sought in vain among the ruins of Uxmal. . . .

. . . We continued the work six hours, and the whole appearance of things was so rude that we began to despair of success, when, on prying up a large flat stone, we saw underneath a skull. . . . I was exceedingly anxious to get the skeleton out entire, but it was impossible to do so. . . . as this [the earth] was removed it all fell to pieces. . . .

. . . I had them [the bones] carried . . . to Uxmal, and thence I bore them away. . . . In their rough journeys on the backs of mules and Indians they were so crumbled and broken . . . and they [the bones] left me one night in a pocket-handkerchief to be carried to Doctor S. G. Morton of Philadelphia.

. . . this gentleman . . . says that this skeleton, dilapidated as it is, has afforded him some valuable facts, and has been a subject of some interesting reflections.

. . . The bones are those of a female. Her height did not exceed five feet three or four inches. The teeth are perfect, and not appreciably worn, while the *epiphyses,* those infallible indications of the growing state, have just become consolidated, and mark the completion of adult age.

. . . The skull was crushed into many pieces, but, by a cautious manipulation, Doctor Morton succeeded in reconstructing the posterior and lateral portions. The occiput is remarkably flat and vertical, while the lateral or parietal diameter measures no less than five inches and eight tenths.

A chemical examination of some fragments of the bones proves them to be almost destitute of animal matter, which, in the perfect osseous structure, constitutes about thirty-three parts in the hundred.

On the upper part of the left tibia there is a swelling of the bone, called, in surgical language, a *node,* an inch and a half in length, and more than half an inch above the natural surface. This morbid condition may have resulted from a variety of causes, but possesses greater interest on account of its extreme infrequency among the primitive Indian population of the country (Stephens 1843:276–282).

An antiquarian enthusiasm for Maya sepulchres led the 19th century excavator-explorer/lawyer-diplomat, John L. Stephens, to develop one of the earliest collaborative investigations of a Maya interment. Eager to learn as much as possible about ancient Maya through the study of their remains, Stephens submitted his find to the premier American physical anthropologist of the day, Dr. Samuel George Morton. Morton carefully described a range of biological attributes, including stature, cranial form, pathology, chemical composition, age, and sex of the deceased, features which continue to interest Mayanists today. The collaboration with Morton stimulated Stephens to address a prominent 19th century theoretical issue, the origin of the peoples who built the great cities of the Americas. The physical similarity of the Maya remains he recovered from the ruins within the *hacienda* of San Francisco (which site he attributed to the ancient Maya city of Ticul) to those of South American mummies caused him to conclude that "these crumbling bones declare, as with a voice from the grave, that we cannot go back to any ancient nation of the Old World for the builders of these cities; they are not the works of people who have passed away, and whose history is lost, but of the same great *race* which, changed . . . still clings around their ruins" (Stephens 1843:284). Just as the study of human skeletal remains led Stephens to examine a key controversy of his day, this volume reports perspectives on competing contemporary models for the development of Maya complexity, for the Maya collapse, and for the impact of the Spanish *entrada* upon indigenous Maya.

The Stephens-Morton discussion also underscores the fragile condition of their "dilapidated" skeleton and the painstaking procedures required to gain human biological data. Although poor preservation continues to challenge Maya bioarchaeologists, the many significant contributions contained in the previous chapters illustrate that the information gained through the excavation and study of Maya burials continues to be well worth the effort.

This volume (Danforth et al.) presents a comprehensive bibliography of Maya physical anthropology, including contributions from virtually all the prominent (physical) anthropologists of the 19th and early 20th centuries. Morton, Virchow, Boas, Hooton, Hrdlička, Comas, and Stewart have each added to our knowledge of ancient Maya. As in the Stephens-Morton example cited above, topical foci ranged widely. Health, stature, sex ratios, and age-at-death have all been considered by scientists who have studied ancient Maya remains.

Yet, as emphasized by Webster in his introductory chapter, only recently have studies of ancient human remains and their contexts become well integrated with archaeological agendas. Webster argues that since his graduate student days of the 1960s "much has changed very rapidly." He attributes the increased prominence of biological anthropology within Maya archaeology to (1) increased archaeological emphasis upon recovery of large samples and detailed contextual data, and (2) recently developed sophisticated biochemical methods. Even so, skeletal samples, some of them large, have accumulated since the days of the Harvard-Peabody (Gordon 1896; 1898) expeditions and have accelerated, especially during the era of excavation begun by the Carnegie Institution during the 1920s. As illustrated by Danforth et al. and to be elaborated below, interpretations of health and disease, as well as genetic relationships, have been amenable to physical anthropological inquiry since the time of Morton and Stephens. Clearly, interpretations of ancient community health *have* become more prominent in recent decades (Buikstra and Cook 1980; Ubelaker 1982), and skeletal biology has in general been a highly descriptive, rather than comparative, interpretive, or theoretical, enterprise, both within the pages of the *American Journal of Physical Anthropology* (Lovejoy et al.

1982) and without (Washburn 1953; Buettner-Janusch 1969). It seems clear, however, that the degree to which physical anthropological data assume prominence in archaeological inquiries *also* has to do with the theoretical orientation of contemporary archaeologists.

When there was interest in establishing a complex set of social statuses appropriate to a city, differences in burial disposal forms were identified (e.g., Morley 1910). As it became important to bolster arguments for a commoner-ruler status dichotomy, priestly and other elite interments were emphasized (e.g., Thompson 1954). One reason for the recent visibility of human biological data within archaeological inquiries develops from a convergence of theoretical interests developed since the 1970s. Skeletal biologists have been concerned with community health and the long-term impact of changing environmental and cultural factors, including diet and culturally mediated differential access to resources. Archaeologists, including those working in the Maya area, influenced by the then "new" or processual archaeology, systems theory, and human ecology, discovered much to their liking within contemporary skeletal biological approaches (Wright 1994). This conjunction has encouraged enhanced cooperation and increased activity. As Webster emphasizes, the linkage may not yet be "mature"

but it has already been remarkably productive, as evidenced by the papers in this state-of-the-art Maya bioarchaeology symposium.

Tempo and Mode

In order to provide a context for the present work, I offer a few observations concerning historical trends in Maya bioarchaeology, based upon the information presented by Danforth et al. in the Appendix. Figure 17.1 summarizes the publications listed by them across decades. There are two points of special interest.

First, the decade between 1930 and 1939 witnessed an unusual increase in physical anthropological publications. In fact, 33 papers were published during that decade, exactly as many published over the previous century. The following two decades were not so productive, with a sustained increase beginning during the sixties and accelerating within recent years. In fact, if the current tempo is maintained, 832 Maya bioarchaeological publications will appear during the 1990s.

Turning first to the initial anomaly, the elevated publication rate during the 1930s, it is intuitively satisfying to attribute this pattern to an increased number of excavations, especially those initiated by the Carnegie during the pre-

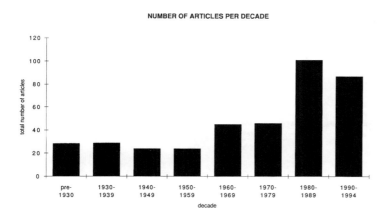

Figure 17.1. Number of Maya bioarchaeology articles per decade from Danforth et al. (this volume).

Table 17.1 Topical Focus of Bioarchaeological Articles

Topic	Pre-1930		1930–1939	
	n[a]	Percent	n[a]	Percent
Isolated cases	7	21	3	9
General syntheses	9	27	2	6
Site reports	5	15	15	45
Special topics	12	36	13	39

[a]n = number of articles.

vious decade (Adams, 1969; Becker 1979; Hay et al. 1940; Willey and Sabloff 1993). To examine this assertion further, Table 17.1 compares the topical emphasis of each article published prior to 1930 with those published between 1930 and 1939. In this example, I assigned each article to either a specialized category, such as syphilis and dental mutilation, or a more inclusive subject label such as general syntheses and site reports. General syntheses include articles such as Breton's (1908) article "Archaeology in Mexico" which includes information about skeletal remains. Site reports

during this period typically described graves and skeletons in appendices without more fully integrating these data with the other archaeological evidence. At this stage, I did not use the Danforth et al. topical assignments because I wanted to compare frequencies of isolated cases vs. site reports explicitly, along with more specialized topics such as syphilis and dental anthropology.

Several trends are obvious, and will be more fully explored in a subsequent section. As a measure of increasing precision in archaeological data gathering, publications of isolated cases, often imperfectly contextualized, decreased while site reports increased by a factor of three. Increased archaeological activity obviously stimulated expanded bioarchaeological reporting.

To explore time trends by topic more fully, I partitioned selected subject assignments made by Danforth et al. by decade of publication (Fig. 17.2). With the exception of highly specialized categories of low frequency and geographical assignments, all subjects were included. As can be seen by comparing the pre-1930 graph with those representing more recent decades, the most popular topics of the pre-1930s era

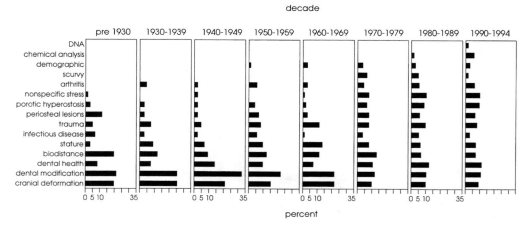

Figure 17.2. Percent of Maya bioarchaeology articles on selected subjects by decade of publication. Subject assignments are from Danforth et al. (this volume).

were maintained during the 1930s: cranial deformation, dental modification, and biological distance/inherited features. Highly visible physical attributes were widely noted and described, in line with archaeology's primarily descriptive perspectives during the 19th and early 20th centuries (Willey and Sabloff 1993).

As we move into more recent times, we see that during the 1960s cranial deformation and dental modifications continue as topics of significance. Following general trends in physical anthropology (Buikstra and Cook 1980; Buikstra et al. 1990; Ubelaker 1982), biological distance becomes less visible while various indicators of health status assume importance. A recent emphasis upon health is apparent when we compare percentages of articles dedicated to health-related topics during the period from 1970 to 1994, increasing from 35% to 65%, as compared to a slight decrease in biological distance articles from 11% during the 1960s to 7% within the present decade. Discussions of cranial deformation have also decreased markedly, from nearly 22% during the 1960s to 9% of published articles during the first five years of this decade.

Although evidence for disease among ancient Maya attracted the attention of such luminaries as Samuel George Morton, Rudolph Virchow, and Franz Boas, the integration of health with competing theories about the Maya collapse was more forcefully articulated by Earnest Hooton. Following the observation of cranial evidence for "a deficiency disease" among many of the children whose remains were recovered from the Cenote at Chichén Itzá, Hooton remarked that it was possible that "osteoporosis caused the downfall of the Maya civilization. I make a present of this idea to Maya archaeologists, who are perennially questing for an explanation" (Hooton 1940:276).

More recently, the health-based inferences of two researchers have been quite influential in archaeological interpretations of the so-called "Maya collapse." The first of these was Haviland's (1967) study of stature differences at Tikal. In this work, he emphasized a general decrease in stature during Late Classic times, especially notable among males. This diminution was linked to nutritional stress, associated perhaps with the causes of the Maya collapse. Haviland's argument, that "Early Classic society may have been fairly simply divided into rulers versus commoners" (1967:322) echoes and reinforces earlier archaeological interpretations, such as those of Thompson. This physical reinforcement of archaeological interpretations no doubt encouraged the visibility of Haviland's study.

A second investigation that had tremendous influence within Maya archaeology was that of Frank Saul. Saul's studies of pathology at the site of Altar de Sacrificios led him to remark that "In fact, one might wonder, not *why* they declined, but rather, *how* they managed to survive for so long" (Saul 1972b:390). As pointed out by Wright (1994), Saul was careful to emphasize the tentative nature of his comments, the absence of a definable chronological trend, and the possibility of compounding social factors. Archaeologists, however, have not always heeded Saul's cautions and have used his data to bolster ecological arguments about the collapse. Santley and colleagues, for example (1986) cite both Saul (1973) and Haviland (1967) as evidence for nutritional stress and demographic instability. Tainter's (1988) discussion of the Maya collapse also uncritically accepts human biological evidence for widespread stress during Terminal Classic times. New data and a further test of the ecological model is offered by papers in this volume.

The Current Volume

Physical evidence said to support (Márquez and Ángel) and to contradict (White, Wright) the ecological model are included here. White's critique of the "myth of the *milpa*" is cogent, as is Wright's caution against projecting ethnohistoric accounts into the distant Maya past. As the archaeological record has filled out, it is clear that no single explanation for the "Maya collapse" will suffice. White points out here, for example, that certain expectations for an ecological model are met at Pacbitun, but not at Lamanai. Her results underscore regional variability, which is currently emphasized by many who interpret ancient Mesoamerica.

Regional variation in diets is also emphasized by Gerry and Krueger, who isolate three dietary patterns for the seven Classic sites which served as a basis for their isotope study. Their use of isotopic signatures from the apatite fraction of bone is important, because *theoretically* this method provides a better estimate of whole diet C_4 plant proportions than the signature from collagen alone. Another important point made by Gerry and Krueger is the need for isotopic characterization of contemporary tropical forest food webs, which is necessary for more precise characterization of ancient diets. In this volume, significant progress in such work is provided by Wright's study from the Pasión lowlands.

Wright's study also underscores site-specificity in diet, noting that her research provides no support for the ecological model. Instead, she argues for transformations of the social and political order, as when Late Classic and Terminal Classic samples are compared. Political or religious factors are also invoked by Massey and Steele in explaining their striking skull pit from the Terminal Classic site of Colha, Belize.

The only authors who favor the ecological model are Márquez and Ángel, who, however, state that the major stature decrease reported for their comprehensive sample occurs between Preclassic and Classic skeletal series. Stronger support would be a notable decrease later in the Classic sequence, when these authors note

only slight changes. This study, while data rich, requires statistical testing for the results to be truly convincing.

As noted by several authors, larger samples would be quite desirable. Chase's estimation of the percentage of the population sampled from the southern lowlands makes it clear that only a minority of those living at the sites have been recovered from archaeological contexts. Chase's figures thus underscore the importance of carefully developed sampling strategies, with physical anthropologists and archaeologists working together from the very early stages of research design, as called for by Webster and by Whittington and Reed.

The emphasis upon health in these studies has encouraged several authors to address the "osteological paradox," which develops from the fact that the death sample is *not* a cross-section of the living population. One of the most creative attempts to address the concerns voiced by Wood et al. in their 1992 article is that of Storey, who carefully evaluates age-specific patterns of pathology among children from elite graves at Copán. While not directly addressing the ecological arguments, she also notes that her data would support a model whereby nutrition and disease affected long-term viability during the Late Classic in Copán. Her results, when compared to those of Wright for the Pasión lowlands and White's Lamanai data, underscore regional variability in health across the Maya world.

The three Late Classic sites investigated by Danforth also provide evidence of developmental stresses, more pronounced than at the Colonial site of Tipu. As articulated by Danforth and by Cohen et al., even in the face of documented epidemics, it appears that the peripheral location of Tipu buffered its Maya from many of the health-related stresses of colonization. To examine the ecological model fully, Danforth's study of enamel microdefects will require a temporal sequence.

A pleasing aspect of many of these presentations is the use of appropriate statistical methods. When faced with small samples, there has been an unfortunate tendency for bioarchaeologists working with Maya materials to over-interpret small differences, when tests would reveal no statistical significance. True tests for differences across age, sex, status, time, and region require sophisticated approaches. Whittington and Reed's log-linear modeling, for example, provides convincing evidence for a similar lifestyle among low-status Maya subpopulations from Copán.

Jacobi's results from Tipu illustrate the presence of kin-based structuring of the Tipu cemetery. In comparisons of Tipu with other Maya sites, his data are useful in examining long-term histories that may reflect population movement or isolation. Wise to chose the relatively abundant dental observations, Jacobi's investigation well illustrates the importance of studying epigenetic features. The other genetic study in the volume is that of Merriwether et al., who report very preliminary mitochondrial DNA results from Maya materials. As Merriwether and colleagues point out, DNA extraction is difficult for the fragile Maya remains, but such procedures hold great promise for establishing the genetic history of this significant world area.

Dental modifications and cranial deformation are reported in the chapters by Saul and Saul, López, Massey and Steele, and Havill et al. Impressive in each of the examples is the nonhomogeneity in patterning. Variation within even small samples occurs in virtually every case, with other individuals not presenting evidence of cultural modification. Although various explanations have been posited, ranging from social status to ethnic markers, we are still far from appreciating the reasons why the Maya chose to alter their appearance. One fascinating observation is Havill et al.'s note that some dental modifications appear to mirror a day-glyph from the 260-day calendar. Examining the technology of modification, as done by Havill and colleagues, may also assist in establishing distributions for specialists in dental modification.

The preoccupation of Mayanists with the more recent portion of the archaeological record is countered here by Saul and Saul's report on the Preclassic skeletons from Cuello. Significant is an emphasis upon variability in health status across Maya sites, established during Preclassic times. They also document evidence for treponemal infection by approximately 1200 to 900 B.C. The Sauls thus continue to explore significant new venues within Maya studies.

As noted by several of the authors, now that sample sizes are increasing and local sequences developing, cross-site and between-observer comparisons become important. It is critical that researchers use standard terminology and minimize inter- and intraobserver error. Among the papers presented in this volume, those of Danforth and Whittington and Reed pay particular attention to the importance of combining data from various sources.

Several authors express appropriate concern about the implications of Wood et al.'s (1992) osteological paradox, but another potential source of confusion relates to archaeological contexts and funerary rituals. As pointed out by Hodder (1982b, 1986a, 1986b) and other post-processualists, status of the deceased is not necessarily reflected in mortuary treatment. After all, as amply illustrated here by Massey and Steele, it *is* the living who inter the dead. An individual's status may be enhanced or inverted, owing to the agendas of those conducting the mortuary ritual. Maya bioarchaeological studies would benefit from this theoretical perspective, newly found in the work of McAnany (1995).

As in any edited volume that includes many authors, differences of opinion are voiced that illustrate the dynamic nature of Maya studies. Some authors, for example Gerry and Krueger, emphasize the central role of maize in Maya diet, citing 16th century accounts of tortillas eaten at most meals. As argued in the chapters by White and Wright, however, such use of analogy is hazardous. Wright notes that Classic Maya polychrome ceramics represent tamales rather than tortillas.

As emphasized by Webster and illustrated in several chapters, bone chemistry has become a highly visible means of estimating ancient Maya diets. Given that Maya bones commonly show evidence of postdepositional physical and chemical alteration, it is crucial that all studies test for evidence of diagenetic change that may have altered experimental results. Biogenic signatures derived from bone apatite may be changed by recrystallization in a manner not reversed by standard treatments with acetic acid. Diagenetic changes of this type have been demonstrated in 1200-year-old Maya bone from the site of Dos Pilas (Wright and Schwarcz 1996). It is therefore possible that the regional patterns for stable carbon isotope spacing reported by Gerry and Krueger reflect similar depositional conditions, especially soil hydrology. Therefore, Gerry and Krueger's unexpected "anomalous" meat signatures may reflect diagenetic change, or they may be attributable to overdependence by the authors upon ethnohistoric analogy.

The Future and Maya Bioarchaeology

As evidenced here, it is clear that Maya bioarchaeology is producing significant results. This symposium develops important new perspectives on regional histories and provides convincing tests of the archaeologically based "ecological model," which is found wanting as a global construct. Skeletal and dental markers of diet and nutrition have provided convincing evidence for regional variation and the significance of local histories in evaluating reasons for the Maya collapse.

It is clear, however, that many potentially informative skeletal biological data sets are underutilized in the development of archaeological models. For example, kinship figures importantly in models for the development of the Archaic state (Henderson and Sabloff 1993; Marcus 1983, 1993; McAnany 1995). Yet studies of inherited phenotypic variation and DNA are seldom cited by archaeologists investigating state formation processes. Such methods hold unique promise for enhancing our knowledge of the history of social, political, and economic formations that created the Maya world. Similarly, further examination of skewing in the composition of burial assemblages and concern for the identity of those subject to elaborate, lengthy mortuary treatment may further enrich our understanding of the mechanisms that created "sacred" ancestors (*sensu* Fortes 1953) from among the many who died. In addition, as noted by Webster in his in introductory remarks, investigations of trauma may help us appreciate the complexities of Maya geopolitics.

Therefore, while diet and health dominate this volume, as they do in skeletal biology generally, bioarchaeologists must not be limited to these data forms. Other potentially informative venues should be explored, depending upon the question at hand. Close collaboration with archaeologists in developing appropriate excavations strategies is essential, as emphasized by Webster in his opening commentary. The scholarship reflected in this volume reinforces the fact that the time spent excavating and studying the frequently fragile ancient Maya remains is well worth the effort today, just as it was when Stephens sent his precious materials to Samuel Morton.

Marie Elaine Danforth,
Stephen L. Whittington,
and Keith P. Jacobi

Appendix. An Indexed Bibliography of Prehistoric and Early Historic Maya Human Osteology: 1839–1994

In his discussion of the burials recovered at Piedras Negras, William Coe noted, "Observations and measurements, when feasible, have been given in the hope that someday there will be sufficient data for a revealing synthesis of Maya skeletal remains" (Coe 1959:121). More than 35 years later, such a synthesis still remains to be produced. Although some might argue that sufficient data will never exist because of poor bone preservation in the region, it also seems that researchers are not always fully aware of the rather substantial literature on prehistoric Maya skeletal biology that has emerged during the last 150 years in the United States, México, and other countries.

With this bibliography, we attempt to remedy this situation by presenting an exhaustive, indexed list of those publications that appeared in print or on microfilm by the end of 1994. Included are references concerning paleodemography, paleopathology, skeletal morphology, and cultural modifications. We hope that this work, the product of extensive exploration of diverse sources from nearly a dozen countries, will allow other researchers to exploit more readily the valuable comparative data and interpretations available in this literature.

We located the publications in various manners. Many of the older references came from review articles of Maya burial practices (Blom 1954; Ricketson 1925; Ruz 1965, 1968; Thompson 1939; Welsh 1988). Several Latin American journals were systematically searched, including *Anales de Antropología* (1964–1983), *Anales del Instituto de Antropología e Historia* (1909–1975), *Ancient Mesoamerica, Antropología e Historia de Guatemala, Boletín de la Escuela de Ciencias Antropológicas de la Universidad de Yucatán* (1973–1990), *Estudios (Universidad de San Carlos)* (1993–1995), *Estudios de Cultura Maya, Latin American Antiquity, Mexicon, Revista Mexicana de Estudios Antropológicos* (1927–1977), and *Yaxkin* (1977–1987). We also examined several extant bibliographies of physical anthropological and Latin American anthropological literature

(Cobb 1944; Genovés et al. 1964; Krogman 1943, 1945; Stewart 1952, 1970; Valle 1971; Villanueva and Serrano 1982). Other useful sources of citations were the San Diego Museum of Man *Paleopathology Citation Database,* which is in development, and *Paleopathology Newsletter.* Finally, a number of references came from personal correspondence, searches of on-line library databases, postings to computer newsgroups, and reviews of others' bibliographies.

From these sources, we further investigated those citations with promising titles and ones that we knew discussed human burials. With only a few exceptions, we personally examined each publication. Our criteria for including citations in the bibliography were: (1) the material had to present data concerning Maya populations, although cultural affiliation was liberally interpreted; (2) the material had to consider osteological evidence, thereby eliminating a variety of entries, including ethnohistoric or artistic treatments of health questions, purely archaeological discussions of mortuary customs, and references in which the author discussed the presence of human remains but gave no further information; and (3) the material had to be published in print or microfilm format by the end of 1994. Research reports distributed only to funding or government agencies and unpublished manuscripts available only by contacting the author directly were excluded. Dissertations awarded in the United States that are available from University Microfilms International have been included, but master's theses, honors papers, and most Latin American and European dissertations do not appear in this bibliography. Abstracts of papers presented at the annual meetings of the American Association of Physical Anthropologists and the annual meetings and European members' meetings of the Paleopathology Association are listed because they are published either in regu-lar issues of, or as supplements to, their respective journals.

We indexed the contents of each reviewed publication according to the type and quality of information contained so that users of the bibliography can judge whether they might be valuable to the particular research being conducted. Each citation is assigned a sequential identification number. The number is in bold print if the primary emphasis of the publication is on Maya skeletal biology. It is in regular print if the publication contains only scattered information of interest. It is in italics if we were unable to locate and review the work.

A citation's identification number appears in the index under one or more categories that reflect geographic, demographic, temporal, health, and cultural variables. In reviewing publications, if a particular pathological condition, cultural modification, or morphological trait was generally even mentioned, then the citation's identification number was included in the index under that category. We took certain liberties in interpreting some of the older literature in which various conditions, such as porotic hyperostosis, are clearly described, although not necessarily labeled with the specific terms used in the index. Works that we could not locate are, of necessity, less completely indexed than those we reviewed.

We are fairly confident that we have not missed any significant studies published as a monograph, in a major journal, or as an appendix to a major archaeological report. Many brief references to osteology were located in published site reports and have subsequently been included in the bibliography, but there is no systematic way to find every last one. Although we also made every effort to ensure the accuracy of each reference, many of the older materials, especially museum publications, have quite complicated citation information appearing in different formats in various bibliographies and library catalogues. Thus, users of the bibliography are encouraged to search for references of interest under all the types of citation information provided.

ADDITIONS. We have created a World Wide Web home page where additions to the bibliography in the form of missed citations from before the end of 1994 and new citations from after the end of 1994 will be available. The address of the home page is http://www.ume.maine.edu/~anthrop/Mayabones.html. Suggestions for additions can be sent via the Internet to either danforth@whale.st.usm.edu or Steve_Whittington@voyager.umeres.maine.edu.

Acknowledgments

We extend our thanks to Rose Tyson and Dan Elerick of the San Diego Museum of Man for sharing their *Paleopathology Citation Database*. Others who graciously provided assistance include Julienne Barker (American Dental Association); Paul Bary and The Latin American Library at Tulane University; Sharon Bennett; Chris Carrelli; Diane Chase (Central Florida); Eve Cockburn (Paleopathology Association); Della Collins Cook (Indiana); Dumbarton Oaks; David Freidel and Charles Suhler (Southern Methodist); Morris Fry (Tozzer Library, Harvard); Veronique Gervais (Caen); Paula Gabbard (Columbia); David Glassman (Southwest Texas); Thomas Hester, Daniel Potter, and Khristaan Villela (Texas at Austin); David Hunt, Maya Riopedre, and Javier Urcid (Smithsonian Institution); Barbara Jones, Libby Soifer, and Christine Whittington (Fogler Library, Maine); Virginia Massey; Frances Matheny, William Erwin, Brenda Adams-Gordon, Matthew Gordon, and Ginger Pendarvis (Southern Mississippi); D. Andrew Merriwether (Michigan); Lourdes Márquez (Esquela Nacional de Antropología e Historia, México); Sandy Rapp (Utah); Eugenia Robinson; Frank and Julie Mather Saul; Pam Smith (Mississippi Dental Association); D. Gentry Steele and Lori Wright (Texas A&M); John Weeks (Minnesota); and Christine White (Western Ontario). Partial support for this project was provided by a University of Southern Mississippi Summer Research Grant.

Bibliography

1. Anon. 1931. Dentistry among Mayans. *El Palacio* 31(12):177–178.
2. ———. 1933. Maya Mummy Tooth. *Contact Point* 11(1):102–103.
3. Adams, R. E. W. 1986. Río Azul, Lost City of the Maya. *National Geographic* 169:420–451.
4. ———. 1990. Archaeological Research at the Lowland Maya City of Río Azul. *Latin American Antiquity* 1:23–41.
5. Adams, R. E. W., and H. R. Robichaux. 1992. Tombs of Río Azul. *National Geographic Research and Exploration* 8:412–427.
6. Adams, R. E. W., and A. S. Trik. 1961. Tikal Report no. 7. Temple 1 (Str. 5D-1): Postconstructional Activities. In *Tikal Reports nos. 5–10*, pp. 113–147. Museum Monograph 20. The University Museum, University of Pennsylvania, Philadelphia.
7. Agrinier, P. 1963. Nuevos casos de mutilaciones dentarias procedentes de Chiapas, México. *Anales del Instituto Nacional de Antropología e Historia* 15:229–243.
8. ———. 1964. *The Archaeological Burials at Chiapa de Corzo and Their Furniture.* Papers of the New World Archaeological Foundation no. 16, publ. 12. Brigham Young University Press, Provo.
9. Agurcia Fasquelle, R., and W. R. Fash, Jr. 1989. A Royal Maya Tomb Discovered. *National Geographic* 176:480–487.
10. Alexanderson, L. 1940. Brief Study of the

Dental Works Done by Ancient Tribes that Inhabited Mexico. *Dental Items of Interest* 62:212–217.

11. Allen, D. J., F. P. Saul, and J. M. Saul. 1982. Scanning Electron Microscopy Study of a Coprolite from Cancun, Mexico: A Pilot Study (abstract). *Abstracts of the Ninth Annual Meeting of the Paleopathology Association, Toledo,* edited by E. Cockburn, p. 15. Paleopathology Association, Detroit.

12. Anderson, A. H. 1959. More Discoveries at Caracol. In *Actas del XXXIII Congreso de Americanistas, 1958,* vol. 2, pp. 211–218. San José, Costa Rica.

13. Anderson, A. H., and H. Cook. 1944. Archaeological Finds near Douglas, British Honduras. In *Notes on Middle American Archaeology and Ethnology,* no. 40, pp. 83–86. Carnegie Institution of Washington, Washington.

14. Andrews, E. W., IV. 1959. Dzibilchaltun: Lost City of the Maya. *National Geographic* 115:91–109.

15. Andrews, E. W., IV, and E. W. Andrews, V. 1980. Burials and Caches. In *Excavations at Dzibilchaltun, Yucatan, Mexico,* pp. 314–325. Middle American Research Institute Publication 48. Tulane University, New Orleans.

16. Anjard, R. 1981. Mayan Dental Wonders. *Journal of Oral Implantology* 9:423–426.

17. Armstrong, C. W. 1991. Statistical Analysis of Postcranial Discrete Traits within the Tipu Population (abstract). *American Journal of Physical Anthropology,* Supplement 12:44–45.

18. Asbell, M. 1964. Dentistry of the Aztecs and Mayas: Vignette in Dental History. *Outlook and Bulletin of the Southern Dental Society of New Jersey* 33:97–98.

19. Ashmead, A. S. 1896. Evidences in Yucatan as to the Possible Connection of Precolumbian Syphilis with Asia. *Journal of Cutaneous and Genito-Urinary Diseases* 14:93–99.

20. Ashmore, W. 1987. Appendix 2—Faunal and Human Osteological Analysis. In *Archaeological Investigations in the North-* *ern Maya Highlands, Guatemala: Interaction and Development of Maya Civilization,* edited by R. J. Sharer and D. W. Sedat, pp. 470–478. University Museum Monograph 59. The University Museum, University of Pennsylvania, Philadelphia.

21. Austin, D. M. 1972. Appendix—Morphology and Dimensions of the Altar de Sacrificios Teeth. In *The Human Skeletal Remains from Altar de Sacrificios: An Osteobiographic Analysis,* by F. P. Saul, pp. 79–81. Papers of the Peabody Museum of Archaeology and Ethnology, vol. 63, no. 2. Harvard University, Cambridge.

22. ———. 1978. The Biological Affinity of the Ancient Populations of Altar de Sacrificios and Seibal. *Estudios de Cultura Maya* 11:57–73.

23. Becker, M. J. 1973. Archaeological Evidence for Occupational Specialization among the Classic Period Maya at Tikal, Guatemala. *American Antiquity* 38:396–406.

24. Becquelin, P. 1969. Appendice C—Description des sépultures de la Vallée de Acul. In *Archéologie de la région de Nebaj (Guatemala),* pp. 130–144. Université de Paris Mémoires de l'Institut d'Ethnologie II. Musée de l'Homme, Paris.

25. ———. 1990. Les sépultures et les caches. In *Tonina, une cité maya du Chiapas (Mexique),* edited by P. Becquelin and E. Taladoire, pp. 1639–1659. Études Mésoaméricaines vol. 6, tome 4. Centre d'Études Mexicaines et Centraméricaines, México.

26. Blom, F. 1923. *Las ruinas de Palenque: Xupa y Finca Encanto.* Instituto Nacional de Antropología e Historia, México.

27. ———. 1954. Ossuaries, Cremation, and Secondary Burials among the Maya of Chiapas. *Journal de la Société des Americanistes* 43:123–145.

28. Blom, F., S. S. Grosjean, and H. Cummins. 1933. A Maya Skull from the Uloa Valley, Republic of Honduras. In *Studies in Middle America,* pp. 1–24. Middle American Research Series Publication no. 5, Pamphlet no. 1. Tulane University, New Orleans.

29. ———. 1933. Una cránea maya del Valle

de Ulúa, República de Honduras. *Anales de la Sociedad de Geografía e Historia* 10:32–40.

30. Blom, F., and O. LaFarge. 1926–1927. *Tribes and Temples.* 2 vols. Middle American Research Institute Publication 1. Tulane University, New Orleans.

31. Boas, F. 1890. Cranium from Progreso, Yucatan. *Proceedings of the American Antiquarian Society* 6:350–359.

32. Bocklage, T. J. 1984. Physical Anthropology of the Ancient Maya Foot (abstract). In *Papers of the Eleventh Annual Meeting of the Paleopathology Association, Philadelphia,* edited by E. Cockburn, p. 15. Paleopathology Association, Detroit.

33. Brady, J. E., L. F. Luin, L. Wright, C. Foncea de Ponciano, and S. Villagrán de Brady. 1992. Descubrimientos recientes en la Cueva de Sangre de Dos Pilas. *IV Simposio de Arqueología Guatemalteca, 1990,* edited by J. P. Laporte, H. L. Escobedo Ayala, and S. Villagrán de Brady, pp. 153–168. Museo Nacional de Arqueología y Etnología, Guatemala.

34. Brand, A. 1941. Dientes mayas mutilados. *Revista Geográfica Americana (Buenos Aires)* 16:83–84.

35. Breton, A. C. 1908. Archaeology in Mexico. *Man* 8(17):34–37.

36. Bullard, W. R., and M. R. Bullard. 1965. *Late Classic Finds at Baking Pot, British Honduras.* Art and Archaeology Occasional Paper 8. Royal Ontario Museum, Toronto.

37. Cáceres, E. 1938. La odontología en la era precolombina. In *Historia de la odontología en Guatemala,* pp. 15–24. Tipografía Nacional, Guatemala.

38. Cadot, S., and J. L. Miquel. 1990. Etude descriptive et approche technique des incrustations dentaires dans le Mexique précolumbian. *Odonto-Stomatologie Tropicale/Tropical Dental Journal* 13(2):41–51.

39. Carmack, R. M. 1981. *The Quiche Maya of Utatlan.* University of Oklahoma Press, Norman.

40. Carrillo y Ancona, D. C. 1886. Las cabezas-chatas. *Anales del Museo Nacional de México,* 1st ser., 3(7a):272–278.

41. [Cave, A. J. E.]. 1939. Cranial Deformation among the Ancient Maya (abstract). *Nature* 144(3644):447.

42. Cave, A. J. E. 1939. Report on Two Skulls from British Honduras. In *Archaeological Investigations in the Corozal District of British Honduras,* by T. W. F. Gann and M. Gann, pp. 59–63. Bulletin 123, Anthropological Papers no. 7. Bureau of American Ethnology, Smithsonian Institution, Washington.

43. Chase, A. F. 1983. A Contextual Consideration of the Tayasal-Paxcaman Zone, El Peten, Guatemala. Ph.D. dissertation, Department of Anthropology, University of Pennsylvania, Philadelphia. University Microfilms International, Ann Arbor.

44. Chase, A. F., and D. Z. Chase. 1987. *Investigations at the Classic Maya City of Caracol, Belize: 1985–1987.* Monograph 3. Pre-Columbian Art Research Institute, San Francisco.

45. ———. 1994. Maya Veneration of the Dead at Caracol, Belize. In *Seventh Palenque Round Table, 1989,* vol. 9, edited by V. M. Fields, pp. 53–60. M. G. Robertson, general editor. Pre-Columbian Art Research Institute, San Francisco.

46. Chase, D. Z. 1982. Spatial and Temporal Variability in Postclassic Northern Belize. Ph.D. dissertation, Department of Anthropology, University of Pennsylvania. University Microfilms International, Ann Arbor.

47. ———. 1994. Human Osteology, Pathology, and Demography as Represented in the Burials of Caracol, Belize. In *Studies in the Archaeology of Carcacol, Belize,* edited by D. Z. Chase and A. F. Chase, pp. 123–138. Monograph 7. Pre-Columbian Art Research Institute, San Francisco.

48. Chase, D. Z., and A. F. Chase. 1988. *A Postclassic Perspective: Excavations at the Maya Site of Santa Rita Corozal, Belize.* Monograph 4. Pre-Columbian Art Research Institute, San Francisco.

49. Cifuentes Aguirre, O. 1963. *Odontología y*

mutilaciones dentarias mayas. Colección
Editorial Universitaria no. 46. Editorial
Universitaria, Guatemala.

50. ———. 1974. Prótesis dental prehispánica
en Guatemala. *Revista Guatemalteca de Estomatología* 4:7–13.

51. Clarke, N. G., S. E. Carey, W. Srikandi,
R. S. Hirsch, and P. I. Leppard. 1986. Periodontal Disease in Ancient Populations.
American Journal of Physical Anthropology
71:173–183.

52. Coe, W. R. 1958. Piedras Negras Archaeol-
ogy: Artifacts, Caches, and Burials. Ph.D.
dissertation, Department of Anthropology,
University of Pennsylvania, Philadelphia.
University Microfilms International, Ann
Arbor.

53. ———. 1959. Burials. In *Piedras Negras Archaeology: Artifacts, Caches, and Burials,*
pp. 120–139. Museum Monographs. The
University Museum, University of Pennsylvania, Philadelphia.

54. ———. 1965. Tikal, Guatemala, and Emer-
gent Maya Civilization. *Science* 147:1401–
1419.

55. Coe, W. R., and V. L. Broman. 1958. Tikal
Report no. 2. Excavations in the Stela 23
Group. In *Tikal Reports nos. 1–4,* pp. 23–
60. Museum Monograph 15. The University
Museum, University of Pennsylvania,
Philadelphia.

56. Coe, W. R., and M. D. Coe. 1956. Excavations at Nohoch Ek, British Honduras.
American Antiquity 21:370–382.

57. Cohen, M. N., C. W. Armstrong, M. E.
Danforth, K. P. Jacobi, and K. A. O'Connor.
1992. Health Indicators on the Fringe of
Spanish Influence: The Maya of Tipu
(abstract). *American Journal of Physical
Anthropology,* Supplement 14:60–61.

58. Cohen, M. N., S. L. Bennett, and C. W.
Armstrong. 1991. Interaction of Classes of
Health Indicators at Tipu (abstract). *American Journal of Physical Anthropology,* Supplement 12:59.

59. Cohen, M. N., K. A. O'Connor, M. E.
Danforth, K. P. Jacobi, and C. W. Armstrong. 1994. Health and Death at Tipu.

In *In the Wake of Contact: Biological Responses to Conquest,* edited by C. S. Larsen
and G. R. Milner, pp. 121–133. Wiley-Liss,
New York.

60. Comas, J. 1960. Datos para la historia de la
deformación craneal en México. *Historia
Mexicana* 9:509–520.

61. ———. 1966. Anthropologie der Sprach-
familie der Maya. *Homo* 17:1–36.

62. ———. 1966. *Características físicas de la
familia lingüística maya.* Cuadernos: Serie
Antropológica, 20. Instituto de Investigaciones Históricas, Universidad Nacional
Autónoma de México, México.

63. ———. 1968. Los restos óseos mexicanos
en el Museo del Hombre, Paris. *Anales de
Antropología* 5:57–74.

64. ———. 1969. Algunos cráneos de la región
maya. *Anales de Antropología* 6:233–248.

65. Cowgill, U., and G. E. Hutchinson. 1963.
Sex-Ratio in Childhood and the Depopulation of the Petén, Guatemala. *Human Biology* 35:90–103.

66. Danforth, M. E. 1987. Dental Microdefects
in a Colonial Maya Population (abstract). In
*Papers on Paleopathology Presented at the
Fourteenth Annual Meeting of the Paleo-
pathology Association, New York,* edited by
E. Cockburn, pp. 13–14. Paleopathology
Association, Detroit.

67. ———. 1988. A Comparison of Health
Patterns in the Classic and Colonial Maya
Using Microscopic Dental Indicators (abstract). *American Journal of Physical Anthropology* 75:201–202.

68. ———. 1989. A Comparison of Childhood
Health Patterns in the Late Classic and Colo-
nial Maya Using Enamel Microdefects. Ph.D.
dissertation, Department of Anthropology,
Indiana University, Bloomington. University
Microfilms International, Ann Arbor.

69. ———. 1989. Enamel Microdefect Formation in Deciduous Teeth (abstract). *American
Journal of Physical Anthropology* 78:209.

70. ———. 1991. Childhood Health Patterns at
Tipu: Evidence from Harris Lines (abstract).
American Journal of Physical Anthropology,
Supplement 12:65

71. ———. 1993. Marriage and Childbirth in Colonial Tipu. *Community College Humanities Review.* Special issue from NEH Summer Institute: Texts of the Pre-Columbian/Spanish Encounters, 1492–1650, pp. 38–44.

72. ———. 1994. Stature Change in Prehistoric Maya of the Southern Lowlands. *Latin American Antiquity* 5:206–211.

73. Danforth, M. E., S. L. Bennett, M. N. Cohen, and H. Melkunas. 1985. Femoral Cortical Involution in a Colonial Maya Population (abstract). *American Journal of Physical Anthropology* 66:162.

74. Dastugue, J., and V. Gervais. 1992. *Paléopathologie du squelette humain.* Société Nouvelle des Editions Boubée, Paris.

75. Dávalos Hurtado, E. 1946. Las deformaciones craneanas. In *México prehispánico: culturas, deidades, monumentos,* edited by J. Abilio Vivo, pp. 831–840. Editorial E. Hurtado, México.

76. ———. 1953. Investigaciones osteopatológicas prehispánicas en México. *Memoria del Congreso Científico Mexicano* 12:78–81.

77. ———. 1964. La patología ósea prehispánica. *Actas y Memorias, XXXV Congreso Internacional de Americanistas, México, 1962,* vol. 3, pp. 79–85. Editorial Libros de México, México.

78. ———. 1965. Las deformaciones craneanas. In *Temas de antropología física,* pp. 13–20. Instituto Nacional de Antropología e Historia, México.

79. ———. 1970. Pre-Hispanic Osteopathology. In *Physical Anthropology,* edited by T. D. Stewart, pp. 68–81. Handbook of Middle American Indians, vol. 9, R. Wauchope, general editor. University of Texas Press, Austin.

80. Dávalos Hurtado, E., and A. Romano Pacheco. 1955. Estudio preliminar de los restos osteológicos encontrados en la tumba del Templo de las Inscripciones, Palenque. *Anales del Instituto Nacional de Antropología e Historia* 6:107–110.

81. ———. 1973. Estudio preliminar de los restos osteológicos encontrados en la tumba del Templo de las Inscripciones, Palenque. In *El Templo de las Inscripciones, Palenque,* edited by A. Ruz Lhuillier, pp. 253–254. Colección Científica Arqueológica 7. Instituto Nacional de Antropología e Historia, México.

82. Demarest, A., H. Escobedo, J. A. Valdes, S. Houston, L. E. Wright, and K. F. Emery. 1991. Arqueología, epigrafía y el descubrimiento de una tumba real en el centro ceremonial de Dos Pilas, Petén, Guatemala. *U tz'ib* 1:14–28.

83. Demarest, A., J. A. Valdes, H. L. Escobedo Ayala, and S. D. Houston. 1992. Una tumba real en el centro ceremonial de Dos Pilas: excavación e implicaciones. In *V Simposio de Investigaciones Arqueológicas en Guatemala, 15–18 de julio de 1991,* edited by J. P. Laporte, H. L. Escobedo Ayala, and S. Villagrán de Brady, pp. 301–315. Museo Nacional de Arqueología y Etnología, Guatemala.

84. Dembo, A. 1937. La decoración dentaria en la América aborigen. Las referencias de los cronistas amplimente confirmados por los hallazgos arqueológicos. *Revista Geográfica Americana (Buenos Aires)* 7:95–100.

85. ———. 1937. La técnica de las mutilaciones dentarias en la América precolumbiana. *Revista Geográfica Americana (Buenos Aires)* 8:195–202.

86. Dembo, A., and J. Imbelloni. 1938. *Deformaciones intencionales del cuerpo humano de carácter étnico.* Sec. A, tomo 3. Humanior, Biblioteca del Americanista Moderno, Buenos Aires.

87. Dillon, B. D., L. Brunker, and K. O. Pope. 1985. Ancient Maya Autoamputation? A Possible Case from Salinas de los Nueve Cerros, Guatemala. *Journal of New World Archaeology* 5(4):24–38.

88. Dingwall, E. J. 1931. Artificial Cranial Deformation in Mexico, Central America and the West Indies. In *Artificial Cranial Deformation,* by E. J. Dingwall, pp. 151–160. Bale and Danielson, London.

89. Donaghey, S., D. C. Pring, R. Wilk, F. P. Saul, L. H. Feldman, and N. Hammond. 1976. Excavations at Cuello, 1976. In

Archaeology in Northern Belize: Corozal Project 1976, Interim Report, edited by N. Hammond, pp. 6–59. Center of Latin American Studies, Cambridge University, Cambridge.

90. Dunning, N., L. E. Wright, K. Emery, E. Secaira, D. Lentz, T. Breach, and D. Rue. 1992. Ecología, agricultura, y nutrición en los siglos 7 y 8 en la región de Petexbatún. In V Simposio de Investigaciones Arqueológicas en Guatemala, 15–18 de julio de 1991, edited by J. P. Laporte, H. L. Escobedo Ayala, and S. Villagrán de Brady, pp. 163–171. Museo Nacional de Arqueología y Etnología, Guatemala.

91. Engerrand, G. 1917. Les mutilations dentaires chez les anciens mayas. Revue Anthropologique 27:488–493.

92. Escobedo H. L., J. M. Samayoa, and O. Gómez. 1994. Las Pacayas: un nuevo sitio arqueológico en la región Petexbatún. In VII Simposio de Investigaciones Arqueológicas en Guatemala, 1993, edited by J. P. Laporte and H. L. Escobedo, pp. 515–538. Museo Nacional de Antropología e Etnología, Guatemala.

93. Evans, D. T. 1973. A Preliminary Evaluation of Tooth Tartar among the Preconquest Maya of the Tayasal Area, El Petén, Guatemala. American Antiquity 38:489–493.

94. Fastlicht, S. 1948. Tooth Mutilations in Pre-Columbian Mexico. Journal of the American Dental Association 36:315–323.

95. ———. 1950. La odontología en el México prehispánico. Revista del Asociación Dental Mexicana 7:67–89.

96. ———. 1960. Las mutilaciones dentarias entre los mayas: un nuevo dato sobre las incrustaciones dentarias. Anales del Instituto Nacional de Antropología e Historia 12:111–130.

97. ———. 1962. Dental Inlays and Fillings among the Ancient Mayas. Journal of the History of Medicine and Allied Sciences 17:393–401.

98. ———. 1974. El pegamento de las incrustaciones dentarias prehispánicas. In Antropología física, época prehispánica, no. 3,

pp. 251–264. Panorama Histórico y Cultural, SEP [Secretaría de Educación Pública] Instituto Nacional de Antropología e Historia, México.

99. ———. 1975. Dental Inlays among the Maya. North Carolina Dental Journal 58:19–21.

100. ———. 1975. Los dientes de los antiguos mexicanos. Gaceta Médica de México 109:223–236.

101. ———. 1976. Tooth Mutilations and Dentistry in Pre-Columbian Mexico, translated by M. Heltzen and E. Comstock. Buch- und Zeitschriften Verlag "Die Quintessenz," Berlin and Chicago.

102. Feindel, W. 1988. Cranial Clues to the Mysterious Decline of the Maya Civilization: The Hippocampal Hypothesis. America Indigena 48:215–221.

103. Ferrer y Ferrer, A. 1949. Mutilaciones dentarias entre los mayas. Revista de la Asociación Dental Mexicana 6:271–277.

104. Folan, W. 1982. La paleoclimatología y la paleoalimentación. Boletín de la Escuela de Ciencias Antropológicas de la Universidad de Yucatán 10:43–47.

105. Fowler, W. B. 1984. Late Preclassic Mortuary Patterns and Evidence for Human Sacrifice at Chalchuapa, El Salvador. American Antiquity 49:603–618.

106. Fry, E. I. 1956. Skeletal Remains from Mayapan. In Current Reports no. 38—Department of Anthropology, pp. 551–571. Carnegie Institution of Washington, Washington.

107. Gamboa Cetina, J. M., and M. E. Peraza López. 1988. Los entierros de Cobá: un ensayo de interpretación osteopatología. Boletín de la Escuela de Ciencias Antropológicas de la Universidad de Yucatán 15:9–22.

108. Gann, T. W. F. 1901. Recent Discoveries in Central America Proving the Pre-Columbian Existence of Syphilis in the New World. Lancet, October 12, pp. 968–970.

109. ———. 1918. The Maya Indians of Southern Yucatan and Northern British Honduras. Bulletin 64. Bureau of American

Ethnology, Smithsonian Institution, Washington.

110. Gann, T. W. F., and M. Gann. 1939. *Archaeological Investigations in the Corozal District of British Honduras.* Bulletin 123, Anthropological Papers no. 7. Bureau of American Ethnology, Smithonian Institution, Washington.

111. Genovés, S. 1964. Antropométrica de Mesoamérica. *Actas y Memorias, XXXV Congreso Internacional de Americanistas, México, 1962.* vol. 3, pp. 87–97. Editorial Libros de México, México.

112. ———. 1970. Anthropometry of Late Prehistoric Remains. In *Physical Anthropology,* edited by T. D. Stewart, pp. 35–49. Handbook of Middle American Indians, vol. 9, R. Wauchope, general editor. University of Texas Press, Austin.

113. Gerry, J. P. 1993. Diet and Status among the Classic Maya: An Isotopic Perspective. Ph.D. dissertation, Department of Anthropology, Harvard University, Cambridge. University Microfilms International, Ann Arbor.

114. Gervais, V. 1988. Étude anthropologique des sites de la Vallée du Rio Chixoy (El Jocote, Chitomax, Los Cimientos, Los Encuentros, La Victoria). In *La Vallée moyenne du Rio Chixoy (Guatemala): occupation préhispanique et problémes actuels,* by A. Ichon, D. Douzat-Rosenfeld, and P. Usselmann. Centre National de la Rechérche Scientifique. Institut D'Ethnologie, Paris. Editorial Piedra Santa, Guatemala.

115. ———. 1989. Exostoses auriculaires précolombiennes. *Actes des 4e Journées Anthropologiques,* pp. 1–6. Dossier de Documentation archéologique no. 13. Éditions du CNRS [Centre National de la Rechérche Scientifique], Paris.

116. Gervais, V., and A. Ichon. 1990. Paléoanthropologie des cimetières de La Campana à Mixco Viejo (Guatemala). *Journal de la Société des Americanistes* 76:55–77.

117. Gervais-Cloris, V. 1985. Annexe 5. Étude anthropologique des ossements humains de la Str. A-7. In *Le protoclassique à La Lagunita, El Quiché (Guatemala),* by A. Ichon and M. C. Arnauld, pp. 243–246. Centre National de la Rechérche Scientifique, Rechérche Cooperative sur Programme 294 et 500. Institut D'Ethnologie, Paris. Editorial Piedra Santa, Guatemala.

118. Ginestet, G. 1933. Mutilations et incrustation dentaire. *Revue de Sintomatologie* 35.

119. Glassman, D. M. 1994. Skeletal Biology of the Prehistoric Maya on Ambergris Cay, Belize (abstract). *American Journal of Physical Anthropology,* Supplement 18:95.

120. Goff, C. W. 1953. New Evidence of Pre-Columbian Bone Syphilis in Guatemala. In *The Ruins of Zaculeu, Guatemala,* vol. 1, edited by R. B. Woodbury and A. S. Trik, pp. 312–319. United Fruit Co., Richmond.

121. ———. 1967. Syphilis. In *Diseases in Antiquity,* edited by D. Brothwell and A. T. Sandison, pp. 279–294. Charles C Thomas, Springfield.

122. Gordon, G. B. 1896. *The Prehistoric Ruins of Copan, Honduras.* Memoirs of the Peabody Museum of American Archaeology and Ethnology, vol. 1, no. 1. Harvard University, Cambridge.

123. ———. 1898. *Researches in the Uloa Valley, Honduras.* Memoirs of the Peabody Museum of American Archaeology and Ethnology, vol. 1, no. 4. Harvard University, Cambridge.

124. Gosse, L. A. 1865. Présentation d'un crâne déformé de Nahoa, trouvé dans la Vallée de Ghovel, Mexique. *Bulletins de la Société d'Anthropologie de Paris* 2:567–577.

125. Graham, E., D. M. Pendergast, and G. D. Jones. 1989. On the Fringes of Conquest: Maya-Spanish Contact in Colonial Belize. *Science* 246:1254–1259.

126. Grazioso S., L. 1992. Entierros clásico tardío de un grupo residencial en el noreste de Petén. In *V Simposio de Investigaciones Arqueológicas en Guatemala, 15–18 de julio de 1991,* edited by J. P. Laporte, H. L. Escobedo Ayala, and S. Villagrán de Brady, pp. 143–154. Museo Nacional de Arqueología y Etnología, Guatemala.

127. Grimm, H. 1991. Rudolf Virchow, a Famous Pathologist: Not Interested in Paleopathology? *Journal of Paleopathology* 3:119–126.

128. Guilbert, H. D. 1943. The Mayan Skulls of Copan. *American Journal of Orthodontics and Oral Surgery* 29:216–222.

129. Guillemin, J. [G.] F. 1961. Un entierro señorial en Iximché. *Anales de la Sociedad de Geografía e Historia de Guatemala* 34:89–105.

130. ———. 1965. *Iximché, capital del antiguo reino cakchiquel*. Publicaciones del Instituto de Antropología e Historia, Guatemala.

131. ———. 1967. The Ancient Cakchiquel Capital of Iximché. *Expedition* 9(2):22–35.

132. ———. 1968. La sépulture d'un chef à Iximché. *Archaeologie* 23.

133. ———. 1969. Exploration du Groupe C d'Iximché (Guatemala). *Bulletin de la Société Suisse des Américanistes* 33:23–33.

134. Gwinnett, A. J., and L. Gorelick. 1979. Inlayed Teeth of the Ancient Mayans: A Tribological Study Using the SEM. *Scanning Electron Microscopy* 3:575–580.

135. Hambly, W. D. 1937. *Skeletal Material from San José Ruin, British Honduras*. Anthropological Series vol. 25, no. 1, publ. 380. Field Museum of Natural History, Chicago.

136. Hammond, N. 1982. Unearthing the Oldest Known Maya. *National Geographic* 162:126–140.

137. Hammond, N., A. Clarke, and C. Robin. 1991. Middle Preclassic Buildings and Burials at Cuello, Belize: 1990 Investigations. *Latin American Antiquity* 2:352–363.

138. Hammond, N., and T. Molleson. 1994. Huguenot Weavers and Maya Kings: Anthropological Assessment Versus Documentary Record of Age at Death. *Mexicon* 16(4):75–77.

139. Hammond, N., K. Pretty, and F. P. Saul. 1975. A Classic Maya Family Tomb. *World Archaeology* 7:57–78.

140. Hammond, N., D. Pring, R. Wilk, S. Donaghey, F. P. Saul, E. S. Wing, A. V. Miller, and L. N. Feldman. 1979. The Earliest Lowland Maya? Definition of the Swasey Phase. *American Antiquity* 44:92–110.

141. Hamy, E. T. 1882. Les mutilations dentaires au Mexique et dans le Yucatan. *Bulletins de la Société d'Anthropologie de Paris*, 3e ser., 5:879–882.

142. ———. 1884. *Anthropologie du Mexique*. Mission Scientifique au Mexique et dans l'Amerique Centrale. Imprimerie Nationale, Paris.

143. Hatch, J. W., and R. A. Geidel. 1985. Status-Specific Dietary Variation in Two World Cultures. *Journal of Human Evolution* 14:469–476.

144. Haviland, W. A. 1967. Stature at Tikal, Guatemala: Implications for Ancient Maya Demography and Social Organization. *American Antiquity* 32:316–325.

145. ———. 1972. Family Size, Prehistoric Population Estimates, and the Ancient Maya. *American Antiquity* 37:135–139.

146. ———. 1972. A New Look at Classic Maya Social Organization at Tikal. *Cerámica de Cultura Maya* 8:1–16.

147. ———. 1981. Dower Houses and Minor Centers at Tikal, Guatemala: An Investigation into the Identification of Valid Units in Settlement Hierarchies. In *Lowland Maya Settlement Patterns*, edited by W. Ashmore, pp. 89–117. University of New Mexico Press, Albuquerque.

148. ———. 1985. Burials. In *Excavations in Small Residential Groups of Tikal, Guatemala: Groups 4F-1 and 4F-2*, by W. A. Haviland, M. J. Becker, A. Chowning, K. A. Dixon, and K. Heider, pp. 123–153. Tikal Report no. 19, University Museum Monograph 58. The University Museum, University of Pennsylvania, Philadelphia.

149. Haviland, W. A., and H. Moholy-Nagy. 1992. Distinguishing the High and Mighty from the Hoi Polloi at Tikal, Guatemala. In *Mesoamerican Elites: An Archaeological Assessment*, edited by D. Z. Chase and A. F. Chase, pp. 50–60. University of Oklahoma Press, Norman and London.

150. Helmuth, H., and D. M. Pendergast. 1986–1987. Lamanai Tomb N9-58/1: Analysis of the Skeletal Evidence. *Ossa* 13:109–118.

151. Hester, T. R., J. D. Eaton, and D. G. Steele. 1983. La fossa dei crania a Colha. In *Colha ei maya dei bassipiani,* edited by T. Hester, G. Ligabue, S. Salvatori, and M. Sartor, pp. 131–133. Erizzo Editrice, Venezia.

152. Hooton, E. A. 1930. Pathology. In *Indians of the Pecos Pueblo,* pp. 306–330. Papers of the Southwestern Expedition no. 4. Yale University Press, New Haven.

153. ———. 1940. Skeletons from the Cenote of Sacrifice at Chichen Itzá. In *The Maya and Their Neighbors: Essays on Middle American Anthropology and Archaeology,* edited by C. L. Hay, R. L. Linton, S. K. Lothrop, H. Shapiro, and G. C. Vaillant, pp. 272–280. Appleton-Century, New York.

154. Housely, R. A., N. Hammond, and I. A. Law. 1991. AMS Radiocarbon Dating of Preclassic Maya Burials from Cuello, Belize. *American Antiquity* 56:514–519.

155. Houston, S., R. Chatham, O. Chinchilla, E. Ponciano, and L. Wright. 1992. Mapeo y sondeos en Tamarindito. In *IV Simposio de Arqueología Guatemalteca, 1990,* edited by J. P. Laporte, H. L. Escobedo, and S. Villagrán de Brady, pp. 169–174. Museo Nacional de Arqueología y Etnología, Guatemala.

156. Hrdlička, A. 1926. The Indians of Panama: Their Physical Relationship to the Maya. *American Journal of Physical Anthropology* 9:1–15.

157. Hummert, J. 1983. Appendix I. Analysis of Faunal Materials from the Protoclassic Project in the Zapotitan Valley, 1978 Season. In *Archeology and Volcanism in Central America,* edited by P. D. Sheets, pp. 295–299. University of Texas Press, Austin.

158. Ichon, A. 1980. Síntesis y conclusiones. In *Rescate arqueológico en la cuenca del Río Chixoy 2 — Cauinal,* by A. Ichon, M. F. Fauvet-Berthelot, C. Plocieniak, R. Hill II, R. González Lauck, and M. A. Bailey, pp. 187–210. Misión Científica Franco-Guatemalteca. Centre National de la Recherche Scientifique R.C.P. 500. Editoria Piedra Santa, Guatemala.

159. Ichon, A., and R. Grignon. 1984. Pratiques funéraires et stratification sociale dans les hautes terres. Les cimetières protohistoriques de La Campana à Mixco Viejo (Guatemala). *Journal de la Société des Américanistes* 70:89–126.

160. Iglesias Ponce de León, M. J. 1993. Reflexiones en torno a ciertos enterramientos en Tikal. In *III Simposio de Investigaciones Arqueológicas en Guatemala, 1989,* edited by J. P. Laporte, H. L. Escobedo, and S. Villagrán de Brady, pp. 183–196. Museo Nacional de Arqueología e Etnología, Guatemala.

161. Imbelloni, J. 1938. Formas, esencia y metódica de las deformaciones cefálicas intencionales. *Revista del Instituto de Antropología, Universidad de Tucumán* 1:1–37.

162. Inomata, T., J. Palka, M. T. Robles, S. Symonds, and L. E. Wright. 1992. Excavaciones en grupos residenciales de Dos Pilas. In *IV Simposio de Arqueología Guatemalteca, 1990,* edited by J. P. Laporte, H. L. Escobedo, and S. Villagrán de Brady, pp. 141–142. Museo Nacional de Arqueología y Etnología, Guatemala.

163. Jacobi, K. P. 1991. Population Affinities and Social Organization of Tipu Individuals through Dental Metrics and Discrete Traits (abstract). *American Journal of Physical Anthropology,* Supplement 12:98.

164. ———. 1994. An Analysis of Genetic Structuring in a Colonial Maya Cemetery, Tipu, Belize, Using Dental Morphology and Metrics (abstract). *American Journal of Physical Anthropology,* Supplement 18:114.

165. Jaén Esquivel, M. T. 1968. El material osteológico de Chiapa de Corzo, Chiapas. *Anales del Instituto Nacional de Antropología e Historia* 19(48):67–77. Secretaría de Educación Pública, México.

166. Jaén Esquivel, M. T., and S. López Alonso.

1974. Algunas características físicas de la
población prehispánica de México. In
Antropología Física, Época Prehispánica,
pp. 115–135. Panorama Histórico y Cultural, III, SEP [Secretaría de Educación
Pública]-Instituto Nacional de Antropología e Historia, México.

167. Katayama, K. 1994. Parte 7. Estudios
osteológicos de los entierros encontrados
en Magoy, Kaminaljuyú. In *Kaminaljuyú
(1991–94),* vol. 2, edited by K. Ohi, pp.
574–597. Museo de Tabaco y Sal, Tokyo.

168. Kennedy, G. E. 1983. Skeletal Remains
from Sarteneja, Belize. In *Archaeological
Excavations in Northern Belize, Central
America,* edited by R. V. Sidrys, pp. 353–
372. Monograph XVII. Institute of Archaeology, University of California at Los
Angeles, Los Angeles.

169. Kidder, A. V. 1937. *Notes on the Ruins of
San Agustin Acasaguastlan, Guatemala.*
Contributions to American Archaeology,
vol. 3, no. 15. Publication 456. Carnegie
Institution of Washington, Washington.

170. Kidder, A. V., J. D. Jennings, and E. M.
Shook. 1946. *Excavations at Kaminaljuyu,
Guatemala.* Publication 561. Carnegie
Institution of Washington, Washington.

171. Lagunas, Z. 1970. Nota sobre el hallazgo
de cráneos con lesión suprainiana en
Cholula. *Boletín del Instituto Nacional de
Antropología e Historia* no. 39, pp. 1–4.

172. Larsen, C. S. 1994. In the Wake of Colum-
bus: Native Population Biology in the Post-
contact Americas. *Yearbook of Physical
Anthropology* 37:109–154.

173. Lentz, D. L. 1991. Cosmetic Dentistry
among the Ancient Maya. *Mississippi Dental Association Journal* 46(3):25.

174. León, N. 1928. La capacidad craneal en algunos tribus indígenas de la República de
México. In *Proceedings of the 20th International Congress of Americanists,* vol. 2,
pp. 37–53.

175. Linné, S. 1940. Dental Decoration in Aboriginal America. *Ethnos* 5:2–28.

176. Littlehales, B. 1961. Treasure Hunt in

the Deep Past. *National Geographic* 120:
550–561.

177. Longyear, J. M. III. 1940. A Maya Old
Empire Skeleton from Copan, Honduras.
American Journal of Physical Anthropology
27:151–154.

178. ———. 1952. Skeletal Data. In *Copan
Ceramics. A Study of Southeastern Maya
Pottery,* p. 87. Publication 597. Carnegie
Institution of Washington, Washington.

179. López, R. F., and G. Martínez Hidalgo.
1992. Excavaciones en el Montículo A-IV-
2, Kaminaljuyú, Guatemala. In *V Simposio
de Investigaciones Arqueológicas en Guatemala, 15–18 de julio de 1991,* edited by
J. P. Laporte, H. L. Escobedo Ayala, and
S. Villagrán de Brady, pp. 3–11. Museo
Nacional de Arqueología y Etnología,
Guatemala.

180. López, R. F., and R. Ortiz. 1994. Excava-
ciones en un palacio residencial en el Grupo
Códice de Nakbe, Petén. In *VII Simposio
de Investigaciones Arqueológicas en Guate-
mala, 1993,* edited by J. P. Laporte and
H. L. Escobedo, pp. 313–333. Museo
Nacional de Arqueología e Etnología,
Guatemala.

181. López Alonso, S. 1968. Material osteológico
de Jaina: cráneos. In *Jaina: la casa en el
agua,* edited by R. Piña Chan, pp. 83–99.
Instituto Nacional de Antropología e Historia, México.

182. López Olivares, N. M. 1992. Los restos
óseos prehispánicos del Valle de Dolores,
Petén. In *V Simposio de Investigaciones
Arqueológicas en Guatemala, 15–18 de
julio de 1991,* edited by J. P. Laporte, H. L.
Escobedo Ayala, and S. Villagrán de Brady,
pp. 237–247. Museo Nacional de Arqueología e Historia, Guatemala.

183. ———. 1993. Huellas vitales y culturales
en los entierros de Uaxactún, Petén. In *III
Simposio de Investigaciones Arqueológicas
en Guatemala, 1989,* edited by J. P. Laporte, H. L. Escobedo, and S. Villagrán de
Brady, pp. 13–31. Museo Nacional de
Arqueología y Etnología, Guatemala.

184. Lowe, G. W. 1964. Burial Customs at Chiapa de Corzo. In *The Archaeological Burials at Chiapa de Corzo and Their Furniture,* pp. 65–75. New World Archaeological Foundation Publ. 12. Brigham Young University Press, Provo.

185. Magennis, A. L., and A. E. Jansen. 1994. Dietary Change at the Lowland Maya Site of Kichpanha, Belize (abstract). *American Journal of Physical Anthropology,* Supplement 18:135.

186. Mandujano Váldez, M. E., and J. J. Izazola Alvarez. 1987. Estomatología y ciencia odontológica en el México prehispánico. *Práctica Odontológica* 8:12–22.

187. Marcus, J. 1992. Royal Families, Royal Texts: Examples from the Zapotec and Maya. In *Mesoamerican Elites: An Archaeological Assessment,* edited by D. Z. Chase and A. F. Chase, pp. 221–241. University of Oklahoma Press, Norman and London.

188. Marden, L. 1959. Dzibilchaltun: Up from the Well of Time. *National Geographic* 115:110–129.

189. Márquez de González, L., A. Benavides Castillo, and P. J. Schmidt. 1982. *Exploración en la gruta de Xcan, Yucatán.* Centro Regional del Sureste, Instituto Nacional de Antropología e Historia, Mérida.

190. Márquez de González, L., and R. Harrington. 1981. Spongy Hyperostosis and Cribra Orbitalia in a Maya Subadult Temple. *Paleopathology Newsletter,* no. 35, pp. 12–13.

191. ———. 1981. Subadult Ossuary in a Chultun at Chichen Itza, Yucatan (abstract). *Papers on Paleopathology Presented at the Annual Meeting of the Paleopathology Association, Detroit,* edited by E. Cockburn, p. D3. Paleopathology Association, Detroit.

192. Márquez Morfín, L. 1984. Distribución de la estatura en colecciones óseas mayas prehispánicas. In *Estudios de antropología biológica (II Coloquio de Antropología Física Juan Comas, 1982),* edited by R. Ramos Galván and R. M. Ramos Rodríguez, pp. 253–271. Antropología Física. Serie Antropológica 75. Instituto de Investiga-

ciones Antropológicas, Universidad Nacional Autónoma de México, México.

193. ———. 1987. Qué sabemos de los mayas peninsulares, a partir de sus restos óseos. In *Memorias del Primer Coloquio Internacional de Mayistas,* pp. 43–56. Universidad Nacional Autónoma de México, México.

194. ———. 1991. La dieta maya prehispánica en la costa yucateca. *Estudios de Cultura Maya* 18:359–394.

195. ———. 1992. Evidencias óseas sobre la dieta maya durante el postclásico. In *Memorias del Primer Congreso Internacional de Mayistas,* pp. 539–549. Instituto de Investigaciones Filológicas, Universidad Nacional Autónoma de México, México.

196. Márquez Morfín, L., and N. González Crespo. 1985. *Las momias de la iglesia de Santa Elena, Yucatán: estudio antropofísico.* Instituto Nacional de Antropología e Historia, México.

197. Márquez, L., and T. Miranda. 1984. Investigaciones osteológicas en la península de Yucatán. In *Investigaciones recientes en el área maya,* tomo 2, pp. 49–62. Memorias de la XVII Mesa Redonda, 1981. Sociedad Mexicana de Antropología, San Cristobal de las Casas.

198. Márquez Morfín, L., M. E. Peraza, J. Gamboa, and T. Miranda. 1982. *Playa del Carmen: una población de la costa oriental en el postclásico (un estudio osteológico).* Colección Científica. Antropología Física 119. Sección de Antropología Física, Centro Regional del Sureste, Instituto Nacional de Antropología e Historia, México.

199. Márquez, L., and P. Schmidt. 1984. Osario infantil en un chultún en Chichén Itzá. In *Investigaciones recientes en el área maya,* tomo 2, pp. 89–103. Memorias de la XVII Mesa Redonda, 1981. Sociedad Mexicana de Antropología, San Cristobal de las Casas.

200. Martin, R., and Saller, K. 1959. *Lehrbuch der Anthropologie,* vol. 2. Gustav Fischer Verlag, Stuttgart.

201. Martínez Lavin, M., J. Mansilla, C. Pineda, C. Pijoan, and P. Ochoa. 1994. Evidence of

Hypertrophic Osteoarthropathy in Human Skeletal Remains from Prehispanic Mesoamerica. *Annals of Internal Medicine* 120: 238–241.

202. Massey, V. K. 1988. Cut Marks on the Colha, Belize, Skull Pit Skeletal Material (abstract). *American Journal of Physical Anthropology* 75:247.

203. ———. 1989. *The Human Skeletal Remains from a Terminal Classic Skull Pit at Colha, Belize.* Papers of the Colha Project, vol. 3. Texas Archeological Research Laboratory, The University of Texas at Austin, and Department of Anthropology, Texas A&M University, College Station.

204. ———. 1994. Osteological Analysis of the Skull Pit Children. In *Continuing Archeology at Colha, Belize,* edited by T. R. Hester, H. J. Shafer, and J. D. Eaton, pp. 209–220. Studies in Archeology 16. Texas Archeological Research Laboratory, The University of Texas at Austin, Austin.

205. Massey, V. K., and D. G. Steele. 1982. Preliminary Notes on the Dentition and Taphonomy of the Colha Human Skeletal Material. In *Archaeology at Colha, Belize: The 1981 Interim Report,* edited by T. R. Hester, H. J. Shafer, and J. D. Eaton, pp. 198–202. Center for Archaeological Research, The University of Texas at San Antonio and Centro Studi e Ricerche Ligabue, Venezia, San Antonio.

206. Mata Amado, G. 1993. Odontología prehispánica en Mesoamérica. *Anales de la Academia de Geografía e Historia de Guatemala* 67.

207. ———. 1994. Dental Treatments in Prehispanic Mesoamerica. In *Seventh Palenque Round Table, 1989,* vol. 9, edited by V. Fields, pp. 257–259. M. G. Robertson, general editor. Pre-Columbian Art Research Institute, San Francisco.

208. Mata Amado, G., and R. D. Hansen. 1992. El diente incrustado temprano de Nakbe. In *V Simposio de Investigaciones Arqueológicas en Guatemala, 15–18 de julio de 1991,* edited by J. P. Laporte, H. L. Escobedo Ayala and S. Villagrán de Brady, pp. 115–

118. Museo Nacional de Arqueología y Etnología, Guatemala.

209. Matheny, D. G. 1988. The Northwest Plaza Burials at Lagartero, Chiapas, Mexico. Ph.D. dissertation, Department of Anthropology, University of Utah, Salt Lake City. University Microfilms International, Ann Arbor.

210. Matthews, W. 1891. The Human Bones of the Hemenway Collection in the U.S. Army Medical Museum at Washington. *Memoirs of the National Academy of Sciences* 6: 141–286.

211. Maudslay, A. P. 1889–1902. *Biologia Centrali-Americana,* vol. 2 (Archaeology Section). R. H. Porter and Dulau, London.

212. Merriwether, D. A. 1994. mtDNA and the Peopling of the New World. *Mother Tongue,* issue 23, November, pp. 22–28.

213. Merriwether, D. A., F. Rothhammer, and R. E. Ferrell. 1992. Mitochondrial DNA Variation in Ancient and Contemporary Amerindians Using the tRNA^{LYS}-COII Deletion and Diagnostic Restriction Sites (abstract). *American Journal of Human Genetics* 51(4):A13.

214. ———. 1994. Genetic Variation in the New World: Ancient Teeth, Bone, and Tissue as Sources of DNA. *Experientia* 50:592–601.

215. Merwin, R. E., and G. C. Vaillant. 1932. *The Ruins of Holmul, Guatemala.* Memoirs of the Peabody Museum of American Archaeology and Ethnology, vol. 3, no. 3. Harvard University, Cambridge.

216. Mock, S. B. 1994. Destruction and Denouement during the Late-Terminal Classic: The Colha Skull Pit. In *Continuing Archeology at Colha, Belize,* edited by T. R. Hester, H. J. Shafer, and J. D. Eaton, pp. 221–231. Studies in Archeology 16. Texas Archeological Research Laboratory, The University of Texas at Austin, Austin.

217. Moedano Koer, H. 1946. Jaina: un cementerio maya. *Revista Mexicana de Estudios Antropológicos* 8:217–242.

218. Moore, S. 1929. The Bone Changes in Sickle Cell Anemia with Note on Similar Changes Observed in Skulls of Ancient

Maya Indians. *Journal of the Missouri State Medical Association* 26:561–564.

219. Morton, S. G. 1839. *Crania americana.* John Pennington, Philadelphia.

220. ———. 1842. Verbal Communications. *Proceedings of the Academy of Natural Sciences* 1:203–204.

221. Muratori, G. 1963. [Ethnic Mutilations. Dental Mutilations in Guatemala]. *Rivista Bimestrale di Scienze Mediche, Arcispedale S. Anna di Ferrara* 16:1191–1200.

222. Nickens, P. R. 1976. Stature Reduction as an Adaptive Response to Food Production in Mesoamerica. *Journal of Archaeological Science* 3:31–41.

223. O'Connor, K. A. 1991. Paleodemography of the Tipu Population (abstract). *American Journal of Physical Anthropology,* Supplement 12:138–139.

224. Ortner, D. J., and W. G. J. Putschar. 1985. Metabolic Disorders. In *Identification of Pathological Conditions in Human Skeletal Remains,* pp. 270–297. Reprinted. Originally published 1981. Smithsonian Contributions to Anthropology no. 28. Smithsonian Institution, Washington.

225. Otis, G. A. 1880. *List of the Specimens in the Anatomical Section of the U.S. Army Medical Museum.* Gibson Brothers, Washington.

226. Paine, R. B. 1993. Population Dynamics at Copan, Honduras, A.D. 450–1250: A Study in Archaeological Demography, Ph.D. dissertation, Department of Anthropology, The Pennsylvania State University, University Park. University Microfilms International, Ann Arbor.

227. Pedersen, P. O. 1944. Om Kunstig Deformering af det Menneskelige Tandsaet: Strejftog det Odontologisk-Ethnografisk Graenseland. *Dens Sapiens* 4:3–12.

228. Peña Saint Martin, F. 1985. Nutrición entre los mayas prehispánicos. Un estudio osteobiográfico. *Cuicuilco* 4(16):5–16. Escuela Nacional de Antropología e Historia, México.

229. Pendergast, D. M. 1969. *Altun Ha, British Honduras (Belize): The Sun God's Tomb.* Art and Archaeology, Occasional Paper 19. Royal Ontario Museum, Toronto.

230. ———. 1979. *Excavations at Altun Ha, Belize, 1964–1970,* vol. 1. Royal Ontario Museum, Toronto.

231. ———. 1982. *Excavations at Altun Ha, Belize, 1964–1970,* vol. 2. Royal Ontario Museum, Toronto.

232. Pendergast, D. M., M. H. Bartley, and G. J. Armelagos. 1968. A Maya Tooth Offering from Yakalche, British Honduras. *Man* 3:635–643.

233. Pijoan Aguadé, C. M., and M. E. Salas Cuesta. 1984. Costumbres funerarias en Mundo Perdido, Tikal. In *Estudios de antropología biológica (II Coloquio de Antropología Física Juan Comas, 1982),* edited by R. Ramos Galván and R.M. Ramos Rodríguez, pp. 237–250. Instituto de Investigaciones Antropológicas, Universidad Nacional Autónoma de México, México.

234. ———. 1984. La población prehispánica de Jaina: análisis osteológico. In *Investigaciones recientes en el área maya,* tomo 2, pp. 471–480. Memorias de la XVII Mesa Redonda, 1981. Sociedad Mexicana de Antropología, San Cristobal de las Casas.

235. Plenot, H. R. 1969. Les mutilations dentaires chez les peuples mesoaméricains. *L'Information Dentaire* 51:2989–2993.

236. Pompa y Padilla, J. A. 1984. Jaina y Chichen Itzá: morfología dentaria normal de dos muestras de la población maya prehispánica. In *Investigaciones recientes en el área maya,* tomo 2, pp. 481–489. Memorias de la XVII Mesa Redonda, 1981. Sociedad Mexicana de Antropología, San Cristobal de las Casas.

237. ———. 1990. *Antropología dental: aplicación en poblaciones prehispánicas.* Serie Antropología Física. Colección Científica 195. Instituto Nacional de Antropología e Historia, México.

238. Popenoe, D. H. 1934. Some Excavations at Playa de los Muertos, Ulua River, Honduras. *Maya Research* 1(2):8–85.

239. Pruner-Bey, M. 1864–1867. Resultats de

craniometrie. *Memoires de la Société d'Anthropologie de Paris* 2:417–432.

240. Quatrefages, A. de, and E. T. Hamy. 1882. *Crania ethnica.* Verlag von A. Asher, Paris.

241. Ramos Rodríguez, R. M. 1978. Algunas observaciones sobre los enterramientos humanos en el sitio "El Rey" (Can Cun). *Anales de Antropología* 15:251–265.

242. Ramos, R. M., and M. Civera C. 1984. La población de Villa Coapa, Chiapas: un estudio osteológico (resumen). In *Investigaciones recientes en el área maya,* tomo 2, pp. 491–497. Memorias de la XVII Mesa Redonda, 1981. Sociedad Mexicana de Antropología, San Cristobal de las Casas.

243. Rands, B. C., and R. L. Rands. 1961. Excavations in a Cemetery at Palenque. *Estudios de Cultura Maya* 1:87–106.

244. Reed, D. M. 1994. Ancient Maya Diet at Copán, Honduras, as Determined through Analysis of Stable Carbon and Nitrogen Isotopes. In *Paleonutrition: The Diet and Health of Prehistoric Americans,* edited by K. D. Sobolik, pp. 210–221. Occasional Papers Series, vol. 22. Center for Archaeological Investigations, Southern Illinois University, Carbondale.

245. Ricketson, O. G., Jr. 1925. Burials in the Maya Area. *American Anthropologist* 27:381–401.

246. ———. 1931. *Excavations at Baking Pot, British Honduras.* Contributions to American Archaeology, vol. 1, no. 1. Publication 403. Carnegie Institution of Washington, Washington.

247. ———. 1937. Human Remains. In *Uaxactun, Guatemala, Group E, 1926–1931,* edited by O. G. Ricketson, Jr. and E. B. Ricketson, pp. 139–149. Publication 477. Carnegie Institution of Washington, Washington.

248. Rivet, P. 1908. Note sur deux crânes du Yucatan. *Journal de la Société des Americanistes* 5:251–259.

249. Robin, C. 1989. *Preclassic Maya Burials at Cuello.* International Series 480. British International Reports, Oxford.

250. Robles Castellano, F. 1980. Entierros encontrados en la Estructura 7-a. In *Informe anual del Proyecto Arqueológico Cozumel: temporada 1980,* pp. 58–61. Instituto Nacional de Antropología e Historia, México.

251. ———. 1981. Entierros hallados en las excavaciones de las estructuras monumentales de San Gervasio, temporada 1980. In *Informe anual del Proyecto Arqueológico Cozumel: temporada 1981,* pp. 106–115. Instituto Nacional de Antropología e Historia, México.

252. Rodríguez Farfán, J. F. 1993. Estudio craneométrico en restos óseos de una región Cakchiquel: Guatemala. *Estudios* no. 1-93, pp. 11–28. Instituto de Investigaciones Históricas, Antropológicas y Arqueológicas, Universidad de San Carlos, Guatemala.

253. Romano Pacheco, A. 1974. Deformación cefálica intencional. In *Antropología física, época prehispánica,* vol. 3, pp. 231–249. Panorama Histórico y Cultural, SEP [Secretaría de Educación Pública]-Instituto Nacional de Antropología e Historia, México.

254. ———. 1979. El material osteológico humano de Toniná, Chiapas: estudio morfológico, descriptivo y comparativo. In *Tonina, une cité maya du Chiapas (Mexique),* edited by P. Becquelin and C. F. Baudez, pp. 179–192. Études Mésoaméricaines vol. 6, tome 1. Mission Archeologique et Ethnologique Francaise au Mexique, México.

255. ———. 1987. Iconografía cefálica maya. *Memorias del Primer Coloquio de Mayistas.* Universidad Nacional Autónoma de México, México.

256. Romano Pacheco, A., and M. T. Jaén Esquivel. 1990. Material óseo humano procedente de diversos sitios arqueológicos del Valle de Ocosingo, estado de Chiapas. In *Tonina, une cité maya du Chiapas (Mexique),* edited by P. Becquelin and E. Taladoire, pp. 1661–1687 and 1968–1976. Études Mésoaméricaines vol. 6, tome 4. Centre d'Études Mexicaines et Centraméricaines, México.

257. Romero Molina, J. 1952. Los patrones de la mutilación dentaria prehispánica. *Anales*

del *Instituto Nacional de Antropología e Historia* 4:177–221.

258. ———. 1958. *Mutilaciones dentarias prehispánicas en México y América en general.* Serie Investigaciones 3. Instituto Nacional de Antropología e Historia, México.

259. ———. 1960. Ultimos hallazgos de mutilaciones dentarias en México. *Anales de Instituto Nacional de Antropología e Historia* 12:151–215.

260. ———. 1965. Recientes adiciones a la colección de dientes mutilados. *Anales del Instituto Nacional de Antropología e Historia* 17:199–256.

261. ———. 1970. Dental Mutilation, Trephination and Cranial Deformation. In *Physical Anthropology,* edited by T. D. Stewart, pp. 50–67. Handbook of Middle American Indians, vol. 9, R. Wauchope, general editor. University of Texas Press, Austin.

262. ———. 1974. La mutilación dentaria. In *Antropología física, época prehispánica,* vol. 3, pp. 231–249. Panorama Histórico y Cultural, SEP [Secretaría de Educación Pública]-Instituto Nacional de Antropología e Historia, México.

263. ———. 1984. Incrustaciones y mutilaciones dentarias. In *México antiguo,* edited by A. López Austin and C. Viesco Trevino, pp. 322–327. Historia general de medicina en México, tomo 1. Universidad Nacional Autónoma de México y Academia Nacional de Medicina, México.

264. ———. 1984. Patrones de mutilación dentaria en la zona maya: observaciones recientes. In *Investigaciones recientes en el área maya,* tomo 1, pp. 3–21. Memorias de la XVII Mesa Redonda. Sociedad Mexicana de Antropología, San Cristobal de las Casas.

265. ———. 1986. *Catálogo de la colección de dientes mutilados prehispánicos, IV parte.* Instituto Nacional de Antropología e Historia, México.

266. Romero Molina, J., and S. Fastlicht. 1951. *El arte de las mutilaciones dentarias.* Enciclopedia mexicana de arte no. 14. Ediciones Mexicanas, México.

267. Rubín de la Borbolla, D. F. 1940. Types of Tooth Mutilation Found in Mexico. *American Journal of Physical Anthropology* 26:349–365.

268. Rue, D., A. C. Freter, and D. A. Ballinger. 1989. The Caverns of Copán Revisited: Preclassic Sites in the Sesesmil River Valley, Copán, Honduras. *Journal of Field Archaeology* 16:395–404.

269. Ruppert, K. 1935. *The Caracol at Chichen Itza, Yucatan, Mexico.* Publication 454. Carnegie Institution of Washington, Washington.

270. Ruz Lhuillier, A. 1954. Exploraciones en Palenque: 1952. *Anales del Instituto Nacional de Antropología e Historia* 6(34):79–106.

271. ———. 1958. Exploraciones arqueológicas en Palenque: 1956. *Anales del Instituto Nacional de Antropología e Historia* 10(39):241–299.

272. ———. 1962. Exploraciones arqueológicas en Palenque: 1957. *Anales del Instituto Nacional de Antropología e Historia* 14(43):35–90.

273. ———. 1965. Tombs and Funerary Practices of the Maya Lowlands. In *Archaeology of Southern Mesoamerica,* part I, edited by G. R. Willey, pp. 441–461. Handbook of Middle American Indians, vol. 2, R. Wauchope, general editor. University of Texas Press, Austin.

274. ———. 1968. *Costumbres funerarias de los antiguos mayas.* Seminaria de Cultura Maya. Universidad Nacional Autónoma de México, México.

275. ———. 1977. Gerontocracy at Palenque? In *Social Process in Maya Prehistory,* edited by N. Hammond, pp. 287–295. Academic Press, New York.

276. Saul, F. P. 1967. Osteobiography of the Lowland Maya of Altar de Sacrificios, Guatemala (abstract). *American Journal of Physical Anthropology* 27:237.

277. ———. 1972. *The Human Skeletal Remains from Altar de Sacrificios, Guatemala: An Osteobiographic Analysis.* Papers of the Peabody Museum of Archaeology and

Ethnology vol. 63, no. 2. Harvard University, Cambridge.

278. ———. 1972. The Physical Anthropology of the Ancient Maya: An Appraisal. In *Verhandlungen des XXXVIII Internationalen Amerikanistenkongresses, Stuttgart-München, 1968,* band IV, pp. 383–394. Kommissionsverlag Klaus Renner, München.

279. ———. 1973. Disease in the Maya Area: The Pre-Columbian Evidence. In *The Classic Maya Collapse,* edited by T. P. Culbert, pp. 301–324. University of New Mexico Press, Albuquerque.

280. ———. 1975. Appendix 8—Human Remains from Lubaantun. In *Lubaantun, a Classic Maya Realm,* edited by N. Hammond, pp. 389–410. Peabody Museum Monographs no. 2. Peabody Museum of Archaeology and Ethnology, Harvard University, Cambridge.

281. ———. 1975. The Maya and Their Neighbors (1974): As Recorded in Their Skeletons. In *The Maya and Their Neighbors,* edited by G. R. Willey, J. A. Sabloff, E. Z. Vogt, and F. P. Saul, pp. 35–40. Peabody Museum Monographs no. 5. Peabody Museum of Archaeology and Ethnology, Harvard University, Cambridge.

282. ———. 1976. Osteobiography: Life History Recorded in Bone. In *The Measures of Man,* edited by E. Giles and S. Friedlaender, pp. 372–382. Peabody Museum Press, Cambridge.

283. ———. 1977. The Paleopathology of Anemia in Mexico and Guatemala. In *Porotic Hyperostosis: An Enquiry,* edited by E. Cockburn, pp. 10–15, 18. Monograph 2. Paleopathology Association, Detroit.

284. ———. 1978. Osteitis or Bone Inflammation and the Question of Pre-Columbian Syphilis (and/or Yaws) among the Maya (abstract). In *Papers and Exhibits on Paleopathology Presented at the Annual Meeting of the Paleopathology Association at the Academy of Medicine, Toronto,* edited by E. Cockburn, pp. T9–T10. Paleopathology Association, Detroit.

285. ———. 1978. Postmortem for an Empire (abstract). In *Papers and Exhibits on Paleopathology Presented at the Annual Meeting of the Paleopathology Association at the Academy of Medicine, Toronto,* edited by E. Cockburn, p. T6. Paleopathology Association, Detroit.

286. ———. 1982. Appendix II—The Human Skeletal Remains from Tancah, Mexico. In *On the Edge of the Sea: Mural Paintings at Tancah-Tulum,* edited by A. G. Miller, pp. 115–128. Dumbarton Oaks Trustees for Harvard University, Washington.

287. Saul, F. P., A. J. Christoforidis, and J. M. Saul. 1980. Maya Paleopathology (abstract). *Papers and Exhibits on Paleopathology Presented at the Annual Meeting of the Paleopathology Association, Niagara Falls,* edited by E. Cockburn, p. NF6. Paleopathology Association, Detroit.

288. ———. 1981. Maya Paleopathology 1981 (abstract). In *Papers on Paleopathology Presented at the Annual Meeting of the Paleopathology Association, Detroit,* edited by E. Cockburn, p. D4. Paleopathology Association, Detroit.

289. ———. 1982. Maya Paleopathology 1982 (abstract). In *Abstracts of the Ninth Annual Meeting of the Paleopathology Association, Toledo,* edited by E. Cockburn, p. 16. Paleopathology Association, Detroit.

290. Saul, F. P., A. J. Christoforidis, J. M. Saul, D. C. Cook, and J. T. Benítez. 1981. The Antiquity of Paget's Disease in the Maya Area (abstract). In *Papers on Paleopathology Presented at the Annual Meeting of the Paleopathology Association, Detroit,* edited by E. Cockburn, p. D3. Paleopathology Association, Detroit.

291. Saul, F. P., and N. Hammond. 1973. A Classic Maya Tooth Cache from Lubaantun, British Honduras. In *Studies in Ancient Mesoamerica,* edited by J. Graham, pp. 31–35. Contributions of the University of California Archaeological Research Facility 18, Berkeley.

292. ———. 1974. A Classic Maya Tooth Cache from Lubaantun, Belize. *Man* 9:123–127.

293. Saul, F. P., and J. M. Saul. 1980. Recent Advances in the Paleopathology of the Maya (abstract). In *Papers and Exhibits on Paleopathology Presented at the Annual Meeting of the Paleopathology Association, Niagara Falls,* edited by E. Cockburn, pp. NF4–NF5. Paleopathology Association, Detroit.

294. ———. 1980. A Year in the Past. *Paleopathology Newsletter* no. 29:7–8.

295. ———. 1983. Mexico and Central America (abstract). *Abstracts of the Tenth Annual Meeting of the Paleopathology Association, Indianapolis,* edited by E. Cockburn, pp. 5–6. Paleopathology Association, Detroit.

296. ———. 1984. La osteopatología de los mayas de las tierras bajas del sur. In *México antiguo,* edited by A. López Austin and C. Viesco Trevino, pp. 313–321. Historia general de la medicina en México, tomo 1. Universidad Nacional Autónoma de México and Academía Nacional de Medicina, México.

297. ———. 1984. Paleobiología en la zona maya. In *Investigaciones recientes en el área maya,* tomo 1, pp. 23–42. Memorias de la XVII Mesa Redonda, 1981. Sociedad Mexicana de Antropología, San Cristobal de las Casas.

298. ———. 1985. Life History as Recorded in Maya Skeletons from Cozumel, Mexico. In *National Geographic Research Reports,* vol. 20, edited by W. Swanson, pp. 583–587. National Geographic Society Press, Washington.

299. Saul, F. P., J. M. Saul, and A. J. Christoforidis. 1985. Maya Paleopathology 1985 (abstract). In *Papers on Paleopathology Presented at the Annual Meeting of the Paleopathology Association, Knoxville,* edited by E. Cockburn, p. 9–10. Paleopathology Association, Detroit.

300. Saul, F. P., and J. M. Saul. 1989. Osteobiography: A Maya Example. In *Reconstruction of Life from the Skeleton,* edited by M. Y. İşcan and K. A. R. Kennedy, pp. 287–302. Alan R. Liss, New York.

301. Saul, F. P., and J. M. Saul. 1991. The Pre-classic Population of Cuello. In *Cuello: An Early Maya Community in Belize,* edited by N. Hammond, pp. 134–158. Cambridge University, Cambridge.

302. Saville, M. H. 1913. Precolumbian Decoration of the Teeth in Ecuador, with Some Account of the Occurrence of the Custom in Other Parts of North and South America. *American Anthropologist* 15:377–394.

303. ———. 1913. *Precolumbian Decoration of the Teeth in Ecuador, with Some Account of the Occurrence of the Custom in Other Parts of North and South America.* New Era Printing, Lancaster.

304. Schellhas, P. 1894. Deformirten Schädel von Ulpan bei Coban, Guatemala, der aus Einem der von Ihm Geöffneten Graber Stammt. *Verhandlungen der Berliner Gesellschaft für Anthropologie, Ethnologie und Urgeschichte* 24:424–425.

305. Schumann, E. A. 1936. A Recent Visit to Southern Mexico. *Maya Research* 3(3–4): 296–305.

306. Schwarcz, H. P., and M. J. Schoeninger. 1991. Stable Isotope Analysis in Human Nutritional Ecology. *Yearbook of Physical Anthropology* 34:283–321.

307. Schwarcz, H. P., C. D. White, and P. F. Healy. 1993. Diversity in Pre-Columbian Diet: The Evidence from Pacbitun, Belize (abstract). *American Journal of Physical Anthropology,* Supplement 16:176.

308. Scott, R. F. 1980. A Note on Miscellaneous Burials from the 1980 Season at Colha. In *The Colha Project, Second Season, 1980 Interim Report,* edited by T. R. Hester, H. J. Shafer, and J. D. Eaton, pp. 353. The University of Texas at San Antonio and Center for Archaeological Research, Centro Studi e Richerche Ligabue, Venezia, San Antonio.

309. Serrano Sánchez, C. 1972. Una serie de cráneos procedentes de Campeche, México. *Anales de Antropología* 9:176–188.

310. ———. 1973. La lesión suprainiana en Mesoamérica: implicaciones arqueológicas. *Estudios de Cultura Maya* 9:29–43.

311. Sharer, R. J. 1978. Archaeology and His-

tory at Quirigua, Guatemala. *Journal of Field Archaeology* 5:51–70.

312. ———. 1978. Special Deposits. In *The Prehistory of Chalchuapa, El Salvador,* vol. 1, edited by R. J. Sharer, pp. 181–194. University of Pennsylvania Press, Philadelphia.

313. Sharer, R. J., and S. E. Sedat. 1987. Special Deposits. In *Archaeological Investigations in the Northern Maya Highlands, Guatemala,* edited by R. J. Sharer and S. E. Sedat, pp. 261–266. University Museum Monograph 59. The University Museum, University of Pennsylvania, Philadelphia.

314. Shook, E. M., and A. V. Kidder. 1952. *Mound E-III-3, Kaminaljuyu, Guatemala.* Contributions to American Anthropology and History, vol. 11, no. 53. Publication 596. Carnegie Institution of Washington, Washington.

315. Smith, A. L. 1937. *Structure A-XVIII, Uaxactun.* Contributions to American Archaeology, vol. 4, no. 20. Publication 483. Carnegie Institution of Washington, Washington.

316. ———. 1950. *Uaxactun, Guatemala: Excavations of 1931–1937.* Publication 588. Carnegie Institution of Washington, Washington.

317. ———. 1972. *Excavations at Altar de Sacrificios: Architecture, Settlement, Burials, and Caches.* Papers of the Peabody Museum of Archaeology and Ethnology, vol. 62, no. 2. Harvard University, Cambridge.

318. Smith, A. L., and A. V. Kidder. 1943. *Explorations in the Motagua Valley, Guatemala.* Contributions to American Anthropology and History, vol. 8, no. 41. Publication 546. Carnegie Institution of Washington, Washington.

319. Smith, R. E. 1937. *A Study of Structure A-1 Complex at Uaxactun, Peten, Guatemala.* Contributions to American Archaeology, vol. 3, no. 19. Publication 456. Carnegie Institution of Washington, Washington.

320. Solares, J. 1993. Incrustaciones dentarias mayas: un análisis preliminar. In *III Simposio de Investigaciones Arqueológicas en Guatemala, 1989,* edited by J. P. Laporte,

H. L. Escobedo, and S. Villagrán de Brady, pp. 3–12. Museo Nacional de Arqueología y Etnología, Guatemala.

321. Soustelle, J. 1936. *Mexique: terre indienne.* Editions Bernard Brassett, Paris.

322. Steele, D. G. 1986. The Skeletal Material from Rio Azul, 1984 Season. In *Rio Azul Reports Number 2, The 1984 Season,* edited by D. G. Steele, pp. 111–116. Center for Archaeological Research, The University of Texas at San Antonio, San Antonio.

323. Steele, D. G., and C. Bramblett. 1988. The Dentition. In *The Anatomy and Biology of the Human Skeleton,* pp. 70–110. Texas A&M University Press, College Station.

324. Steele, D. G., J. D. Eaton, and A. J. Taylor. 1980. The Skulls from Operation 2011 at Colha: A Preliminary Examination. In *The Colha Project, Second Season, 1980 Interim Report,* edited by T. R. Hester, H. J. Shafer, and J. D. Eaton, pp. 163–172. The University of Texas at San Antonio and Center for Archaeological Research, Centro Studi e Ricerche Liguabue, Venezia, San Antonio.

325. Steinbock, R. T. 1976. *Paleopathological Diagnosis and Interpretation.* Charles C Thomas, Springfield.

326. Stephens, J. L. 1843. *Incidents of Travel in Yucatan.* Harper Brothers, New York.

327. Stewart, T. D. 1941. New Examples of Tooth Mutilation from Middle America. *American Journal of Physical Anthropology* 28:117–124.

328. ———. 1943. Skeletal Remains from Tajumulco, Guatemala. In *Excavations at Tajumulco, Guatemala,* edited by B. P. Dutton and H. R. Hobbs, pp. 111–114. School of American Research Monograph 9, University of New Mexico Press, Albuquerque.

329. ———. 1947. The Cultural Significance of Lambdoid Deformity in Mexico (abstract). *American Journal of Physical Anthropology* 5:233–234.

330. ———. 1948. Distribution of the Type of Cranial Deformity Originally Described under the Name "Tête Trilobée." In *El occidente de México: Cuarta Reunión de Mesa*

Redonda, celebrada en el Museo Nacional de Historia del 23 al 28 de septiembre de 1946, pp. 17–20. Sociedad Mexicana de Antropología, México.

331. ———. 1948. The True Form of the Cranial Deformation Originally Described Under the Name "Tête Trilobée". *Journal of the Washington Academy of Sciences* 38(2):66–72.

332. ———. 1949. Notas sobre esqueletos humanos prehistóricos hallados en Guatemala. *Antropología e Historia de Guatemala* 1(1):23–34.

333. ———. 1951. Appendix B—Notes on Skeletal Material. In *Excavations at Nebaj, Guatemala,* edited by A. L. Smith and A. V. Kidder, pp. 86–87. Publication 594. Carnegie Institution of Washington, Washington.

334. ———. 1953. Skeletal Remains from Zaculeu, Guatemala. In *The Ruins of Zaculeu, Guatemala,* vol. 1, edited by R. B. Woodbury and A. S. Trik, pp. 295–311. United Fruit Co., Richmond.

335. ———. 1975. *Human Skeletal Remains from Dzibilchaltun, Yucatan, Mexico, with a Review of Cranial Deformity Types in the Maya Region.* Middle American Research Institute Publ. 31, no. 7. Tulane University, New Orleans.

336. Storey, R. 1985. La paleodemografía de Copán. *Yaxkin* 8:151–160.

337. ———. 1985. Precolumbian Child and Infant Mortality in Teotihuacan and Copan (abstract). *American Journal of Physical Anthropology* 66:234–235.

338. ———. 1986. Entierros y clase social en Copán, Honduras: aspectos biológicas. *Yaxkin* 9:55–61.

339. ———. 1988. Prenatal Enamel Defects in Teotihuacan and Copan (abstract). *American Journal of Physical Anthropology* 75:275–276.

340. ———. 1992. The Children of Copan: Issues in Paleopathology and Paleodemography. *Ancient Mesoamerica* 3:161–167.

341. ———. 1992. Patterns of Susceptibility to Dental Enamel Defects in the Deciduous Dentition of a Precolumbian Skeletal Population. In *Recent Contributions to the Study of Enamel Developmental Defects,* edited by A. H. Goodman and L. L. Capasso, pp. 171–183. Journal of Paleopathology Monographic Publications 2. Associazione Antropologica Abruzze, Chieti.

342. ———. 1994. Developmental Defects of Enamel and Children of Privilege in One Late Classic Maya Center (abstract). *American Journal of Physical Anthropology,* Supplement 18:189.

343. Stromsvik, C. 1941–1942. Honduras. *Carnegie Institution Year Book* 41:249–250. Carnegie Institution of Washington, Washington.

344. Sweet, A. P. S., M. G. Buonocore, and I. F. Buck. 1963. Prehispanic Indian Dentistry. *Dental Radiography and Photography* 36:3–12, 19–21.

345. Thompson, E. H. 1897. *Explorations in the Cave of Loltun, Yucatan.* Memoirs of the Peabody Museum of American Archaeology and Ethnology vol. 1, no. 2. Harvard University, Cambridge.

346. ———. 1904. *Archaeological Researches in Yucatan.* Memoirs of the Peabody Museum of American Archaeology and Ethnology vol. 3, no. 1. Harvard University, Cambridge.

347. Thompson, J. E. S. 1931. *Archaeological Investigations in the Southern Cayo District, British Honduras.* Anthropological Series, vol. 17, no. 3, Publ. 301. Field Museum of Natural History, Chicago.

348. ———. 1932. Some Jade Inlaid Teeth of Ancient Mayas. *Field Museum News* 3(3):3.

349. ———. 1938. Notes on the Report. In *The High Priest's Grave, Chichen Itza, Yucatan, Mexico,* by E. H. Thompson, pp. 45–53. Anthropological Series, vol. 27, no. 1. Publ. 412. Field Museum of Natural History, Chicago.

350. ———. 1939. *Excavations at San Jose, British Honduras.* Publication 506. Carnegie Institution of Washington, Washington.

351. ———. 1940. *Late Ceramic Horizons at Benque Viejo, British Honduras.* Contribu-

tions to American Anthropology and History, vol. 7, no. 35. Publication 528. Carnegie Institution of Washington, Washington.

352. Toriello, J. 1965. La deformación craneal cultural de los antiguos indígenes. *La Revista del Colegio Médico de Guatemala,* 16:36–44.

353. Tourtellot, G., III. 1990. *Excavations at Seibal: Burials: A Cultural Analysis.* Memoirs of the Peabody Museum of Archaeology and Ethnology, vol. 17, no. 2. Harvard University, Cambridge.

354. Trik, A. S. 1953. Graves. In *The Ruins of Zaculeu, Guatemala,* edited by R. B. Woodbury and A. S. Trik, pp. 77–111. United Fruit Co., Richmond.

355. Turner, C. G., II. 1985. The Dental Search for Native American Origins. In *Out of Asia: Peopling the Americas and the Pacific,* edited by R. Kirk and E. Szathmary, pp. 31–78. The Journal of Pacific History, Canberra.

356. Urcid, J. 1993. Bone and Epigraphy: The Accurate Versus the Fictitious? *Texas Notes on Precolumbian Art, Writing and Culture* no. 42, pp. 1–5. The University of Texas at Austin, Austin.

357. van Rippen, B. 1917. Pre-Columbian Operative Dentistry of the Indians of Middle and South America. *Dental Cosmos* 59: 861–873.

358. ———. 1918. Mutilations and Decorations of Teeth among Indians of North, Central and South America. *Journal of the Allied Dental Society* 13:219–242.

359. van Tuerenhout, D., R. Méndez, I. Verhagen, and P. Aldritt. 1994. Investigaciones arqueológicas en Quim Chi Hilan: temporadas de 1992 y 1993. In *VII Simposio de Investigaciones Arqueológicas en Guatemala, 1993,* edited by J. P. Laporte and H. L. Escobedo, pp. 471–493. Museo Nacional de Antropología e Etnología, Guatemala.

360. Vargas P., E., and P. Santillon S. 1992. Sistema de enterramientos en Tulum. *Estudios de Cultura Maya* 19:67–112.

361. Velásquez, J. L. 1993. Un entierro dedicatorio a finales del preclásico medio en Kami-naljuyú, Guatemala. In *III Simposio de Investigaciones Arqueológicas en Guatemala, 1989,* edited by J. P. Laporte, H. L. Escobedo, and S. Villagrán de Brady, pp. 199–208. Museo Nacional de Arqueología y Etnología, Guatemala.

362. Virchow, R. 1887. Schädel von Merida, Yucatan. *Zeitschrift für Ethnologie, Verhandlungen* 19:451–455.

363. von Luschan, F. 1901. Siebzehn Schädel aus Chaculá in Guatemala. In *Die Alten Ansiedelungen von Chaculá im Distrikte Nenton des Departments Huehuetenango der Republik Guatemala,* edited by E. Seler, pp. 207–213. Verlag von Dietrich Reimer (Ernst Vohsen), Berlin.

364. Wauchope, R. 1934. *House Mounds of Uaxactun, Guatemala.* Contributions to American Archaeology, vol. 2, no. 7. Publication 436. Carnegie Institution of Washington, Washington.

365. ———. 1942. *Cremations at Zacualpa, Guatemala.* Instituto Nacional de Antropología e Historia, México.

366. Weeks, J. M. 1980. Dimensions of Social Differentiation at Chisalin, El Quiche, Guatemala, A.D. 1400–1524. Ph.D. dissertation, Department of Anthropology, State University of New York at Albany, Albany. University Microfilms International, Ann Arbor.

367. ———. 1983. *Chisalin: A Late Postclassic Maya Settlement in Highland Guatemala.* International Series 169. British Archaeological Reports, Oxford.

368. Weiss, P. 1967. Ensayo de osteología cultural en Guatemala. *Antropología e Historia de Guatemala* 19:14–26.

369. Welsh, W. B. M. 1988. *An Analysis of Classic Lowland Maya Burials.* International Series 409. British Archaeological Reports, Oxford.

370. ———. 1988. A Case for the Practice of Human Sacrifice among the Classic Lowland Maya. In *Recent Studies in Precolumbian Archaeology,* pp. 143–165. International Series 421. British Archaeological Reports, Oxford.

371. White, C. D. 1988. The Ancient Maya from Lamanai, Belize: Diet and Health Over 2000 Years. *Canadian Review of Physical Anthropology* 6(2):1–21.

372. ———. 1988. Diet and Health in the Ancient Maya at Lamanai. In *Diet and Subsistence: Current Archaeological Perspectives,* edited by B. E. Kennedy and G. M. LeMoine, pp. 288–296. Archaeology Association, University of Calgary, Calgary.

373. ———. 1990. Patterns of Anemia and Diet Before and After the Conquest of the Maya (abstract). *American Journal of Physical Anthropology* 81:316.

374. ———. 1994. Dietary Dental Pathology and Culture Change in the Maya. *Strength in Diversity: A Reader in Physical Anthropology,* edited by A. Herring and L. Chan, pp. 279–302. Canadian Scholar's Press, Toronto.

375. White, C. D., P. F. Healy, and H. P. Schwarcz. 1993. Intensive Agriculture, Social Status and Maya Diet at Pacbitun, Belize. *Journal of Anthropological Research* 49:347–375.

376. White, C. D., and H. P. Schwarcz. 1989. Ancient Maya Diet: as Inferred from Isotopic and Elemental Analysis of Human Bone. *Journal of Archaeological Science* 16:451–474.

377. White, C. D., L. E. Wright, and D. M. Pendergast. 1994. Biological Disruption in the Early Colonial Period at Lamanai. In *In the Wake of Contact: Biological Responses to Conquest,* edited by C. S. Larsen and G. R. Milner, pp. 135–145. Wiley-Liss, New York.

378. Whitsley, H. G. 1935. History and Development of Dentistry in Mexico. *Journal of the American Dental Association* 22:989–995.

379. Whittington, S. L. 1988. Use of Event History Analysis to Expose Statistically Significant Demographic Differences Between Populations (abstract). *American Journal of Physical Anthropology* 75:287–288.

380. ———. 1989. Characteristics of Demography and Disease in Low-Status Maya from Classic Period Copan, Honduras. Ph.D. dissertation, Department of Anthropology, The Pennsylvania State University, University Park. University Microfilms International, Ann Arbor.

381. ———. 1991. Detection of Significant Demographic Differences between Subpopulations of Prehispanic Maya from Copan, Honduras, by Survival Analysis. *American Journal of Physical Anthropology* 85:167–184.

382. ———. 1991. Enamel Hypoplasia in the Low Status Maya Population of Copan, Honduras, around the Time of the Collapse (abstract). *American Journal of Physical Anthropology,* Supplement 12:183.

383. ———. 1992. Enamel Hypoplasia in the Low Status Maya Population of Prehispanic Copan, Honduras. In *Recent Contributions to the Study of Enamel Developmental Defects,* edited by A. H. Goodman and L. L. Capasso, pp. 185–205. Journal of Paleopathology Monographic Publications 2. Associazone Antropologica Abruzze, Chieti.

384. Whittington, S. L., and D. M. Reed. 1994. Los esqueletos de Iximché. In *VII Simposio de Investigaciones Arqueológicas en Guatemala, 1993,* edited by J. P. Laporte and H. L. Escobedo, pp. 23–28. Museo Nacional de Arqueología y Etnología, Guatemala.

385. Wiercinski, A. 1971. Racial Affinities of Some Ancient Populations in Mexico. In *Anthropological Congress Dedicated to Aleš Hrdlička, 30th August–5th September 1969, Praha, Humpolec,* pp. 485–499. Academia, Praha.

386. Willey, G. R. 1965. Human Burials. In *Prehistoric Settlement Patterns in the Belize Valley,* edited by G. R. Willey, W. R. Bullard, J. B. Glass and J. C. Gifford, pp. 530–558. Papers of the Peabody Museum of Archaeology and Ethnology, vol. 54. Harvard University, Cambridge.

387. Williams, H. U. 1929. Human Paleopathology. *Archives of Pathology* 7:839–902.

388. Wright, L. E. 1990. An Archaeological Application of Cementum Annulation at Tipu,

Belize (abstract). *American Journal of Physical Anthropology* 81:320.

389. ———. 1990. Stresses of Conquest: A Study of Wilson Bands and Enamel Hypoplasias in the Maya of Lamanai, Belize. *American Journal of Human Biology* 2:25–35.

390. ———. 1993. La dieta antigua en la región del Río de la Pasión. In *VI Simposio de Investigaciones Arqueológicas en Guatemala, 1992,* edited by J. L. Laporte, H. L. Escobedo, and S. Villagrán de Brady, pp. 201–208. Museo Nacional de Arqueología y Etnología, Guatemala.

391. ———. 1993. Prehistoric Diet in the Collapse of the Pasion Maya (abstract). *American Journal of Physical Anthropology,* Supplement 16:213.

392. ———. 1993. Prehistoric Health Status in the Pasión Maya Lowlands: Ecological Collapse Reconsidered (abstract). *Papers on Paleopathology Presented at the Annual Meeting of the Paleopathology Association, Toronto,* edited by E. Cockburn, pp. 27–28. Paleopathology Association, Detroit.

393. ———. 1994. Enfermedad, salud y el colapso maya en las tierras bajas. In *VII Simposio de Investigaciones Arqueológicas en Guatemala, 1993,* edited by J. L. Laporte and H. L. Escobedo, pp. 553–562. Museo Nacional de Arqueología y Etnología, Guatemala.

394. ———. 1994. The Sacrifice of the Earth? Diet, Health and Inequality in the Pasión Maya Lowlands. Ph.D. dissertation, Department of Anthropology, University of Chicago, Chicago. University Microfilms International, Ann Arbor.

395. Young, D. 1994. Analysis of Human Skeletal Remains from Operation 2031, Colha, Belize. In *Continuing Archeology at Colha, Belize,* edited by T. R. Hester, H. J. Shafer, and J. D. Eaton, pp. 59–63. Studies in Archeology 16. Texas Archeological Research Laboratory, The University of Texas at Austin, Austin.

396. Zimbrón, A., and M. Feingold. 1988. *Algunas prácticas odontológicas en la época prehispánica.* Aportes de Investigaciones no. 28. Centro Regional de Investigaciones Multidisciplinarias, Universidad Nacional Autónoma de México, México.

Index to the Bibliography

105, 109, 118, 119, 122, 126, 128, 134,
135, 139, 140, 141, 147, 148, 151, 159,
160, 162, 167, 173, 175, 178, 181, 182,
183, 184, 186, 205, 206, 207, 208, 215,
217, 221, 233, 235, 243, 245, 246, 247,
249, 254, 256, 257, 258, 261, 262, 263,
264, 266, 267, 273, 274, 278, 280, 286,
293, 294, 296, 297, 298, 300, 302, 303,
308, 311, 316, 317, 319, 320, 327, 332,
333, 343, 344, 346, 348, 350, 353, 357,
358, 364, 365, 378, 380, 384, 386, 396

Demographic analysis, 15, 65, 138, 145, 146,
149, 184, 187, 223, 226, 242, 273, 275,
278, 279, 286, 298, 334, 336, 337, 339,
340, 356, 379, 380, 381

DNA analysis, 180, 212, 213, 214

Metrics and morphology

craniometrics, 6, 31, 41, 42, 49, 52, 53, 61,
62, 64, 80, 81, 107, 109, 112, 114, 116,
117, 120, 135, 140, 142, 156, 165, 166,
167, 174, 177, 178, 181, 189, 193, 198,
209, 225, 234, 238, 239, 240, 246, 247,
248, 252, 256, 272, 277, 278, 282, 286,
300, 309, 319, 322, 332, 333, 334, 335,
362, 363, 385, 386, 395

dental morphology, 21, 22, 43, 104, 106, 114,
116, 126, 139, 153, 163, 164, 167, 168,
183, 203, 204, 209, 236, 237, 246, 247,
249, 254, 256, 277, 280, 281, 282, 286,
291, 292, 301, 319, 364, 366, 367, 384,
395

discrete traits, 17, 27, 31, 32, 47, 52, 53, 64,
74, 79, 104, 106, 112, 114, 115, 116, 117,
120, 135, 148, 149, 153, 158, 167, 168,
182, 183, 209, 234, 246, 247, 254, 286,
304, 328, 332, 333, 334, 352, 363

odontometrics, 20, 21, 135, 163, 164, 256,
282

postcranial metrics, 6, 32, 52, 53, 80, 81, 107,
109, 111, 112, 114, 135, 146, 165, 168,
177, 189, 192, 198, 209, 238, 246, 247,
254, 277, 278, 286, 319, 322, 332, 333,
335, 364, 380, 386, 395

stature, 3, 6, 7, 8, 52, 53, 57, 58, 59, 61, 62,
72, 80, 81, 82, 83, 92, 104, 105, 107, 109,
111, 112, 114, 116, 119, 129, 132, 135,
140, 144, 146, 147, 148, 149, 150, 153,

160, 165, 166, 167, 177, 179, 184, 189,
192, 193, 194, 197, 209, 220, 222, 234,
238, 241, 242, 243, 246, 247, 249, 254,
256, 270, 272, 277, 278, 286, 295, 297,
300, 301, 310, 314, 319, 322, 332, 333,
334, 335, 337, 343, 353, 364, 386, 395

Paleonutrition

coprolite analysis, 11

isotope analysis, 113, 172, 244, 306, 307,
371, 372, 373, 374, 375, 376, 377, 384,
390, 391, 394

trace element analysis, 143, 195, 287, 295,
372, 376, 394

Paleopathology

anemia. *See* porotic hyperostosis *under* Paleopathology

ankylosing spondylitis. *See* vertebral pathology
under Paleopathology

arthritis, 3, 5, 7, 9, 15, 32, 45, 47, 55, 57, 58,
82, 106, 107, 114, 116, 117, 135, 150, 151,
165, 168, 176, 182, 183, 193, 197, 198, 201,
209, 234, 242, 246, 247, 249, 254, 256,
277, 285, 286, 296, 300, 301, 308, 310,
322, 325, 332, 334, 335, 384, 388, 395

calculus, 7, 20, 27, 43, 45, 47, 48, 52, 53, 82,
90, 93, 107, 109, 128, 167, 168, 172, 182,
183, 185, 189, 193, 194, 195, 198, 203,
209, 228, 246, 249, 254, 256, 277, 300,
301, 384

caries, 7, 20, 27, 29, 31, 43, 45, 47, 49, 52,
53, 55, 57, 58, 73, 89, 90, 106, 107, 109,
114, 116, 117, 126, 128, 135, 139, 140,
148, 151, 153, 158, 165, 167, 168, 170,
172, 177, 178, 182, 183, 184, 185, 189,
193, 198, 203, 204, 205, 209, 220, 224,
228, 231, 232, 234, 246, 247, 249, 254,
256, 269, 277, 279, 280, 285, 286, 287,
291, 292, 295, 296, 297, 300, 301, 310,
313, 320, 324, 328, 332, 333, 366, 367,
371, 372, 374, 377, 380, 384, 386, 393,
395, 396

cementum annulation, 388

congenital dysraphism, 281, 282, 285, 287,
300

cortical bone maintenance, 73, 150

cribra orbitalia. *See* porotic hyperostosis *under*
Paleopathology

151, 155, 162, 165, 169, 178, 181, 182,
184, 190, 191, 193, 197, 199, 202, 204,
209, 216, 217, 226, 233, 234, 236, 237,
243, 244, 246, 254, 259, 260, 270, 280,
286, 290, 291, 292, 300, 308, 310, 313,
315, 319, 324, 337, 338, 339, 340, 342,
345, 348, 349, 350, 351, 353, 356, 359,
363, 364, 379, 382, 392, 393, 394

Postclassic, 6, 15, 21, 22, 25, 39, 43, 46, 48,
62, 72, 93, 106, 107, 116, 120, 121, 129,
130, 131, 132, 133, 135, 144, 166, 168,
172, 176, 183, 185, 192, 193, 194, 198,
205, 209, 215, 222, 228, 229, 230, 231,
232, 233, 237, 241, 246, 250, 251, 254,
256, 257, 265, 273, 274, 276, 277, 278,
279, 288, 297, 298, 306, 308, 310, 312,
313, 316, 317, 332, 333, 334, 335, 350,
352, 353, 354, 360, 363, 365, 366, 367,
371, 372, 373, 374, 375, 376, 377, 381,
383, 384, 385, 386, 389, 391

Historic, 14, 17, 43, 57, 58, 59, 66, 67, 68,
69, 70, 71, 73, 116, 125, 127, 142, 159,
163, 164, 172, 174, 188, 196, 223, 240,
242, 248, 252, 286, 297, 298, 309, 312,
326, 371, 372, 373, 374, 376, 377, 384,
388, 389

References Cited

Abrams, E. M., and D. J. Rue. 1988. The Causes and Consequences of Deforestation among the Prehistoric Maya. *Human Ecology* 16: 377–396.

Adams, R. E. W. 1969. Maya Archaeology 1958–1968, a Review. *Latin American Research Review* 4(2):3–45.

———. 1971. *The Ceramics of Altar de Sacrificios*. Papers of the Peabody Museum of Archaeology and Ethnology, vol. 63, no. 1. Harvard University, Cambridge.

———. 1983. Ancient Land Use and Culture History in the Pasión River Region. In *Prehistoric Settlement Patterns,* edited by E. Z. Vogt and R. M. Leventhal, pp. 319–335. University of New Mexico Press, Albuquerque, and Peabody Museum of Archaeology and Ethnology, Harvard University, Cambridge.

Adams, R. E. W., and H. R. Robichaux. 1992. Tombs of Río Azul, Guatemala. *National Geographic Research and Exploration* 8: 412–427.

Alter, G., and J. C. Riley. 1989. Frailty, Sickness, and Death: Models of Morbidity and Mortality in Historical Populations. *Population Studies* 43:25–45.

Ambrose, S. H. 1990. Preparation and Characterization of Bone and Tooth Collagen for Isotopic Analysis. *Journal of Archaeological Science* 17:431–451.

———. 1993. Isotopic Analysis of Paleodiets: Methodological and Interpretative Considerations. In *Investigations of Ancient Human Tissue: Chemical Analyses in Anthropology,* edited by M. K. Sandford, pp. 59–130. Food and Nutrition in History and Anthropology, vol. 10, S. H. Katz, series editor. Gordon and Breach, Langhorne.

Ambrose, S. H., and L. Norr. 1992. On Stable Isotopic Data and Prehistoric Subsistence in the Soconusco Region. *Current Anthropology* 33:401–404.

———. 1993. Experimental Evidence for the Relationship of the Carbon Isotope Ratios of Whole Diet and Dietary Protein to Those of Bone Collagen and Carbonate. In *Prehistoric Human Bone: Archaeology at the Molecular Level,* edited by J. B. Lambert and G. Grupe, pp. 1–37. Springer-Verlag, Berlin.

Anderson, S., A. T. Bankier, B. G. Barrel, M. H. L. DeBulin, A. R. Coulson, J. Drouin, I. C. Eperon, D. P. Nierlich, B. A. Roe, F. Sanger,

P. H. Schreier, A. J. H. Smith, R. Staden, and I. G. Young. 1981. Sequence and Organization of the Human Mitochondrial Genome. *Nature* 290:457–465.

Ángel E., A. del, and H. Cisneros R. 1991. Corrección de las ecuaciones de regresión para estimar estatura elaboradas por S. Genovés (1967). Ms. on file, Instituto de Investigaciones Antropológicas, Universidad Nacional Autónoma de México, México.

Ángel E., A. del, C. S. Serrano, and A. S. Castro. 1993. Dental Morphology from Two Mayan Ethnic Groups in Chiapas, Mexico. *Dental Anthropology Newsletter* 7(2):13.

Aranzadi, T. D., and L. Hoyos Sainz. 1894. Vorläufige Mittheilung zur Anthropologie von Spanien. *Archiv für Anthropologie* 22:425.

Armstrong, C. 1989. Pathological Analysis of Long Bones within the Tipu Population. Master's thesis, State University of New York at Plattsburgh, Plattsburgh.

Ashmore, W. (editor). 1981. *Lowland Maya Settlement Patterns.* University of New Mexico Press, Albuquerque.

Atran, S. 1993. Itza Maya Tropical Agro-Forestry. *Current Anthropology* 34:633–700.

Austin, D. M. 1970. Dental Microevolution in Two Ancient Maya Communities. Master's thesis, Department of Anthropology, The Pennsylvania State University, University Park.

———. 1978. The Biological Affinity of the Ancient Populations of Altar de Sacrificios and Seibal. *Estudios de Cultura Maya* 11:57–73.

Baker, B. J., and G. J. Armelagos. 1988. The Origin and Antiquity of Syphilis: Paleopathological Diagnosis and Interpretation. *Current Anthropology* 29:703–737.

Baker, S. J., and V. I. Mathan. 1975. Prevalence, Pathogenesis, and Prophylaxis of Iron Deficiency in the Tropics. In *Iron Metabolism and Its Disorders,* edited by H. Kief, pp. 145–157. Excerpta Medica, Amsterdam.

Barksdale, J. T. 1972. Appendix III: A Descriptive and Comparative Investigation of Dental Morphology. In *Physical Anthropology of the Eastern Highlands of New Guinea,* edited by R. A. Littlewood, pp. 113–174. University of Washington Press, Seattle.

Barrera, A. 1979. El manejo de las selvas por los mayas: sus implicaciones silvícolas y agrícolas. *Programa Indicativo de Ecología.* CONACYT, México.

Barrera, A., A. Gómez-Pompa, and C. Vázquez-Yanes. 1977. El manejo de las selvas por los mayas: sus implicaciones silvícolas y agrícolas. *Biótica (México)* 2(2):47–60.

Bass, W.M. 1971. *Human Osteology: A Laboratory and Field Manual of the Human Skeleton.* Missouri Archaeological Society, Columbia.

Becker, M. J. 1979. Priests, Peasants, and Ceremonial Centers: The Intellectual History of a Model. In *Maya Archaeology and Ethnohistory,* edited by N. Hammond and G. R. Willey, pp. 3–20. University of Texas Press, Austin.

Béhar, M. 1968. Food and Nutrition of the Maya before the Conquest and at the Present Time. In *Biomedical Challenges Presented to the American Indians,* pp. 114–119. Scientific Publication 165. Pan American Health Organization, Washington.

Beighton, P. 1978. *Inherited Disorders of the Skeleton.* Churchill Livingstone, Edinburgh.

Benedict, F. G., and M. Steggerda. 1937. *The Food of the Present-Day Maya Indians of Yucatan.* Contributions to American Archaeology, vol. 3, no. 18. Publication 456. Carnegie Institution of Washington, Washington.

Bennett S., and M. N. Cohen. 1985. Social Patterns in the Colonial Population from Tipu. Paper presented at the 84th Annual Meeting of the American Anthropological Association, Washington.

Berry, A. C., and R. J. Berry. 1967. Epigenetic Variation in the Human Cranium. *Journal of Anatomy* 101:361–379.

———. 1972. Origins and Relationships of the Ancient Egyptians. Based on a Study of Non-Metrical Variations in the Skull. *Journal of Human Evolution* 1:199–208.

Blake M., B. S. Chisholm, J. E. Clark, B. Voorhies, and M. W. Love. 1992. Prehistoric Subsistence in the Soconusco Region. *Current Anthropology* 33:83–94.

Blakey, M. L., and G. J. Armelagos. 1985. Deciduous Enamel Defects in Prehistoric Americans from Dickson Mounds: Prenatal and Postnatal

Stress. *American Journal of Physical Anthropology* 66:371–380.

Blom, F. 1954. Ossuaries, Cremation, and Secondary Burials among the Maya of Chiapas. *Journal de la Société des Américanistes* 43:123–145.

Boyd, R. C. 1972. Appendix IV: An Odontometric and Observational Assessment of the Dentition. In *Physical Anthropology of the Eastern Highlands of New Guinea,* edited by R. A. Littlewood, pp. 175–212. University of Washington Press, Seattle.

Breton, A. C. 1908. Archaeology in Mexico. *Man* 8(17):34–37.

Brin, I., and Y. Ben-Bassat. 1989. Appearance of a Labial Notch in Maxillary Incisors: A Population Survey. *American Journal of Physical Anthropology* 80:25–29.

Bronson, B. 1966. Roots and the Subsistence of the Ancient Maya. *Southwestern Journal of Anthropology* 22:251–279.

Brown, J. A. 1987. Quantitative Burial Analyses as Interassemblage Comparison. In *Quantitative Research in Archaeology: Progress and Prospects,* edited by M. S. Aldenderfer, pp. 294–308. Sage Publications, London.

Buettner-Janusch, J. 1969. The Nature and Future of Physical Anthropology. *Transactions of the New York Academy of Sciences* 31:128–138.

Buikstra, J. E. 1976. *Hopewell in the Lower Illinois Valley: A Regional Approach to the Study of Human Biological Variability and Prehistoric Mortuary Behavior.* Scientific Papers no. 2. Northwestern University Archaeological Program, Evanston.

Buikstra, J. E., and D. C. Cook. 1980. Paleopathology: An American Account. *Annual Review of Anthropology* 9:433–470.

Buikstra, J. E., S. R. Frankenberg, and L. W. Konigsberg. 1990. Skeletal Biological Distance Studies in American Physical Anthropology: Recent Trends. *American Journal of Physical Anthropology* 82:1–8.

Calvin, M., and A. A. Benson. 1948. The Path of Carbon in Photosynthesis. *Science* 107:476–480.

Campillo, D. 1977. *Paleopatología del cráneo en Cataluña, Valencia y Baleares.* Editorial Montblanc-Martin, Barcelona.

Cannon, A. 1989. The Historical Dimension in Mortuary Expressions of Status and Sentiment. *Current Anthropology* 30:437–458.

Chase, A. F. 1983. A Contextual Consideration of the Tayasal-Paxcaman Zone, El Peten, Guatemala. Ph.D. dissertation, Department of Anthropology, University of Pennsylvania, Philadelphia.

———. 1985. Archaeology in the Maya Heartland. *Archaeology* 38(1):32–39.

———. 1990. Maya Archaeology and Population Estimates in the Tayasal-Paxcaman Zone, Peten, Guatemala. In *Precolumbian Population History in the Maya Lowlands,* edited by T. P. Culbert and D. S. Rice, pp. 149–165. University of New Mexico Press, Albuquerque.

———. 1992. Elites and the Changing Organization of Classic Maya Society. In *Mesoamerican Elites: An Archaeological Assessment,* edited by D. Z. Chase and A. F. Chase, pp. 30–49. University of Oklahoma Press, Norman.

Chase, A. F., and D. Z. Chase. 1987. *Investigations at the Classic Maya City of Caracol, Belize: 1985–1987.* Monograph 3. Pre-Columbian Art Research Institute, San Francisco.

———. 1994a. Details in the Archaeology of Caracol, Belize: An Introduction. In *Studies in the Archaeology of Caracol, Belize,* edited by D. Z. Chase and A. F. Chase, pp. 1–11. Pre-Columbian Art Research Institute, San Francisco.

———. 1994b. Maya Veneration of the Dead at Caracol, Belize. In *Seventh Palenque Round Table, 1989,* vol. 9, edited by V. Fields, pp. 53–60. M. G. Robertson, general editor. Pre-Columbian Art Research Institute, San Francisco.

———. 1996. A Mighty Maya Nation: How Caracol Built an Empire by Cultivating Its "Middle Class." *Archaeology* 49(5):66–72.

Chase, A. F., and P. M. Rice. 1985. *The Lowland Maya Postclassic.* University of Texas Press, Austin.

Chase, D. Z. 1982. Spatial and Temporal Variability in Postclassic Northern Belize. Ph.D.

dissertation, Department of Anthropology, University of Pennsylvania, Philadelphia.

———. 1990. The Invisible Maya: Population History and Archaeology at Santa Rita Corozal, Belize. In *Precolumbian Population History in the Maya Lowlands,* edited by T. P. Culbert and D. S. Rice, pp. 199–213. University of New Mexico Press, Albuquerque.

———. 1994. Human Osteology, Pathology, and Demography as Represented in the Burials of Caracol, Belize. In *Studies in the Archaeology of Caracol, Belize,* edited by D. Z. Chase and A. F. Chase, pp. 123–138. Monograph 7. Pre-Columbian Research Institute, San Francisco.

Chase, D. Z., and A. F. Chase. 1988. *A Postclassic Perspective: Excavations at the Maya Site of Santa Rita Corozal, Belize.* Monograph 4. Pre-Columbian Art Research Institute, San Francisco.

——— (editors). 1994. *Studies in the Archaeology of Caracol, Belize.* Monograph 7. Pre-Columbian Art Research Institute, San Francisco.

———. 1996. Maya Multiples: Individuals, Entries, and Tombs in Structure A34 of Caracol, Belize. *Latin American Antiquity* 7:61–79.

Cheverud, J. M., and J. E. Buikstra. 1982. Quantitative Genetics of Skeletal Non-Metric Traits in the Rhesus Macaques on Cayo Santiago. III. Relative Heritability of Skeletal Non-Metric and Metric Traits. *American Journal of Physical Anthropology* 59:151–155.

Cheverud, J. M., J. E. Buikstra, and E. Twichell. 1979. Relationships between Non-Metric Skeletal Traits and Cranial Size and Shape. *American Journal of Physical Anthropology* 50:191–198.

Coale, A. J. 1972. *The Growth and Structure of Human Populations.* Princeton University Press, Princeton.

Cobb, W. M. 1944. Bibliography in Physical Anthropology: July 1, 1943–June 30, 1944. *American Journal Physical Anthropology* 2: 381–421.

Coe, M. D. 1992. *Breaking the Maya Code.* Thames and Hudson, New York.

Coe, W. R. 1959. Burials. In *Piedras Negras Archaeology: Artifacts, Caches, and Burials,* pp. 120–139. Museum Monographs. The University Museum, University of Pennsylvania, Philadelphia.

Cogolludo, D. 1955. *Historia de Yucatán.* 3 vols. Gobierno del Estado de Campeche, México.

Cohen, M. N. 1989. *Health and the Rise of Civilization.* Yale University Press, New Haven.

Cohen, M. N., and G. J. Armelagos (editors). 1984. *Paleopathology at the Origins of Agriculture.* Academic Press, New York.

Cohen, M. N., S. Bennett, and C. Armstrong. 1989. Health and Genetic Relationships in a Colonial Maya Population. Submitted to National Science Foundation, Grant BNS 85-06785.

Cohen, M. N., S. Bennett, C. Armstrong, M. E. Danforth, and J. Armstrong. 1987. Paleopathological Diagnosis of the Scurvy Syndrome. Paper presented at the 27th Annual Meeting of the Northeast Anthropological Association, Amherst.

Cohen, M. N., K. A. O'Connor, M. E. Danforth, K. P. Jacobi, and C. W. Armstrong. 1994. Health and Death at Tipu. In *In the Wake of Contact,* edited by C. S. Larsen and G. R. Milner, pp. 121–133. Wiley-Liss, New York.

Colby, R. A., D. A. Kerr, and H. B. G. Robinson. 1971. *Color Atlas of Oral Pathology.* 3d ed. J. B. Lippincott, Philadelphia.

Coleman, D. C., and B. Fry (editors). 1991. *Carbon Isotope Techniques.* Academic Press, San Diego.

Comas, J. 1960. *Manual of Physical Anthropology.* Charles C Thomas, Springfield.

———. 1966. *Características físicas de la familia lingüística maya.* Cuadernos: Serie Antropológica, 20. Instituto de Investigaciones Históricas, Universidad Nacional Autónoma de México, México.

———. 1983. *Manual de antropología física.* Instituto de Investigaciones Antropológicas, Universidad Nacional Autónoma de México, México.

Comas, J. and P. Marquer. 1969. *Cráneos deformados de la Isla de Sacrificios, Veracruz, México.* Cuadernos: Serie Antropológica, 23. Instituto de Investigaciones Históricas, Universidad Nacional Autónoma de México, México.

Condon, K. W. 1981. Correspondence of Development Enamel Defects between the Mandibular Canine and First Premolar. Master's thesis, University of Arkansas, Fayetteville.

Condon, K. and J. C. Rose. 1992. Intertooth and Intratooth Variability in the Occurrence of Developmental Enamel Defects. In *Recent Contributions to the Study of Enamel Developmental Defects,* edited by A. H. Goodman and L. L. Capasso, pp. 61–78. Journal of Paleopathology Monographic Publications 2. Associazone Antropologica Abruzze, Chieti.

Conner, M. D. 1984. Population Structure and Biological Variation in the Late Woodland of West-Central Illinois. Ph.D. dissertation, University of Chicago, Chicago.

———. 1990. Population Structure and Skeletal Variation in the Late Woodland of West-Central Illinois. *American Journal of Physical Anthropology* 82:31–43.

Cook, D. C. 1981. Mortality, Age Structure and Status in the Interpretation of Stress Indicators in Prehistoric Skeletons: A Dental Example from the Lower Illinois Valley. In *The Archaeology of Death,* edited by R. Chapman, I. Kinnes, and K. Randsborg, pp. 133–144. Cambridge University Press, New York.

———. 1990. Epidemiology of Circular Caries: A Perspective from Prehistoric Skeletons. In *A Life in Science: Papers in Honor of J. Lawrence Angel,* edited by J. Buikstra, pp. 64–86. Scientific Papers no. 6. Center for American Archeology, Kampsville.

Cook, D. C., and J. E. Buikstra. 1979. Health and Differential Survival in Prehistoric Populations: Prenatal Defects. *American Journal of Physical Anthropology* 51:649–664.

Corruccini, R. S. 1983. Pathologies Relative to Subsistence and Settlement at Casas Grandes. *American Antiquity* 48:609–610.

Culbert, T. P. 1973. Introduction. In *The Classic Maya Collapse,* edited by T. P. Culbert, pp. 3–21. University of New Mexico Press, Albuquerque.

———. 1988. The Collapse of Classic Maya Civilization. In *The Collapse of Ancient States and Civilizations,* edited by N. Yoffee and G. L. Cowgill, pp. 69–101. University of Arizona Press, Tucson.

——— (editor). 1991. *Classic Maya Political History: Hieroglyphic and Archaeological Evidence.* Cambridge University Press, Cambridge.

Culbert, T. P., and D. S. Rice (editors). 1990. *Precolumbian Population History in the Maya Lowlands.* University of New Mexico Press, Albuquerque.

Culbert, T. P., L. Kosakowsky, R. E. Fry, and W. A. Haviland. 1990. The population of Tikal, Guatemala. In *Precolumbian Population History in the Maya Lowlands,* edited by T. P. Culbert and D. S. Rice, pp. 103–122. University of New Mexico Press, Albuquerque.

Dahlberg, A. A. 1951. The Dentition of the American Indian. In *Papers on the Physical Anthropology of the American Indian,* edited by W. S. Laughlin, pp. 138–176. The Viking Fund, New York.

———. 1956. *Materials for the Establishment of Standards for Classification of Tooth Characters, Attributes and Techniques in Morphological Studies of Dentition.* Zoller Laboratory of Dental Anthropology at the University of Chicago, Chicago.

Danforth, M. E. 1989. A Comparison of Childhood Health Patterns in the Late Classic and Colonial Maya Using Enamel Microdefects. Ph.D. dissertation, Department of Anthropology, Indiana University, Bloomington.

———. 1991. Childhood Health Patterns at Tipu: Evidence from Harris Lines. Poster presented at the 60th Annual Meeting of the American Association of Physical Anthropologists, Milwaukee.

———. 1994. Stature Change in the Prehistoric Maya of the Southern Lowlands. *Latin American Antiquity* 5:206–211.

Danforth, M. E., S. Bennett, M. N. Cohen, and H. Melkunas. 1985a. Femoral Cortical Involution in a Colonial Maya Population. Paper presented at the 54th Annual Meeting of the American Association of Physical Anthropologists, Knoxville.

———. 1985b. Femoral Cortical Involution in a Colonial Maya Population (abstract). *American Journal of Physical Anthropology* 66:162.

Danforth, M. E., K. P. Jacobi, and M. N. Cohen. 1991. Gender and Health in the Prehistoric and Early Contact Lowland Maya. Paper presented at the 90th Annual Meeting of the American Anthropological Association, Chicago.

Danforth, M. E., D. Light, M. N. Cohen, and C. W. Armstrong. 1985. Genetic Distance between Subgroups in the Tipu Population. Paper presented at the 25th Annual Meeting of the Northeastern Anthropological Association, Lake Placid.

Demarest, A. A. 1992. Ideology in Ancient Maya Cultural Evolution: The Dynamics of Galactic Polities. In *Ideology and Pre-Columbian Civilizations,* edited by A. A. Demarest and G. Conrad, pp. 135–157. School of American Research Press, Santa Fe.

Demarest, A., H. Escobedo, J. A. Valdés, S. Houston, L. E. Wright, and K. F. Emery. 1991. Arqueología, epigrafía y el descrubrimiento de una tumba real en el centro ceremonial de Dos Pilas, Petén, Guatemala. *U tz'ib* 1(1):14–28.

Demarest, A., and S. Houston (editors). 1989. *Proyecto Arqueológico Regional Petexbatún. Informe preliminar #1. Primera temporada.* Submitted to Instituto de Antropología e Historia de Guatemala.

——— (editors). 1990. *Proyecto Arqueológico Regional Petexbatún. Informe preliminar #2. Segunda temporada.* Submitted to Instituto de Antropología e Historia de Guatemala.

Demarest, A., T. Inomata, and H. Escobedo (editors). 1992. *Proyecto Arqueológico Regional Petexbatún. Informe preliminar #4. Cuarta temporada.* Submitted to Instituto de Antropología e Historia de Guatemala.

Demarest, A., T. Inomata, H. Escobedo, and J. Palka (editors). 1991. *Proyecto Arqueológico Regional Petexbatún. Informe preliminar #3. Tercera temporada.* Submitted to Instituto de Antropología e Historia de Guatemala.

Dembo, A., and J. Imbelloni. 1938. *Deformaciones intencionales del cuerpo humano de carácter étnico.* Sec. A, tomo 3. Humanior, Biblioteca del Americanista Moderno, Buenos Aires.

Deniker, J. 1907. *The Races of Man.* Walter Scott, London.

DeNiro, M. J. 1985. Postmortem Preservation and Alteration of *in vivo* Bone Collagen Isotope Ratios in Relation to Palaeodietary Reconstruction. *Nature* 317:806–809.

———. 1987. Stable Isotopy and Archaeology. *American Scientist* 75:182–191.

DeNiro, M. J., and S. Epstein. 1978. Influence of Diet on the Distribution of Carbon Isotopes in Animals. *Geochimica et Cosmochimica Acta* 42:495–506.

———. 1981. Influence of Diet on the Distribution of Nitrogen Isotopes in Animals. *Geochimica et Cosmochimica Acta* 45:341–351.

DeNiro, M. J., and M. J. Schoeniger [*sic*]. 1983. Stable Carbon and Nitrogen Isotope Ratios of Bone Collagen: Variations within Individuals, between Sexes, and within Populations Raised on Monotonous Diets. *Journal of Archaeological Science* 10:199–203.

DeNiro, M. J. and S. Weiner. 1988. Chemical, Enzymatic and Spectroscopic Characterization of Collagen and Other Organic Fractions from Prehistoric Bones. *Geochimica et Cosmochimica Acta* 52:2197–2206.

Dillon, B. D. 1988. Meatless Maya? Ethnoarchaeological Implications for Ancient Subsistence. *Journal of New World Archaeology* 7(2/3):59–70.

Ditch, L. E., and J. C. Rose. 1972. A Multivariate Dental Sexing Technique. *American Journal of Physical Anthropology* 37:61–64.

Douglass, W. A. 1969. *Death in Murelaga.* University of Washington Press, Seattle.

Droessler, J. 1981. *Craniometry and Biological Distance.* Center for American Archeology at Northwestern University, Evanston.

Dunning, N. P., and T. Beach. 1994. Soil Erosion, Slope Management, and Ancient Terracing in the Maya Lowlands. *Latin American Antiquity* 5:51–69.

Duray, S. M. 1992. Enamel Defects and Caries Etiology: An Historical Perspective. In *Recent Contributions to the Study of Enamel*

Developmental Defects, edited by A. H. Goodman and L. L. Capasso, pp. 307–320. Journal of Paleopathology Monographic Publications 2. Associazone Antropologica Abruzze,
Chieti.

Eaton, J. D. 1980. Architecture and Settlement at
Colha. In *The Colha Project. Second Season.*
1980 Interim Report, edited by T. R. Hester,
J. D. Eaton, and H. J. Shafer, pp. 41–50. The
University of Texas at San Antonio and Center
for Archaeological Research, Centro Studi e
Ricerche Ligabue, Venezia, San Antonio.

———. 1982. Colha: An Overview of Architecture and Settlement. In *Archaeology at Colha.*
Belize: The 1981 Interim Report, edited by
T. R. Hester, H. J. Shafer, and J. D. Eaton,
pp. 198–202. Center for Archaeological Research, The University of Texas at San Antonio
and Centro Studi e Ricerche Ligabue, Venezia,
San Antonio.

El-Najjar, M. Y., and A. L. Robertson, Jr. 1976.
Spongy Bones in Prehistoric America. *Science*
193:141–143.

El-Najjar, M. Y., D. J. Ryan, C. G. Turner II, and
B. Lozoff. 1976. The Etiology of Porotic Hyper-
ostosis among the Prehistoric and Historic
Anasazi Indians of Southwestern United States.
American Journal of Physical Anthropology
44:477–488.

El-Nofely, A. A., and M. Y. İşcan. 1989. Assess-
ment of Age from the Dentition of Children. In
Age Markers in the Human Skeleton, edited by
M. Y. İşcan, pp. 237–254. Charles C Thomas,
Springfield.

Emery, K. 1991. Análisis preliminar de los restos
óseos de fauna de la región de Petexbatún. In
Proyecto Arqueológico Regional Petexbatún.
Informe preliminar #3. Tercera temporada,
tomo 2, edited by A. A. Demarest, T. Inomata,
H. Escobedo, and J. Palka, pp. 813–828. Submitted to Instituto de Antropología e Historia
de Guatemala.

Evans, D. T. 1973. A Preliminary Evalutation of
Tooth Tartar among the Preconquest Maya of
the Tayasal Area, El Petén, Guatemala. *American Antiquity* 38:489–493.

Falkner, F. T., and J. M. Tanner (editors). 1986.

Human Growth: A Comprehensive Treatise.
Plenum, New York.

Fancourt, C. S. J. 1854. *The History of the Yucatan from Its Discovery to the Close of the
Seventeenth Century.* John Murray, London.

Fanning, E. A., and T. Brown. 1971. Preliminary
and Permanent Tooth Development. *Australian
Dental Journal* 16:41–43.

Farriss, N. M. 1984. *Maya Society under Colonial Rule.* Princeton University Press, Princeton.

Fastlicht, S. 1948. Tooth Mutilations in Pre-
Columbian Mexico. *Journal of the American
Dental Association* 36:315–323.

———. 1962. Dental Inlays and Fillings among
the Ancient Mayas. *Journal of the History of
Medicine and Allied Sciences* 17:393–401.

———. 1976. *Tooth Mutilations and Dentistry
in Pre-Columbian Mexico.* Quintessence
Books, Chicago.

Fleming, A. F. 1977. Iron-Deficiency in the Tropics. In *Ferastras, Iron-Poly (Sorbitol-Gluconic
Acid) Complex,* edited by J. Fielding, pp. 315–
321. Scandinavian Journal of Haematology
Supplementum no. 32.

Foias, A. E. 1993. Resultados preliminares del
análisis cerámico del Proyecto Petexbatún.
Apuntes Arqueológicos 3(1):37–54.

Ford, A. 1990. Maya Settlement in the Belize
River Area: Variations in Residence Patterns
of the Central Maya Lowlands. In *Precolumbian Population History in the Maya Lowlands,* edited by T. P. Culbert and D. S. Rice,
pp. 167–181. University of New Mexico Press,
Albuquerque.

Ford, A., and S. Fedick. 1992. Prehistoric Maya
Settlement Patterns in the Upper Belize River
Area: Initial Results of the Belize River Archae-
ological Settlement Survey. *Journal of Field
Archaeology* 19:35–47.

Fortes, M. 1953. The Structure of Unilineal
Descent Groups. *American Anthropologist*
55:17–41.

Gamero Idiaquez, I. 1978. *Mamíferos de mi tie-
rra.* Banco Central de Honduras, Tegucigalpa.

Gann, T. W. F. 1900. Mounds in Northern
Honduras. *Nineteenth Annual Report, 1897–
1898, Bureau of American Ethnology,* part

2, pp. 661–692. Smithsonian Institution, Washington.

———. 1911. Explorations Carried on in British Honduras in 1908–9. *Liverpool Annals of Archaeology and Anthropology* 4:72–87.

———. 1914. Report on Some Excavations in British Honduras. *Liverpool Annals of Archaeology and Anthropology* 7:28–42.

———. 1918. *The Maya Indians of Southern Yucatan and Northern British Honduras.* Bulletin 64. Bureau of American Ethnology, Smithsonian Institution, Washington.

Garza, M. de la (editor). 1983. *Relaciones histórico-geográficas de la gobernación de Yucatán (Mérida, Valladolid y Tabasco).* Centro de Estudios Mayas, Instituto de Investigaciones Filológicas, Universidad Nacional Autónoma de México, México.

Genovés, S. 1964. Introducción al estudio de la proporción entre los huesos largos y la reconstrucción de la estatura en restos mesoamericanos. *Anales de Antropología* 1:47–62. Instituto de Investigaciones Históricas, Universidad Nacional Autónoma de México, México.

———. 1967. Proportionality of Long Bones and Their Relation to Stature among Mesoamericans. *American Journal of Physical Anthropology* 26:67–77.

Genovés, S., T. Comas, and J. Comas. 1964. *La antropología física en México, 1943–64: inventario bibliográfico.* Cuadernos: Serie Antropológica, 17. Instituto de Investigaciones Históricas, Universidad Nacional Autónoma de México, México.

Gerry, John. 1993. Diet and Status among the Classic Maya: An Isotopic Perspective. Ph.D. dissertation, Department of Anthropology, Harvard University, Cambridge.

Giles, E. 1970. Discriminant Function Sexing of the Human Skeleton. In *Personal Identification in Mass Disasters,* edited by T. D. Stewart, pp. 99–109. National Museum of Natural History, Smithsonian Institution, Washington.

Ginther, C., D. Corach, G. A. Penacino, J. A. Rey, F. R. Carnese, M. H. Hutz, A. Anderson, J. Just, F. M. Salzano, and M. C. King. 1993. Genetic Variation among the Mapuche Indians from the Patagonian Region of Argentina: Mitochondrial DNA Sequence Variation and Allele Frequencies of Several Nuclear Genes. In *DNA Fingerprinting: State of the Science,* edited by S. R. J. Pena, R. Chakraborty, J. T. Epplen, and A. J. Jeffreys, pp. 211–219. Birkhauser Verlag, Basel.

Glassman, D. M. 1994. Skeletal Biology of the Prehistoric Maya on Ambergris Cay, Belize (abstract). *American Journal of Physical Anthropology,* Supplement 18:95.

Goodman, A. H. 1993. On the Interpretation of Health from Skeletal Remains. *Current Anthropology* 34:281–288

Goodman, A. H., and G. J. Armelagos. 1985. Factors Affecting the Distribution of Enamel Hypoplasias within the Human Permanent Dentition. *American Journal of Physical Anthropology* 68:479–493.

Goodman, A. H., and L. L. Capasso (editors). 1992. *Recent Contributions to the Study of Enamel Developmental Defects.* Journal of Paleopathology Monographic Publications 2. Associazone Antropologica Abruzze, Chieti.

Goodman, A. H., D. L. Martin, G. J. Armelagos, and G. Clark. 1984. Indicators of Stress from Bone and Teeth. In *Paleopathology at the Origins of Agriculture,* edited by M. N. Cohen and G. J. Armelagos, pp. 13–50. Academic Press, New York.

Goodman, A. H., D. L. Martin, C. P. Klein, M. S. Peele, N. A. Cruse, L. R. McEwen, A. Saeed, and B. M. Robinson. 1992. Cluster Bands, Wilson Bands, and Pit Patches: Histological and Enamel Surface Indicators of Stress in the Black Mesa Anasazi Population. In *Recent Contributions to the Study of Enamel Developmental Defects,* edited by A. H. Goodman and L. L. Capasso, pp. 115–129. Journal of Paleopathology Monographic Publications 2. Associazone Antropologica Abruzze, Chieti.

Goodman, A. H., G. H. Pelto, L. H. Allen, and A. Chavez. 1992. Socioeconomic and Anthropometric Correlates of Linear Enamel Hypoplasia in Children from Solis, Mexico. In *Recent Contributions to the Study of Enamel Developmental Defects,* edited by A. H. Goodman and L. L. Capasso, pp. 373–380. Journal of Paleopathology Monographic Publications 2. Associazone Antropologica Abruzze, Chieti.

Goodman, A. H., and J. C. Rose. 1990. Assessment of Systemic Physiological Perturbations from Dental Enamel Hypoplasias and Associated Histological Structures. *Yearbook of Physical Anthropology* 33: 59–110.

———. 1991. Dental Enamel Hypoplasias as Indicators of Nutritional Status. In *Advances in Dental Anthropology,* edited by M. A. Kelley and C. S. Larsen, pp. 279–294. Wiley-Liss, New York.

Gordon, G. B. 1896. *The Prehistoric Ruins of Copan, Honduras.* Memoirs of the Peabody Museum of American Archaeology and Ethnology, vol. 1, no. 1. Harvard University, Cambridge.

———. 1898. *Researches in the Uloa Valley, Honduras.* Memoirs of the Peabody Museum of American Archaeology and Ethnology, vol. 1, no. 4. Harvard University, Cambridge.

Graham, E., D. M. Pendergast, and G. D. Jones. 1989. On the Fringes of Conquest: Maya-Spanish Contact in Colonial Belize. *Science* 246:1254–1259.

Green, R. F., and J. M. Suchey. 1976. The Use of Inverse Sine Transformations in the Analysis of Non-Metric Data. *American Journal of Physical Anthropology* 45:61–68.

Gustafson, A. G. 1959. A Morphologic Investigation of Certain Variations in the Structure and Mineralization of Human Dental Enamel. *Odontologisk Tidskrift* 67:361–472.

Guthe, C. E. 1921. Report of Dr. Carl E. Guthe. *Carnegie Institution of Washington Yearbook* 20:364–368. Washington.

———. 1922. Report on the Excavations at Tayasal. *Carnegie Institution of Washington Yearbook* 21:318–319. Washington.

Gwinnett, A.J., and L. Gorelick. 1979. Inlayed Teeth of the Ancient Mayans: A Tribological Study Using the SEM. *Scanning Electron Microscopy* 3:575–580.

Hall, G. D. 1989. Realm of Death: Royal Mortuary Customs and Polity Interaction in the Classic Maya Lowlands. Ph.D. dissertation, Harvard University, Cambridge.

Hammond, N. (editor). 1991. *Cuello: An Early Maya Community in Belize.* Cambridge University Press, Cambridge.

Hammond, N., A. Clarke, and F. Estrada Belli. 1992. Middle Preclassic Maya Buildings and Burials at Cuello, Belize. *Antiquity* 66:955–964.

Hammond, N., K. Pretty, and F. P. Saul. 1975. A Classic Maya Family Tomb. *World Archaeology* 7:57–78.

Hamy, E. T. 1882. Les mutilations dentaires au Mexique et dans le Yucatan. *Bulletins de la Société d'Anthropologie de Paris,* 3e ser., 5:879–882.

———. 1883. Mutilations dentaires des huaxteques modernes. *Bulletins de la Société d'Anthropologie de Paris,* 3e ser., 6:644–645.

Handler, J. S., R. S. Corruccini, and R. J. Mutaw. 1982. Tooth Mutilation in the Caribbean: Evidence from a Slave Burial Population in Barbados. *Journal of Human Evolution* 11:297–313.

Harris, D. 1978. The Agricultural Foundations of Lowland Maya Civilization. In *Pre-Hispanic Maya Agriculture,* edited by P. D. Harrison and B. L. Turner, pp. 301–324. University of New Mexico Press, Albuquerque.

Harris, E. F., and H. L. Bailit. 1987. Odontometric Comparisons among Solomon Islanders and Other Oceanic Peoples. In *The Solomon Islands Project: A Long-Term Study of Health, Human Biology and Culture Change,* edited by J. S. Friedlaender, pp. 215–264. Clarendon Press, Oxford.

Harris, J. E., and K. R. Weeks. 1973. *X-Raying the Pharaohs.* Charles Scribner's Sons, New York.

Harrison, P. D., and B. L. Turner II (editors). 1978. *Pre-Hispanic Maya Agriculture.* University of New Mexico Press, Albuquerque.

Hatch, M. D., and C. R. Slack. 1966. Photosynthesis by Sugarcane Leaves. A New Carboxylation Reaction and the Pathway of Sugar Formation. *Biochemical Journal* 101:103–111.

Hauser, G., and G. F. De Stefano. 1989. *Epigenetic Variants of the Human Skull.*

E. Schweizerbasrtsche Verlagsbuchhandlung, Stuttgart.

Haviland, W. A. 1967. Stature at Tikal, Guatemala: Implications for Ancient Maya Demography and Social Organization. *American Antiquity* 32:316–325.

———. 1972. A New Look at Classic Maya Social Organization at Tikal. *Cerámica de Cultura Maya* 8:1–16.

———. 1981. Dower Houses and Minor Centers at Tikal, Guatemala: An Investigation into the Identification of Valid Units in Settlement Hierarchies. In *Lowland Maya Settlement Patterns,* edited by W. Ashmore, pp. 89–117. University of New Mexico Press, Albuquerque.

———. 1988. Musical Hammocks at Tikal: Problems with Reconstructing Household Composition. In *Household and Community in the Mesoamerican Past,* edited by R. Wilk and W. Ashmore, pp. 121–134. University of New Mexico Press, Albuquerque.

Haviland, W. A., M. J. Becker, A. Chowning, K. A. Dixon, and K. Heider. 1985. *Excavations in Small Residential Groups of Tikal: Groups 4F-1 and 4F-2,* Tikal Report no. 19, University Museum Monograph 58. The University Museum, University of Pennsylvania, Philadelphia.

Hay, C. L., R. L. Linton, S. K. Lothrop, H. Shapiro, and G. C. Vaillant. 1940. *The Maya and Their Neighbors: Essays on Middle American Anthropology and Archaeology.* Appleton-Century, New York.

Healy, P. F., J. D. Lambert, J. T. Arnason, and R. J. Hebda. 1983. Caracol, Belize: Evidence of Ancient Maya Agricultural Terraces. *Journal of Field Archaeology* 10:397–410.

Helms, M. W. 1979. *Ancient Panama.* University of Texas Press, Austin.

Henderson, J. S., and. J. A. Sabloff. 1993. Reconceptualizing the Maya Cultural Tradition: Programmatic Comments. In *Lowland Maya Civilization in the Eighth Century A.D.,* edited by J. A. Sabloff and J. S. Henderson, pp. 445–476. Dumbarton Oaks, Washington.

Hendon, J. 1992. Status and Power in Classic Maya Society: An Archaeological Study. *American Anthropologist* 93:894–918.

Hester, T. R., J. D. Eaton, and H. J. Shafer (editors). 1980. *The Colha Project. Second Season, 1980 Interim Report.* The University of Texas at San Antonio and Center for Archaeological Research, Centro Studi e Ricerche Ligabue, Venezia, San Antonio.

Hester, T. R., G. Ligabue, S. Salvatori, and M. Sartor (editors). 1983. *Colha ei maya dei bassipiani.* Erizzo, Venezia.

Hester, T. R., and H. J. Shafer. 1984. Exploitation of Chert Resources by the Ancient Maya of Northern Belize, Central America. *World Archaeology* 16:157–173.

Hester, T. R., H. J. Shafer, and J. D. Eaton (editors). 1982. *Archaeology at Colha, Belize: The 1981 Interim Report.* Center for Archaeological Research, The University of Texas at San Antonio and Centro Studi e Ricerche Ligabue, Venezia, San Antonio.

——— (editors). 1994. *Continuing Archeology at Colha, Belize.* Studies in Archeology 16. Texas Archeological Research Laboratory, The University of Texas at Austin, Austin.

Hillson, S. 1986. *Teeth.* Cambridge University Press, Cambridge.

Hinton, R. J. 1981. Form and Patterning of Anterior Tooth Wear among the Aboriginal Human Groups. *American Journal of Physical Anthropology* 54:555–564.

Hodder, I. 1982a. The Identification and Interpretation of Ranking in Prehistory: A Contextual Perspective. In *Ranking, Resource, and Exchange: Aspects of the Archaeology of Early European Society,* edited by C. Renfrew and S. Shennan, pp. 150–154. Cambridge University Press, Cambridge.

———. 1982b. *Symbolic and Structural Archaeology.* Cambridge University Press, Cambridge.

———. 1986a. *Archaeology as Long Term History.* Cambridge University Press, Cambridge.

———. 1986b. *Reading the Past.* Cambridge University Press, Cambridge.

Hodges, D. C. 1985. Dental Pathology in a Late Classic Sample from the Copan Valley, Honduras. Paper presented at the 84th Annual Meeting of the American Anthropological Association, Washington.

Hodges, D., and R. M. Leventhal. n.d. *Copan Settlement Pattern Project: Burials.* Papers of the Peabody Museum of Archaeology and Ethnology, vol. 81. Harvard University, Cambridge. In preparation.

Hole, F. 1989. Patterns of Burial in the Fifth Millennium. In *Upon This Foundation: The 'Ubaid Reconsidered,* edited by E. Henrickson and I. Thuesen, pp. 149–180. Museum Tusculanum Press, University of Copenhagen, Copenhagen.

Holliday, D. Y. 1993. Occipital Lesions: A Possible Cost of Cradleboards. *American Journal of Physical Anthropology* 90:283–290.

Hooton, E. A. 1930. *The Indians of Pecos Pueblo.* Papers of the Southwestern Expedition no. 4. Yale University Press, New Haven.

———. 1940. Skeletons from the Cenote of Sacrifice at Chichen Itzá. In *The Maya and Their Neighbors: Essays on Middle American Anthropology and Archaeology,* edited by C. L. Hay, R. L. Linton, S. K. Lothrop, H. Shapiro, and G. C. Vaillant, pp. 272–280. Appleton-Century, New York.

Horai, S., R. Kondo, Y. Nakagawa-Hattori, S. Hayasaki, S. Sonoda, and K. Tajima. 1993. Peopling of the Americas, Founded by Four Major Lineages of Mitochondrial DNA. *Molecular Biology and Evolution* 10(1):23–47.

Houston, S. D. 1989. Archaeology and Maya Writing. *Journal of World Prehistory* 3(1):1–31.

———. 1993. *Hieroglyphs and History at Dos Pilas: Dynastic Politics of the Classic Maya.* University of Texas Press, Austin.

Houston, S. D., and P. Mathews. 1985. *The Dynastic Sequence of Dos Pilas, Guatemala.* Monograph 1. Pre-Columbian Art Research Institute, San Francisco.

Howell, J. D. 1993. Concepts of Heart-Related Diseases. In *Cambridge World History of Human Disease,* edited by K. F. Kiple, pp. 91–102. Cambridge University Press, Cambridge.

Huss-Ashmore, R., A. H. Goodman, and G. J. Armelagos. 1982. Nutritional Inference from Paleopathology. In *Advances in Archaeological Method and Theory,* vol. 5, edited by M. B. Schiffer, pp. 395–474. Academic Press, New York.

Hutchinson, D. L., and C. S. Larsen. 1985. Determination of Stress Episode Duration from Linear Enamel Hypoplasias: A Case Study from St. Catherine's Island, Georgia. *Human Biology* 60:93–110.

Inomata, T. 1995. Archaeological Investigations at the Fortified Center of Aguateca, El Peten, Guatemala: Implications for the Study of the Classic Maya Collapse. Ph.D. dissertation, Vanderbilt University.

Irish, J. D., and C. G. Turner II. 1987. More Lingual Surface Attrition of the Maxillary Teeth in American Indians: Prehistoric Panamanians. *American Journal of Physical Anthropology* 73:209–213.

Jacobi, K. P. 1996. An Analysis of Genetic Structuring in a Colonial Maya Cemetery, Tipu, Belize, Using Dental Morphology and Metrics. Ph.D. dissertation, Indiana University.

Jaén Esquivel, M. T. 1968. El material osteológico de Chiapa de Corzo, Chiapas. *Anales del Instituto Nacional de Antropología e Historia* 19(48):67–77. Secretaría de Educación Pública, México.

Johansson, S. R., and S. Horowitz. 1988. Estimating Mortality in Skeletal Populations. Influence of the Growth Rate on the Interpretation of Levels and Trends During the Transition to Agriculture. *American Journal of Physical Anthropology* 71:233–250.

Johnson, A. L., and N. C. Lovell. 1994. Biological Differentiation at Predynastic Naqada, Egypt: An Analysis of Dental Morphological Traits. *American Journal of Physical Anthropology* 93:427–433.

Johnston, K. 1985. Maya Dynastic Territorial Expansion: Glyphic Evidence for Classic Centers of the Pasión River, Guatemala. In *Fifth Palenque Round Table, 1983,* vol. 3, edited by V. M. Fields, pp. 49–56. M. G. Robertson, general editor. Pre-Columbian Art Research Institute, San Francisico.

———. 1994. The "Invisible" Maya: Late Classic Minimally-Platformed Residential Settlement at Itzan, Peten, Guatemala. Ph.D. dissertation, Yale University.

Jones, G. D. 1989. *Maya Resistance to Spanish Rule.* University of New Mexico Press, Albuquerque.

Jones, G., and R. Kautz. 1981a. Archaeology

and Ethnohistory on a Spanish Colonial Frontier: The Macal Tipu Project in Western Belize. Paper presented at the XVII Mesa Redonda de la Sociedad Mexicana de Antropología, San Cristobal de las Casas.

———. 1981b. Native Elites on the Colonial Frontiers of Yucatan. Paper presented at the 80th Annual Meeting of the American Anthropological Association, Los Angeles.

Jones, G., R. Kautz, and E. Graham. 1986. Tipu: A Maya Town on the Spanish Colonial Frontier. *Archaeology* 39(1):40–47.

Joyce, T. A. 1914. *Mexican Archaeology*. P. L. Warner, London.

Katz, S. H., M. L. Hediger, and L. A. Valleroy. 1974. Traditional Maize Processing Techniques in the New World. *Science* 184:763–765.

———. 1975. The Anthropological and Nutritional Significance of Traditional Maize Processing Techniques in the New World. In *Biosocial Interrelations in Population Adaptation,* edited by E. S. Watts, F. E. Johnston, and G. W. Lasker, pp. 195–231. Mouton, The Hague.

Katzenberg, M. A. 1992. Advances in Stable Isotope Analysis of Prehistoric Bones. In *Skeletal Biology of Past Peoples: Research Methods,* edited by S. R. Saunders and M. A. Katzenberg. Wiley-Liss, New York.

Keegan, W. F. 1989. Stable Isotope Analysis of Prehistoric Diet. In *Reconstruction of Life From the Skeleton,* edited by M. Y. İşcan and K. A. R. Kennedy, pp. 223–36. Alan R. Liss, New York.

Kennedy, G. E. 1983. Skeletal Remains from Sarteneja, Belize. In *Archaeological Excavations in Northern Belize, Central America,* edited by R. V. Sidrys, pp. 353–372. Monograph XVII. Institute of Archaeology, University of California at Los Angeles, Los Angeles.

Kieser, J. A. 1990. *Human Adult Odontometrics*. Cambridge University Press, Cambridge.

Klecka, W. R. 1982. *Discriminant Analysis*. Sage University Papers Series on Quantitative Applications in the Social Sciences, no. 07-019. Sage Publications, Beverly Hills.

Knoke, D., and P. J. Burke. 1980. *Log-Linear Models*. Sage University Papers Series on Quantitative Applications in the Social Sciences, no. 07-020. Sage Publications, Beverly Hills.

Krogman, W. M. 1943. Bibliography in Physical Anthropology: July 1, 1942–June 30, 1943. *American Journal Physical Anthropology* 1:437–486.

———. 1945. Bibliography in Physical Anthropology: July 1, 1944–June 30, 1945. *American Journal Physical Anthropology* 3:367–417.

———. 1962. *The Human Skeleton in Forensic Medicine*. Charles C Thomas, Springfield.

Krogman, W. M., and M. Y. İşcan. 1986. *The Human Skeleton in Forensic Medicine*. Charles C Thomas, Springfield.

Krueger, H. W. 1991. Exchange of Carbon with Biological Apatite. *Journal of Archaeological Science* 18:355–361.

Krueger, H. W., and C. H. Sullivan. 1984. Models for Carbon Isotope Fractionation between Diet and Bone. In *Stable Isotopes in Nutrition,* edited by J. R. Turnlund and P. E. Johnson, pp. 205–220. ACS Symposium Series, vol. 258. American Chemical Society, Washington.

Lallo, J. W., G. J. Armelagos, and R. P Mensforth. 1977. The Role of Diet, Disease, and Physiology in the Origin of Porotic Hyperostosis. *Human Biology* 49:471–483.

Landa, D. de. 1978 [1566]. *Relación de las cosas de Yucatán*. Porrúa, México.

Lang, C. A. 1990. The Dental Morphology of the Maya from Lamanai and Tipu. Master's thesis, Trent University.

Laporte, J. P. 1992. Los sitios arqueológicos del Valle de Dolores en las Montañas Mayas. *Mesoamérica* 13:413–440. Centro de Investigaciones Regionales de Mesoamérica [CIRMA], Antigua, Guatemala.

Layrisse, M., and M. Roche. 1964. The Relationship between Anemia and Hookworm Infection. *American Journal of Hygiene* 79:279–287.

Lee-Thorp, J. A., J. C. Sealy, and N. J. van der Merwe. 1989. Stable Carbon Isotope Ratio Differences between Bone Collagen and Bone Apatite, and Their Relationship to Diet. *Journal of Archaeological Science* 16:585–599.

Lentz, D. L. 1991. Maya Diets of the Rich and Poor: Paleoethnobotanical Evidence from Copán. *Latin American Antiquity* 2:269–287.

Linares, O. 1976. "Garden Hunting" in the American Tropics. *Human Ecology* 4:331–349.

Linné, S. 1940. Dental Decoration in Aboriginal America. *Ethnos* 5:2–28.

Littlewood, R. A. (editor). 1972. *Physical Anthropology of the Eastern Highlands of New Guinea.* University of Washington Press, Seattle.

Longyear, J. M., III. 1952. *Copan Ceramics. A Study of Southeastern Maya Pottery.* Publication 597. Carnegie Institution of Washington, Washington.

Lovejoy, C. O., R. S. Meindl, R. P. Mensforth, and T. J. Barton. 1985. Multifactorial Determination of Skeletal Age at Death: A Method and Blind Tests of Its Accuracy. *American Journal of Physical Anthropology* 68:1–14.

Lovejoy, C. O., R. S. Meindl, T. R. Pryzbeck, T. J. Barton, and D. Kotting. 1977. Paleobiology of the Libben Site, Ottawa Co., Ohio. *American Journal of Physical Anthropology* 55:529–542.

Lovejoy, C. O., R. P. Mensforth, and G. J. Armelagos. 1982. Five Decades of Skeletal Biology as Reflected in the American Journal of Physical Anthropology. In *A History of American Physical Anthropology 1930–1980,* edited by F. Spencer, pp. 329–336. Academic Press, New York.

Lovell, W. G. 1982. Collapse and Recovery: A Demographic Profile of the Cuchumatan Highlands of Guatemala (1520–1821). In *The Historical Demography of Highland Guatemala,* edited by R. M. Carmack, J. Early, and C. Lutz, pp. 103–120. Publication 6. Institute for Mesoamerican Studies, State University of New York at Albany, Albany.

Lowe, J. W. G. 1985. *The Dynamics of the Apocalypse: A Simulation of the Classic Maya Collapse.* University of New Mexico, Albuquerque.

Lukacs, J. R., and B. E. Hemphill. 1991. The Dental Anthropology of Prehistoric Baluchistan: A Morphometric Approach to the Peopling of South Asia. In *Advances in Dental Anthropology,* edited by M. A. Kelly and C. S. Larsen, pp. 77–119. Wiley-Liss, New York.

Lukacs, J. R., and M. R. Joshi. 1992. Enamel Hypoplasia Prevalence in Three Ethnic Groups of Northwest India: A Test of Daughter Neglect and a Framework for the Past. In *Recent Contributions to the Study of Enamel Developmental Defects,* edited by A. H. Goodman and L. L. Capasso, pp. 359–372. Journal of Paleopathology Monographic Publications 2. Associazone Antropologica Abruzze, Chieti.

Lynott, M. J., T. W. Boutton, J. E. Price, and D. E. Nelson. 1986. Stable Carbon Isotopic Evidence for Maize Agriculture in Southeast Missouri and Northeast Arkansas. *American Antiquity* 51:51–65.

Marcus, J. P. 1973. Territorial Organization of the Lowland Classic Maya. *Science* 180:911–916.

———. 1982. The Plant World of the 16th and 17th Century Maya. In *Maya Subsistence,* edited by K. Flannery, pp. 239–273. Academic Press, New York.

———. 1983. Lowland Maya Archaeology at the Crossroads. *American Antiquity* 48:454–488.

———. 1992. Royal Families, Royal Texts: Examples from the Zapotec and Maya. In *Mesoamerican Elites: An Archaeological Assessment,* edited by D. Z. Chase and A. F. Chase, pp. 221–241. University of Oklahoma Press, Norman.

———. 1993. Ancient Maya Political Organization. In *Lowland Maya Civilization in the Eighth Century A.D.,* edited by J. A. Sabloff and J. S. Henderson, pp. 111–184. Dumbarton Oaks, Washington.

Márquez, L. 1993. Xcaret. Estudio osteológico de un sitio arqueológico maya. Ms. on file. Dirección de Antropología Física, Instituto Nacional de Antropología e Historia, México.

Márquez, L., and P. Schmidt. 1984. Osario infantil en un chultún en Chichén Itzá. In *Investigaciones recientes en el área maya,* tomo 2, pp. 89–103. Memorias de la XVII Mesa Redonda, 1981. Sociedad Mexicana de Antropología, San Cristobal de las Casas.

Márquez de González, L., A. Benavides Castillo,

and P. J. Schmidt. 1982. *Exploración en la gruta de Xcan, Yucatán.* Centro Regional del Sureste, Instituto Nacional de Antropología e Historia, Mérida.

Márquez Morfín, L. 1984. Distribución de la estatura en colecciones óseas mayas prehispánicas. In *Estudios de antropología biológica (II Coloquio de Antropología Física Juan Comas. 1982),* edited by R. Ramos Galván and R. M. Ramos Rodríguez, pp. 253–271. Antropología Física. Serie Antropológica 75. Instituto de Investigaciones Antropológicas, Universidad Nacional Autónoma de México, México.

———. 1992. Evidencias óseas sobre la dieta maya durante el Postclásico. In *Memorias del Primer Congreso International de Mayistas,* pp. 539–549. Instituto de Investigaciones Filológicas, Universidad Nacional Autónoma de México, México.

Márquez Morfín, L., M. E. Peraza, J. Gamboa, and T. Miranda. 1982. *Playa del Carmen: una población de la costa oriental en el Postclásico (un estudio osteológico).* Colección Científica. Antropología Física 119. Sección de Antropología Física, Centro Regional del Sureste, Instituto Nacional de Antropología e Historia, México.

Massey, V. K. 1989. *The Human Skeletal Remains from a Terminal Classic Skull Pit at Colha, Belize.* Papers of the Colha Project, vol. 3. Texas Archeological Research Laboratory, The University of Texas at Austin, and Department of Anthropology, Texas A&M University, College Station.

———. 1994. An Osteological Analysis of the Skull Pit Children. Ms. on file at the Center for Archaeological Research, The University of Texas at San Antonio.

Massey, V. K., and D. G. Steele. 1982. Preliminary Notes on the Dentition and Taphonomy of the Colha Human Skeletal Material. In *Archaeology at Colha, Belize: The 1981 Interim Report,* edited by T. R. Hester, H. J. Shafer, and J. D. Eaton, pp. 198–202. Center for Archaeological Research, The University of Texas at San Antonio and Centro Studi e Ricerche Ligabue, Venezia, San Antonio.

Massler, M., I. Schour, and H. G. Poncher. 1941. Development Pattern of the Child as Reflected in the Calcification Pattern. *American Journal of Diseases of Children* 62:33–67.

Mathews, P. and G. R. Willey. 1991. Prehistoric Polities of the Pasión Region: Hieroglyphic Texts and Their Archaeological Settings. In *Classic Maya Political History: Hieroglyphic and Archaeological Evidence,* edited by T. P. Culbert, pp. 30–71. Cambridge University Press, New York.

May, R. L., A. H. Goodman, and R. S. Meindl. 1993. Response of Bone and Enamel Formation to Nutritional Supplementation and Morbidity among Malnourished Guatemalan Children. *American Journal of Physical Anthropology* 92:37–51.

McAnany, P. A. 1995. *Living with the Ancestors.* University of Texas Press, Austin.

McCormick, S. K. 1994. Evidence of Association between Cranial Modification and Supra-Inion Depressions (abstract). *American Journal of Physical Anthropology,* Supplement 18:142.

McKern, T. W., and T. D. Stewart. 1957. *Skeletal Age Changes in Young American Males. Analysed from the Standpoint of Age Identification.* Environmental Protection Research Division, Technical Report EP-45. Quartermaster Research and Development Command, U.S. Army, Natick.

Mensforth, R. P., C. O. Lovejoy, J. W. Lallo, and G. J. Armelagos. 1978. The Role of Constitutional Factors, Diet, and Infectious Disease in the Etiology of Porotic Hyperostosis and Periosteal Reactions in Prehistoric Infants and Children. *Medical Anthropology,* vol. 2, issue 1, part 2.

Merriwether, D. A. 1993. Mitochondrial DNA Variation in South American Indians. Ph.D. dissertation, University of Pittsburgh, Pittsburgh.

Merriwether, D. A., A. G. Clark, S. W. Ballinger, T. G. Schurr, H. Soodyall, T. Jenkins, S. T. Sherry, and D. C. Wallace. 1991. The Structure of Human Mitochondrial DNA Variation. *Journal of Molecular Evolution* 33:543–555.

Merriwether, D. A., F. Rothhammer, and R. E. Ferrell. 1994. Genetic Variation in the New

World: Ancient Teeth, Bone, and Tissue as Sources of DNA. *Experientia* 50:592–601.

———. 1995. Distribution of the Four Founding Lineage Haplotypes in Native Americans Suggests a Single Wave of Migration for the New World. *American Journal of Physical Anthropology* 98:411–430.

Merwin, R. E., and G. C. Vaillant. 1932. *The Ruins of Holmul, Guatemala.* Memoirs of the Peabody Museum of American Archaeology and Ethnology, vol. 3, no. 3. Harvard University, Cambridge.

Miles, A. E. W. 1963. Dentition in the Estimation of Age. *Journal of Dental Research* 42:255–263.

Millard, A. V. 1994. A Causal Model of High Rates of Child Mortality. *Social Science and Medicine* 38:253–268.

Miller, A. G., and N. M. Farriss. 1979. Religious Syncretism in Colonial Yucatan: The Archaeological and Ethnohistorical Evidence from Tancah, Quintana Roo. In *Maya Archaeology and Ethnohistory,* edited by N. Hammond and G. R. Willey, pp. 223–240. University of Texas Press, Austin.

Millon, R. 1976. Social Relations in Ancient Teotihuacán. In *The Valley of Mexico,* edited by E. R. Wolf, pp. 205–248. University of New Mexico Press, Albuquerque.

Milner, G. R., and C. S. Larsen. 1991. Teeth as Artifacts of Human Behavior: Intentional Mutilation and Accidental Modification. In *Advances in Dental Anthropology,* edited by M. A. Kelley and C. S. Larsen, pp. 357–378. Wiley-Liss, New York.

Mock, S. B. 1994. Destruction and Denouement during the Late-Terminal Classic: The Colha Skull Pit. In *Continuing Archeology at Colha, Belize,* edited by T. R. Hester, H. J. Shafer, and J. D. Eaton, pp. 221–231. Studies in Archeology 16. Texas Archeological Research Laboratory, The University of Texas at Austin, Austin.

Moore, J. A., and A. S. Keene (editors). 1983. *Archaeological Hammers and Theories.* Academic Press, New York.

Moorrees, C. F. A. 1957. *The Aleut Dentition.* Harvard University Press, Cambridge.

Morley, S. G. 1910. A Group of Related Structures at Uxmal, Mexico. *American Journal of Archaeology,* 2d ser., 14(1):1–18.

———. 1946. *The Ancient Maya.* Stanford University Press, Stanford.

Morley, S. G., and G. Brainerd. 1983. *The Ancient Maya.* Revised by R. J. Sharer. Stanford University Press, Stanford.

Murphy, T. R. 1959. Gradients of Dentine Exposure in Human Tooth Attrition. *American Journal of Physical Anthropology* 17:179–185.

Nations, J. D., and R. B. Nigh. 1980. The Evolutionary Potential of Lacandon Maya Sustained-Yield Tropical Forest Agriculture. *Journal of Anthropological Research* 36:1–30.

Nichol, C. R., and C. G. Turner II. 1986. Intra- and Interobserver Concordance in Classifying Dental Morphology. *American Journal of Physical Anthropology* 69:299–315.

Nickens, P. R. 1976. Stature Reduction as an Adaptive Response to Food Production in Mesoamerica. *Journal of Archaeological Science* 3:31–41.

Nikiforuk, G., and D. Fraser. 1981. The Etiology of Enamel Hypoplasia: A Unifying Concept. *Journal of Pediatrics* 98:888–893.

Norr, L. 1991. Nutritional Consequences of Prehistoric Subsistence Strategies in Lower Central America. Ph.D. dissertation, University of Illinois at Urbana-Champaign, Urbana-Champaign.

O'Connor, K. 1991. Paleodemography of the Tipu Population. Paper presented at the 60th Annual Meeting of the American Association of Physical Anthropologists, Milwaukee.

———. 1995. The Age Pattern and Level of Mortality in Paleodemographic Samples: Identifying Characteristics and Sources of Error. Ph.D. dissertation, Department of Anthropology, State University of New York at Albany, Albany.

O'Leary, M. H. 1988. Carbon Isotopes in Photosynthesis. *Bioscience* 38:328–336.

Oloriz y Aguilera, D. F. 1896. La talla humana en España. *Discursos leidos en la Real Academia de Medicina.* Madrid.

Ortner, D. J., and W. G. J. Putschar. 1985. *Identification of Pathological Conditions in*

Human Skeletal Remains. Reprinted. Originally published 1981. Smithsonian Contributions to Anthropology no. 28. Smithsonian Institution, Washington.

Ortner, D. J., and A. C. Aufderheide. 1991. Introduction. In *Human Paleopathology: Current Syntheses and Future Options,* edited by D. J. Ortner and A. C. Aufderheide, pp. 1–2. Smithsonian Institution Press, Washington.

O'Shea, J. M. 1984. *Mortuary Variability.* Academic Press, New York.

Pagden, A. R. (editor and translator). 1975. *The Maya: Diego de Landa's Account of the Affairs of Yucatan.* J. Philip O'Hara, Chicago.

Pearson, M. P. 1982. Mortuary Practices, Society and Ideology: An Ethnoarchaeological Study. In *Symbolic and Structural Archaeology,* edited by I. Hodder, pp. 99–113. Cambridge University Press, Cambridge.

Peña Saint Martin, F. 1985. Nutrición entre los mayas prehispánicos. Un estudio osteobiográfico. *Cuicuilco* 4(16):5–16. Escuela Nacional de Antropología e Historia, México.

Pendergast, D. M. 1986. Stability through Change: Lamanai, Belize, from the 9th to the 17th Century. In *Late Lowland Maya Civilization: Classic to Postclassic,* edited by J. A. Sabloff and E. W. Andrews, pp. 223–249. University of New Mexico Press, Albuquerque.

Perou, M. L. 1964. *Cranial Hyperostosis (Hyperostosis Cranii or H. C.).* Charles C Thomas, Springfield.

Pijoan Aguade, C. M., and M. E. Salas Cuesta. 1980. Datos de estatura: Colección Jaina. Ms. on file, Dirección de Antropología Física, Instituto Nacional de Antropología e Historia, México.

———. 1984. La población prehispánica de Jaina: análisis osteológico. In *Investigaciones recientes en el área maya,* tomo 2, pp. 471–480. Memorias de la XVII Mesa Redonda, 1981. Sociedad Mexicana de Antropología, San Cristobal de las Casas.

Pindborg, J. J. 1970. *Pathology of the Dental Hard Tissues.* W. B. Saunders, Philadelphia.

———. 1982. Aetiology of Developmental Enamel Defects Not Related to Fluorosis. *International Dental Journal* 32:123–134.

Podo-Ledezma, L. F. 1985. Enfermedades transmitidas por el agua y el colapso de la civilización maya clásica. *Mesoamérica* 10:391–410. Centro de Investigaciones Regionales de Mesoamérica [CIRMA], Antigua, Guatemala.

Pohl, M. (editor). 1985a. *Prehistoric Lowland Maya Environment and Subsistence Economy.* Papers of the Peabody Museum of Archaeology and Ethnology, vol. 77. Harvard University, Cambridge.

Pohl, M. 1985b. The Privileges of Maya Elites: Prehistoric Vertebrate Fauna from Seibal. In *Prehistoric Lowland Maya Environment and Subsistence Economy,* edited by M. Pohl, pp. 133–145. Papers of the Peabody Museum of Archaeology and Ethnology, vol. 77. Harvard University, Cambridge.

———. 1990. *Excavations at Seibal: The Ethnozoology of the Maya: Faunal Remains from Five Sites in Peten, Guatemala.* Memoirs of the Peabody Museum of Archaeology and Ethnology, vol. 17, no. 3. Harvard University, Cambridge.

Pompa y Padilla, J. A. 1990. *Antropología dental: aplicación en poblaciones prehispánicas.* Serie Antropología Física. Colección Científica 195. Instituto Nacional de Antropología e Historia, México.

Prewitt, C. T. 1988–1989. Geophysical Laboratory. The Director's Essay. *Carnegie Institution of Washington Year Book* 88:125–146.

Puleston, D. E. 1982. The Role of Ramón in Maya Subsistence. In *Maya Subsistence,* edited by K. Flannery, pp. 353–366. Academic Press, New York.

———. 1983. *The Settlement Survey of Tikal,* edited by W. A. Haviland. Tikal Report no. 13. University Museum Monograph 48. The University Museum, University of Pennsylvania, Philadelphia.

Rathje, W. 1970. Socio-Political Implications of Lowland Maya Burials: Methodology and Tentative Hypotheses. *World Archaeology* 1:359–374.

Reed, D. M. 1992. Ancient Maya Diet at Copán, Honduras, as Determined through the Analysis of Stable Carbon and Nitrogen Isotopes. Paper presented at the conference Paleonutrition: Diet and Health of Prehistoric Americans.

Center for Archaeological Investigations, Southern Illinois University, Carbondale.

———. 1994. Ancient Maya Diet at Copán, Honduras, as Determined through Analysis of Stable Carbon and Nitrogen Isotopes. In *Paleonutrition: The Diet and Health of Prehistoric Americans,* edited by K. D. Sobolik, pp. 210–221. Occasional Papers Series, vol. 22. Center for Archaeological Investigations, Southern Illinois University, Carbondale.

Reyment, R. A., R. E. Blackith, and N. A. Campbell. 1984. *Multivariate Morphometrics.* Academic Press, London.

Ricketson, O. G., Jr. 1925. Burials in the Maya Area. *American Anthropologist* 27:381–401.

———. 1931. *Excavations at Baking Pot, British Honduras.* Contributions to American Archaeology, vol. 1, no. 1. Publication 403. Carnegie Institution of Washington, Washington.

Riley, J. C. 1993. Measuring Morbidity and Mortality. In *The Cambridge World History of Human Disease,* edited by K. F. Kiple, pp. 230–238. Cambridge University Press, Cambridge.

Roberts, C. A. 1987. Case Report no. 9. *Paleopathology Newsletter* no. 57, pp. 14–15.

Roemer, E., Jr. 1984. A Late Classic Maya Lithic Workshop at Colha, Belize. Master's thesis, Texas A&M University, College Station.

Roksandic, Z., M. Minagawa, and T. Akazawa. 1988. Comparative Analysis of Dietary Habits between Jomon and Ainu Hunter-Gatherers from Stable Carbon Isotopes of Human Bone. *Journal of the Anthropological Society of Nippon* 96:391–404.

Romero Molina, J. 1958. *Mutilaciones dentarias prehispánicas en México y América en general.* Serie Investigaciones 3. Instituto Nacional de Antropología e Historia, México.

———. 1970. Dental Mutilation, Trephination and Cranial Deformation. In *Physical Anthropology,* edited by T. D. Stewart, pp. 50–67. Handbook of Middle American Indians, vol. 9, R. Wauchope, general editor. University of Texas Press, Austin.

———. 1986. *Catálogo de la colección de dientes mutilados prehispánicos, IV parte.* Instituto Nacional de Antropología e Historia, México.

Rose, J. C. 1973. Analysis of Dental Micro-defects of Prehistoric Populations from Illinois. Ph.D. dissertation, University of Massachusetts, Amherst.

———. 1977. Defective Enamel Histology of Prehistoric Teeth from Illinois. *American Journal of Physical Anthropology* 46:439–446.

Rose, J. C., G. J. Armelagos, and J. W. Lallo. 1978. Histological Enamel Indicator of Childhood Stress in Prehistoric Skeletal Samples. *American Journal of Physical Anthropology* 49:511–516.

Roys, R. L. 1972. *The Indian Background of Colonial Yucatan.* University of Oklahoma Press, Norman.

Rubín de la Borbolla, D. F. 1940. Types of Tooth Mutilation Found in Mexico. *American Journal of Physical Anthropology* 26:349–365.

Rue, D. 1987. Early Agriculture and Early Postclassic Maya Occupation in Western Honduras. *Nature* 326:285–286.

Ruz Lhuillier, A. 1965. Tombs and Funerary Practices of the Maya Lowlands. In *Archaeology of Southern Mesoamerica,* part I, edited by G. R. Willey, pp. 441–461. Handbook of Middle American Indians, vol. 2, R. Wauchope, general editor. University of Texas Press, Austin.

———. 1968. *Costumbres funerarias de los antiguos mayas.* Seminaria de Cultura Maya. Universidad Nacional Autónoma de México, México.

———. 1973. *El Templo de las Inscripciones, Palenque.* Colleción Científica Arqueología 7. Instituto Nacional de Antropología e Historia, México.

———. 1977. Gerontocracy at Palenque? In *Social Process in Maya Prehistory,* edited by N. Hammond, pp. 287–295. Academic Press, New York.

Sabloff, J. A. 1975. *Excavations at Seibal: Ceramics.* Memoirs of the Peabody Museum of Archaeology and Ethnology, vol. 13, no. 2. Harvard University, Cambridge.

Sabloff, J. A., and G. R. Willey. 1967. The Collapse of Maya Civilization in the Southern Lowlands: A Consideration of History and Process. *Southwestern Journal of Anthropology* 23:311–336.

Saiki, R. K., D. H. Gelfland, S. Stoffel, S. J. Scharf, R. Higuchi, G. T. Horn, K. B. Mullis, and H. A. Erlich. 1988. Primer-Directed Enzymatic Amplification of DNA with a Thermostable DNA Polymerase. *Science* 239:487–491.

Sanders, W. T. 1962. Cultural Ecology of the Maya Lowlands (part I). *Estudios de Cultura Maya* 2:79–121.

———. 1963. Cultural Ecology of the Maya Lowlands (part II). *Estudios de Cultura Maya* 3:203–241.

———. 1973. The Cultural Ecology of the Lowland Maya: A Reevaluation. In *The Classic Maya Collapse,* edited by T. P. Culbert, pp. 325–366. University of New Mexico Press, Albuquerque.

Sanders, W. T., and B. J. Price. 1968. *Mesoamerica: The Evolution of a Civilization.* Random House, New York.

Santley, R. S., T. W. Killion, and M. T. Lycett. 1986. On the Maya Collapse. *Journal of Anthropological Research* 42:123–159.

Sattenspiel, L., and H. Harpending. 1983. Stable Populations and Skeletal Age. *American Antiquity* 48:489–498.

Saul, F. P. 1972a. *The Human Skeletal Remains of Altar de Sacrificios: An Osteobiographic Analysis.* Papers of the Peabody Museum of Archaeology and Ethnology, vol. 63, no. 2. Harvard University, Cambridge.

———. 1972b. The Physical Anthropology of the Ancient Maya: An Appraisal. In *Verhandlungen des XXXVIII Internationalen Amerikanistenkongresses, Stuttgart-München, 1968,* Band 4, pp. 383–394. Kommissionsverlag Klaus Renner, München.

———. 1973. Disease in the Maya Area: The Pre-Columbian Evidence. In *The Classic Maya Collapse,* edited by T. P. Culbert, pp. 301–324. University of New Mexico Press, Albuquerque.

———. 1974. Datos inéditos de las enfermedades encontradas en el material óseo del Cenote Sagrado de Chichén Itzá. Ms. on file, Dirección de Antropología Física, Instituto Nacional de Antropología e Historia, México.

———. 1975a. Appendix 8—Human Remains from Lubaantun. In *Lubaantun, a Classic Maya Realm,* edited by N. Hammond, pp. 389–410. Peabody Museum Monographs no. 2. Peabody Museum of Archaeology and Ethnology, Harvard University, Cambridge.

———. 1975b. The Maya and Their Neighbors (1974): As Recorded in Their Skeletons. In *The Maya and Their Neighbors,* edited by G. R. Willey, J. A. Sabloff, E. Z. Vogt, and F. P. Saul, pp. 35–40. Peabody Museum Monographs no. 5. Peabody Museum of Archaeology and Ethnology, Harvard University, Cambridge.

———. 1977. The Paleopathology of Anemia in Mexico and Guatemala. In *Porotic Hyperostosis: An Enquiry,* edited by E. Cockburn, pp. 10–15, 18. Monograph 2. Paleopathology Association, Detroit.

———. 1982. Appendix II—The Human Skeletal Remains from Tancah, Mexico. In *On the Edge of the Sea: Mural Paintings at Tancah-Tulum,* edited by A. G. Miller, pp. 115–128. Dumbarton Oaks Trustees for Harvard University, Washington.

Saul, F. P., and J. M. Saul. 1984. Paleobiología en la zona maya. In *Investigaciones recientes en el área maya,* tomo 1, pp. 23–42. Memorias de la XVII Mesa Redonda, 1981. Sociedad Mexicana de Antropología, San Cristobal de las Casas.

———. 1985. Life History as Recorded in Maya Skeletons from Cozumel, Mexico. In *National Geographic Research Reports,* vol. 20, edited by W. Swanson, pp. 583–587. National Geographic Society Press, Washington.

———. 1989. Osteobiography: A Maya Example. In *Reconstruction of Life from the Skeleton,* edited by M. Y. İşcan and K. A. R. Kennedy, pp. 287–302. Alan R. Liss, New York.

———. 1991. The Preclassic Population of Cuello. In *Cuello: An Early Maya Community in Belize,* edited by N. Hammond, pp. 134–158. Cambridge University Press, Cambridge.

Saunders, S. R., and R. D. Hoppa. 1993. Growth Deficit in Survivors and Non-Survivors: Biological Mortality Bias in Subadult Skeletal Samples. *Yearbook of Physical Anthropology* 36:127–152.

Saville, M. H. 1913. Precolumbian Decoration of the Teeth in Ecuador. *American Anthropologist* 15:377–394.

Schele, L., and D. Freidel. 1990. *A Forest of Kings: The Untold Story of the Ancient Maya.* William Morrow, New York.

Schoeninger, M. J., and M. J. DeNiro. 1984. Nitrogen and Carbon Isotopic Composition of Bone Collagen from Marine and Terrestrial Animals. *Geochimica et Cosmochimica Acta* 48:625–639.

Schoeninger, M. J., and K. Moore. 1992. Bone Stable Isotope Studies in Archaeology. *Journal of World Prehistory* 6:247–296.

Schour, I., and M. Massler. 1941. The Development of the Human Dentition. *Journal of the American Dental Association* 28:1153–1160.

———. 1944. *Development of the Human Dentition* (chart). 2d ed. American Dental Association, Chicago.

Schurr, T. G., S. W. Ballinger, Y. Y. Gan, J. A. Hodge, D. A. Merriwether, D. N. Lawrence, W. C. Knowler, K. M. Weiss, and D. C. Wallace. 1990. Amerindian Mitochondrial DNAs Have Rare Asian Mutations at High Frequencies Suggesting a Limited Number of Founders. *American Journal of Human Genetics* 46:613–623.

Schwarcz, H. P. 1991. Some Theoretical Aspects of Isotope Paleodiet Studies. *Journal of Archaeological Science* 18:261–275.

Schwarcz, H. P., J. Melbye, M. A. Katzenberg, and M. Knyf. 1985. Stable Isotopes in Human Skeletons of Southern Ontario. *Journal of Archaeological Science* 12:187–206.

Schwarcz, H. P., and M. J. Schoeninger. 1991. Stable Isotope Analyses in Human Nutritional Ecology. *Yearbook of Physical Anthropology* 34:283–321.

Scrimshaw, N. S., and C. Tejada. 1970. Pathology of Living Indians Seen in Guatemala. In *Physical Anthropology,* edited by T. D. Stewart, pp. 203–225. Handbook of Middle American Indians, vol. 9, R. Wauchope, general editor. University of Texas Press, Austin.

Sealy, J. C. 1989. Reconstruction of Later Stone Age Diets in the Southwestern Cape, South Africa: Evaluation and Application of Five Isotopic and Trace Element Techniques. Ph.D. dissertation, University of Cape Town.

Sealy, J. C., and N. J. van der Merwe. 1988. Social, Spatial and Chronological Patterning in Marine Food Use as Determined by δ^{13}C Measurements of Holocene Human Skeletons from the South-Western Cape, South Africa. *World Archaeology* 20:87–102.

Sempowski, M. L. 1992. Economic and Social Implications of Variations in Mortuary Practices at Teotihuacan. In *Art, Ideology, and the City of Teotihuacan,* edited by J. Berlo, pp. 27–58. Dumbarton Oaks, Washington.

Shafer, H. J., and T. R. Hester. 1983. Ancient Maya Chert Workshops in Northern Belize, Central America. *American Antiquity* 48:519–543.

———. 1986. Maya Stone-Tool Craft Specialization and Production at Colha, Belize: Reply to Mallory. *American Antiquity* 51:158–166.

Shafer, W. G., M. K. Hine, and P. M. Levy. 1974. *A Textbook of Oral Pathology.* W. B. Saunders, Philadelphia.

Sharer, R. 1994. *The Ancient Maya.* 5th ed. Stanford University Press, Palo Alto.

Shattuck, G. C. 1938. *A Medical Survey of the Republic of Guatemala.* Publication 499. Carnegie Institution of Washington, Washington.

Shields, G. F., K. Hecker, M. I. Voevoda, and J. K. Reed. 1992. Absence of the Asian-Specific Region V Mitochondrial Marker in Native Beringians. *American Journal of Human Genetics* 50:758–765.

Shields, G. F., A. M. Schmiechen, B. L. Frazier, A. Redd, M. I. Voevoda, J. K. Reed, and R. H. Ward. 1993. mtDNA Sequences Suggest a Recent Evolutionary Divergence for Beringian and Northern North American Populations. *American Journal of Human Genetics* 53:549–562.

Shimkin, D. B. 1973. Models for the Downfall: Some Ecological and Culture-Historical Considerations. In *The Classic Maya Collapse,* edited by T. P. Culbert, pp. 269–300. University of New Mexico Press, Albuquerque.

Siemens, A. H., and D. E. Puleston. 1972. Ridged Fields and Associated Features in Southern Campeche: New Perspectives on the Lowland Maya. *American Antiquity* 37: 228–239.

Sillen, A., J. C. Sealy, and N. J. van der Merwe. 1989. Chemistry and Paleodietary Research: No More Easy Answers. *American Antiquity* 54:504–512.

Sjøvold, T. 1973. The Occurrence of Minor Non-Metrical Variants in the Skeleton and Their Quantitative Treatment for Population Comparison. *Homo* 24:204–233.

Skinner, M., and A. H. Goodman. 1992. Anthropological Uses of Developmental Defects of Enamel. In *Skeletal Biology of Past Peoples: Research Methods,* edited by S. R. Saunders and M. A. Katzenberg, pp. 153–174. Wiley-Liss, New York.

Skinner, M., and J. T. W. Hung. 1989. Social and Biological Correlates of Localized Enamel Hypoplasia of the Human Deciduous Canine Tooth. *American Journal of Physical Anthropology* 79:159–175.

Smith, A. L. 1950. *Uaxactun, Guatemala: Excavations of 1931–1937.* Publication 588. Carnegie Institution of Washington, Washington.

———. 1972. *Excavations at Altar de Sacrificios: Architecture, Settlement, Burials, and Caches.* Papers of the Peabody Museum of Archaeology and Ethnology, vol. 62, no. 2. Harvard University, Cambridge.

Smith, A. L., and A. V. Kidder. 1943. *Explorations in the Motagua Valley, Guatemala.* Contributions to American Anthropology and History, vol. 8, no. 41. Publication 546. Carnegie Institution of Washington, Washington.

Smith, B. H. 1984. Patterns of Molar Wear in Hunter-Gatherers and Agriculturalists. *American Journal of Physical Anthropology* 63: 39–56.

Sofaer, J. A., P. Smith, and E. Kaye. 1986. Affinities between Contemporary and Skeletal Jewish and Non-Jewish Groups Based on Tooth Morphology. *American Journal of Physical Anthropology* 70:265–275.

Solares Aguilar, J. 1990. Incrustaciones dentarias mayas. Análisis preliminar. Paper presented at the Seminario de la Investigación Socio-Epidemiología de Enfermedades Orales en Guatemala, Antigua, Guatemala.

SPSS, Inc. 1988. *SPSS-X User's Guide.* 3d ed. SPSS, Chicago.

Steele, D. G. 1970. Estimation of Stature from Fragments of Long Limb Bones. In *Personal Identification in Mass Disasters,* edited by T. D. Stewart, pp. 85–97. National Museum of Natural History, Smithsonian Institution, Washington.

Steele, D. G., and C. Bramblett. 1988. *The Anatomy and Biology of the Human Skeleton.* Texas A&M University Press, College Station.

Steele, D. G., J. D. Eaton, and A. J. Taylor. 1980. The Skulls from Operation 2011 at Colha: A Preliminary Examination. In *The Colha Project, Second Season, 1980 Interim Report,* edited by T. R. Hester, H. J. Shafer, and J. D. Eaton, pp. 163–172. The University of Texas at San Antonio and Center for Archaeological Research, Centro Studi e Ricerche Liguabue, Venezia, San Antonio.

Steggerda, M. 1932. *Anthropometry of Adult Maya Indians. A Study of Their Physical and Physiological Characteristics.* Publication 434. Carnegie Insitution of Washington, Lancaster.

———. 1941. *Maya Indians of Yucatan.* Publication 531. Carnegie Institution of Washington, Washington.

Steinbock, R. T. 1976. *Paleopathological Diagnosis and Interpretation: Bone Diseases in Ancient Human Populations.* Charles C Thomas, Springfield.

Stephens, J. L. 1843. *Incidents of Travel in Yucatan,* vol. 1. Harper and Brothers, New York.

Stewart, T. D. 1942. Persistence of the African Type of Tooth Pointing in Panama. *American Anthropologist* 44:328–330.

———. 1949. Notas sobre esqueletos humanos prehistóricos hallados en Guatemala. *Antropología e Historia de Guatemala* 1(1):23–34.

———. 1952. *A Bibliography of Physical Anthropology in Latin America: 1937–48.* Wenner-Gren, New York.

———. 1953. Skeletal Remains from Zaculeu, Guatemala. In *The Ruins of Zaculeu, Guatemala,* vol. 1, edited by R. B. Woodbury and A. S. Trik, pp. 295–311. United Fruit Company, New York.

————— (editor). 1970. References. In *Physical An-thropology,* pp. 235–271. Handbook of Middle American Indians, vol. 9, R. Wauchope, general editor. University of Texas Press, Austin.

Stewart, T. D. 1979. *Essentials of Forensic Anthropology Especially as Developed in the United States.* Charles C Thomas, Springfield.

Stini, W. A. 1969. Nutritional Stress and Growth: Sex Differences in Adaptive Response. *American Journal of Physical Anthropology* 31: 417–426.

Stinson, S. 1985. Sex Differences in Environmental Sensitivity during Growth and Development. *Yearbook of Physical Anthropology* 28:123–148.

Stone, A. 1989. Disconnection, Foreign Insignia, and Political Expansion: Teotihuacan and the Warrior Stelae of Piedras Negras. In *Mesoamerica after the Decline of Teotihuacan, A.D. 700–900,* edited by R. A. Diehl and J. C. Berlo, pp. 153–172. Dumbarton Oaks, Washington.

Stone, A. C., and M. Stoneking. 1994. Ancient DNA from a Pre-Columbian Amerindian Population. *American Journal of Physical Anthropology* 92:463–471.

Storey, R. 1985. An Estimate of Mortality in a Pre-Columbian Urban Population. *American Anthropologist* 87:519–534.

————. 1992a. The Children of Copan: Issues in Paleopathology and Paleodemography. *Ancient Mesoamerica* 3:161–167.

————. 1992b. *Life and Death in the Ancient City of Teotihuacan: A Modern Paleodemographic Synthesis.* University of Alabama Press, Tuscaloosa.

————. 1992c. Patterns of Susceptibility to Dental Enamel Defects in the Deciduous Dentition of a Precolumbian Skeletal Population. In *Recent Contributions to the Study of Enamel Developmental Defects,* edited by A. H. Goodman and L. L. Capasso, pp. 171–183. Journal of Paleopathology Monographic Publications 2. Associazone Antropologica Abruzze, Chieti.

Stuart, D. 1993. Historical Inscriptions and the Maya Collapse. In *Lowland Maya Civilization in the Eighth Century A.D.,* edited by J. Sabloff and J. Henderson, pp. 321–354. Dumbarton Oaks, Washington.

Stuart-Macadam, P. 1985. Porotic Hyperostosis: Representative of a Childhood Condition. *American Journal of Physical Anthropology* 66:391–398.

————. 1987. Porotic Hyperostosis: New Evidence to Support the Anemia Theory. *American Journal of Physical Anthropology* 74: 521–526.

————— (organizer). 1994. Female Biological Superiority: Fact or Fiction? Symposium held at the 63d Annual Meeting of the American Association of Physical Anthropologists, Denver.

Suckling, G. W. 1989. Developmental Defects of Enamel: Historical and Present Day Perspectives on Their Pathogenesis. *Advances in Dental Research* 3:87–94.

Suckling, G. W., D. C. Elliot, and D. C. Thurley. 1986. The Macroscopic Appearance and Associated Histological Changes in the Enamel Organ of Hypoplastic Lesions of Sheep Incisor Teeth Resulting from Induced Parasitism. *Archives of Oral Biology* 31:427–439.

Suga, S. 1992. Hypoplasia and Hypomineralization of Tooth Enamel. In *Recent Contributions to the Study of Enamel Developmental Defects,* edited by A. H. Goodman and L. L. Capasso, pp. 269–292. Journal of Paleopathology Monographic Publications 2. Associazone Antropologica Abruzze, Chieti.

Tainter, J. A. 1975. Social Inference and Mortuary Practices: An Experiment in Numerical Classification. *World Archaeology* 7:1–15.

————. 1988. *The Collapse of Complex Societies.* Cambridge University Press, Cambridge.

Tanner, M. 1973. *Growth at Adolescence.* Blackwell Scientific, Oxford.

Taube, K. A. 1989. The Maize Tamale in Classic Maya Diet, Epigraphy, and Art. *American Antiquity* 54:31–51.

Tedlock, D. (translator). 1985. *Popol Vuh: The Mayan Book of the Dawn of Life.* Simon and Schuster, New York.

Thompson, J. E. S. 1939. *Excavations at San Jose, British Honduras.* Publication 506. Carnegie Institution of Washington, Washington.

————. 1954. *The Rise and Fall of Maya Civilization.* University of Oklahoma Press, Norman.

———. 1970. *Maya History and Religion.* University of Oklahoma Press, Norman.

Tieszen, L. L., T. W. Boutton, K. G. Tesdahl, and N. A. Slade. 1983. Fractionation and Turnover of Stable Carbon Isotopes in Animal Tissues: Implication for δ^{13}C Analysis of Diet. *Oecologia* 57:32–37.

Tieszen, L. L., and T. Fagre. 1993a. Carbon Isotopic Variability in Modern and Archaeological Maize. *Journal of Archaeological Science* 20:25–40.

———. 1993b. Effect of Diet Quality and Composition on the Isotopic Composition of Respiratory CO_2, Bone Collagen, Bioapatite, and Soft Tissues. In *Prehistoric Human Bone: Archaeology at the Molecular Level*, edited by J. B. Lambert and G. Grupe, pp. 121–155. Springer-Verlag, Berlin.

Torroni, A., Y. S. Chen, O. Semino, A. S. Santachiara-Benerecetti, C. R. Scott, M. T. Lott, M. Winter, and D. C. Wallace. 1994. mtDNA and Y-Chromosome Polymorphisms in Four Native American Populations from Southern Mexico. *American Journal of Human Genetics* 54:303–318.

Torroni, A., J. V. Neel, R. Barrantes, T. G. Schurr, and D. C. Wallace. 1994. Mitochondrial DNA "Clock" for the Amerinds and Its Implications for Timing Their Entry into North America. *Proceedings of the National Academy of Sciences USA* 91:1158–1162.

Torroni, A., T. G. Schurr, M. F. Cabell, M. D. Brown, J. V. Neel, M. Larsen, D. G. Smith, C. M. Vullo, and D. C. Wallace. 1993. Asian Affinities and Continental Radiation of the Four Founding Native American Mitochondrial DNAs. *American Journal of Human Genetics* 53:563–590.

Torroni, A., T. G. Schurr, C. C. Yang, E. J. E. Szathmary, R. C. Williams, M. S. Schanfield, G. A. Troup, W. C. Knowler, D. N. Lawrence, K. M. Weiss, and D. C. Wallace. 1992. Native American Mitochondrial DNA Analysis Indicates that the Amerind and the Nadene Populations Were Founded by Two Independent Migrations. *Genetics* 130:153–162.

Torroni, A., R. I. Sukernik, T. G. Schurr, Y. B. Starikovskaya, M. F. Cabell, M. H. Crawford, A. G. Comuzzie, and D. C. Wallace. 1993. Mitochondrial DNA Variation of Aboriginal Siberians Reveals Distinct Affinities with Native Americans. *American Journal of Human Genetics* 53:591–608.

Tourtellot, G., III. 1988. *Excavations at Seibal: Peripheral Survey and Excavation: Settlement and Community Patterns.* Memoirs of the Peabody Museum of Archaeology and Ethnology, vol. 16. Harvard University, Cambridge.

———. 1990a. *Excavations at Seibal: Burials: A Cultural Analysis.* Memoirs of the Peabody Museum of Archaeology and Ethnology, vol. 17, no. 2. Harvard University, Cambridge.

———. 1990b. Population Estimates for Preclassic and Classic Seibal, Peten. In *Precolumbian Population History in the Maya Lowlands*, edited by T. P. Culbert and D. S. Rice, pp. 83–102. University of New Mexico Press, Albuquerque.

Tozzer, A. L. (editor and translator). 1941. *Landa's Relación de las cosas de Yucatán.* Papers of the Peabody Museum of American Archaeology and Ethnology no. 18. Harvard University, Cambridge.

Trotter, M., and G. C. Gleser. 1958. A Re-Evaluation of Estimation of Stature Taken during Life and of Long Bones after Death. *American Journal of Physical Anthropology* 16:79–123.

Turner, B. L., II. 1974. Prehistoric Intensive Agriculture in Mayan Lowlands. *Science* 185:118–123.

———. 1979. Agricultura intensiva en las tierras bajas mayas: una lección del pasado. Paper presented at the XLIII Reunión del Congreso Internacional de Americanistas, Vancouver.

Turner, B. L., II, and P. D. Harrison (editors). 1983. *Pulltrouser Swamp: Ancient Maya Habitat, Agriculture, and Settlement in Northern Belize.* University of Texas Press, Austin.

Turner, C. G., II. 1979. Dental Anthropological Indications of Agriculture among the Jomon People of Central Japan. X. Peopling of the Pacific. *American Journal of Physical Anthropology* 51:619–636.

———. 1985. The Dental Search for Native American Origins. In *Out of Asia: Peopling the Americas and the Pacific,* edited by R. Kirk and E. Szathmary, pp. 31–78. The Journal of Pacific History, Canberra.

Turner, C. G., II, and L. M. C. Machado. 1983. A New Dental Wear Pattern and Evidence for High Carbohydrate Consumption in a Brazilian Archaic Skeletal Population. *American Journal of Physical Anthropology* 61: 125–130.

Turner, C. G., II, C. R. Nichol, and G. R. Scott. 1991. Scoring Procedures for Key Morphological Traits of the Permanent Dentition: The Arizona State University Dental Anthropology System. In *Advances in Dental Anthropology,* edited by M. A. Kelly and C. S. Larsen, pp. 13–31. Wiley-Liss, New York.

Ubelaker, D. H. 1982. The Development of American Paleopathology. In *A History of American Physical Anthropology 1930–1980,* edited by F. Spencer, pp. 337–356. Academic Press, New York.

Valdés, J. A., A. Foias, T. Inomata, H. Escobedo, and A. A. Demarest (editors). 1993. *Proyecto Arqueológico Regional Petexbatún. Informe preliminar #5. Quinta temporada.* Submitted to Instituto de Antropología e Historia de Guatemala.

Valle, R. H. 1971. *Bibliografía maya.* Reprinted. Burt Franklin Bibliography and Reference Series 436. Selected Essays in History, Economics, and Social Sciences 306. B. Franklin, New York. Reprint of the 1937–1941 edition, Boletín bibliográfico de antropología americana, Instituto Panamericana de Geografía e Historia, México.

van der Merwe, N. J. 1982. Carbon Isotopes, Photosynthesis, and Archaeology. *American Scientist* 70:596–606.

van der Merwe, N. J., and J. C. Vogel. 1978. ^{13}C Content of Human Collagen as a Measure of Prehistoric Diet in Woodland North America. *Nature* 292:815–816.

Vaughan, H. H., A. S. Deevy, Jr., and S. E. Garrett-Jones. 1985. Pollen Stratigraphy of Two Cores from the Petén Lake District, with an Appendix on Two Deep-Water Cores. In *Prehistoric Lowland Maya Environment and Subsistence Economy,* edited by M. Pohl,

pp. 73–89. Papers of the Peabody Museum of Archaeology and Ethnology, vol. 77. Harvard University, Cambridge.

Veblen, T. T. 1982. Native Population Decline in Totonicapan, Guatemala. *The Historical Demography of Highland Guatemala,* edited by R. M. Carmack, J. Early, and C. Lutz, pp. 81–102. Publication 6. Institute for Mesoamerican Studies, State University of New York at Albany, Albany.

Villagutierre Soto-Mayor, J. de. 1983 [1701]. *History of the Conquest of the Province of the Itzá.* Translated by R. D. Wood. Labyrinthos, Culver City.

Villanueva, M., and C. Serrano Sánchez. 1982. Inventario de antropología física: 1930–1979 (por autores). In *Estudios de antropología biológica. (I Colóquio de Antropología Física Juan Comas. 1980),* edited by M. Villanueva and C. Serrano Sánchez, pp. 84–124. Serie Antropológica. Antropología Física 51. Instituto de Investigaciones Antropológicas, Universidad Nacional Autónoma de México, México.

Vogt, E. Z. 1990. *The Zinacantecos of Mexico: A Modern Maya Way of Life.* Holt, Rinehart and Winston, Fort Worth.

Wallace, D. C., K. Garrison, and W. C. Knowler. 1985. Dramatic Founder Effects in Amerindian Mitochondrial DNAs. *American Journal of Physical Anthropology* 68:149–155.

Ward, R. H., B. L. Frazier, K. Dew-Jager, and S. Paabo. 1991. Extensive Mitochondrial Diversity within a Single Amerindian Tribe. *Proceedings of the National Academy of Sciences USA* 88:8720–8724.

Ward, R. H., A. Redd, D. Valencia, B. Frazier, and S. Paabo. 1993. Genetic and Linguistic Differentiation in the Americas. *Proceedings of the National Academy of Sciences USA* 90:10663–10667.

Washburn, S. 1953. The Strategy of Physical Anthropology. In *Anthropology Today,* edited by A. L. Kroeber, pp. 1–14. University of Chicago Press, Chicago.

Weaver, M. P. 1981. *The Aztecs, Maya, and Their Predecessors.* 2d ed. Academic Press, New York.

Webster, D. (editor). 1989a. *The House of the Bacabs.* Studies in Pre-Columbian Art and

Archaeology no. 29. Dumbarton Oaks, Washington.

Webster, D. 1989b. The House of the Bacabs: Its Social Context. In *The House of the Bacabs*, edited by D. Webster, pp. 5–40. Studies in Pre-Columbian Art and Archaeology no. 29. Dumbarton Oaks, Washington.

―――. 1994a. Classic Maya Architecture: Implications and Comparisons. Paper presented at the Dumbarton Oaks Symposium on Form and Function in Maya Architecture, Washington.

―――. 1994b. Cultural Ecology and Culture History of Resource Management at Copán, Honduras. Paper presented at the School of American Research Symposium on the Archaeology of Copán, Albuquerque.

Webster, D., and A. Freter. 1990a. The Demography of Late Classic Copan. In *Precolumbian Population History in the Maya Lowlands*, edited by T. P. Culbert and D. S. Rice, pp. 37–61. University of New Mexico Press, Albuquerque.

―――. 1990b. Settlement History and the Classic Collapse of Copán: A Redefined Chronological Perspective. *Latin American Antiquity* 1:66–85.

Webster, D., and N. Gonlin. 1988. Household Remains of the Humblest Maya. *Journal of Field Archaeology* 15:169–190.

Webster, D., W. T. Sanders, and P. van Rossum. 1992. A Simulation of Copan Population History and Its Implications. *Ancient Mesoamerica* 3:185–197.

Weiss, K. M. 1973. *Demographic Models for Anthropology*. Memoirs no. 27. Society for American Archaeology, Washington.

Welsh, W. B. M. 1988. *An Analysis of Classic Lowland Maya Burials*. International Series 409. British Archaeological Reports, Oxford.

White, C. D. 1986. Paleodiet and Nutrition of the Ancient Maya at Lamanai, Belize: A Study of Trace Elements, Stable Isotopes, Nutritional and Dental Pathology. Master's thesis, Trent University, Peterborough.

White, C. D., P. F. Healy, and H. P. Schwarcz. 1993. Intensive Agriculture, Social Status, and Maya Diet at Pacbitun, Belize. *Journal of Anthropological Research* 49:347–375.

White, C. D., and H. P. Schwarcz. 1989. Ancient Maya Diet: as Inferred from Isotopic and Elemental Analysis of Human Bone. *Journal of Archaeological Science* 16:451–474.

White, C. D., L. E. Wright, and D. M. Pendergast. 1994. Biological Disruption in the Early Colonial Period at Lamanai. In *In the Wake of Contact: Biological Responses to Conquest*, edited by C. S. Larsen and G. R. Milner, pp. 135–145. Wiley-Liss, New York.

Whittington, S. L. 1989. Characteristics of Demography and Disease in Low-Status Maya from Classic Period Copan, Honduras. Ph.D. dissertation, Department of Anthropology, The Pennsylvania State University, University Park.

―――. 1992. Enamel Hypoplasia in the Low Status Maya Population of Prehispanic Copan, Honduras. In *Recent Contributions to the Study of Enamel Developmental Defects*, edited by A. H. Goodman and L. L. Capasso, pp. 185–206. Journal of Paleopathology Monographic Publications 2. Associazone Antropologica Abruzze, Chieti.

Whittington, S. L., and D. M. Reed. 1993. Preliminary Results of Analysis of Human Skeletal Remains from Iximche, Guatemala. Paper presented at the 58th Annual Meeting of the Society for American Archaeology, St. Louis.

Wilken, G. C. 1971. Food-Producing Systems Available to the Ancient Maya. *American Antiquity* 36:432–448.

Wilkinson, L., M. A. Hill, and E. Vang. 1992. *SYSTAT: Statistics, Version 5.2 Edition*. SYSTAT, Evanston.

Willey, G. R. 1973. *The Altar de Sacrificios Excavations: General Summary and Conclusions*. Papers of the Peabody Museum of Archaeology and Ethnology, vol. 64, no. 3. Harvard University, Cambridge.

―――. 1990. *Excavations at Seibal: General Summary and Conclusions*. Memoirs of the Pea-body Museum of Archaeology and Ethnology, vol. 17, no. 4. Harvard University, Cambridge.

Willey, G. R., W. R. Bullard, Jr., J. B. Glass, and J. C. Gifford. 1965. *Prehistoric Maya Settlements in the Belize Valley*. Papers of the Peabody Museum of Archaeology and Ethnology, vol. 54. Harvard University, Cambridge.

Willey, G. R., and R. Leventhal. 1979. Prehistoric Settlement at Copan. In *Maya Archaeology and Ethnohistory,* edited by N. Hammond and G. R. Willey, pp. 75–102. University of Texas Press, Austin.

Willey, G. R., and J. A. Sabloff. 1993. *A History of American Archaeology.* W. H. Freeman, San Francisco.

Willey, G. R., and D. B. Shimkin. 1973. The Maya Collapse: A Summary View. In *The Classic Maya Collapse,* edited by T. P. Culbert, pp. 457–503. University of New Mexico Press, Albuquerque.

Willey, G. R., and A. L. Smith. 1969. *The Ruins of Altar de Sacrificios, Department of Peten, Guatemala: An Introduction.* Papers of the Peabody Museum of Archaeology and Ethnology, vol. 62, no. 1. Harvard University, Cambridge.

Williams, G. D. 1931. *Maya-Spanish Crosses in Yucatan.* Papers of the Peabody Museum of American Archaeology and Ethnology, vol. 13, no. 1. Harvard University, Cambridge.

Wilson, D. P., and P. R. Schroff. 1970. The Nature of Striae of Retzius as Seen with the Optical Microscope. *Australian Dental Journal* 15:162–171.

Wing, E. S. 1981. A Comparison of Olmec and Maya Foodways. In *The Olmec and Their Neighbors: Essays in Memory of Matthew W. Stirling,* edited by E. P. Benson, pp. 21–28. Dumbarton Oaks, Washington.

Wing, E. S., and A. B. Brown. 1979. *Paleonutrition: Method and Theory in Prehistoric Foodways.* Academic Press, New York.

Wingard, J. D. 1992. The Role of Soils in the Development and Collapse of Classic Maya Civilization at Copan, Honduras. Ph.D. dissertation, Department of Anthropology, The Pennsylvania State University, University Park.

Wiseman, F. M. 1973. The Artificial Rain Forest. Paper presented at the 38th Annual Meeting of the Society for American Archaeology, San Francisco.

———. 1983. Subsistence and Complex Societies: The Case of the Maya. In *Advances in Archaeological Method and Theory,* vol. 6, edited by M. B. Schiffer, pp. 143–189. Academic Press, New York.

———. 1985. Agriculture and Vegetation Dynamics of the Maya Collapse in Central Peten, Guatemala. In *Prehistoric Maya Environment and Subsistence,* edited by M. D. Pohl, pp. 63–71. Papers of the Peabody Museum of Archaeology and Ethnology, vol. 77. Harvard University, Cambridge.

Wolley, C., and L. E. Wright. 1990. Operación DP7: investigaciones en el Grupo L4-4. In *Proyecto Arqueológico Regional Petexbatún. Informe preliminar #2. Segunda temporada,* edited by A. Demarest and S. Houston, pp. 44–65. Submitted to Instituto de Antropología e Historia de Guatemala.

Wood, J. W., and G. R. Milner. 1994. Reply. *Current Anthropology* 35:631–637.

Wood, J. W., G. R. Milner, H. C. Harpending, and K. M. Weiss. 1992. The Osteological Paradox: Problems of Inferring Prehistoric Health from Skeletal Samples. *Current Anthropology* 33:343–370.

Wright, L. E. 1989. Cementum Annulation: A Test of Its Application to the Colonial Maya of Tipu, Belize. Master's thesis, University of Chicago, Chicago.

———. 1990. Stresses of Conquest: A Study of Wilson Bands and Enamel Hypoplasias in the Maya of Lamanai, Belize. *American Journal of Human Biology* 2:25–35.

———. 1994. The Sacrifice of the Earth? Diet, Health, and Inequality in the Pasión Maya Lowlands. Ph.D. dissertation, Department of Anthropology, University of Chicago, Chicago.

———. 1995. La dieta antigua y la evolución social de los Mayas del río Pasión: Una visión isotópica. *VIII Simposio de Investigaciones Arqueológicas en Guatemala, 1994,* vol. 1, edited by J. P. Laporte and H. L. Escobedo, pp. 301–314. Ministerio de Cultura y Deportes, Instituto de Antropología e Historia, and Asociación Tikal, Guatemala.

Wright, L. E., and H. P. Schwarcz. 1996. Infrared and Isotopic Evidence for Diagenesis of Bone Apatite at Dos Pilas, Guatemala: Paleodietary Implications. *Journal of Archaeological Science* 23:933–944.

Index

Page numbers in italics refer to *figures,* and those in boldface refer to **tables.**

Acbi phase, 158, **158**, 161, **161**, *163* (12.5), 167, **167**
Age-at-death, 23, 30, **31**, 62–64, **63**, 81–82, 85–86, 115, 118–19, *124,* 125, 158, 159, 165, **165**, **166**, *166,* 167–68
Agricultural practices, 171–72, 181, 184, 194, 226
Aguateca, Guatemala, 182–83, 185, 188, **189**, 191, *191,* 192, 193
Ajsac phase, Late Classic, 185, **189**, 191, *191,* 193
Altar de Sacrificios, Guatemala, 35, 36, 38, 39, 43, 44, 45, 46, 48, **48**, 49, **49**, 52, 54, **54**, **55**, 58, 59, 127, 150, **151**, 165, 173–74, 175, 179, 182, 185, 188, **189**, *189,* 190, 191–92, *191, 192* (14.6), 193–94, *193,* 197, 199, **203**, 204, **204**, *204, 205,* 225
Alta Verapaz, Guatemala, 112
Anemia. *See* Porotic hyperostosis
Ankylosing spondylitis. *See* Vertebral pathology
Apatite, 197, 198–99, *199,* 200–3, *201,* **201**, *202,* **203**, 204–7, **204**, *205,* 228
Arthritis, 38–39, *224*
Ayn phase, Early Classic, 185, 188, **189**, *189*

Baking Pot, Belize, 197, 199, **203**, 204–6, **204**, *204, 205*
Barton Ramie, Belize, 52, 127, 128–29, **130**, 131–33, *132,* **133**, 134–35, 136, 197, 199, **203**, 204–6, **204**, *204, 205*

Bayal phase, Terminal Classic, 151, 185, **189**, 190–91, *190* (14.4), 193, *193*
Bioarchaeological publications, 222–28, *223,* **224**, *224*
Biodistance, 61, 139, 151–52, *224,* 225. *See also* DNA analyses
Bladen phase, Middle Preclassic, 28, 29, **31**, 32, **32**, 34, **34**, 35, **37**, 39, 42, **42**, 43, 44, **44**, *45,* 46, *47,* **47**, 48, **48**, **49**
Boca phase, Terminal Classic, 185, 188, **189**, *189,* 193, *193*

Calculus, 24, 42–43, 46, 49, 63, 64, *65,* 76
Cancún (El Rey), Quintana Roo, 53–54, **54**, *59*
Cantutse phase, Late Preclassic-Protoclassic, 185, **189**, 190–91, *190* (14.4)
Caracol, Belize, 9, 15–16, 18, 19, **19**, 20–22, 23, 24, 25, 26–27
Caries, 24, 39, 42–43, **42** (3.5), 46, 49, 63, 64, 65–66, *65,* **66**, *67,* 124–25, 173–74, *174–75,* 176, **176**, 177–78, **178**, *178,* 179–80
Ceibal, Guatemala. *See* Seibal, Guatemala
Cenote Sagrado. *See* Chichén Itzá, Yucatán
Chau Hiix, Belize, 92, 93–95, **93**, 99–100, 101, 102, 104
Chiapa de Corzo, Chiapas, 53–54, **54**
Chicanel phase, Late Preclassic-Protoclassic, 28–29, 30, **31**, 32–33, **32**, 34–35, **34**, **37**, *38,* 39, *39,* 42, **42**, 43–44, **44**, *45,* 46–48, *47,* **47**, **48**, **49**, 108–9, *109,* **110**